Gallica
Volume 4

CHRISTINE DE PIZAN'S CHANGING OPINION

A QUEST FOR CERTAINTY IN THE MIDST OF CHAOS

Gallica

ISSN 1749–091X

General Editor: Sarah Kay

Gallica aims to provide a forum for the best current work in medieval French studies. Literary studies are particularly welcome and preference is given to works written in English, although publication in French is not excluded.

Proposals or queries should be sent in the first instance to the editor, or to the publisher, at the addresses given below; all submissions receive prompt and informed consideration.

Professor Sarah Kay, Department of French and Italian, Princeton University, 303 East Pyne, Princeton, NJ 08544, USA

The Managing Editor, Gallica, Boydell & Brewer Ltd., PO Box 9, Woodbridge, Suffolk IP12 3DF, UK

Already Published

1 *Postcolonial Fictions in the 'Roman de Perceforest': Cultural Identities and Hybridities*, Sylvia Huot
2 *A Discourse for the Holy Grail in Old French Romance*, Ben Ramm
3 *Fashion in Medieval France*, Sarah-Grace Heller

CHRISTINE DE PIZAN'S CHANGING OPINION

A QUEST FOR CERTAINTY IN THE MIDST OF CHAOS

Douglas Kelly

D. S. BREWER

© Douglas Kelly 2007

All Rights Reserved. Except as permitted under current legislation no part of this work may be photocopied, stored in a retrieval system, published, performed in public, adapted, broadcast, transmitted, recorded or reproduced in any form or by any means, without the prior permission of the copyright owner

The right of Douglas Kelly to be identified as the author of this work has been asserted in accordance with sections 77 and 78 of the Copyright, Designs and Patents Act 1988

First published 2007
D. S. Brewer, Cambridge

ISBN 978 1 84384 111 1

D. S. Brewer is an imprint of Boydell & Brewer Ltd
PO Box 9, Woodbridge, Suffolk IP12 3DF, UK
and of Boydell & Brewer Inc.
668 Mt Hope Avenue, Rochester, NY 14620, USA
website: www.boydellandbrewer.com

A catalogue record for this title is available from the British Library

This publication is printed on acid-free paper

Typeset by Carnegie Book Production, Lancaster
Printed in Great Britain by
Antony Rowe Ltd, Chippenham, Wiltshire

CONTENTS

	Preface	vii
	Abbreviations	xi
	Introduction	1
1	Opinion as a Concept: Definition and Cognition	7
2	Opinion as a Personification: Description and Invention	41
3	Misogyny, Introspection, and Radical Opinion	77
4	Love, Reason, and Debatable Opinion	107
5	Self-Interest, Common Opinion, and Corrective Encomia	142
6	Opinion and Subjectivity	169
	Bibliography	181
	Index	213

Wie van ons kan ten volle navoelen wat voor degenen die toen leefden concepties als die van de Rede en van het Gevoel betekend hebben? wat voor een omwenteling en innerlijke tegenstrijdigheden die veroorzaakt hebben in van huis uit door starre rechtzinnigheid, standsvooroordelen en rigide seksuele opvattingen beheerste gemoederen?

Hella S. Haasse

[Who among us can fully sense what notions like Reason and Feeling meant to people living in those days? What an upheaval and inner conflict they aroused in minds dominated by an inflexible sense of rectitude, class prejudices, and rigid conceptions of sexuality?]

Mit dem Wort 'gewiß' drücken wir die völlige Überzeugung, die Abwesenheit jedes Zweifels aus, und wir suchen damit den Andern zu überzeugen. Das ist *subjektive* Gewißheit.

Ludwig Wittgenstein

[With the word 'certain' we express complete conviction, the total absence of doubt, and thereby we seek to convince other people. That is *subjective* certainty.]

PREFACE

> Nous ne supposerons à aucun moment de rencontre
> particulière entre la pensée ou la sensibilité médiévales
> et les nôtres.[1]

Christine de Pizan's focus on opinion in her writings corresponds with a new emphasis in late medieval French literature. As Claude Gauvard has noted, '"*Ut opinor*", jamais cette expression chère à Nicolas de Clamanges n'a été aussi actuelle'.[2] Christine herself clearly reflects the importance of opinion in her writings, for example, in her description of Lady Opinion, a personification that appears in the second part of the *Advision Cristine* (1405). This 'shade' is continually changing, in shape like a cloud, in color as if under shifting stage lighting. Around it, or her, swarm clouds of similar shades that illustrate diverse opinions on all manner of subjects by their own variegated, changing hues and shapes. Like Lady Opinion, opinions are in constant flux. Christine too changes her opinions, replicating the attribute of change in both Lady Opinion and her attendants. Her writings develop, modify, and correct her views of the world around her and their effect on her life and thought. Simply put, this book studies 'changing opinion' in the writings of Christine de Pizan.

Christine de Pizan flourished, and languished, during the terrible years for France between the death of Charles V in 1380 and the advent of Joan of Arc in 1429. Much as she likens her own fate in the *Mutacion de Fortune* (1403) to a shipwreck in stormy seas followed by a strenuous recovery, so too did France, already reeling from the Schism, shipwreck on the rocks of Charles VI's madness and under the steady pounding of war and rebellion. The social and moral realm was in chaos.[3] The full autumn tide, 'es levens felheid'[4] [the violence of life], as Huizinga portrayed the late Middle Ages, ramped over Christine's world and her work, blighting her happiness, undermining her certainties, and often suspending life and thought in the rough seas of a chaotic world. Perhaps this accounts for her heightened awareness of the role of opinion and changing opinions in human affairs.

---

[1] M. Zink 1985, p. 8.
[2] Gauvard 1995, p. 121.
[3] See Krynen 1981, pp. 43–48; Rossiaud 1986.
[4] Huizinga 1997, p. 13. Cf. *Advision*, II.xxii.64: 'tu es venue en mauvais temps' [you came into this world in bad times].

Hella S. Haasse's questions, cited in the epigraph to this book,[5] suggest how difficult it is to understand opinions that were formed and defended in bygone times. Let me illustrate this issue with another modern novelist's approach to the issues she raises. In Thomas Mann's *Doktor Faustus* a character relates an anecdote that offers a 'humane' reading of a woman burned at the stake for having allegedly engaged in illicit sexual concourse with an incubus three times each week while in bed with her unwitting husband. Confessing her sin, she and her inquisitor agree that the stake is the best solution because it liberates the woman from contact with the demon and from eternal torture in Hell, rewarding her confession with Heaven, thanks to God's forgiveness.[6] Do not such opinions evoke the mentality and the world Huizinga so tellingly describes in his scholarly masterpiece on the late Middle Ages? They also reveal something of the world Christine de Pizan knew and experienced. She too confronted issues of humanity such as the one Thomas Mann evokes fictionally. Her originality, as I hope to show, consists in relying on reason and experience in order to adapt her views to the diverse opinions she knew, some of which she shared, others which she rejected or modified. In the end she emerges in her writings as a remarkably enlightened writer for her times – enlightened in a more modern sense than we find in Mann's inquisitor and his victim.

Just as Christine's opinions about the *Roman de la rose* differed sharply from the opinions of those whom she called the 'disciples' of Jean de Meun, so too nowadays opinions differ and spark controversy on the meaning of Christine's own opinions and their significance for her time and ours.[7] To be sure, understanding thought and emotion in past times is as problematical as Haasse suggests. Yet, 'to say that one cannot read a medieval text "on its own ground" ... does not mean that one is entitled to ignore evidence of what that ground might have been'.[8] Parsing opinion in Christine's writings gives us insight into her thought on often controversial issues. This book attempts to

---

[5] Haasse 1996, p. 34. Widespread medieval and cool modern reception of Christine de Pizan's moralistic *Epistre Othea* is a good illustration of the issue Haasse raises. For an enlightened approach to *Othea* reception, see Parussa, ed., *Othea*, pp. 28–30, 81.

[6] 'Welche warme Humanität aus der Genugtuung darüber, diese Seele noch im letzten Augenblick durch das Feuer dem Teufel entrissen und ihr die Verzeihung Gottes verschafft zu haben!' (*Faustus*, p. 155) [What sincere human feeling emerges from satisfaction in having, at the last moment through fire, wrenched this soul free from the devil and gained it God's forgiveness!]

[7] For representative illustrations of scholarly differences regarding Christine's opinions about women and their roles, see Delany 1987 and 1992 vis-à-vis Quilligan 1991, pp. 7–10, and Reno 1992a. Such opposing views suggest that 'Christine as a reader and a writer was both resistant to and complicitous with medieval construction of femininity' (Krueger 1993, pp. 237–38). For mediating positions on Christine's alleged anti- versus profeminism, see Solente 1974, pp. 372–73; Gottlieb 1985; Huot 1985; Hicks 1988 and 1995b; Brown-Grant 1999b and 2003; Stedman 2002; Haidu 2004, pp. 303–13; Waaldijk 2004.

[8] Patterson 2001, p. 679. Recent studies illustrate this approach; see Gauvard 1991; the articles in *Anger* and *Emoties*, especially Frijda 1998 (on the subject of emotions in medieval French writing, see Van Gijsen 1998 and Stuip 1998); Burrow 2002; Cheyette and Chickering

illuminate evidence for Christine's opinion making. In having to convince others, she provides us with that evidence while highlighting opinions that were and, indeed, often still are controversial and subjective. While seeking certainty, a lifelong quest depicted in her writings, Christine discovered her own limits; at the same time, she knew and came to understand subjective certainty much as Wittgenstein describes it in the second epigraph.[9] Christine de Pizan reflected deeply on the subject of opinion while analyzing, evaluating, challenging, and changing her own and others' opinions in a lifelong quest for certainty, that is, 'complete conviction' and 'the total absence of doubt'. How Christine defines opinion, how she evaluates opinions as well as how she argues for the validity of or error in diverse opinions she shared, modified, or rejected – all this is accessible through close attention to her thinking and writing. Whenever she changed or modified an opinion, Christine revealed how she evaluated opinions in her own mind and in debate with others.

*

Note on text
Translations are mine, unless otherwise identified; I have, however, not translated quotations in modern French. In some cases, I have modified quoted translations; the modifications are italicized in those translations.

Acknowledgements
Parts of Chapter 2 were presented at the Tenth Triennial Congress of the International Courtly Literature Society in Tübingen, 2001, while parts of Chapter 5 were presented at the Third International Conference on the Medieval Chronicle sponsored by the University of Utrecht and held at Driebergen, The Netherlands, in 2002. I am grateful for observations by those who attended. Prior to its publication, Liliane Dulac kindly provided me with a copy of the *Advision Cristine* that she and Christine Reno edited. SunHee Kim Gertz subjected a nearly final version of my book to thorough, probing scrutiny. Others have been helpful in various ways. I am especially thankful to Frank Brandsma, Keith Busby, and Lori J. Walters. Finally, I have profited from the contributions and critical engagement of students since the 1960s while teaching Christine de Pizan and Jean de Meun's *Roman de la rose*, two authors who provoked marvel, controversy, and heated debate in their times, and who continue to generate diverse and conflicting opinions even today. No medieval authors remain as current today as these two, where, in the interplay of reason and passion, they continue to promote and challenge opinions and opinion making.

2005. Although these studies do not treat Christine de Pizan specifically, they do seek grounds for actions and emotions depicted in medieval evidence.
[9] Wittgenstein 1970, p. 56.

Abbreviations

(Abbreviations of editions appear in Bibliography, primary texts)

Apogée	*Apogée et déclin: Actes du Colloque de l'URA 411, Provins 1991.* Ed. Claude Thomasset and Michel Zink. Cultures et civilisations médiévales, 8. Paris: Presses de l'Université de Paris Sorbonne, 1993.
Archéologie	*Archéologie du signe.* Ed. Lucie Brind'Amour and Eugene Vance. Recueil d'Etudes médiévales, 3. Toronto: Pontifical Institute of Medieval Studies, 1983.
Au champ	*Au champ des escriptures: IIIe Colloque International sur Christine de Pizan, Lausanne, 18–22 juillet 1998.* Ed. Eric Hicks, with Diego Gonzalez et Philippe Simon. Etudes Christiniennes, 6. Paris: Champion, 2000.
AW	*Tobler-Lommatzsch Altfranzösisches Wörterbuch.* 11 vols. Berlin: Wiedmann, Wiesbaden: Steiner, 1925–.
CAIEF	*Cahiers de l'Association Internationale des études françaises.*
Casebook	*Christine de Pizan: A Casebook.* Ed. Barbara K. Altmann and Deborah L. McGrady. Routledge Medieval Casebooks, 34. New York, London: Routledge, 2003.
CFMA	Classiques français du moyen âge.
Chaucer's Contemporaries	*Chaucer's French Contemporaries: The Poetry/Poetics of Self and Tradition.* Ed. R. Barton Palmer. Georgia State Literary Studies, 10. New York: AMS Press, 1999.
Christine Categories	*Christine de Pizan and the Categories of Difference.* Ed. Marilynn Desmond. Medieval Cultures, 14. Minneapolis, London: University of Minnesota Press, 1998.
Christine Lyric	*Christine de Pizan and Medieval French Lyric.* Ed. Earl Jeffrey Richards. Gainesville: University Press of Florida, 1998.
Christine 2000	*Christine de Pizan 2000: Studies on Christine de Pizan in Honour of Angus J. Kennedy.* Ed. John Campbell and Nadia Margolis. Faux Titre, 196. Amsterdam, Atlanta: Rodopi, 2000.

Christine vrouw	*Christine de Pizan, een bijzondere vrouw.* Ed. R. E. V. Stuip. Utrechtse Bijdragen tot de Mediëvistiek, 19. Hilversum: Verloren, 2004.
Città	*Christine de Pizan: une città per se.* Ed. Patrizia Caraffi. Biblioteca Medievale: saggi, 10. Rome: Carocci, 2003.
City of Scholars	*The City of Scholars: New Approaches to Christine de Pizan.* Ed. Margarete Zimmermann and Dina De Rentiis. European Cultures: Studies in Literature and the Arts, 2. Berlin, New York: de Gruyter, 1994.
Condición	*La Condición de la mujer en la edad media: Actas del Coloquio celebrado en la Casa de Velásquez, del 5 al 7 noviembre de 1984.* Ed. Yves-René Fonquerne and Alfonso Esteban. Madrid: Casa de Velásquez, Universidad Complutense, 1986.
Contexts	*Contexts and Continuities: Proceedings of the IVth International Colloquium on Christine de Pizan (Glasgow 21–27 July 2000), Published in Honour of Liliane Dulac.* Ed. Angus J. Kennedy with Rosalind Brown-Grant, James C. Laidlaw, and Catherine M. Müller. Glasgow University Medieval French Texts and Studies, 1. 3 vols. Glasgow: University of Glasgow Press, 2002.
Courtly Literature	*Courtly Literature and Clerical Culture–Höfische Literatur und Klerikerkultur–Littérature courtoise et culture cléricale. Selected Papers from the Tenth Triennial Congress of the International Courtly Literature Society, Universität Tübingen, Deutschland, 28. Juli–3. August 2001.* Ed. Christoph Huber and Henrike Lähnemann, with Sandra Linden. Tübingen: Attempto, 2002.
Emoties	*Emoties in de Middeleeuwen.* Ed. R. E. V. Stuip and C. Vellekoop. Utrechtse Bijdragen tot de Mediëvistiek, 15. Hilversum: Verloren, 1998.
Femme de lettres	*Une Femme de lettres au moyen âge: études autour de Christine de Pizan.* Ed. L. Dulac and B. Ribémont, Medievalia, 16: Etudes Christiniennes. Orléans: Paradigme, 1995.
Femmes	*Femmes: mariages – lignages XIIe–XIVe siècles. Mélanges offerts à Georges Duby.* Bibliothèque du Moyen Age, 1. Brussels: De Boeck Université, 1992.
FEW	*Französisches Etymologisches Wörterbuch.* Ed. Walter von Wartburg. 25 vols. Berlin: Teubner, Basel: Zbinden, 1928–.
Gender and Text	*Gender and Text in the Later Middle Ages.* Ed. Jane Chance. Gainesville: University Press of Florida, 1996.

GRLMA	*Grundriß der romanischen Literaturen des Mittelalters.* Heidelberg: Winter, 1968–.
Hommage Dufournet	*Et c'est la fin pour quoy sommes ensemble: hommage à Jean Dufournet. Littérature, histoire et langue du Moyen Âge.* Nouvelle Bibliothèque du moyen âge, 25. 3 vols. Paris: Champion, 1993.
HWR	*Historisches Wörterbuch der Rhetorik.* Ed. Gert Ueding [et alii]. Tübingen: Niemeyer, 1992–.
Ideals	*Ideals for Women in the Works of Christine de Pizan.* Ed. Diane Bornstein. Medieval and Renaissance Monograph Series, Michigan Consortium for Medieval and Early Modern Studies, 1. Detroit: Fifteenth-Century Symposium, 1981.
Medieval Lyric	*Medieval Lyric: Genres in Historical Context.* Ed. William D. Paden. Illinois Medieval Studies. Urbana, Chicago: University of Illinois Press, 2000.
Miscellanea Mediaevalia	*Miscellanea Mediaevalia: mélanges offerts à Philippe Ménard.* Ed. J. Claude Faucon, Alain Labbé, and Danielle Quéruel. Nouvelle Bibliothèque du moyen âge, 46. 2 vols. Paris: Champion, 1998.
Mittelalterbilder	*Mittelalterbilder aus neuer Perspektive: Diskussionsanstöße zu amour courtois, Subjektivität in der Dichtung und Strategien des Erzählens.* Ed. Ernstpeter Ruhe and Rudolf Behrens. Beiträge zur romanischen Philologie des Mittelalters, 14. Munich: Fink, 1985.
Musique	*Musique naturele: Interpretationen zur französischen Lyrik des Spätmittelalters.* Ed. Wolf-Dieter Stempel. Romanistisches Colloquium, 7. Munich: Fink, 1995.
Mythographic	*The Mythographic Art: Classical Fable and the Rise of the Vernacular in Early France and England.* Ed. Jane Chance. Gainesville: University of Florida Press, 1990.
Novum Glossarium	*Novum Glossarium mediae latinitatis ab anno DCCC ad annum MCC.* Ed. Franz Blatt and Yves Lefèvre. Copenhagen: Munksgaard, 1983–.
Penser	*Penser le pouvoir au Moyen Age (VIIIe–XVe siècle): études d'histoire et de littérature offertes à Françoise Autrand.* Ed. Dominique Boutet and Jacques Verger. Paris: Editions Rue d'Ulm/Presses de l'Ecole Normale Supérieure, 2000.
Politics	*Politics, Gender, and Genre: The Political Thought of Christine de Pizan.* Ed. Margaret Brabant. Boulder, CO, San Francisco, Oxford: Westview, 1992.

Recherches	*Recherches sur la littérature du XVe siècle: Actes du VIe Colloque International sur le Moyen Français, Milan, 4–6 mai 1988, vol. III.* Ed. Sergio Cigada and Anna Slerca. Contributi del 'Centro sulla letteratura medio-francese e medio-inglese', 9, Scienze filologiche e letteratura, 46. Milan: Vita e Pensiero, 1991.
Reinterpreting Christine	*Reinterpreting Christine de Pizan.* Ed. Earl Jeffrey Richards, with Joan Williamson, Nadia Margolis, and Christine Reno. Athens, GA, London: University of Georgia Press, 1992.
Riens ne m'est seur	*'Riens ne m'est seur que la chose incertaine': études sur l'art d'écrire au moyen âge offertes à Eric Hicks par ses élèves, collègues, amies et amis.* Ed. Jean-Claude Mühlethaler and Denis Billotte, with Alain Corbellari, Marie-Thérèse Bonadonna, and Barbara Wahlen. Travaux des Universités Suisses, 9. Geneva: Slatkine, 2001.
Robert	*Dictionnaire historique de la langue française.* Ed. Alain Rey. 2 vols. Paris: Robert, Montréal: Dicorobert, 1992.
SATF	Société des Anciens Textes français.
Strong Voices	*Strong Voices, Weak History: Early Women Writers and Canons in England, France, and Italy.* Ed. Pamela Joseph Benson and Victoria Kirkham. Ann Arbor: University of Michigan Press, 2005.
Sur le chemin	*Sur le chemin de longue étude … : Actes du Colloque d'Orléans juillet 1995.* Ed Bernard Ribémont. Etudes Christiniennes, 3. Paris: Champion, 1998.
TLF	Textes littéraires français.
Traduction	*Traduction et adaptation en France à la fin du Moyen Age et à la Renaissance: Actes du Colloque organisé pas l'Université de Nancy II, 23–25 mars 1995.* Ed. Charles Brucker. Colloques, Congrès et Conférences sur la Renaissance, 10. Paris: Champion, 1997.
Violence	*Violence in Medieval Society.* Ed. Richard W. Kaeuper. Woodbridge: Boydell, 2000.
What Is Literature?	*What Is Literature? France 1100–1600.* Ed. François Cornilliat, Ullrich Langer, and Douglas Kelly. The Edward C. Armstrong Monographs on Medieval Literature, 7. Lexington, KY: French Forum, 1993.

INTRODUCTION

> Ne scez tu que les tres meilleurs choses sont les plus debatues et les plus arguees?[1]

In the second part of the *Advision*, Christine relates her encounter with 'une grant ombre femmenine sans corps' (II.i.9) [a great, disembodied feminine shade]. This is Lady Opinion. Christine recognizes her from previous encounters, notably in the debate about the *Roman de la rose*. 'Ne fus je celle', Lady Opinion asks,

> qui mist le debat entre les clers, disciples de Maistre Jehan de Meun ... et toy sur la compillacion du *Romant de la Rose*, duquel entre vous contradictoirement escripsistes l'un a l'autre, chascune partie soustenant ses raisons, si comme il appert par le livret qui en fu fait? (*Advision*, II.xxi.25–29)
>
> [Was I not she who started the debate between the clerics, disciples of Master Jean de Meun, and you on the compilation called the *Roman de la rose*, a work about which you exchanged opposing interpretations, each party defending its arguments, as one can see in the book containing them?]

In the debate, Christine defends the opinion that the *Roman de la rose* uses vulgar and obscene language to exhort its readers to lewdness and lewd acts, whereas Jean's 'disciples' claim that the romance dissuades such conduct. Although a debate about contradictory opinions, only Christine de Pizan regularly refers to 'opinion' and its synonyms; Jean's 'disciples' use this terminology far less frequently.[2] She was obviously more concerned than they seem to have been about the prominence of opinion in argument.

Christine distinguished between opinion and 'certainne science' (*Débat*, p. 131:510–11); she also distinguished between opinion and religious faith, as is apparent in statements such as 'chose qui est dicte par oppinion et non de loy commandee' (*Débat*, p. 12:32–33) [something expressing an opinion, but

---

[1] *Cité*, p. 48: 'Don't you know that the most excellent topics are the ones most hotly debated and argued?'

[2] *Débat*, Gautier Col: p. 9:12; Pierre Col: pp. 100:387, 101:458, 154:30. Christine de Pizan's examples are so numerous that cataloguing them here is superfluous; many will be discussed in what follows. I find no occurrence of the word in Gerson's contributions.

not dictated by religion]. *Loy*, as religion, clearly does not fall within the semantic range of opinion. Christine's use of the word 'opinion' conforms to French usage in her time as an assertion or belief that falls between ignorance or error, on the one hand, and certainty on the other. In Brunetto Latini's *Tresor*, for example, opinion denotes a judgment of greater or lesser certainty,[3] especially in moral issues.[4] Moreover, in this work, which Christine knew, opinion is not synonymous with presumption, since it is founded on probability or verisimilitude.[5] As we shall see, Christine avers that certain passages in the *Rose* are expressly condemned and forbidden by her religion; she thinks they incite to lust, a mortal sin. That lust is wrong is a religious truth embodied in the Ten Commandments; that the *Rose* incites to lust is her opinion. She insists that the poem lures into sin those of weak moral character, including the young and inexperienced, as well as the morally 'soft', or *mous*.[6] Jean Gerson agrees with her opinion, but Jean de Meun's 'disciples' do not. Rather they hold that their master's romance turns its readers away from sin and its temptations. Following 'protocol', each disputant produces contemporary examples that support his or her opinion on the work's effects.[7] Not surprisingly, perhaps, given the debate form, it does not occur to any of the disputants that reading the *Rose* might produce both results.[8]

Christine describes Lady Opinion, her personification of the notion, in Chapter Two of the *Advision Cristine*. But she also attaches to this major figure numerous opinions that personify diverse opinions. The description of Lady Opinion and the multicolored, polymorphous opinions that flit about and accompany her provides the model for my book. In the first two chapters I treat Christine's definition and description of Lady Opinion and the opinions that swirl about her. In the following chapters I turn to Christine's own opinions. Here we perceive that the changing colors and shapes of opinions that are part of the description of Lady Opinion are not mere literary inventions. Allegorically, they illustrate Christine's own intellectual experience. Her opinions changed too, as her thought evolved and, in many ways, matured.

Chapter 1 begins with Christine's use of the term 'opinion' in the *Rose* debate because that is where the notion first becomes prominent in her writings.

---

[3] Messelaar 1963, pp. 25, 210, and 282. In what follows, I rely heavily on Messelaar's excellent study of Brunetto's intellectual vocabulary.

[4] Messelaar 1963, pp. 38, 65, 143, and 323; on opinion and pride, see pp. 41, 161, 343, and 377.

[5] Messelaar 1963, p. 60. For the semantic range of *opinio* and *opinor* in medieval Latin, see *Novum Glossarium*, cols. 551–56. Issues involving opinion are raised frequently in John of Salisbury's *Policraticus*; see the French translation, *Policratique*, by Denis Foulechat, p. 422, s.v. 'Op(p)inion.' On opinion in early Christian and Scholastic thought, see von Moos 2002.

[6] On *mollesse* in this sense, see Kelly 1995a, pp. 119–21.

[7] *Débat*, Pierre Col: p. 106:598–606; Christine: pp. 139:799–140:812.

[8] On such selective partiality in reading the *Rose* in the Middle Ages, see Huot 1993a.

Christine grounds her reflections on opinion on the thought processes by which humans seek certainty. Perhaps most importantly, Chapter 1 reveals that the movement in her thought from one opinion to another, extending from more controversial to more acceptable opinions in her times, has a cumulative resonance, permitting us to articulate and even evaluate the grounds on which she founded her opinions.[9]

Chapter 2 examines Christine's description of the personification of Opinion in the *Advision Cristine*.[10] Description is a feature of the art of rhetoric. Rhetoric as the art of arguing plausible opinions looms large. This requires a thorough study of the art of topical invention she uses to describe personifications such as Lady Opinion that exemplify evidence for her thinking and opinion making. Important here is the process by which Christine actually changes her opinion. The *Advision Cristine* illustrates such changes by showing how, influenced by Boethius and Thomas Aquinas, she changed her opinion on the role of fortune in her life. Thus, in discussing the process in this chapter, I examine how Lady Opinion and Lady Philosophy convince the character, Christine, that Opinion, not Fortune, is the source of her political, intellectual, and personal difficulties.

In each of the following chapters, I treat an important change or modification of her opinion, thus exploring her changing views on misogyny, ideal love, and self-interest in French history and politics; in these instances, conflicting opinion is a central issue. Thus, Chapter 3 treats opinions on misogyny through the lens of 'vray sentement'. More specifically, it examines the role of individual opinion in the face of misogyny, a majority opinion in Christine's time[11] and itself an expression of *vray sentement*. Although relatively straightforward, this line of argument is inherently slippery and controversial, being based in part on 'passionate' feeling; after all, did not both Martin Luther King and Hitler feel passionately the opinions they promoted? The same question can be asked of the misogynists, lovers, and French knights in Christine's age. From this perspective, Christine described herself, perhaps ironically, as 'passionnee comme femme' as she set out to write the very sober *Corps de policie* (p. 1:7).[12] When we examine this statement, it will be apparent that passion is a vice; it is not suitable as a moral foundation, and is, therefore, a shaky foundation for opinion. How Christine evaluates 'passionate' feelings like hers is an important factor in defending her opinions. The rehabilitation of the vice passion depends on the opinion the vice promulgates.

Chapter 4 focuses on an obvious passion, love. To correct Jean de Meun, Christine has Reason come back down from her tower to debate and resolve

---

[9] Cf. the incisive analysis of infratextuality in Christine's *œuvre* in Hauck 1995.

[10] Laidlaw 1983, p. 544, notes that the *Advision* 'does not seem ever to have been included by Christine in a collection of her works'. It survives in only three manuscripts (Reno and Dulac, ed., *Advision*, p. xi).

[11] Angeli 2002, p. 115.

[12] Cf. Blanchard 1986b, p. 57; Dulac 1991a.

matters of opinion on love and lovemaking. On this topic, as in the *Rose* and the *Rose* debate, issues are controversial and opinions diverge. Chapter 4 also explores Christine's opinions on love as *raison* construes it in her love poetry. Christine's own opinions on love evolve over time from the idealistic, chivalric love she admires in the *Rose* debate to, finally, a categorical denial of any good love outside of, at times, marriage. In particular, the commonplace that love, a passion, is justifiable if it promotes chivalry, an opinion that Christine defends in her early writing, is later abandoned in the light of experience.

Chapter 5 considers France's political troubles during the dark years of the Hundred Years War in the light of *loy* and the epideictic mode. Here we discover an evolution in Christine's opinion on the place of self-interest in the body politic and in the commonweal. She comes to realize that the self-interest she criticized in the warring parties could actually be a source of union and restoration of the kingdom. This occurs when, as enlightened self-interest, different social groups unite for the common good. Christine's opinions on France's plight were generally received or accepted in her time, even if they were not always followed, especially when narrow views of self-interest prevailed even when they did not benefit the body politic. An important feature of Christine's thought in this context is the distinction between inherited nobility and true nobility founded on virtue.

Finally, in Chapter 6, Christine's conception of opinion finds its place in recent work on the emergence of a sense of subjectivity in medieval literature. Taking subjectivity in Michel Zink's sense of the word – 'le produit d'une conscience particulière'[13] – Christine's evaluation of opinion is unique in ways that place her opinions in an evolving medieval context that modern scholarship has identified as the emerging significance of subjective truth in late medieval and early modern literature. Christine promotes her views as woman. As such, her opinions are indeed subjective. They also oppose traditional opinions that, by the fifteenth century, have become virtual *idées reçues* on misogyny and love. To state her case, she attaches great significance to her own experiences and to the impact of those experiences on her opinions as they emerge, evolve, and change, as well as when she rejects them outright. She takes account of contingencies, anomalies, and contradictions in her opinions and in those of others. In the evolution of medieval subjectivity, Christine's changing opinions mark a major stage on the way to Rabelais and Montaigne.

Over the last twenty or more years, Christine scholarship evinces three principal approaches.[14] Her return to prominence, for example, owes much to feminist readings that locate her opinions in the context of current feminist theory. Other studies endeavor to show, by internal textual analysis, the development and coherence of Christine's thought on the diverse subjects she treated. Finally, more traditional studies explore the place and significance of

---

[13] M. Zink 1985, p. 8.
[14] Ruhe 2000, pp. 92–93.

her thought as it might have been perceived and understood by medieval audiences and readers in the late fourteenth and early fifteenth centuries. My study belongs in the third group. To be sure, the three approaches are not hermetically sealed from one another, nor is there universal agreement among scholars within each of the three groups. Therefore, although emphasizing the third approach, I have tried to make good use of what the other two offer to elucidate Christine's thought on and use of opinion in the often controversial contexts in which she wrote, while not forgetting Haasse's reminder of how inscrutable earlier thinkers can seem today when treating moral and social issues.

1
Opinion as a Concept: Definition and Cognition

> Einsi par: 'non a, – si a, – non fu, – si fu', fais gens entreoccire souventesfois.[1]

Many of Christine de Pizan's opinions remain controversial today. They are debated in the same arena as in the *Advision Cristine*: the university classroom and its extension, academic symposia and publications. Such debates focus on what Christine's opinions are, how she arrives at them, and how valid they may be today. My intention here is to examine criteria she used for making and changing opinion in order that she might distinguish true from false opinion, an examination that will allow us to appreciate and evaluate the grounds and rigor of her opinions as she defined and articulated them in an ongoing quest for certainty.

Late medieval writers wrote their treatises using formulae that suggest how they construed their subject matter.[2] Among these criteria, the *modi tractandi* were in common use among vernacular writers in Christine's time. In Dante's well-known examples, the *modi tractandi* include the allegorical (*poeticus*), fictional (*fictivus*), descriptive (*descriptivus*), digressive (*digressivus*), and metaphorical (*transumptivus*) modes; supplementing these are additional modes, such as definition (*diffinitivus*), demonstrative logic (*probativus vel improbativus*), and supporting examples (*exemplorum positivus*).[3] Christine used all these modes at various places in her writings.[4] Two that both Christine and Jean de Meun used are prominent in their treatment of opinion: definition and description, or *modus diffinitivus* and *modus descriptivus*.[5] In the second part of her *Advision*, for example, Christine first sets out an extensive description of Lady Opinion as a personification; she then concludes with a definition of

---

[1] *Advision*, II.xvii.48–49: So by dint of 'No he doesn't', 'Yes he does', 'No he wasn't', 'Yes he was', I often cause people to kill one another.
[2] Minnis 1984; see also Kelly 1985; Cerquiglini 1988a, pp. 91–92.
[3] Allen 1982, pp. 71–74; Minnis 1984, pp. 144–45.
[4] McLeod 1992; Brown-Grant 2000b. Cf. Schreiner 2000 on Christine's original adaptation of received images or the topoi *locus* and *tempus*.
[5] For Jean de Meun, see Kelly 1995a, pp. 56–65, 100–22.

the concept the Lady personifies. Here, I will treat Christine's definition of opinion in this chapter, and, in the next chapter, her description of Lady Opinion.[6]

Christine's definition of opinion

What does Christine de Pizan mean by opinion?[7] What is its place in her thought and writings? What are the sources of her ideas and how does she adapt them to her own thought? Christine treats the subject of opinion extensively in the second part of her three-part *Advision Cristine*. She links it there to the first part of this treatise on Fama, or reputation, especially France's reputation in a chaotic world (*Advision*, I.iv.10–13, v. 6–9), and to the last part on firm truth based on the harmonious union of reason as philosophy and of faith as theology.

In the second part, the *Advision* describes Christine's encounter with Lady Opinion, complete with numerous examples of variously shaped and colored attendant opinions flitting about her. When Christine finally recognizes the personification, she proposes the following definition:

> Comme la descripcion de vous meismes m'en apprengne la diffinicion, je dis ... et conclus que vous estes adhesion a une partie, laquelle adhesion est causee de l'apparence d'aucune raison prouvable, soit que l'oppinant ait doubte de l'autre partie, soit que non. (*Advision*, II.xxii.72–73, 80–83)

> [As your description teaches me how to define you, I state ... and conclude that you are adherence to one side in a dispute, adherence that stems from reasoning that seems demonstrable, whether the person holding the opinion has doubts regarding the other side or not.]

The ability to comprehend is limited by the inability to detect with certainty whether an analysis reveals truth or not. Consequently, opinions may be true or false, and opposing parties – 'une partie' and 'l'autre partie' – may disagree (cf. *Tresor*, III.9.1.2–4). Christine recognized this inherent human limitation when she concluded that the debate on the *Roman de la rose* led to a deadlock: they say it's good; she says it's bad.[8]

Before examining opinion as Christine uses the concept in the *Advision*, it will be helpful to look at the role of opinion in the *Rose* debate, where she

---

[6] Christine was perhaps placing the anonymous description before the definition in order to create audience suspense and anticipation before identifying and defining the personification.

[7] The best study of her use of opinion before the Reno–Dulac edition of the *Advision* is Badel 1980, pp. 436–47. Brown-Grant 1999a, ch. 3, focuses on Christine's political opinions. See also Blanchard 1986a and Brown-Grant 1992; Reno and Dulac, ed., *Advision*, pp. 162–63, n. I–II, and 164, n. IV.

[8] Cf. Brownlee 1992, p. 257; Brown-Grant 1999a, pp. 31–32.

first expresses her views on it. The debate mode, common in allegory, registers diverse opinions. It was widespread in literal writing too because the mode is suitable for treating diverse opinions (*Tresor*, III.9).⁹

Clashing opinions in the *Rose* debate

The *Rose* debate between the opponents and defenders of Jean de Meun's romance turns on the truth or falsity of the opinion that the romance is a moral treatise.¹⁰ Did Jean intend to write a guide for and praise of seduction? This thorny problem is as controversial today as it was in Christine's time.¹¹ According to Christine, if he had intended the *Rose* to be a guide to moral conduct, he failed. The poem incites to lust, she firmly believes, making it morally reprehensible, since incitement to lust is a sin contrary to religion, or *loy*. Her standards are accepted by opponents and defenders of Jean de Meun. However, although the latter accept those standards, they deny the faults Christine and Jean Gerson impute to the romance. Consonant with Christine, Gerson reads the poem as a source,

> trop grant en occasions de erreurs, en blaphemes, en venimeuses doctrines, en destruccions et desolacions de povres ames crestiennes, en illicite perdicion de tamps qui est tant precieux, au prejudice de Chasteté, en la disipacion de loyaulté hors mariaige et ens, ou dechassement de Paour et de Honte, ou diffame de Raison, ou grant deshonneur de vous, dame Justice Canonique ... (*Débat*, p. 86:678–84)

> [too great an incitement to errors, blasphemies, poisonous teachings, it destroys and devastates poor Christian souls through illicit waste of precious time; all this opposes Chastity and weakens fidelity both in and out of

---

⁹ Potansky 1972, pp. 195–201; Hauck 1995; Strubel 2002, pp. 177–79. Christine uses debate in her debate poems as well as debates between lovers such as that in the *Cent ballades d'amant et de dame*.

¹⁰ Badel 1980, pp. 418–31. On the 'scholastic literary principles' that 'determined some of the parameters of the debate', see Minnis 1991 (quote from p. 36). I set aside the issue of which *Rose* manuscript, and therefore which illustrations, the disputants may have known, an issue that cannot be resolved with certainty on the basis of evidence available today. The illustrations in *Rose* manuscripts are one of the faults Gerson finds in the work; he seems to assume that Jean is the actual source for those illustrations (*Débat*, pp. 63:103–06, 68:238–46, 73:355, 87:700–02). On the scholarship on these illustrations, see McMunn 2000, who finds no evidence that Christine was offended by illustrations. On the repercussions of the *Rose* debate among English writers through Hoccleve, see Fleming 1971, pp. 21–40, and Kooper 2004; they follow earlier English quarrels about Chaucer (Erler 1990, pp. 160–67). Jean de Meun alludes to debate in his own time while responding to accusations of vulgarity, misogyny, and anti-religious sentiments (*Rose*, v. 15105–272; cf. Hicks, ed., *Débat*, pp. xx–xxiii; Kelly 1995a, pp. 98–99). For the relation of the *Rose* debate to the longer-lasting discussion about French Humanism instigated by Petrarch's criticism of French writing, see Margolis 2000; cf. Badel 1980, pp. 462–82; Solterer 1995, pp. 151–56.

¹¹ See Arden 1993.

marriage, driving away Fear and Shame, defaming Reason, to your great dishonor, Lady Canon Law.]

Pierre Col counters Gerson. For this 'disciple'[12] of Jean de Meun, his 'maistre' is 'ce tres devolt catholique et tres eslevey theologien, ce tres divin orateur et poete et tres parfait philozophe' (*Débat*, p. 89:11–13) [this very devout Catholic and most distinguished theologian, this most divine orator and poet and most perfect philosopher]. With opponents at such loggerheads, little wonder that Christine for her part could only exclaim: 'et si n'est ce pas article de foy … si en *croie* chascun ce qui luy plaist le mieulx qu'i porra' (*Débat*, p. 149:1116–18; my emphasis) [this is not an article of faith, so let each *believe* what pleases him as best he can]. Since divine truth cannot resolve such differences of opinion, each person must adhere to the view that seems to offer the more reasonable demonstration to him or her (cf. *Advision* II.xxii.72–83, partially quoted above).

In matters of opinion such as these, rhetoric, not logic or moral theology, is the art used to argue one's case, since rhetoric is the art of arguing the plausible.[13] Both sides in the debate agree on this, and they evoke rhetorical procedures and rules that govern such debate. Indeed, Christine admires her opponents' eloquence.[14] She evaluates and judges effective rhetorical ploys that they use.[15] Yet effective rhetoric and eloquence are not in and of themselves sufficient to force conviction or alter the opinions of any of the debaters.

> Vueil que tu saches, tout soient tes raisons bien conduites a la fin de ton entencion contraires a la mienne oppinion, ycelles, non obstant la belle eloquence, ne mouvent en riens mon couraige ne troublent mon sentement au contraire de ce que autrefoys ay escript sus la matiere.
> (*Débat*, p. 115:16–20)

> [I want you to know that although your argument is well developed according to the goal you have set for yourself, it is opposed to my opinion and it has

---

[12] On 'disciple', see De Rentiis 1994.

[13] On rhetoric's prominence in Christine's time, see Meyenberg 1992; Gauvard 1995, pp. 118–19; G. Zink 1995. Besides the works in G. Zink's bibliography (p. 395 n. 6), see on rhetorical style Auerbach 1958, especially ch. 3; Meyenberg 1992, pp. 159–62. There is no systematic study of Christine's knowledge of the art of rhetoric or her use of it in her writing, although some studies treat features of the art (Curnow 1992; Fenster 1992; McLeod 1992; Enders 1994; Arden 1997, especially pp. 11–15; Margolis 1997). On epistolary debates in Christine's time, see Cerquiglini 1993b, p. 154; Richards 1993 and 1998b. We have only anecdotal or circumstantial information about her education or how she acquired her knowledge and skills; see Willard 1984, pp. 33–34; Zühlke 1994, pp. 48–62. Stuip 2004 offers a wide-ranging survey of what her education could have been, and as part of her ongoing desire to know and learn.

[14] *Débat*, pp. 12:10–12, 33–36, 49:11–12, 50:33–35; cf. *Mutacion*, v. 7975–8070.

[15] For example, Jehan Johannez is 'expert de rethorique' (*Débat*, pp. 11:5–12:6) and Pierre Col expresses himself with 'belle eloquence' (*Débat*, p. 115:18).

in no way swayed me in spite of your fine eloquence, nor troubled me, nor made me think the opposite of what I have written earlier on the subject.]

Christine's opponents stand just as firm in the opinions of Jean de Meun's 'disciples'. Christine's and Gerson's 'hault entendement, cler engien, et ... eloquance' (*Débat*, p. 89:4–5) [profound understanding, clear intellect,[16] and eloquence] do not sway them at all (*Débat*, pp. 111:793–112:810).

Elsewhere, Christine argues that Jean failed to adhere to decorum.[17] Here too opinions differ. The debate turns on how decorously Jean describes diverse personifications, including the language they use to refer to lovers and lovemaking and the import of the advice they offer. Christine is especially critical of Reason's referring to genitalia in crude language.[18] In response, Pierre Col claims that, on the contrary, Reason's language is entirely appropriate when speaking to a Fol Amoureux.

> Si ne fault ja dire qu'il garda mal les regles de rethorique, car il monstre evidemmant qu'il les avoit naturelement et par estude: j'ose dire que qui le lit et entent, il entendra avec maistre Jehan de Meung ne devoir autrement parler qu'il parla. (*Débat*, p. 98:325–29)
>
> [One must not claim that he did not adhere to rhetorical decorum, for he shows quite obviously that he possessed the art both naturally and through study. I dare say that his attentive reader will agree with master Jean de Meun that one must not speak other than he did.]

Christine nonetheless rejects this argument on the grounds that, even if Jean satirizes Fol Amoureux in this way, the 'ordre de rethorique' (*Débat*, p. 135:641; see ll. 636–46), or decorum, requires that he also explain his strategy and offer counter-examples.[19]

Through her responses, the debate on the *Roman de la rose* falls for Christine in the realm of opinion, not in that of certain knowledge or of faith. It centers 'upon questions of language and social responsibility, on what an author allegedly intended and what various audiences heard'.[20] Given human limitations

---

[16] On *engien* in this sense, cf. Reno and Dulac, ed., *Advision*, p. 224 s.v. *engin*; on the word's semantic range of positive and negative meanings, see Messelaar 1963, especially pp. 25, 56, 260, 360.

[17] *Débat*, pp. 124:299–303, 135:640–44; Gerson makes the same claim (*Débat*, p. 85:641–56). Cf. Minnis 1991, pp. 14–22; Edsall 2000.

[18] Christine names genitalia when necessary, as, for example, for the castration of Saturn, but her choice of words differs from Reason's; see Kelly 1995a, pp. 46–47. Apart from the objection to Reason's language Christine lauds Reason's criticism of foolish love in her *Deux amants*, v. 961–77.

[19] Cf. *Tresor*, III.46, 64.16–17. An example of such decorum is her description of Charles V's youth in *Charles V*; I treat this description below, pp. 119–22. On decorum and the *style clergial* and/or *prosal*, see Zumthor 1955, pp. 246–47; Potansky 1972, p. 188; Burnley 1986; Laird and Richards 1998; and on clerical and court styles, Margolis 1998.

[20] Fenster 1998, p. 96.

that prevent understanding from rising to full comprehension and contemplation of eternal truths, Christine concludes that one must judge products of imagination like the *Rose* by opinion rather than by certain knowledge: 'convient par oppinion plus que de certainne science determiner des choses ymaginees plus voirsamblables' (*Débat*, p. 115:6–8) [one must decide by opinion rather than with certain knowledge regarding the credibility of products of the imagination]. As an allegorical construct, the *Rose* is a product of the imagination, or, more precisely, the faculty known as imagination in medieval faculty theory. This faculty perceives and retains the forms of visible things in the mind.[21] Thus, debate turns on what the *Rose*, a visible thing, represents, and the image that it projects will be more or less a matter of opinion. The poem's rhetoric is eloquent, but ineffective, according to Christine.

This is not the fault of rhetoric itself. We must strive to clear our minds of the current, often pejorative connotations of words like 'rhetoric' and 'eloquence' that are frequently evoked to criticize political debates nowadays. Such negative connotations did not prevail in Christine de Pizan's times. Indeed, Jean Gerson acknowledges rhetorical appeal by personifying Eloquence Theologienne. The art of rhetoric is a perfectly acceptable mode for debate and, potentially, judgment in disputes regarding opinions (*Tresor*, I.4.9–10). Its failure in such debates does not mean that rhetoric *per se* supports the negative connotations that attend it today. Yet it cannot always overcome strongly held opinions such as those expressed in the *Rose* debate. Even compromise on such 'contraires choses'[22] seems impossible. As Christine herself puts it to Pierre Col: 'Je ne say a quoy tant nous debatons ces questions, car je croy ne toy ne moy n'avons talent de mouvoir nos oppinions: tu dis qu'il est bon; je dis qu'il est mauvais' (*Débat*, p. 145:971–73) [I don't know why we debate these issues so much, for I believe that neither one of us wishes to change our opinions; you say it's good, I say it's bad]. In cases such as this, one is left with a hung jury, or with having to appeal to authority, as Christine does when she brings the *Rose* debate to an end by sending the relevant documents to the Queen (*Débat*, pp. 5–6).[23]

Although the *Rose* debate does not invalidate rhetoric as an effective instrument, it does raise the issue of how the art should be used and the credibility of rhetoricians practicing the art. Traditionally, the orator should be a *vir bonus dicendi peritus* – a good and eloquent man.[24] If he is only eloquent,

---

[21] See Kelly 1978, ch. 3.

[22] On 'contraires choses' see Paré 1947, pp. 31–32; Regalado 1981; Poirion 1983a, pp. 181–83; Weil 1995; Adams 2000. I discuss Christine's use of the principle below, pp. 123–24.

[23] Her ploy may not have been as high-handed as one might suppose. Contemporary writers, including Christine, frequently curried favor by proposing that a potential benefactor resolve a debate (Dulac 1992a; Altmann 1999, Kelly 1999c). Gerson was also a force in concluding the debate; see Potansky 1972, pp. 192–94.

[24] Christine adopts the definition from Isidore's *Etymologies* (*Mutacion*, v. 8033–40; see Solente, ed., vol. 2, p. 354 n. 8007–58). The definition goes back to Roman times; see

however, his rhetoric can serve perverse ends. This is the basis for Christine's *ad hominem* argument against the *Roman de la rose*. She argues that, because of his lewd intentions, Jean de Meun does not measure up to the standard of the *vir bonus dicendi peritus*, or the ideal orator. She does not doubt his skill as poet and rhetorician; *dicendi peritus*, Jean de Meun clearly mastered the art of rhetoric. But she claims that he is not a *vir bonus* because his intentions in writing the *Rose* were immoral. In other words, Jean's art of love is written in the Ovidian mode; as an art of seduction, the poem is licentious and, indeed, pornographic. In rhetorical manner, Christine extrapolates that Jean de Meun was a licentious man unacquainted with good women or good love who was bent only on luring others into a sensual, and thus sinful, life.[25] Christine goes on to accuse Jean of misogyny,[26] alleging that he never met a good, morally upright woman.[27] Of course, such *ad hominem* allegations are also personal opinions that rely on the intentional fallacy. The admixture of good and sophistic rhetoric Christine finds in the *Rose*[28] is evidence of its author's duplicity or *faux semblant* – something Jean de Meun was effective at, according to Christine.[29] Finally, she presents as proof Jean's subsequent writings in which, she asserts, he repents for having written the romance.[30]

Opinion about the *Rose*, often a personal opinion even today, is an issue that, I believe, can never be resolved. It is in the nature of moralist writing to be unsettling and to provoke the reader by satire and invective.[31] 'C'est que l'ambiguïté caractérise la satire pour le moraliste: la marge est étroite entre la mise à jour des vices à des fins dénonciatrices et la peinture complaisante de

---

Lausberg 1973, pp. 550–51. The union of *sagesse* and eloquence produces in Christine's time the conviction that 'l'homme sage est un homme éloquent' (Meyenberg 1992, p. 111; see pp. 111–14, 127–28).

[25] See *Débat*, pp. 66:194–200, 130:491–96. Jean's disciples claim the opposite: *Débat*, pp. 9:8–10:13, 89:12–16.

[26] *Débat*, p. 26:55–64.

[27] *Débat*, pp. 19:256–58, 55:215–25.

[28] *Débat*, pp. 53:155–62, 130:504–131:517. Christine also attacks this vice in depicting false lovers in her *Epistre au dieu d'amour*, v. 23–66, 519–32, 771–75. On the deceit Faux Semblant personifies in the *Rose*, see Stakel 1991.

[29] She expresses admiration for his representation of Faux Semblant, while recycling Jean's depiction of it in her own description of the mendicant orders (*Mutacion*, v. 5581–92; see Badel 1980, p. 415; Chance 1993, p. 24 n. 12). *Faux semblant* is a neutral notion that can serve vice, as in the *Rose*, or virtue, as in the *Trois Vertus*; see below, p. 146 n. 18. In both instances, it requires self-mastery (Dulac 2000, pp. 616–21). In service of vice it appears as Fraude in the *Advision*'s first part.

[30] *Débat*, p. 121:191–214. This is a reference to Jean's Retraction in his *Testament* (ed. Buzzetti Gallarati, pp. 10–14).

[31] Cf. Jean de Montreuil on 'satiricum illum perseverum magistrum Johannem de Magduno' (*Débat*, p. 38:4–5) [that stern satirist, master Jean de Meun]; satire is Jean's mode according to his 'disciples' (*Débat*, p. 36:16, 42:26–28). They also term Christine's criticism as invective (*Débat*, p. 9:6).

ces mêmes débauches.'[32] Christine acknowledges, in the words quoted above, that the two sides will never agree, and that, in the final analysis, the *Roman de la rose* and the debate about its meaning are too frivolous to merit further attention. If Jean's disciples intend to continue following their master as they understand him, so be it. 'Quant a moy, je renonce a sa discipline, car je tens a aultre que je cuide estre plus prouffitables et qui mieux m'est agreable' (*Débat*, p. 145:988–90)[33] [As for me, I renounce his teaching, for I have other inclinations which, in my opinion, are more profitable and agreeable to me]. *De gustibus non est disputandum.*[34] Christine admits as much when she proclaims that 'ne toy ne moy n'avons talent de mouvoir nos oppinions' (*Débat*, p. 145:972–73) [neither you nor I are inclined to change our opinions]. True enough. Still, Christine would continue to reflect on opinion. In doing so, she would even contemplate altering her opinion on the *Roman de la rose*.

Changing opinion, the *Mutacion de Fortune*, and Boethius

Between the *Rose* debate and the *Advision*, a period from about 1401 to 1405, Christine continually returned to the problems raised by opinions. As she did so, her awareness of the role of opinion in human thought and actions evolved. In the *Mutacion*, an especially important document, the word 'opinion' occurs only twice. In the first instance, it appears in its usual sense to refer to diverse opinions on the length of time between King David's reign and the Babylonian exile.

> ... les aucteurs en union
> Ne sont mie du nombre, ainçois,
> Selon qu'es escriptures vois,
> Trop se different les aucteurs,
> Qui des aages sont escripteurs. (*Mutacion*, v. 8384–88)
>
> [The authorities do not at all agree on the number. Rather, as far as my reading goes, those who write about chronology diverge greatly from the one to the other.]

Christine gives a figure 'Selon aucune oppinion' (v. 8383) but makes no claim for it over the many others she does not report. Further on, in the *Mutacion*'s only other instance of *opinion*, she condemns the 'oppinions plus sotes' (*Mutacion*, v. 6075) [more foolish opinions] of irrational, illogical, and

---

[32] Wolf-Bonvin 1998, p. 120; cf. Kelly 1995a, pp. 152–58; Minnis 2001; Monahan 2002; and, in general, the articles on *Les Moralistes français des XVIIe et XVIIIe siècles* in the 'Deuxième Journée', *CAIEF*, 30 (May 1978), pp. 105–94.

[33] Cf. *Débat*, pp. 116:47–48, 150:1122–23; *Enseignemens*, 77.

[34] Cf. Stierle 1972, pp. 188–89, on taste judgment, a notion he borrows from Kant to refer to aesthetic ideas.

uneducated clerics who 'Pou prisent la [science] speculative, / Ou l'entendement se parfait' (*Mutacion*, v. 6080–81) [hold little esteem for speculative knowledge, where understanding is perfected].[35]

Although the word *opinion* is almost absent from the *Mutacion*, a narrower cognate, *cuidier*, is omnipresent. *Cuidier* is presumption; for example, it can be the opinion that people can keep what they do not truly possess, an opinion (*cuidier*) that exposes them to fortune's inevitable turns.[36] In the *Mutacion*, Christine illustrates this in the description of Fortune's castle and in the chronicle of misfortunes that befell the four kingdoms of Assyria, Carthage, Macedonia, and Rome.

For example, Cyrus was raised, then brought down by Fortune because of his presumption (*cuidier*).

> Bien cuidoit estre affin né
> Que tout le monde deust conquerre,
> Mais follie lui faisoit querre
> Ce que Fortune donne et tolt,
> Et change et mue tart ou tost!   (*Mutacion*, v. 9798–802)
>
> [He presumed indeed that he was destined to conquer the
> whole world. But folly drove him to seek what Fortune gives
> and takes away, changing and metamorphosing it sooner or
> later.]

In her earlier *Epistre Othea*, Christine foreshadows this sense of *cuidier* as opinion. There Cyrus was 'si oultrecuidiez qu'il n'ait doubte que mescheoir lui puist par aucune fortune' (57:27–28) [so presumptuous as to have no fear that his Fortune can turn bad in some way].

That this opinion, or presumption, exposes Cyrus to fortune's twists and turns is even more explicit in the *Advision*. But there is also something new in this treatise. After showing how Fortune raises Cyrus up (*Advision*, II.xv.42–52), Lady Opinion illustrates his downfall with another illustration: Xerxes's defeats in Greece (II.xvi.7–15). Although Fortune brought him down, she, Opinion, was 'la premiere naiscence de celle emprise' (II.xvi.16–17) [gave birth to that undertaking]. Philosophy corroborates this analysis in general terms: 'ainsi pues tu veoir que le mal ou le bien que les gens ont leur vient pour cuidier et par opinion, et non mie des choses' (III.xxi.41–42) [the evil or good that befalls people comes to them through presumption and by opinion, and not from things themselves]. The entire argument of the *Advision*, Part Three, corrects Christine's view that her own misfortunes are real; that they are misfortunes is only a matter of opinion. Her thought on the subject has evolved

---

[35] I return to *entendement* below, pp. 25–26.
[36] See as well *Prouverbes*, 18, 21, 28, 60, 65; *Policie*, p. 31:17–36. Cf. Blanchard and Quereuil 1999, p. 103 s.v. *cuider*: 'S'imaginer, se figurer'; cf. *cuidance*: 'présomption, outrecuidance'.

into an entirely Boethian perspective, completing a reevaluation of her opinion begun in the *Mutacion* on Fortune as the first cause of misfortune.

Christine had read Boethius and knew how he resisted fortune (*Mutacion*, v. 6857–66).[37] According to her, Boethius teaches that opinion gives value to false goods that do not belong naturally to human beings, but rather are the gifts of fortune. Such false goods are the very goals of *cuidier* in the *Mutacion*. Book Two of Boethius's *Consolation of Philosophy* treats five false goods: wealth, honor, power, fame, and bodily pleasures. All are granted, but also withdrawn, by Fortune. As unnatural goods, they are not part of human nature. False opinion, however, holds that they bring happiness to those who possess them. But, being foreign to the natural human being, they can be lost, leaving in their wake misfortune and a depressing, albeit false sense of loss.

In the *Mutacion*, it is Christine's opinion that the trials of the world, including both the turmoil in France during her own time and her own losses, illustrate Fortune's power. Modifying gradually her opinion regarding goods she once possessed and then lost, Christine reviews Boethius's five false goods in the *Advision*: desire inspired by opinion makes men presume (*cuidier*) the worth not only of false goods such as wealth (*flourins*) and sensual pleasure (*avoir belles dames*), but even more positive goods such as knowledge (*science*), knighthood (*chevalerie*), and a virtuous life (*vivre vertueusement, bien faire*) (*Advision*, II.xvii.57–71; cf. III.xxiii.8–15). Moreover, opinion with regard to honor or fame can be granted or withdrawn by others as it pleases them (*Advision*, III.xxv.5–17). This is pure Boethius, as Christine points out in the same place. Hence her recurrent quandary in matters of opinion; although most people are of the opinion that the virtuous life is the best of all, even Jesus Christ's perfect life failed to please everyone (*Advision*, II.xvii.72–75).

Glynnis M. Cropp identifies these and other passages in Christine de Pizan's writings that are indebted to Boethius's *Consolation of Philosophy*.[38] She also notes two important factors in Christine's rewriting of Boethius and, by implication, of other authors she used: compilation and inspiration.[39] Christine refers to the *Roman de la rose* as a compilation,[40] a work that brings together material from diverse sources into a coherent whole. There are different ways of doing

---

[37] Deschamps likens Christine's life to Boethius's; see his *Balades*, Ballade 1242, v. 35–36.

[38] Cropp 1981; see also Blanchard 1986a, pp. 428–33; Sazaki 1988, pp. 374–77; Willard 1990a; Semple 1995; Walters 1996; Holderness 2002; Ribémont 2003; and Reno and Dulac, ed., *Advision*, pp. xxviii–xxxi. Christine refers to the *Consolation of Philosophy* in the *Rose* debate (*Débat*, p. 139:795).

[39] Cropp 1981, pp. 416–17. On compilation and inspiration, see as well Cerquiglini 1993b, pp. 89–95; Zimmermann 2003b, especially pp. 38–41.

[40] See *Advision*, II.xxi.27; *Fais d'armes*, p. 144. She refers as well to her own 'compillacions et volumes' (II.xxii.19). On this term, see Minnis 1984, pp. 94–98; Blanchard 1988; Dulac and Reno 1997; Holderness 2000; Paupert 2002a. Blanchard 1988, p. 150, likens Christine to Proba, the poetess who rewrote the Old and New Testaments with a mosaic of Vergil's verse. Christine lauds Proba in the *Cité*, pp. 156–58.

this. For example, by conjoining Boethius with Thomas Aquinas and Aristotle,

> Christine ... n'a pas suivi servilement l'argument de Boèce, mais a choisi au hasard les passages utiles à son propre argument. Au fur et à mesure elle a volontairement modifié, resserré ou cité mot à mot la traduction [à laquelle elle a emprunté tel passage]; parfois elle s'est trompée dans son interprétation.[41]

Christine may have erred; but, more positively, such 'unfaithful' quoting or cross-referencing may also result from the author's intentional, even original reflection on the chosen passage and its modification or adaptation to fit other sources and her own thought.[42] As Cropp puts it: 'en joignant ainsi à l'autorité de Boèce celle des saints docteurs, elle a réuni philosophie et théologie'.[43] For example, Christine reviews the errors of philosophers and theologians in Part Two of the *Advision*; in Part Three, she corrects her own errors with the authority of Boethius and authoritative Church fathers and theologians.

A. J. Minnis has noted the different kinds of literary activities performed by the scribe, the compiler, the commentator, and the author. 'The *auctor* contributes most, the *scriptor* contributes nothing of his own.'[44] However, these activities may alternate in the same work. Compilation in one part may simply collect, as in a florilegium, what others have written. Yet the cumulative effect may produce something new or original, as Proba did in collecting lines from Vergil into a life of Christ (cf. *Cité*, pp. 157–59). Ruth Morse has noted this feature in Christine de Pizan's compilations. For example, the *Mutacion* is 'a stealthy demonstration of the compiler's art'. And Morse goes on to describe such compilation in an illuminating paragraph.

> The compiler's options are complex. Christine can change the story by rewriting it (a) on her own (i.e. by changing the facts, suppressing them,

---

[41] Cropp 1981, p. 409. On Christine's knowledge of Latin – neither profound nor negligible – see Willard 1992, pp. 20–21; Dulac and Reno 1995; Stuip 2004, pp. 148–49. Within this range, about which there is debate, it is difficult to draw firm conclusions; see Parussa 1997 (with bibliography). Christine's knowledge of the commentary tradition would speak in favor of her command of some Latin; see Minnis 1991, pp. 35–36. She alludes to 'les rumigacions du latin' (*Advision*, III.viii.5–6) she heard from her parents, but of which she retained very little because of her domestic duties. Reno and Dulac, ed., *Advision*, p. 248, translate *rumigacion* 'rappel à la mémoire, rumination'; Blanchard and Querueil 1999, p. 345, translate the word 'action de réciter par cœur, en chuchotant.' Did Christine's parents speak to her in Latin? In *Advision*, III.xvii, Christine refers to the 'rumignacion de son savoir' [recall and reflection on his knowledge] that she retained from her father. Cf. Plebani 2003, p. 51.

[42] Blanchard 1985, pp. 11–27; Cerquiglini 1993a; Pagot 1995.

[43] Cropp 1981, p. 409; see also Blanchard 1985, pp. 24–27; Reno and Dulac, ed., *Advision*, p. xxxi; for examples, see Reno and Dulac, ed., *Advision*, pp. 184 n. XIX/5–9; 187 ns. XXI/42–43 and XXI/50–52.

[44] Minnis 1984, p. 94.

recasting them, offering new interpretations or motives), or (b) by choosing one version over others (and suppressing the rejected ones); she can reproduce the story in the old way but reinterpret it or offer counter-examples (as fickleness of men against inconstancy of women); reorient it (by seeing it from another character's point of view, absorbing it in another story); recontextualize it, (a) by its position in a sequence or (b) by the permutations available by contrast to other stories told in the same sequence. She uses style to achieve some of her effects: register, metaphor, semantic field – all the resources of poetry in order to change the tone.[45]

We come across this art of compilation in most of Christine's works examined in this book.

Christine's original approach to compilation as Morse delineates it points to the inspiration Cropp sees as informing Christine's rewriting of Boethius.

> En composant *La Mutacion de Fortune*, Christine s'est assurément inspirée de la tradition de la *Consolatio*, mais en esquissant ou en développant librement quelques thèmes. Il est erroné d'attribuer ses emprunts à l'une ou l'autre des traductions, car leur rapport avec le texte de Boèce est assez vague.[46]

Inspiration does indeed play a role in Christine's emulation (*aemulatio*) of Boethius.[47] It is particularly evident in the sections on Philosophy's rent garment and Fortune's power and impotence vis-à-vis opinion.

In the *Consolation*, Philosophy's robe is rent in such a way as to separate the Greek letters Θ and Π (*De consolatione*, I Pr. i.3–5).[48] Simply put, theory is divorced from practice. As a result, various 'philosophers' emerge holding onto pieces of her robe. Yet such snippets contain only parts of philosophy (*De consolatione*, I Pr. iii). Importantly, Christine rewrites this image in the *Advision* as the colors in Lady Opinion's shifting shapes. She ascribes these colors to

---

[45] Morse 1996, pp. 96–97; cf. Meyenberg 1992, pp. 53–54.

[46] Cropp 1981, p. 392.

[47] On inspiration in the sense of 'inspiring mode', see Muckelbauer 2003; by *aemulatio* one strives to equal or surpass another, while by *imitatio* one follows a model (Cizek 1994; Kelly 1999a, ch. 2). In the *Advision*, Christine is that kind of rewriter defined in the Middle Ages as an author (*auctor*) who 'writes both his own materials and those of others, but his own as the principal materials, and the materials of others annexed for the purpose of confirming his own' (Minnis 1984, p. 94, quoting Saint Bonaventure); such authors are inspired by their sources and, ultimately for Christine, by faith. The result recalls Macrobius's sense of *conspiratio*, or the harmonious, original blending of diverse sources (Kelly 1999a, pp. xi–xii).

[48] This image is common throughout the Middle Ages; see Courcelle 1967. Christine uses it in, for example, the *Mutacion* (Courcelle 1967, p. 139). Alain Chartier rewrites it in his *Quadrilogue*, p. 8:9–29, a work that is a veritable mine of fortune commonplaces. The Wheel of Fortune appears in illustrations to Christine's autograph manuscripts; see Hindman 1986, especially plates 43–44, from manuscripts that are autograph presentations (Laidlaw 2003, p. 244).

heretical sects that falsify the true faith as well as to erroneous philosophies, thereby rewriting Boethius's description of the rags torn from Lady Philosophy as the various shades and shapes attending Lady Opinion. Christine depicts these sects and philosophies as attempts to explain God and first causes, thereby occupying a major role in Lady Opinion's illustrations of true and false opinions. The partial nature of these teachings – they are 'rent' from whole cloth – makes them inadequate; the absence of faith makes their opinions uncertain or false. Ultimately, faith relies on and is one of the theological virtues that confirm true opinion among human beings and, therefore, elevate it to certain truth (*Advision* II.iii.41–42; cf. II.iv.65–68, III.xxvi.67–71).

More radically, compilation and inspiration play a role in Christine's portrayal of Fortune. In the *Advision*, Lady Opinion corrects the *Mutacion de Fortune*.[49] In this poem Fortune enters the world and establishes her dominion at the moment Adam and Eve commit original sin: 'Fortune estoit tres doncques nee' (*Mutacion*, v. 8198) [Fortune was born at that very moment]. In Part Two of the *Advision*, however, Lady Opinion argues that she is prior to Fortune in the mortal realm: 'saches que, des adonc que Adam fu fourmez, je fus creé' (*Advision*, II.iii.12; cf. II.xiv) [know that I was created at the same time Adam was shaped]. In Part Three, Philosophy corrects Christine's views on Fortune's role in her own life, in society, and in world history, a pointed and systematic correction of the opinion Christine set out at length in the *Mutacion*. Although Christine attributes her own *historia calamitatum*[50] and, indeed, all human calamities to Fortune in the *Advision*, Lady Philosophy shows that it is actually Opinion, not Fortune, that is at fault (*Advision*, III.xvi–xxvi). Thereupon Christine changes her own opinion. Boethius authorizes the change, as do the Bible and Church fathers.

We can see the change described dramatically in the *Chemin de long estude* (1403). There Christine evokes the power of Fortune in her life and world, before rereading Boethius's *Consolation*; upon this rereading, she perceives her error.

> Ainsi pris a Boëce garde
> Et pensay que cellui n'a garde
> Qui de vertus peut estre plains;
> En joye sont tournez ses plains. (*Chemin*, v. 291–94)[51]

---

[49] Kiehl 2002, pp. 450–51, notes this correction but does not otherwise discuss fortune as opinion. Strubel 2002, p. 333, states that Christine is unique among vernacular writers in opposing Fortune and Opinion. Angeli 1996, p. 28, points out that Christine's views on fortune vary from work to work; actually, they evolve. As we shall see, she drew her views from Thomas Aquinas.

[50] Angeli 1993, p. 35.

[51] The episode is fully described in *Chemin*, v. 61–450. It leads to the vision in which the Sibyl launches Christine's learning process. She seems to mark the change poetically by replacing the heptasyllabic verse that evokes Fortune's power with octosyllabic verse in v. 253.

> [In this way I took notice of what Boethius teaches, realizing that the person who possesses many virtues has nothing to worry about. His or her complaints are transformed into joy.]

True felicity does not depend on the false goods Fortune bestows and withdraws capriciously. Only virtue can offer assurance and felicity. This episode deserves a place among the great moments of illumination in Christine's life. As with her reflection in the *Cité des dames* on Matheolus, from reading and thinking on what one learns one derives rational understanding of how the world works and how opinions stand or fall. In the *Chemin de long estude*, Christine describes, externally as it were, her first steps towards reassessment of fortune. The *Advision* completes the change.

In concluding this section, it is necessary to note that Christine further revised her opinion on some of Boethius's false goods in the *Corps de policie*. Such goods as renown and honor, she reasoned, may derive from virtue and virtuous conduct. They are not vices when serving a just cause (*Policie*, p. 83:13–18). Covetousness itself is a virtue if one covets virtue (pp. 82–83).

Intellectual virtues: consideration, discretion, retention, and memory

Christine de Pizan investigates the mind and thought that generate and evaluate opinion in the *Mutacion*. Her investigation includes the intellectual virtues with which one is born. These are consideration, discretion, retention, and memory (*consideracion, discrecion, retentive, memoire*: see *Mutacion*, v. 567–640).[52] In the same poem, Christine also investigates the intellectual faculties that, sharpened by her education and upbringing, permit her to define and describe the opinions she considers. These faculties are reason, eloquence, and rational understanding (*raison, loquence, entendement de raison*: see *Mutacion*, v. 652–58). This terminology describes her thought in the crucial treatise on opinion, the *Advision*, especially with regard to the evolution of and changes in her opinions on misogyny, love, and political issues. The terminology Christine uses to refer to the intellectual virtues and faculties corresponds to that found in Brunetto Latini's *Tresor*, a work, as mentioned above, that she knew.[53] I shall therefore use the *Tresor* to interpret her terminology, relying heavily on P. A. Messelaar's valuable analysis of Brunetto's intellectual vocabulary as well as Paul Zumthor's work on the vocabulary of ideas.[54]

---

[52] I have inverted the order in which she treats the first two virtues by taking up *consideracion* before *discrecion*, since this is the order in which she envisages their being used.

[53] See Solente, ed., *Mutacion*, vol. 1, pp. l–lv; Willard, ed., *Paix*, p. 40.

[54] Messelaar 1963; Zumthor 1955, 1956. Cf. Mühlethaler 1992.

According to the *Mutacion*,[55] Nature bestowed the intellectual virtues – *discrecion, consideracion, retentive,* and *memoire* – on Christine at birth. These are 'biens de Nature' (*Mutacion*, v. 647). But, because they are natural to her, Christine also terms them 'vertus de l'ame' (*Mutacion*, v. 681). They fall accordingly among the goods that Boethius identifies as virtues natural to all human beings. Moreover, they are God-given (*Mutacion*, v. 665–69); Nature merely transmits them to mortals like Christine. Nature's intermediary role explains why their effectiveness varies from person to person. Although the virtues bestowed by God are perfect in themselves, the bodies Nature shapes to receive them differ in organization, composition, and proportions (v. 670–77, 698–702). This is obvious when the mind of the fool (mental or moral) is compared with that of the sage; fools may possess *consideracion*, but not as a person of sound mind does who is also gifted with greater discretion (*Mutacion*, v. 597–99).

The distinction between God's gifts and Nature's bodies that receive the gifts explains an otherwise curious passage in which Christine describes both her physical and mental person. She likens her virtues to a small crown. God 'me donna ce chappellet / Assis en mon chief crespellet, / Qui bel fu, selon mon degré' (*Mutacion*, v. 729–31) [gave me this little crown set on my curly head, which was beautiful in proportion to my station]. Her physical beauty, bestowed by Nature, is commensurate with the quality of her mind.[56]

> Si n'ay je pas beau corps, n'abile,
> Ne l'entendement de sebile;
> Mais, tel qu'il est il me souffist,
> J'en regraci Dieu, qui le fist,
> Et les vertus que j'ay nommees.   (*Mutacion*, v. 659–63)[57]

> [I don't have a beautiful or agile body, nor the understanding
> of a sibyl. But I am content with my understanding such as it
> is, as God made it and the virtues I referred to.]

She thus explains the relation between physical features and intellectual qualities, introducing Nature as God's agent who fashions the imperfect body that receives the God-given virtues.

In the *Advision*, Christine is somewhat more positive about her body, although she still maintains the distinction between her perfect, God-given virtues and

---

[55] See Zühlke 1994, pp. 77–79. These virtues are named in a commentary on Boethius that Christine may have known; see Holderness 2002, p. 427.

[56] Cf. Brown-Grant 2003, pp. 85–88.

[57] Christine makes the connection elsewhere between physical beauty and virtues; for example, she relates the beauty of Judith and Esther to their virtues (*Mutacion*, v. 10149–52, 11424–25, 11549–54). Eve's intelligence was on a par with her physical perfection (*Epistre Dieu*, v. 591–616). In the *Dit de Poissy*, Christine uses stereotypical description in elaborate, virtually textbook illustration of a man (v. 1078–1236) and a woman (v. 1479–1608); see Schilperoort 1936, pp. 35–36, 37–38; Altmann, ed., *Poissy*, pp. 204–05.

the imperfect body they are located in. There Philosophy tells Christine how fortunate she is to 'avoir corps sans nulle difformité et assez plaisant, saintif et non maladis, mais bien complexionné et de competant discrecion et entendement' (*Advision*, III.xvii.24–26)[58] [have a body without any deformity, but attractive, in good health, well balanced and with competent discretion and understanding]. Here Christine maintains the distinction and relation between God-given mind and natural body that she set out in the *Mutacion*.

How did Christine define the four intellectual virtues, and how did they facilitate her understanding of and evaluation of opinions? We can begin to elucidate her thought by seeking definitions that fit the description of her mind in the *Mutacion*.

Consideracion means that one literally considers something. That is, this intellectual virtue applies a person's attention to an object of thought so as to know it better.[59] Moreover, it precedes *discrecion* that actually evaluates the object of thought. Christine further contrasts *consideracion* in the young with the faculty's greater maturity in adults (cf. *Mutacion*, v. 763–70). She fears, for example, that her son's return from his privileged life in England will make him want to return to that country. This, she feels, is because young people, lacking mature discretion, have a more superficial opinion of what is good for them (*Advision*, III.xi.59–62). But even age does not promise perfection. Philosophers too err when they fail to consider the causes of what they observe (*Advision*, II.xi.35–46). Aristotle criticized earlier philosophers because they failed to explain motion. Although they did indeed consider motion because 'toute naturelle consideracion enquiert de mouvement' (*Advision*, II.xi.42) [every natural act of consideration inquires into motion], they left out of consideration the fact that all motion has a cause. By failing to consider this, they erred. They resemble the fool in the *Mutacion* who possesses *consideracion* but lacks discretion. Correction of the failure allows for full and complete consideration, which must be thorough and complete to be fully developed.

Discrecion, the intellectual virtue that actually evaluates the object of thought, acquires knowledge intuitively and discursively.[60] The discrete mind distinguishes objects of thought from one another and in relation to one another.[61] *Discrecion* makes the person prudent, eloquent, and capable of exercising self-control; without it, one is bereft of intelligence or wit (*Mutacion*, v. 568–73).[62] More importantly for Christine, discretion distinguishes between good and

---

[58] Cf. as well *Advision*, III.xvii.58–62. Philosophy underscores continually the place of *entendement* in her lessons in Part Three of the *Advision*; see, for example, III.xviii.16–21. I discuss Christine's use of *entendement* under the intellectual faculties.

[59] Messelaar 1963, p. 50.

[60] Messelaar 1963, p. 25.

[61] Messelaar 1963, p. 57.

[62] Cf. Brunetto Latini: 'Povretés de sens et de discretion est achoison de mal' (*Tresor*, II.18.5) [Poverty of wit and discretion is a source of evil].

evil[63] – that is, it includes moral judgment and discernment.[64] Such fully developed discretion evaluates opinions sanely and with a level head, distinguishing in an opinion what is acceptable or unacceptable, what is good or evil. Discretion is the intellectual virtue that, in fact, revealed original sin to Adam and Eve. It is, according to the *Advision*, the origin of opinion.[65]

Christine's use of the term 'discretion' conforms to these meanings of the word in Brunetto Latini's *Tresor*. The early demise of Charles V, for example, left the French court subject to opposing wills, a debate Christine visualized as a confrontation among personified authorities in the last part of the *Chemin de long estude*. This chaotic state of affairs is also manifest in Part One of the *Advision*, where Christine suggests that France's chaos is partly attributable to a lack of discretion (cf. *Advision*, III.v.15–19).

Retentive and *memoire*, the remaining two intellectual virtues, are easier to explain. In effect, retention, as Christine uses the term, grasps and holds onto what memory retrieves when needed. That is to say that what the senses perceive and the mind construes (*Mutation*, v. 614–16) is stored as memory, where it is retained and available for recall (*Mutacion*, v. 624–28). Of course, the two words overlap in meaning and usage,[66] but Christine makes the distinction obvious. Her distinction is itself an instance of her discretion.

Christine continues to refer to the four intellectual virtues in forming thought and evaluating opinions in works she wrote after the *Mutacion*. Two are especially important. In the *Livre de la paix* (1412–13), under prudence (I.v), a synonym for discretion, Christine counsels Louis de Guyenne to use careful consideration, a faculty that she relates to 'circonspection' (*Paix*, p. 67), in order to prepare for the discretion that allows reason to operate effectively.[67] In *Paix*, III.xxx she treats the same virtues under *largesse*. There she also shows how ill-considered opinion can lead to great harm.

> Tost deliberant sans consideracion, entreprenant sans circonspection à voulenté et non regart de raison, de brief conseil, de grans menaces pleines de sang, de cuidier legier tost meue à bataille. (*Paix*, p. 73)
>
> [Rapid deliberation without consideration, enterprises without circumspection wilfully undertaken with no attention to reason, peremptory counsel with bloody threats and ill-considered opinion quickly moved to conflict.]

---

[63] Messelaar 1963, p. 65.

[64] Messelaar 1963, pp. 27, 342.

[65] I return to this interpretation of original sin below (p. 83).

[66] Messelaar 1963, pp. 66–67. Cf. Zimmermann 2003a. On the relation between memory in these senses and rational thought, see Carruthers 1990, especially pp. 197–294. These pages relate the process of *cogitatio* to composition. See also Carruthers 1998, pp. 116–19.

[67] As early as her *Enseignemens*, 4, Christine counsels prudence as a bulwark against fortune.

Finally, in the *Epistre de la prison humaine* (1418), written for Marie de Berry, Christine returns to discretion, retention, and memory in consolation, all the while providing abundant examples for consideration in achieving consolation (*Epistre prison*, pp. 34–37).[68]

Intellectual faculties: reason, eloquence, and rational understanding

When the four intellectual virtues function well, a person possesses 'loquence et raison / Et entendement de raison' (*Mutacion*, v. 653–54) [eloquence, reason, and understanding of reason]. Christine's choice of words requires clarification.

Raison has two common meanings in Old and Middle French. They are illustrated in rhymes such as:

> '... tous contre lui yront,
> S'il leur demande fors raison';
> Quant entendi ceste raison,
> Nabugodonosor, sanz faille,
> Dit 'qu'il les aura par bataille.' (*Mutacion*, v. 9934–38)

> ['All will oppose him if he asks anything but what reason (*raison*) demands of them.' When Nebuchadnezzar heard these words (*raison*), he said that, for sure, 'he will get them by combat.']

As this passage shows, *raison* can refer to both the rational faculty (v. 9935) and language (v. 9936). The faculty manifests itself through language, including the language of speculative thought.[69] The two meanings point to the distinction between two other faculties Christine names: *loquence* and *entendement de raison*.

The second faculty, *loquence*, is 'eloquence' (*Mutacion*, v. 8011), or what Christine also calls 'belle parleure' (*Mutacion*, v. 8005).[70] Eloquence comes from using the art of rhetoric effectively (*Mutacion*, v. 8017–20). After all, rhetoric

> science est de bien dire,
> Pour la coppie d'eloquence,
> Ordre de droicte consequance

---

[68] Christine does not mention consideration or circumspection here, but she alludes to the faculty in describing discretion that prudently considers past, present, and future factors: 'pour tant que sa proprieté est de faire loing et pres et environ soy regarder' (*Epistre prison*, p. 35:748–49) [since its function is to make one observe near and far and all round about]. This is also analogous to her sense of circumspection.

[69] Messelaar 1963, pp. 289–90; cf. Wolfzettel 1995, pp. 87–88.

[70] Cf. 'bonne parleure' in the *Tresor*, III.1.7, and Messelaar 1963, p. 283.

> Neccessaire en toutes similes
> Questions, plaines ou soubtilles,
> A persuader choses bonnes
> Et justes es fais des personnes. (*Mutacion*, v. 8010–16)
>
> [is the science of using the abundant resources of eloquence to
> speak well, setting out in good order that is essential in all
> such questions, be they plain or subtle, so as to persuade what
> is good and right in human actions.]

Such good order, moreover, relies on reason (the first faculty) to advance an argument (*Mutacion*, v. 7977–82).

But reason must be understood, both by the speaker and by the audience. This consideration leads Christine to emphasize *entendement de raison*. One must not only have the rational faculty, one must also understand how to use it well. *Entendement de raison* activates *consideracion* and *discrecion*, *retentive* and *memoire*, the four intellectual virtues that can become sources of *coppie d'eloquence*. Such *coppie*, or *copia*, is understood traditionally as the wealth of subject matter and grammatical or rhetorical devices writers and speakers can draw on in order to elaborate their thought.[71] More specifically, Brunetto Latini defines *entendement de raison* as understanding that does not come through the senses (*Tresor*, I.xv.4). It is what Christine understands by speculative thought. 'Reason, for Christine, is not oriented toward original social analysis: it is a merely administrative virtue (*l'administreresse*) that puts into operation the orders of a good understanding.'[72] Such understanding is especially important in moral judgment.

A well-known moment in Reason's lesson to Amant in the *Roman de la rose* will clarify Christine's distinction between *raison* and *entendement de raison*.[73] The narrator interrupts the debate between Reason and Fol Amoureux to describe Amour's actions while Reason is preaching:

> hors de ma teste, a une pele,
> quant au sarmon seant m'aguiete,
> par l'une des oreilles giete
> quan que Reson en l'autre boute,
> si qu'ele i pert sa peine toute. (*Rose*, v. 4608–12)
>
> [when he, Love, catches me listening to her sermon, he shovels
> out of my head through one ear what Reason thrusts into the
> other ear, with the result that she, Reason, totally wastes her
> time.]

---

[71] See Blanchard and Quereuil 1999, p. 94; cf. Moss 2002.
[72] Haidu 2004, p. 311.
[73] This episode is part of the *Rose*'s Reason that Christine recommends in *Deux amants*.

Amant hears, but fails to understand Reason's words. This also occurs when, for example, he fails to grasp the *contraires* in Reason's description of love: 'Amors, ce est pez haïneuse, / Amors, c'est haïne amoureuse' (*Rose*, v. 4263–64) [Love is hateful peace, Love is loving hatred]. There is too much *contraire* in the description for him to learn anything from what Reason teaches (*Rose*, v. 4334–35). As a result, he does not understand her definition of love either, since definitions are established by the principle of *contraires choses*.[74]

>   Ainsinc va des contreres choses,
>   les unes sunt des autres gloses;   = *consideracion*
>   et qui l'une an veust defenir,
>   de l'autre li doit souvenir,   = *retentive* and *memoire*
>   ou ja, par nule antancion,
>   n'i metra diffinicion;
>   car qui des .II. n'a connoissance,
>   ja n'i connoistra differance,   = *discrecion*
>   san quoi ne peut venir en place
>   diffinicion que l'an face.   (*Rose*, v. 21543–52)[75]

[This is the way opposites function: the one glosses the other
(= *consideracion*). If one wishes to define the one, do not
forget the other (= *retentive* and *memoire*). Otherwise there will
be no definition whatsoever. For without knowledge of both,
the difference between them (= *discrecion*) is not perceptible,
and without that perception no definition can be satisfactory.]

To be sure, Amant 'considers' what Reason teaches. But, as he says later of his experience in plucking the rose: 'de Reson ne me souvint' (*Rose*, v. 21730) [I didn't remember Reason]. Indeed, this Fol Amoureux has what, according to Christine, even fools may possess: consideration. But, more importantly, he sorely lacks the discretion and retention that might have permitted him to understand the different kinds of love Reason goes on to describe[76] and make a sensible choice from among them. Reason's argument only makes him angry (*Rose*, v. 4613), and, therefore, unable to make reasonable distinctions. This is obvious when Amant exclaims after hearing Reason's admonitions: 'ou j'ameré ou je harré' (*Rose*, v. 4625)[77] [either I love or I hate]. Having failed to retain Reason's advice, Amant clearly lacks discretion.

---

[74] By contrast, in the *Advision* the description of Lady Opinion makes it possible for Christine to define the concept of opinion; see above, pp. 7–8.

[75] Nature too alludes to such defining (*Rose*, v. 16048–52).

[76] Kelly 1995a, pp. 56–70.

[77] Cf. *Othea*, 17:36–38, 41–42: 'yre est un mortel vice ou si mauvais que cellui qui en est forment attaint n'a nulle cognoissance de raison ... Et pour ce dit Aristote: "Garde toy d'ire, car elle trouble l'entendement et destourne raison"' [anger is a mortal vice, one so bad that he who is afflicted by it has no understanding of reason ... Hence, Aristotle says: 'Avoid anger, for it troubles one's understanding and rejects reason'].

Subtlety

Moreover, Amant, now a Fol Amoureux, also lacks the subtlety that so appeals to Christine in both poetry and moral judgment. Christine realizes that subtle reading and writing are a gift that Nature bestowed on her, a gift that she became aware of while reading poets.

> Puis me pris aux livres des pouetes, et comme de plus en plus alast croissant le bien de ma congnoissance, adonc fus je aise quant j'oz trouvé le stille a moy naturel, me delictant en leurs soubtilles couvertures et belles matieres mucees soubz fictions delictables et morales, et le bel stille de leurs mettres et proses deduites par belle et polie rethorique aournee de soubtil langage et proverbes estranges; pour laquelle science de poesie Nature en moy resjouie me dist: 'Fille, solace toy quant tu as attaint en effait le desir que je te donne.' (*Advision*, III.x.23–31)

> [Then I turned to books by poets. As my knowledge and experience grew, how pleased I was to discover the mode of writing that came naturally to me. I took delight in their subtle integumenta and beautiful subjects hidden under pleasing moral fictions, as well as in their fine verse and prose composed using beautiful, polished rhetoric and embellished with subtle language and striking proverbs. My knowledge of poetics delighted Nature: 'Daughter, be content in realizing in practice the desire I give you.']

The desire Nature instils in her daughter[78] is quite different from the desire Amant delights in, he who rejects 'les integumanz aus poetes' (*Rose*, v. 7138) [the poets' integuments]: 'Mes des poetes les sentances, / les fables et les methaphores / ne bé je pas a gloser ores' (v. 7160–62) [But I don't desire now to gloss the poets' teachings, fables, and metaphors]. Amant's lack of discretion deprives him of the poetic subtlety that appeals to Christine.

Reading subtle poetry is not sufficient. Nature wants Christine to write her own subtle, ornate poetry (*Advision*, III.x.38–39). She does so, Christine assures her readers, 'amendant mon stille en plus grant soubtilleté et plus haulte matiere' (*Advision*, III.x.49–50) [improving my style with greater subtlety and more elevated subject matter]. For Brunetto Latini, *soutilleté* is that 'ingéniosité avec laquelle l'esprit sait utiliser des connaissances professionnelles'.[79] It manifests itself, he implies elsewhere, in the poet's 'bon engien et soutil entendement' (*Tresor*, III.lxxv.5) [genius for invention and subtle understanding]. These words fit Christine's usage and further clarify her sense of *entendement de raison* as the natural ability to learn, recall, examine, and distinguish (*Advision*, II.xxi.12–22). By such subtle understanding she can sift and winnow, or *esplucher*, as she often puts it.

---

[78] Nature is Christine's mother in the *Mutacion* (v. 339–68).
[79] Messelaar 1963, p. 63; cf. pp. 297, 306; cf. M. Zink 1985, pp. 12–13.

Christine de Pizan's emphasis on *soutilleté* is not unique to her.[80] The prose prologue to Alain de Lille's *Anticlaudianus*, for example, offers an authoritative model for Christine's progress in subtle reading and writing. In this prologue, Alain names three levels on which his poem can be read. Importantly, each level corresponds to a stage in a pupil's growing proficiency in reading subtle allegories. 'In hoc etenim opere litteralis sensus suauitas puerilem demulcebit auditum, moralis instructio perficientem imbuet sensum, acutior allegorie subtilitas proficientem acuet intellectum' (*Anticlaudianus*, p. 56) [For in this work the sweetness of the literal sense will soothe the ears of boys, the moral instruction will inspire the mind on the road to perfection, and the sharper subtlety of the allegory will whet the advanced intellect (Sheridan, pp. 40–41)].

Christine's first major effort in this style of writing, the *Epistre Othea*, illustrates a similar program in its layout. Each fable is summarized in a literal, four-line poem. Each poem is then glossed literally and morally, after which an allegorical gloss cites biblical and patristic authorities on deeper matters of morality and faith.[81] Thus, in language reminiscent of Alain's, Christine claims regarding the Pygmalion fable that a number of interpretations are possible. This is true for all such fables: 'et pour ce les firent les poetes que les entendemens des hommes s'aguisassent et soubtillassent a y trouver diverses exposicions' (*Othea*, 22:25–27)[82] [poets wrote them so that human understanding might become sharper and more subtle in inventing different interpretations]. *Othea* illustrates Christine's progress in subtle reading and writing by attaching a moral gloss and a religious allegory to each literal fable.

This is not the only instance of Christine's attention to a three-stage approach to subtlety. She returns to this program in the *Advision*. In the first part, she treats the tribulations of France, victim of Fortune, especially the lives and actions of virtuous and evil kings, as evidence of Fortune's mutability. In the second part, she inquires into the ways of opinion, relying on the teachings of philosophers, their errors and their approach to truth, Boethius among them, thereby bringing to her readers' attention useful philosophical assessment. She also considers religious heresies. Both these emphases anticipate Part Three where the lessons of Boethius's *Consolation* are grounded in Holy Scripture (*Advision*, III.xxiii.6–8).[83] Accordingly, Philosophy becomes Theology as Christine adapts Boethius's teachings to Christian doctrine and faith as expressed in the Bible and the Church fathers. The three-part work thus mirrors the fables

---

[80] On subtlety in poetry, especially allegorical poetry, see Kelly 1992, pp. 124–25.

[81] Tuve 1966, pp. 33–45, 285–311; Hindman 1986, ch. 1; Parussa, ed., *Othea*, pp. 13–30.

[82] See also *Othea*, 1:82–85, 3:63–68, etc. Cf. Messelaar 1963, p. 62, on *soutillité*: 'Perspicacité, la faculté de concevoir ce qui est caché à bien d'autres.'

[83] As the notes of Reno and Dulac show, Christine's reading of Boethius is validated by medieval commentaries that give a theological sense to his instruction.

in the *Epistre Othea*, each of which contains a poem, a moral gloss, and a religious or spiritual allegory.

Although Christine delights in subtle allegory, she does not venture to speculate on profound lessons authoritatively. Rather she quotes authorities, especially for the allegories in *Othea*. Elsewhere, she confines her subject matter within the limits of her geocentric universe. We observe this at the end of the *Mutacion*, in which, like Dante in the *Divine Comedy*, Alexander is shown in flight looking down at the world dominated by Fortune, 'Si qu'il luy ert vis que le monde / Ne fust fors une boule ronde' (*Mutacion*, v. 23003–04)[84] [so that it seemed to him that the world was no more than a round ball]. The analogy is also found in Christine's *Chemin de long estude*.

> Il me sembloit, je vous plevi,
> Que quant contre val regardoie,
> Que toute la terre veoye
> Comme une petite pellote,
> Aussi ronde que une balote. (*Mutacion*, v. 1700–04)
>
> [I assure you that when I looked down it seemed to me that the whole world resembled a little spool of yarn as round as a small ball.]

Unlike Alexander, but like Dante, Christine knows that more lies above and beyond her world. However, unlike the Italian poet, she does not venture beyond the confines of the geocentric universe. Rather, in the *Chemin de long estude* Christine applies her subtle mind to the solution of moral and social problems that infest parts of that little ball she looks down on from the sphere in which Reason dwells.

Indeed, Christine's emphasis on moral allegory positions the conscience as a source of subtle understanding and as judge of conduct. Conscience is the 'faculté par laquelle l'homme juge, dans le domaine du concret, de ce qu'il faut faire ou éviter en vertu de la loi divine, et qui provoque des souffrances morales à la suite d'une transgression de cette loi'.[85] As such, Christine's conscience is critical to the formation of opinions. Opinion, that is, operates under the aegis of morality and moral judgment, thereby generating a range of subtle considerations, from interpretation of *loy* as religion through conscience,

---

[84] Cf. Dante's glance back before entering Heaven in the *Divine Comedy*, Paradiso XXVII, v. 76–87. On the sphericity of the earth in medieval cosmology, see Lindberg 1992, p. 253, and note 15 (p. 392).

[85] Messelaar 1963, p. 143; cf. p. 65. See Blanchard and Mühlethaler 2002, p. 44: 'Christine ... entend se poser en voix et conscience du royaume tout entier en partageant ses craintes et son *amor patriae* avec le public.'

judgment, and opinion to error.[86] Conscience, critically, requires clarity. To achieve it, one uses the virtues and faculties one is endowed with.[87]

We now have an overview of Christine's intellectual equipment, that is, the virtues and faculties by which she thinks, evaluates, and promotes or criticizes opinions. They authorize and illuminate her subtle reading and writing. Endowed with the ability to retain and retrieve what she learns and experiences while heeding the voice of reason, she seeks understanding in making philosophical and, especially, moral decisions. To be sure, her thought is informed by her faith. Much as, in *Othea*, Christine's subtle reading proceeds programmatically from the mutable to the spiritual, from glossing to allegory, so Philosophy metamorphoses into Theology in the *Advision*. This is the process that confirms her faith beyond reason:[88] 'O Dame Sainte Theologie, tu m'as donné certaineté …' (*Advision*, III.xxvii.55–56) [Oh! Holy lady Theology, you have given me certainty]. In the final analysis, understanding by both faith and reason makes it possible for Christine to evaluate her own experience and that of others, both in the world around her and in her reading. The subtlety she appreciates, demonstrates, and seeks gives weight to her perceptions. She knows, moreover, that she can promote her opinions in full awareness of the precarious nature of human thought. She is, finally, ready to confront opinion as a major force in human thought and life. The confrontation takes place in the *Advision Cristine*.[89]

Opinion's scope in relation to faith, reason, and experience

As we have seen, Christine de Pizan recognizes the 'grande ombre femmenine' (*Advision*, II.1.9) in the second part of the *Advision* as Lady Opinion because she has already met her in the debate on the *Roman de la rose*, a debate that arose from contrary opinions as to the morality of the poem (*Advision*, II. xxi.25–29). It also gave Christine a clear conception of opinion before she personified the notion in the *Advision*, as is evident in the opening lines of her last document in the *Rose* debate.

> Pour ce que entendement humain ne puet estre eslevé jusques a haultesse de clere cognoissance d'enterine veritey entendre des choses occultes (par

---

[86] Messelaar 1963, pp. 41, 142–43, 161. Cf. Zumthor 1955, p. 177: in study of the semantic range of ideas, 'l'adoption d'un ou plusieurs sens (une ou plusieurs *idées*) constitue le phénomène primaire; l'adoption d'une forme donnée (un *mot*), le phénomène secondaire.'

[87] In the *Advision*, Christine distinguishes between 'la bonne conscience adrecee a Dieu' (*Advision*, p. 9:254), and 'viles consciences … mauvaises' (III.vi.178).

[88] Tuve 1966, pp. 287–88.

[89] I have not discussed here how Christine uses her subtle intelligence to write poetry. This subject, which relies on the *aviser–deviser* paradigm, is treated in Chapter 2 as description.

l'ofuscacion grosse et terrestre qui l'empesche et tolt vraie clarté[90]), convient par oppinion plus que de certainne science determiner des choses ymaginees plus voirsamblables: pour celle cause souventefois sont esmeues diverses questions – mesmement entre les plus subtilz – par oppinions contraires, et chascun s'efforce de monstrer par vive raison son oppinion estre vraye. (*Débat*, p. 115:3–11)

[Because human understanding cannot be lifted to heights from which it can comprehend the full truth of things hidden (this is because gross, material obfuscation deprives it of a clear view of the truth), we must evaluate by opinion more than by certain knowledge whether the things that imagination construes are verisimilar. For this reason, various issues frequently arise, even among the most subtle minds, because of opposing opinions, and each person strives to demonstrate by rational argument that his or her opinion is true.]

This is a clear statement of subjective certainty. The evaluation of personal opinion is grounded in logical thought and personal experience that admits subjectivity in serious debate.

That opinions can be variously qualified is illustrated by the way Christine uses the word and its synonyms *avis* and *cuidier*. Collecting the author's own terms, the contrast between positive and negative opinions in the *Rose* debate is apparent in the two sets listed below, each of which reproduces Christine's language. The judgments are Christine's own. The first set refers to Christine's own opinions about the *Roman de la rose*; the second set refers to the opinions of Jean's 'disciples' that she rejects.

Christine's good opinions about the *Rose*

'vraies oppinions' (7:27) [true opinions]

' selon mon foible avis, en doit estre parlé sobrement' (14:90, 51:87–88) [in my weak opinion, it ought to be discussed soberly]

'bon advis' (15:107, 52:104) [good opinion]

'ma veritable oppinion justement meue' (24:7–8) [my true opinion rightly formed]

'nostre oppinion bonne' (148:1058) [our good opinion]

Her opponents' bad opinions about the *Rose*

'oppinions a honnesteté contraires' (6:28) [opinions opposed to good morals]

'oppinion de gent'[91] (124:286) [common opinion]

---

[90] Cf. the distinction noted above in the *Mutacion* between the perfect intellectual gifts bestowed by God and the imperfect, 'obfuscating' body Nature locates them in.

[91] Cf. von Moos 2002, pp. 15–16, on this fault.

'home deceu par oppinion volomptaire' (131:532) [man deceived by arbitrary opinion]

Jean's 'disciples, however, attribute only negative value to opinion. For example, Pierre Col asserts that 'tu as parlé par oppinion ou presumpcion oultrageuse. O tres fole oultrecuidance!' (*Débat*, p. 100:387–88) [you spoke from opinion or with outrageous effrontery. What most foolish presumption!] In another passage anticipating the *Advision*, Col evokes the philosophers Aristotle condemns for holding 'oppinions ... contenans erreurs en philozophie' (*Débat*, pp. 101:458–102:459) [opinions that contained errors in philosophy], words Christine notes and does not forget. Aristotle, she states elsewhere, refuted 'l'oppinion des anciens philozophes contenans erreurs' (133:595–96) [the opinion of ancient philosophers that contained errors]; so she too refutes the opinions of Jean's defenders by denying the moral integrity of the *Roman de la rose*. Indeed, she recalls Aristotle's refutation anew in the *Advision*, amplifying on the topic using Aquinas's Commentary on the *Metaphysics* in Lady Opinion's review of philosophical and religious errors.

Christine's references to opinion in the *Rose* debate anticipate the *Advision* by distinguishing between opinion and articles of faith. She excludes articles of faith from the realm of opinion. Referring to a recent debate on the Virgin's Immaculate Conception, for example, she concludes: 'si n'est ce pas article de foy; aussy n'est cecy [that is, opinion on the *Rose*]: si en croie chascun ce qui luy plaist le mieulx qu'i pourra' (*Débat*, p. 149:1116–18)[92] [but this matter is not an article of faith; nor is this, so each of us may believe whatever pleases as best he or she can]. But Christine nuances the distinction further by also considering 'certain knowledge'. In Isidore of Seville's *Etymologies*, a work Christine knew,[93] philosophy combines knowledge of human and divine matters ('rerum humanarum divinarumque cognitio') with moral philosophy ('cum studio bene vivendi') (*Etymologiae*, II.xxiv.1). Philosophy's role in the *Advision* conforms to this analysis, as when, in evaluating Christine's life, she shifts responsibility for her troubles from Fortune to Opinion.[94] Isidore goes on to affirm that philosophy relies on knowledge (*scientia*), which is based on reason and opinion (*opinatio*), opinion again being less certain because it is not founded on firm reason (*Etymologiae*, II.xxiv.2). This too is consistent with Christine's distinction between certain truth and true opinion. Like Isidore, Christine argues that knowledge is certain, but that opinion, although uncertain, is not necessarily false. Isidore further lists several questions that opinion, not knowledge, must answer. For example, is the sun as big as it appears, or is it bigger than the earth? Is the moon convex or concave? Do the stars adhere to the heavenly

---

[92] See Hicks, ed., *Débat*, p. 228 n. 149/1116.
[93] Solente, ed., *Mutacion*, vol. I, pp. l–lix; Reno-Dulac, ed., *Advision*, p. xxxix. Christine also mentions Isidore's *Synonyms* (*Advision*, I.xxvi.7).
[94] The *Chemin* treats *rerum humanarum ... cognitio*, as we shall see (pp. 36–37, 149–52). Cf. *Charles V*, vol. 2, p. 170.

sphere or do they move freely through the air (*Etymologiae*, II.xxiv.2)? In the *Advision*, Christine likewise evokes 'scientific' issues that can only be responded to speculatively; for example, in treating the First Material Cause, she asks which came first – earth, air, fire, or water? Not all these questions are issues today. We are sure, for example, that the sun is bigger than the earth; for us, this is certain knowledge, not opinion. On the other hand, what the basic material of the universe may have been and how it came about – Christine's issue – are still controversial, making them matters of opinion in Isidore's and Christine's terminology. Speculation in moral philosophy also belongs to the realm of opinion. Today opinions about morality are often as opposed and uncertain as Isidore's about a convex or concave moon.

Argument for and against an opinion classifies points of view such as those proposed by Christine for the meaning of the *Roman de la rose*. It does so by trying to sway emotions in order to change opinions – *mouvoir opinions*, in Christine's words.[95] In the *Advision* Christine further dissects opinions by naming three factors in opinion making: *loy*, *raison*, and *vray sentement*.

Loy can be ambiguous in Christine's usage as well as in Old and Middle French in general. It refers to both the rules established in society by the ruler and God's laws promulgated through religion and command.[96] However, the apparent ambiguity of her usage actually reveals the coherence of her thought in its medieval context. That is, the word's sense of 'established law' fits into the same hierarchy in which Christine locates herself in relation to her faith and by which she understands the divine right of kings.[97] There is, or should be, harmony between God's law and the ruler's, for God protects those who accept their place and status in His scheme of things.[98] Christine illustrates this in Part Three of the *Advision* by conjoining Philosophy and Theology as arbiter of truth. Here, an opinion is validated by what we know of God's plan and the fit of that opinion in His plan. God's word is made known through faith, the Bible, and ecclesiastical authority founded on a hierarchy extending from God to the Pope, the king, and other mortals beneath them. When Christine as author lets Philosophy speak as Theology at the end of the *Advision*, she proceeds much as Jean Gerson does when he puts the condemnation of Jean's 'disciples' in the mouth of Eloquence Theologienne and, later, in his own sermons. Within the hierarchy deriving from God, Theology gives certainty to Eloquence, even though human limitations imposed by Nature may prevent us from recognizing that truth or from fully comprehending it;[99] this is apparent, for example, in the heresies referred to in Part Two of the *Advision*. Lack of education is another

[95] *Débat*, pp. 12:19 and 30–31, 24:7–8, 49:19 and 30.
[96] Both senses of the word *loy* are found in Christine's writings; see Blanchard and Quereuil 1999, p. 242; cf. Messelaar 1963, pp. 274, 326.
[97] Forhan 2002, pp. 77–81, 84–85.
[98] Klee 1997, pp. 374–75; Quillet 2002, p. 690.
[99] For the problem of ascertaining truth in Christine's historical context, see Pons 2000.

impediment; Sibyl refers to such inadequacy in the *Chemin de long estude* when she acknowledges that Christine's lack of a formal education denies her access to theological speculation (cf. *Chemin*, v. 2023–26; *Advision*, III.i.15–19, and viii–ix). Otherwise, 'chose qui est dicte par oppinion et non de loy commandee se puet redarguer sans prejudice' (*Débat*, p. 12:32–33; cf. p. 50:31–33) [something expressed as a matter of opinion but not imposed by law as faith can be criticized without prejudicing one's argument].

Likewise, Gerson's Eloquence Theologienne evokes the faculty *raison* and its corollary, speech, in evaluating opinion.[100] In Old and Middle French, *raison*, as both the rational faculty and as human speech, comprises not only logical discourse but also rhetorical discourse designed to sway emotion. In the context of medieval faculty psychology, reason defines and thus informs the imagination and the senses. For Christine, Reason leads not to certain truth, but to probable opinion. As Lady Opinion puts it: 'tant que je seray en toy fondee sur loy, raison et vray sentement, tu ne mesprendras es fondacions de tes oeuvres es choses plus voir semblables, non obstant de plusieurs les divers jugemens' (*Advision*, II.xxii.39–42) [as long as I am grounded in you on divine law, reason, and valid experience, you will not err in founding your works on verisimilar evidence despite the various judgments of different people]. The credible or verisimilar *semblance*, or appearance of things, is the form an opinion takes, an opinion that is based on rational criteria and definitions. In debate, verisimilar examples can appear to illustrate such opinions.[101]

The last of the factors in opinion making, *vray sentement*, can refer to actual feelings one has with regard to a matter of opinion. Informed by faith and by reason, it includes conscience; the feeling's validity is also confirmed by experience. The feeling can, moreover, be direct, as in Christine's response to Jean de Meun's disciples about her direct knowledge and experience of women's feelings (*Débat*, pp. 123:253–77, 139:775–84); it can be very personal, as in her response to misogyny in the opening section of the *Cité des dames*.[102] Rhetoric is an effective instrument for advancing opinion based on *vray sentement* because, by swaying the emotions, it translates personal experience into language that can arouse analogous emotions in others, even across gender barriers. That is, it communicates experience vicariously.

But *sentement* (and *de sentement* as well as *sentir*) requires further clarification in the light of the word's relation to reason and thought. *De sentement* was a commonplace phrase used to underscore the sincerity of the poet's affection in courtly poetry.[103] Brunetto Latini shows that this meaning includes a kind of cognition applying to sensations,[104] thereby connoting the understanding of one's feelings, including a rational understanding of them. Indeed,

---

[100] *Débat*, pp. 71:321–72:324, 81:563–82:582, 85:664–86:669.
[101] See Kleinschmidt 1974, pp. 79–90.
[102] Blumenfeld-Kosinski 1990, pp. 289–92.
[103] Kelly 1978, pp. 245–48; Cerquiglini 1985, pp. 190–97.
[104] Messelaar 1963, pp. 25, 232–33. This meaning applies as well to *sentir*.

as Reno and Dulac note in the glossary to their edition of the *Advision*, *sentement* can be defined as 'intelligence, esprit', 'jugement', and 'sentiment' (p. 249 s.v. *sentement*) while *sentir* includes the meanings of 'comprendre' and 'ressentir' (p. 250 s.v. *sentir*).

By the thirteenth century, the word *sentement* had taken on the meaning 'capacité d'apprécier un ordre de choses, une valeur morale, esthétique', and, more particularly, 'une tendance affective stable et durable, d'où l'emploi également courant (XIIIe s.) à propos de l'inclination d'une personne pour une autre, qu'il s'agisse d'amour ou d'amitié'.[105] By 1390, the word also appears designating the faculty of thought.[106] This is how Christine uses it. *Sentement*, especially *vray sentement*, is the faculty by which the action of *esplucher* functions in matters of feeling and sensation. This is, in the French sense, *apprécier*.

The limits of Christine's inquiry

Although Christine does not question, interpret, or speculate on matters of faith, she does seek to understand where she can while accepting what she must.[107] We can observe this by contrasting her expedition into the breadth and depth of human knowledge in the *Chemin de long estude* with Alain de Lille's similar excursion in the *Anticlaudianus*, a work she may have known.[108] In Alain's poem, the narrator comes to a crucial moment in relating the ascent of Reason and Prudence to the edge of the finite geocentric universe. Thus far, they are accompanied by the five senses and sustained and borne along by the seven liberal arts. At the edge of the geocentric universe, however, Prudence leaves all behind her except for the sense of hearing and advances into the *aevum*. But before describing this realm outside time and space the narrator inserts a remarkable intervention. He announces that he is setting aside the language of the poet for the words of the prophet (*Anticlaudianus*, V, v. 268–69). In Alain's terminology, 'prophet' can mean not only 'one who foresees or tells the future' but also 'one who proclaims biblical or theological truth'.[109] As prophet in the latter sense, Alain tells what Prudence[110] and Hearing apprehend in the Great Beyond: incontrovertible articles of faith and theology such as the Trinity, the

---

[105] *Robert*, p. 1921.

[106] *Robert*, p. 1922.

[107] Christine's religious beliefs are not so conventional as has been claimed. This point is made by Forhan 2002, pp. 88–89.

[108] On Christine and this work, see Kottenhoff 1994. Gerson refers to Alain's *De planctu Naturae* in the *Rose* debate (p. 80:527–28); Christine mentions it in the *Chemin*, v. 5205–12.

[109] See Alain's *Distinctiones*, col. 912. On this passage in the *Anticlaudianus*, V, v. 265–305, see Meier 1979, especially p. 82.

[110] On Prudence here and for Christine, see Brown-Grant 1999a, p. 167. Prudence is Minerva in Christine's *Cité*; see Zühlke 1994, ch. 3.

Virgin birth, the harmony of the four elements, and similar mysteries. These are not matters of opinion. Alain's visions are not speculation. They are literal, not allegorical statements, albeit pronounced within an allegorical framework. That is, Alain states literally what Reason, left behind, cannot explain: the prophet speaks the truth and the poet's pen records it (V, v. 273–77). Thus, Prudence *sees* the Virgin birth and Immaculate Conception – givens that exceed human understanding. That is why Prudence must view them in a mirror that represents them literally, not mystically or spiritually. To give voice to the prophet, Alain merely pens the literal truth.

Christine too assumes a prophetic role in the *Epistre Othea* by establishing a connection between past (albeit partially fictional) events and the future. Christine can assume a prophetic voice despite her humble status and limited education because, as she claims in the work's dedication, she will express authorized truths.[111] Thus, although the words she puts in Othea's mouth are expressed 'En esperit de prophecie' (*Othea*, 1:68), 'riens ne diray qui n'aviengne, / S'avenu n'est' (1:70–71)[112] [in the spirit of prophecy ... I shall say nothing that will not come to pass if it has not already happened]. In this fictional context, Othea's lessons to Hector announce his loves, combats, and death – past events in Christine's time. But her words also fit *Othea*'s allegorical context. Christine uses euhemerism, or moral allegory applicable to both the knight and the human soul (see Chapter 2), by compiling and citing biblical and ecclesiastical statements of her faith's truths. In this, she resembles Alain de Lille, the prophet or speaker of truth. However, she applies her faith only to practical moral teachings useful for the common good, not to the mysteries in the Great Beyond.[113]

Although faith is a guide amidst conflicting opinions, Christine does not presume to ascend to the heights Alain the prophet does. In the *Chemin de long estude*, she declines to rise on Imagination's Ladder of Speculation beyond the firmament that separates the finite universe from the *aevum* that Alain's Prudence knew. Indeed, she abides on an even lower plane than Reason does in the *Anticlaudianus* (V, v. 76–78). Off-limits to her are both the crystalline sphere at the limits of the geocentric universe where Alain's Reason stops, and the 'hault ciel' (*Chemin*, v. 2041) into which Prudence and Hearing pass: 'Il ne te loit passer un pas / Oultre ce ciel; tant que tu portes / Ce corps, closes te sont les portes' (*Chemin*, v. 2036–38) [You may not pass on beyond this sphere; as long as you have this body, the gates beyond are closed to you].

---

[111] Alain does the same when enunciating truths seen by Prudence in Heaven.

[112] On Christine as prophet who repeats and/or interprets earlier prophecies, see Mühlethaler 1983; Tarnowski 1993; Laennec 1995, pp. 131–38; Dulac 1999, pp. 88–89; Margolis 2000, pp. 304–08; Blanchard and Mühlethaler 2002, pp. 42–58. Cf. Minnis 1984, p. 101; Solterer 1995, pp. 165–71.

[113] Forhan 2002, pp. 87–93.

Christine even declines to repeat future events that Sibyl allegedly revealed to her.[114]

> Car sillence tres commandee
> Me fu. Si sera bien gardee,
> Car n'appartient a reveller
> Le secrés de Dieu, n'a parler
> De ce fors a ceulx qui commis
> Y a Dieux comme ses amis. (*Chemin*, v. 2173–78)
>
> [For I was ordered to keep silent, and I shall do so. It is not proper for anyone to reveal or state God's mysteries except those to whom God assigned the task.]

Instead, the Sibyl leads Christine to a different task where she confronts France's political quandary (*Chemin*, v. 2031–35).

To understand better the limitations Christine the author sets for herself in the *Chemin*'s allegory, let us look briefly at two vernacular examples of crossover into the *aevum*: Dante's *Divine Comedy* and Jean de Meun's *Rose*. Christine knew both poems. Indeed, they served as models that she adapts to her own vision in the *Chemin de long estude*.

Like Prudence, Dante the Pilgrim went all the way through Paradise.[115] Leaving the earth far behind, he rose up through the spheres of the planets, the fixed stars, and the firmament into the Great Beyond. But unlike Alain, Dante does not describe this realm in literal terms. Rather he inverts the concentric spheres of the geocentric universe in order to describe Heaven allegorically. Beginning with what is literally closest to earth, he describes the sphere of the moon as the most distant (given Heaven's 'place' beyond time and space) from the Trinity. Thus, not surprisingly, the physical reality becomes the grounds for a greater theological reality as Dante reads into the cosmos God's sense of order. Likewise, Dante's view of Heaven, like that of Purgatory and Hell, focuses on faith, with consequences for mortals that depend on the life each one leads before death. It certainly seems as if the *Divine Comedy* was on Christine's mind as she described her fictional ascent into higher regions.[116] However, adapting Dante's vision to her purposes, Christine wrote on subjects accessible on her own lower status as 'poet' in the *Chemin*.

Following the Sibyl up the Ladder of Speculation lowered by Imagination, then, Christine observes the heavenly spheres as physical realities, not in theological terms. Her discoveries are, in other words, 'scientific'; she does not gloss them as moral lessons or reaffirmations of faith. In this her experience

---

[114] Is she alluding allegorically to some astrological predictions that her father may have once communicated to her?

[115] See Brownlee 1995a, pp. 131–34.

[116] *Chemin*, v. 1127–52; cf. *Débat*, pp. 141:868–142:876 (pp. 226–27 n. 142/871); *Advision*, I.xvi.38–41 (p. 157 n. XVI/38–40). See Zühlke 1994, pp. 150–59.

of the heavens (not Heaven) is analogous to that presented in the *Anticlaudianus* before Prudence passes on and her narrator changes from poet to prophet.[117] Christine learns about the spheres of the air, ether, and fire, as well as the sphere on which she stops to survey all creation. She looks, but does not venture beyond, convinced that the realm of the angelic hierarchies Alain and Dante describe in theologically informed images is not meant for her pen. As we have seen, Christine rises no higher on the Ladder of Speculation, not because she lacks intelligence, but because she lacks education. As the Sibyl explains to her,

> Monter ou firmament te fault,
> Combien que autres montent plus hault;
> Mais tu n'as mie le corsage
> Abille a ce. Toutefoiz say ge
> Que de toy ne vient le deffault,
> Mais la force qui te deffaut
> Est pour ce que tart a l'escole[118]
> Es venue.   (*Chemin*, v. 1677–84)

[You are to ascend to the firmament, although others ascend even higher. But you do not have the qualifications to do so. I know that this is through no fault of your own; rather, you lack the wherewithal because you began to acquire an education late in life.]

Christine's speculation is therefore confined to the physical and moral universe of time and space. In this context, she focuses on political opinions in the context of the troubled French monarchy.

Christine's other model for imaginative speculation, Jean de Meun's *Rose*, is, interestingly, almost the antiphrasis of Dante's *Comedy*. Nature's description of the universe in the *Rose* is modeled on that set out in Alain's other major poetic work, *De planctu Naturae*.[119] For Nature in both Alain's *De planctu* and Jean's French adaptation of Alain's prosimetrum, God's universe functions as it should except in the case of man. Christine goes even further in the *Chemin de long estude*, asserting there that all things, from humanity to the elements, are in rebellion.

---

[117] Christine's prophetic stance stands out more forcefully in works like the *Livre de la paix* that attempt to predict France's future. See Van Hemelryck 2000, especially pp. 667, 675, 682; and Suard 1993 on prophecy in the *Ditié de Jehanne d'Arc*.

[118] Christine's lack of a clerical education makes her, as poet, a forerunner of those lay persons the arts of the second rhetoric taught; cf. Jung 1971; Wolfzettel 1995, especially p. 91.

[119] In the *Chemin*, v. 2668–71, Christine briefly contrasts the image of the non-human world of plants, animals, and inanimate things doing their assigned tasks with man's failure to do so; see Ribémont 1995, pp. 247–50, and Brucker 1995, pp. 265–69.

> Tout y va a rebellion,
> Et non pas seulement li hom;
> Ains y va ainsi estrivant
> Toute creature vivant
> Et mesmement li element. (*Chemin*, v. 399–403)[120]
>
> [Everything is in rebellion, and not just men; rather all living creatures are in strife, as are even the elements.]

Even the angels revolted against God at one time (v. 427–36). To be sure, the war among the elements is part of God's plan to create order out of chaos. Although disorder and rebellion among men are not part of His plan, they occur in the exercise of free will and, therefore, Christine reports them in the *Chemin de long estude*. Interestingly, she rewrites the same disorder and rebellion in the description of Chaos at the beginning of the *Advision*.[121]

Genius is another of Jean de Meun's adaptations of Alain de Lille. Genius, a personification that includes in its semantic range Imagination,[122] is the faculty that, personified as Imagination, lowered the Ladder of Speculation to Christine in the *Chemin*. The enlightened Genius of the *De planctu*, however, becomes the besotted imagination of the *Rose* personification preaching unbridled lust and sexual intercourse as the path to Heaven. This is the Genius Christine found so offensive in the *Rose* debate.[123] The opinion that vigorous sexual indulgence leads to Paradise would have been obviously ironic and, therefore, preposterous to anyone of Christian faith reading the *Roman de la rose* in the Middle Ages.

But Jean's Genius can also be read allegorically, as Laurent de Premierfait does in claiming that Dante's vision of the ascent through the spheres is modeled on Jean's.[124] Of course, Dante's white rose in 'Paradiso' Canto 30 is hardly the red rose plucked at the end of Jean's poem. In Laurent's view of the *Rose*'s influence on Dante's *Comedy*, the Italian poet rewrote the red rose of the French poem, transformed *in bono* by antiphrasis, as the white rose in 'Paradiso' Canto 30; antiphrasis could be a legitimate technique for reading the *Rose*,

---

[120] The discord among the elements in the world contrasts with their harmony in Heaven in the *Anticlaudianus*, V, v. 311–72. The 'rebellion' of the sub-lunar world conforms to Nature's description of this changeable realm in the *Rose* and human responsibility for its defects.

[121] See Dudash 2003, pp. 818–19.

[122] Wetherbee 1976.

[123] See, for example, *Débat*, pp. 141:849–145:970.

[124] Christine may have known this statement inserted in Laurent's translation of Boccaccio's *De casibus*, but not at the time she wrote the *Chemin*. Laurent's earlier, 1400 translation, which she may also have known, does not contain the claim (Badel 1980, pp. 484–87). The 'second edition' translation is dated 1409; the *Chemin* was written ca. 1402.

according to Christine (*Cité*, p. 48).¹²⁵ For his part, Laurent also perceived there, but did not develop as a central theme, the principle of the three orders in society.¹²⁶ Since the Christine persona in the *Chemin* did not launch herself into the *aevum*, she opted for the political context that she felt competent to speculate about and form opinions on. For this she came down to Reason's realm.

In the *Advision*, Christine analyzes opinion as concept using theology and philosophy – or, to be more precise, theologies and philosophies. To her mind, truth and error are absolute. However, the two are generally confused in human minds. As a result, not only have there been different theologies and different philosophies, there have been differences among individuals who adhere to the same theological or philosophical opinion. Differences in human understanding explain diverse human activities, from military activities to the arts and trades. In the *Advision*, however, such diversity is the model for Christine's description of Lady Opinion, her activities, her genealogy, and her progeny. When Christine finally recognizes Lady Opinion and can name her, she can also see beyond mutable variety to define the concept the lady personifies. For, as Matthew of Vendôme says, 'argumentum sive locus a nomine est quando per interpretationem nominis de persona aliquid boni vel mali persuadetur' (*Ars versificatoria*, 1.78) [*an argument* drawn from a name is a matter of interpreting a person's name to suggest something good or bad about the person (Galyon, p. 48)]. The description preceding the naming allows the reader to understand the full significance of the personification. That understanding makes definition possible.

---

¹²⁵ Brown-Grant 1999a, pp. 145, 149–50; see pp. 56–78 on *Othea*, and pp. 84–85 below. Christine rewrote Matheolus as well; see Luff 1999, pp. 369–70.
¹²⁶ Badel 1980, pp. 484, 486; Forhan 2002, pp. 59–65.

2
Opinion as a Personification: Description and Invention

> Le revers de la verité a cent mille figures et un champ
> indefiny.   (*Essais,* I.ix, p. 38)

In the *Advision* Christine defines opinion as a more or less credible view that one may accept or reject. It follows that opinion can represent any view that comes up in debate, serving to 'faire bouger les catégories mentales',[1] or, as Christine herself puts it, to 'mouvoir nos oppinions' (*Débat*, p. 145:972–73) [change our opinions]. Human limitations explain why opinion rather than certain knowledge prevails in human thought. The desire to know impels humans to form opinions and defend them when attacked. Since, however, an opinion may be true or false, and since its truth or falsity is a matter of opinion, there is always some uncertainty registered when opinions differ. These are factors that Christine took into account in describing her personification of opinion.

Description in medieval French allegory relies on a scheme often identified as *aviser* followed by *deviser*. Before the Fountain of Wisdom, for example, Christine remarks that 'm'arrestay pour aviser / Ce que vous m'orrés deviser' (*Chemin*, v. 811–12) [I paused to construe what you will hear me describe]. Descriptions facilitate understanding of the object of description (*Policie*, p. 3:3–5). To construe and then describe in this manner is important in delineating and resolving matters of opinion. Again, in the *Chemin de long estude*, Christine relates the technique to her description of the debate on the ideal ruler that concludes the poem.

> Car oppinions moult diverses
> Y a, et l'une a l'autre averses.
> Si a bien cy a deviser
> Pour mieulx choisir et aviser.   (*Chemin,* v. 3451–54)

---

[1] Cerquiglini 2000, p. 603.

> [For there are many diverse, and divergent, opinions. There is much to describe here in order better to perceive[2] and construe them.]

These lines extend the *aviser–deviser* paradigm to include an audience's *aviser* – that is, the author's conception (*aviser*) is represented in words that describe it (*deviser*) and, in this way, permit the audience to understand and evaluate (*aviser*).

As a commonplace attendant to allegory, *aviser* comprises all the intellectual virtues and faculties identified with thought and described in the preceding chapter. But because, for Christine, it also includes 'imagination', *aviser* leads, in allegory, to *deviser*, in the specific sense of description informed by the artist's *avis*. In the *Livre de la paix*, Christine explains how she describes prudence in this way.

> De ceste vertu, pour mieulx descripre que c'est et dont elle vient et dessent, est assavoir qu'entendement qui est puissance et operacion de l'ame ... est son commencement. L'office de cest entendement est d'ymaginer toutes choses veues ou non veues selon la quantité de sa force par lesquelles ymaginacion, par bien investiguer, est engendrée congnoissance laquelle s'approche plus des choses ouvrales, c'est assavoir des choses que on veult mectre à euvre, congnoistre, et entendre les manieres de les faire et entreprendre. De ceste congnoissance vient Discrecion.   (*Paix*, pp. 65–66)

> [In order to describe that virtue and its origin and derivation, know that it begins with understanding, a power and function of the soul. It is the office of such understanding to form a mental image of all things seen and not seen; by careful investigation, using imagination in this way, cognition is born. Cognition then turns to the tasks to be done, that is to say, the tasks one wants to accomplish, knowing and understanding how to do and carry them out. Discretion comes from that cognition.]

In this way, prudence as discretion considers a subject matter that it seeks to understand (*aviser*) and, as a result, invents a description (*deviser*) that illustrates coherently that subject matter.[3] This chapter will examine Christine's art of description and its relation to her views on opinion and opinion making. We begin with Christine's description of Lady Opinion in the *Advision*.

---

[2] 'To perceive' rather than 'to choose' seems to be the best translation given the descriptive mode Christine evokes in these lines.

[3] Cf. Kelly 1978, p. 39, and 1983, pp. 117–19. See also *Chemin*, v. 1603–05, 3269–70, 3453–54, 4571–72, 4921–22; *Enseignemens*, 99–100.

The description of Lady Opinion

Christine describes the personification of Lady Opinion at the beginning of the *Advision*'s second part.

> Avisay ... une grant ombre femmenine sans corps, si comme chose esperituelle de trop estrange nature ...; car celle chose veoie estre une seulle ombre, mais plus de cent mil milions, voire innombrables parties, les unes grandes, les autres mendres, autres plus petites de soy elle faisoit; puis s'assembloient les parties d'ombre comme par grans tourbes si que font nuees ou ciel ou oyselles volans par tas ensemble. (*Advision*, II.i.9–15)

> [I recognized a great feminine shade, incorporeal as would be something spiritual of a very unusual kind. For I saw it as a single shape with a hundred thousand million, nay with countless parts, some big, others less so, and still other smaller versions of herself. Then these parts of shade came together in great masses as clouds do in the sky or birds flying in flocks.]

The word *ombre* that Christine uses to describe Lady Opinion in the *Advision* refers to an 'appearance' and a 'shade'; she is not only a 'shadow', she is also a 'shape', and, indeed, a shape that is constantly shifting like a cloud or a flock of birds.[4] But, as 'shade', she connotes both 'shadow' and 'color'. Her color is ever changing too, being determined by the different schools of thought her colors refer to allegorically, 'as well as a fluidity in the types of knowledge to which authority is to be assigned'.[5] Shapes and shades of diverse color and hue – her parts – swarm about Lady Opinion, blending, intermingling, and separating before Christine's astonished eyes.

> Et tout ainsi comme les couleurs d'icelles ombres par tourbes se differoient, semblablement faisoient leurs fourmes. Car il n'est corps de creature humaine ne d'estrange beste, oysel, monstre de mer, serpent ne chose que Dieux formast oncques, voire des plus haultes choses celestielles et de tout quanque pensee puet presenter a la fantasie, dont n'y eust la fourme. Si en avoit tant d'estranges qu'il n'est cuer qui le peust penser. (*Advision*, II.i.30–36)

---

[4] Dulac 2001, pp. 188–89. On *ombre*, see *FEW*, vol. 14, p. 21: 'modèle', 'apparence trompeuse'; *Robert*, p. 1365: 'Le mot s'applique notamment à l'ombre par opposition au corps qui la produit: de là, les sens d'"image sans consistance, apparence, semblant", et "spectre, mort".' In *AW*, vol. 6, col. 1086, ll. 43–49, the word carries over from 'shadow' the notion of something that can darken vision. On the relation between a word's semantic range and the changing figure that personifies the word and that range, see Kelly 1978, p. 25, and 1995a, p. 56. Christine evokes the same image to describe flatterers in the *Corps de policie*; they hide their vices 'soubz fainte simulacion en ombre et en couleur de bien' (p. 16:23) [beneath feigned disguise as the shadow and color of good]. See also *Paix*, p. 122, where dissimilation is likened to a shade that colors its appearance so as to hide its true nature. This comparison recalls Jean de Meun's Faux Semblant.

[5] Semple 1998b, p. 115.

[And just as the colors of these masses differed from one another, so did the shapes they assumed. For there was no human or strange beast ever fashioned by God that was not depicted there – whether bird, sea-monster, or serpent or any of the highest things in the heavens or whatever fantasy may conjure up in the mind. Indeed, there were some so bizarre that no mind could conceive them.]

In this way, the personification of opinion illustrates the consistencies and nuances, as well as the diversity, inconsistencies, and enormities, of human thought. Opinions may be very strange beasts.

By contrast, in the *Advision*'s first part, Christine shows how virtues and vices form a 'normative array' in the medieval sense of 'adequacy of evidence'[6] – that is, 'they converge into a definition of human nature in society as something morally based on both acts and words'.[7] Virtues constitute an orderly array, analogous to a genealogical tree that correlates the one with the other. 'Les vertus descendent les unes des autres et s'entreacompaignent et attraient' (*Advision*, I.xxvii.2–3) [The virtues descend the one from the other, forming groups by mutual attraction]. Such order characterizes Christine's allegorical descriptions. In the *Advision* in particular, there are the three contexts she envisages in her gloss, humanity in general, her own life, and France; but she does not exclude other readings that one may find there (*Advision*, pp. 3:4–4:46). As for the vices, their relation is less orderly because they 'trebuchent de l'une en l'autre et s'entresachent et apparient' (I.xxxvii.3–4) [stumble along from the one to the other, jostling and pairing up in heterogeneous combinations]. This description anticipates the description of Lady Opinion in her various shapes. Indeed, such instability characterizes the undesirable personifications such as Chaos and the vices that populate the first part of the *Advision*.[8]

Since opinion is especially at home in the University, Christine locates Lady Opinion and her various 'shades' in that setting, populated as it is by clerics ever debating conflicting opinions (*Advision*, II.i.3–6). Christine herself belongs to that realm, as Lady Opinion perceives in addressing her as 'Fille d'escolle' (*Advision*, II.iii.4). Since, however, as a woman, Christine cannot attend the University,[9] this title must refer to her as daughter of a school of thought and, therefore, of opinion.[10] Charity Cannon Willard paraphrases 'fille d'escole' as

---

[6] Allen 1982, p. 101.

[7] Allen 1982, p. 104. See as well Hicks 2000, pp. 228–29; Parussa, ed., *Othea*, pp. 19–20.

[8] Nature is a shade that variously produces human shapes (*Advision*, I.ii). Fraude is like Faux Semblant: 'tu te transfigures en trop d'estranges fourmes' (I.xix.27–28) [you transform yourself into too many strange shapes].

[9] See Stuip 2004, p. 155.

[10] Christine extends the realm of opinion beyond the medieval university; it has a place among practitioners of mechanical arts as well as in warfare and knighthood (*Advision*, II. ii.41–46, iii.15–20, iv.19–25). The shades as different 'schools' may therefore represent

'bluestocking', that is, an intellectual but not necessarily a student.[11] This is consistent with the role Christine assigns herself in the *Rose* debate. As daughter of a school of thought, Christine is among Lady Opinion's daughters. Her own quest for truth locates her, both as an individual and as a member of a particular school of thought, among the numberless and diverse shades of Opinion.

Lady Opinion has her own parents. They are Ignorance, her mother, and Désir de Savoir, her father. She was conceived, that is, created or formed, as soon as Adam was created (*Advision*, II.iii.12–13).[12] Encouraged by Opinion, and eager to know what the fruit of the Tree of Knowledge of Good and Evil might teach them in their ignorance, the first man and woman tasted the forbidden fruit (II.iii.13–14).[13] Opinion, however, is not always a false teacher. She taught Adam and Eve how to cultivate the earth and order their life (II.iii.16–18). Indeed, she is the source of all invention, including poetic invention.[14] As time passed, more opinions emerged; eventually philosophy and its philosophers came along (II.iii.19–25). These thinkers also appear in the *Chemin de long estude* (v. 1647–48), but they operate in the realm of speculation. Lady Opinion prevails until certain truth is found. She will disappear only at the end of the world, for she has no place in Heaven or Hell, where absolute and certain truth prevails (*Advision*, II.iii.31). There is no opinion in God's mind.

The admixture of truth and error in human opinions derives from the human admixture of speculative soul and ignorant body (*Advision*, II.iv.70–75).[15] When Reason reigns, the soul's inclinations dominate the body and the mind approaches certain truth (*Advision*, II.iv.60–62). Lady Opinion illustrates this dynamic with a survey of some true and false faiths, including religious errors such as Manicheism and Arianism, and philosophical errors, especially the errors of the philosophers she compares unfavorably with the more certain perception of truth she finds in Aristotle.[16]

---

diverse techniques, trades, and activities as well as schools of thought to which Christine herself might belong. In the *Chemin*, the Sibyl, 'ma maistrece' (v. 1545), claims Christine for her own school (v. 656–58, 1587–88, 1682–84, 6294; cf. v. 1506–10); see Zühlke 1994, pp. 302 n. 249, 306 n. 293, and 309 n. 317.

[11] Willard 1984, p. 100. Cf. Schilperoort 1936, pp. 34–38. 'Bluestocking' can, therefore, be laudatory or negative, depending on context – and opinion. Cf. Hicks 1995a, pp. 234–35.

[12] Cf. *Advision*, III.ix.35–42. On this correction of the *Mutacion*, see *Advision*, II.xiv.4–11, and above, pp. 14–20. Opinion's 'parents' are evoked in the speculative part of the *Chemin* in v. 1620–22, 1654, 1751–53, 1809–11, 1984–88.

[13] Christine seems to imply that the devil is one of Opinion's shapes.

[14] Cerquiglini 1993a, p. 212.

[15] See Cerquiglini 1993b, pp. 105–07; cf. Brown-Grant 1999a, pp. 121–22; and Chapter 1, pp. 21–22.

[16] On Christine's indebtedness here to Aristotle's *Metaphysics* and Thomas Aquinas's commentary on it, see Dulac and Reno 1995; Reno and Dulac, ed., *Advision*, pp. xxxii–xxxiii; Richards 2000a, pp. 201–02.

Opinion and rhetoric

To sway opinion, one relies on the noble art of rhetoric (*Cité*, p. 160). Christine recognizes this function, perhaps influenced by Boethius's Philosophy who supports her own lessons by 'rhetoricae suadela dulcedinis' (*De consolatione*, II Pr. i.8) [the sweet persuasion of rhetoric (Green, p. 21)]. For example, Lady Opinion adapts her rhetorical demonstration to her pupil as audience.[17] First, she confines her discussion of philosophical opinions on first causes to the 'cause de matiere' (*Advision*, II.vi.12 and x.22) or 'cause materielle' (II.x.27),[18] that is, the Material Cause.[19] Second, she adopts the *ars arengandi*: 'Et tres ore soit changié l'ordre de nostre rethorique en plus vulgare et elegant parleure en retournant a nostre premiere arrenge' (II.xiii.12–14) [And let the order of our rhetorical demonstration be altered to fit a more common, elegant discourse by returning to our first point]. *Arenga* refers to the order in which an argument is set forth.[20] Thus, the speaker defines his or her subject, arranges the evidence, and illustrates it with appropriate examples that clarify and sway opinion. The *arenga* was commonly used in debates; this is obvious in the *Rose* debate, in which Christine uses the term, pointing out that although she cannot 'user de belle arenge et mos polis bien ordennéz qui mes raisons rendissent luisans' (*Débat*, pp. 12:35–36 and 50:34–35) [express myself by beautiful discourse and well-disposed, polished speech that might illuminate my argument], she will argue her opinions solidly and straightforwardly.[21] The *Advision* makes the same

---

[17] Philosophy does so in Boethius's *Consolation* when she precedes her harsh medicine with milder cures (*De consolatione*, I Pr. v. 11–12; cf. II Pr. i.7, III Pr. i.2–3). The *Rose* too takes account of diverse audiences (Kelly 1995a, pp. 17–19). In the *Chemin* the Sibyl recognizes Christine's limitations as a result of her education, adapting her instruction to her pupil's level of accomplishment (v. 1668–90). Audience is a major point of dispute in the *Rose* debate, as discussed above.

[18] These expressions translate *causa materialis* in Aquinas's Commentary on Aristotle's *Metaphysics* (*Expositio*, especially Book I, Lessons 4–17), one of Christine's sources on opinion; see Dulac and Reno 1997; Reno and Dulac, *Advision*, p. xxxiii.

[19] On the Four Causes – Efficient, Formal, Material, and Final – see Minnis 1984 and Brown-Grant 2000b; for their place in the composition of the *Rose*, see Kelly 1995a. Christine refers only briefly to the other causes in treating Aristotle's criticism of his predecessors. The formal cause is evoked in the *Advision*, II.xi.47–52, the final cause in II.xii.3–18, and the efficient cause as God in II.xii.1831. See also Dulac and Reno 1997, pp. 125–26. Lady Opinion describes herself as the efficient cause of human activities in explaining her own relation to Fortune (II.xiv). Thomas Aquinas treats extensively all four causes in Christine's source, in the Commentary on Aristotle's *Metaphysics*.

[20] McLeod 1991, pp. 114–16, shows how the disposition of the *Cité des dames* fits the order prescribed by Cicero in his *De inventione*; cf. as well *Paix*, p. 167. This passage is also translated in Brunetto Latini's *Tresor*, III.15; he also explains it at some length.

[21] Cf. p. 115:14–116:30 and Richards 1998b. By the time she wrote the *Advision* Christine was more confident in using the *ars arengandi*. Her use of the art is related to the art of letter-writing (*ars dictaminis*); see Almeida Ribero 1989; Richards 1993; LeBlanc 1995; Margolis 1996. On the relationship between the *ars arengandi* and the *ars dictaminis* in general, see Camargo 1991, p. 40, and Koch, *HWR*, 1, 1035–36. Christine knows that the

point because Christine's discussion with Lady Opinion is said to take place in a University setting.

The University Lady Opinion occupies lies in the middle ground between France's Chaos in the *Advision*'s Part One and the small chamber of Philosophy in Part Three. France, personified by a figure named Libera,[22] deplores the chaos of the realm, starkly visualized in the depiction of human life as a descent through all-consuming Chaos and the final, startling elimination of its material self as excrement. In Part Three, Philosophy depicts the limits of opinion as she moves on to the solid ground of faith and herself acquires the new name Theology (*Advision*, III.xxvii).[23] Faith, founded on biblical, and therefore infallible, truth for Christine, shows false opinion emerging among mortals at the moment the devil convinced Adam and Eve to sin. To be sure, they did acquire knowledge through sin, since they came to know good and evil by disobedience. Sinning always teaches something. But presumption, a variety of opinion, counters God's will and reveals their error through knowledge of their sin.

Philosophy is more akin to theology in the *Advision* than she is in Boethius's *Consolation*, as well as to the philosophies about the Material Cause evoked in *Advision*, Part Two.[24] Born before Lady Opinion, Philosophy is the daughter of God.[25] At her best, Opinion is chambermaid to Philosophy, striving to express the latter's God-given truths. Christine herself exemplifies this effort in passing from the truths of opinion in Part Two of the *Advision* to the truth of philosophy and theology in Part Three. As a 'fille d'escolle' and herself a daughter of opinion, Christine strives to distinguish true from false opinion by the process

---

arenga also designates a critical introduction to a discourse. The art flourished in Italy, spreading from there to France and elsewhere. See Segre 1968, pp. 121–23, and Koch, *HWR*, vol. 1, cols. 1033–40 (on the *ars arengandi*) and cols. 877–89 (on *arenga*).

[22] Libera foreshadows Chartier's France in the *Quadrilogue invectif*. See Cerquiglini 1993b, p. 158; cf. Auerbach 1958, p. 153. On Christine's influence on Chartier, see Willard 1984, pp. 202, 212–23.

[23] Philosophy is also named Sapience and Serenité in the *Advision*, III.ii.4 and iii.2. Changing the name of personifications or other exemplary figures to fit the semantic range of the idea personified or exemplified is analogous to Christine's description of Opinion's 'colors'. For example, Prudence in Alain's *Anticlaudianus* also goes by the names Phronesis, Sapientia, and Sophia; similarly, in the *Advision* Lady Philosophy becomes Lady Theology. Minerva alias Pallas refers to different roles for the same goddess; see González Doreste 1997. Fortune in the *Roman de Fauvel* also has different names depending on whether it represents providence, destiny, or chance (Angeli 1996, pp. 23–24). On this subject, see Whitman 1987, pp. 4–8, 269–72. Penthesilea may also be renamed, and newly described, as with Othea in *Othea* (see Parussa 1993, p. 483). Such adaptation is analogous to Froissart's inventions using, among other techniques, renaming (Kelly 1981, 1998). Cf. Heitmann 1963.

[24] Cf. Reno and Dulac, *Advision*, p. xxxi.

[25] *Advision*, II.iii.26–27; cf. III.xxvii.28–29: 'O Theologie que je vueil louer, Dame, en toy, souveraine Philosophie ...' [Oh! Theology whom I wish to praise in you, sovereign Lady Philosophy]; and 55: 'Sainte Theologie ...' [Holy Theology]; cf. III.xxvii.17–19.

she frequently refers to as *esplucher*,²⁶ or careful sifting and winnowing. Thanks to Philosophy alias Theology in the *Advision*'s third part, Christine corrects her own false opinions. We shall examine instances of such correction below and in the remaining chapters.

Since, as Christine reminds Lady Opinion, 'vous estes ambigue et pouez estre deceue' (*Advision*, II.xxii.79–80) [you are ambiguous and can be deceived], specific opinions arising out of ignorance are never entirely free from doubt because of their relation to Opinion's mother, Ignorance. As we have seen, she found criteria for evaluating opinions in religion, reason, and personal experience.²⁷ Lady Opinion encourages her 'fille d'escole' to ground her quest of true opinion on these three criteria.

> Si te conseil que ton oeuvre tu continues, comme elle soit juste, et ne te doubtes d'errer en moy. Car tant que je seray en toy fondee sur *loy, raison* et *vray sentement*, tu ne mesprendras es fondacions de tes oeuvres es choses plus voir semblables, non obstant de plusieurs les divers jugemens, les ungs par moy simplement, les autres par Envie.
> (*Advision*, II.xxii.38–43; my emphasis)
>
> [I advise you to persevere, as is right, and not to fear erring through me. For as long as you rely on *religion, reason*, and *personal experience*, you will not err by basing your works on credible foundations, in spite of diverse judgments either pure and simple through me, or by others arising out of envy.]

As noted above, *loy* includes religion; reason is the human faculty whereas *vray sentement* is personal experience and a sense or feeling for what is right or true; it is based on conscience and one's emotional response to experience. Conscience distinguishes between right and wrong emotions; for example, envy clouds judgment and leads to error when aligned with mere opinion not grounded in conscience informed by reason and faith. Although Christine accepts her human and personal limitations, she can learn using reason and faith, as she does under Philosophy–Theology's tutelage in Part Three of the *Advision*. Religion is a firm foundation for Christine de Pizan. It does not admit of doubt, although one can err in trying to understand it, falling into heresies like those Opinion mentions (*Advision*, II.v).

---

²⁶ Pierre Col uses this word in the *Rose* debate (*Débat*, p. 93:161); Christine adopts it to refer to her own investigation of opinions (*Débat*, pp. 129:468–69, 135:650; cf. *Cité*, p. 42). However, *esplucher* does not appear in the *Advision*. Montaigne uses 'esplucher' in an analogous manner; see his *Essais*, I.xl, p. 245, and, in general, Leake 1981, p. 424. Cf. Fumaroli 1997, p. 15; *Robert*, p. 74 s.v. *éplucher*. *Débat*, pp. 93:161 (Pierre Col), and 129:468–69 and 135:650 (Christine de Pizan). Cf. *Robert*, p. 711 s.v. *éplucher*, which 'signifie d'abord "nettoyer, en enlevant les parties inutiles"'; it therefore anticipates Christine's *aviser* as *consideracion* and *discrecion*.

²⁷ For example, she had a good marriage because all these criteria came together in the decision for her to marry (Zühlke 1994, p. 63).

Christine's changing opinions and her ongoing education

Christine illustrates opinion both true and false in the debates on the first cause in the *Advision*'s Part Two. Moreover, Lady Opinion too explains how Christine's own complaint about Fortune in the *Mutacion* is erroneous. Although Fortune may rule over things, including the body, opinion errs in making Fortune out to be the first cause and an evil. We remember that in the *Mutacion*, Fortune changed Christine from a woman to a man because she had to assume a man's conventional role as head of her household.[28] The trials and tribulations attributed to Fortune there, however sincerely they were felt, are in fact the fruit of wrong opinion. They conflict with Boethius's teachings. Although Christine accepted this view in Part Two of the *Advision*, she is still victim of the same error in Part Three, apparently having forgotten what she learned, as Boethius does at the beginning of the *Consolation*.[29] Philosophy–Theology shows Christine how philosophical truth corrects errors regarding the power of Fortune in her own life.

Lady Opinion encourages Christine to seek true opinion, distinguishing sharply between it and false opinions that prevail in the world. Christine agrees with Lady Opinion in Part Two. Yet her lengthy complaint in Part Three about the havoc Fortune wrought in her own life shows that she has not applied that knowledge to understanding her own experiences. Philosophy corrects her false opinion using the very combination of religion, reason, and personal experience that Opinion told Christine she needed in order to get at truth. Here again we recognize the subjective certainty that, like Lady Opinion, changes as Christine's quest for truth progresses.

Philosophy's argument is thus closely modeled on the *Consolation*. Good and bad fortune 'vient par cuidier et par opinion' (*Advision*, III.xxi.42) [comes from presumption and opinion], whereas sufficiency is contentment with what God grants (*Advision*, III.xxi.44–45). Such gifts would include the virtues God bestowed on Christine. Although 'l'extimacion et opinion des gens' (*Advision*, III.xxv.7) [people's opinion] may determine what people value, these are false values when they do not rest on religion, reason, and personal experience. Christine's Philosophy gathers 'flowers' from Boethius's *Consolation* to teach her disciple a profound lesson (*Advision*, III.xxv.30–33). Going beyond the *Consolation*, she includes arguments gleaned from Scripture. In doing so, Philosophy appears as the highest knowledge, acquiring a new name, Theology (*Advision*, III.xxvi.1–2, 11–17).[30] As mentioned earlier, such renaming occurs not infrequently in allegorical poetry. It is analogous to Christine's metamorphosis from woman to man in the *Mutacion*. Philosophy–Theology's lessons, like manna from Heaven (*Advision*, III.xxvii.68–71), restore Christine's faith,

---

[28] See Zühlke 1994, pp. 86–90; Kelly 1996; Brown-Grant 1999a, pp. 121–22.
[29] On weak memory, see Brown-Grant 1999a, pp. 153, 161–62.
[30] Christine seems to replace the changing sizes of Boethius's Philosophy (*De consolatione*, I Pr. i.2) by changing the name of her personification (*Advision*, III.xxvii.17–34).

giving her practical understanding of her life's course. Her changed opinion about the place of fortune in her life and in the world she lives in allows her to turn to the political and moral issues that interest her most and to which she devotes her later writings.[31] With Aristotle, she corrects opinions in matters of faith, philosophy, and politics; with Boethius, she corrects her own false opinions about the role of fortune in her life.

Different voices express opinions in Christine's writings. In the debate mode characteristic of her work on opinion, as well as in the *Rose* debate, she adapts the traditional modes of deliberative rhetoric. The debate mode was common in medieval court poetry before and in her time; it was, therefore, familiar to Christine's readers. Debate as 'dialogue presents different points of view and various possibilities of thought' – and, we might infer, of opinions; since, however, 'dialogue is situational and the speakers' moods are generally transparent',[32] character becomes a factor in debate, and, more specifically, in the style of debate. In Christine's case, style is a feature of her character. As she puts it, she prefers 'le stille a moy naturel', a 'bel stille' (*Advision*, III.x.25, 27) because of her scholarly, rather reclusive character (III.x.9–13; cf. *Débat*, p. 148:1077). This 'natural style' is the allegorical mode that poets use.

> J'oz trouvé le stille a moy naturel, me delictant en leurs soubtilles couvertures et belles matieres mucees soubz fictions delictables et morales, et le bel stille de leurs mettres et proses deduites par belle et polie rethorique aournee de soubtil langage et proverbes estranges.   (*Advision*, III.x.25–29)[33]
>
> [I had found the style natural to me, wherein I took delight in their subtle integuments and beautiful subject matter lying beneath pleasing moral fictions, and the beautiful style of their verse and prose drawn out in lovely, polished rhetorical flourishes using subtle language and unusual proverbs.]

Her personifications and exemplary figures also speak in character, an issue that looms large in the *Rose* debate on Jean de Meun's decorum as well. In the terminology of medieval rhetoric, this is Material Style.[34] This term refers to the conformity between character and level of discourse in description of a person or personification. In Christine's time, such description was part of invention.

---

[31] Kelly 1996; Paupert 2000.
[32] Echtermann and Nagel 2000, p. 496.
[33] See Strubel 1995. For early examples of this style, see *CB* 61, 86, 90; *AB* 7, 14.
[34] Kelly 2000, pp. 197–200; on Material Style in general, see Quadlbauer 1962; Kelly 1983, 1991, pp. 71–78.

Opinion and description as topical invention: common places and commonplaces

Description in medieval poetics is the art of topical invention. To understand such description as it was practiced by Christine de Pizan and many other medieval authors, we must make the critical distinction between what I have termed the commonplace and the common place. Commonplace refers 'to a conventional image, thought, or action an author repeats or paraphrases in a new work', whereas a common place identifies 'places in a person, thing, or action common to all persons, things, or actions of the same kind'; each work describes such places according to its author's intention.[35] In this book, I use these terms as they are defined here. In medieval poetics, topos is synonymous with 'common place'; that is, it designates a 'place' common to any thing, whether human, animal, vegetable, mineral, or intellectual – 'en somme, toutes les conditions ou circonstances de l'existence'.[36] The 'place' is identified by a definition. What is defined is a feature or 'property' common to all persons, things, actions, or ideas of a particular kind, but a feature that can vary from person to person.[37] For example, an obviously important topos in Christine's writings is gender (*sexus*).[38] Gender is an attribute of human nature like, among other such topoi, nationality, language, age, and family. Once the feature is identified, the writer gives it substance by means of a description that characterizes the person, thing, or action as individual or type.

Did, however, Christine de Pizan know and consciously use topical invention? We know little about her actual education, which appears to have included both what she gleaned from her father and what her mother imparted as part of the upbringing of a young woman being prepared for marriage and motherhood. Deschamps refers to a more ambitious role for her father in what Zühlke terms a *translatio studii* from father to daughter.[39] According to Deschamps, this included instruction in the seven liberal arts.[40] If this is so, her education would have included grammar and rhetoric, arts that, in the Middle Ages, offered instruction and practice in topical invention.[41]

---

[35] Kelly 1999b, pp. 62–63.

[36] Zumthor 1972, p. 83; cf. Kelly 1983; Edwards 1989, especially interchapter 2. On the meanings of the term topos since the Middle Ages, see the articles on *Lieux communs et littérature* in the 'Première Journée', *CAIEF*, 49 (May 1997), pp. 13–150.

[37] It can also support comparisons; for example, 'le chien a maintes proprietez a quoy le bon homme d'armes doit retraire et ressembler' (*Policie*, p. 15:19–20) [a dog has many features the good soldier should imitate and resemble]. As examples, Christine names loving the master, protecting him, and remaining constantly alert.

[38] On *sexus* as a variable attribute of human nature, see Richards 1996, pp. 101–12.

[39] See Zühlke 1994, pp. 57–58; cf. *Mutacion*, v. 651–58; cf. *Advision*, III.ii.8–11.

[40] See Ballade 1242, v. 19, in *Balades*.

[41] Her comparison of composition to architecture in *Charles V* (vol. 1, p. 191; cf. Desmond 1994, pp. 209–12; Richards 2000b, p. 117) recalls Geoffrey of Vinsauf's use of the analogy in *Poetria nova*, v. 43–70; see Willard 1984, pp. 125–26. Perhaps this accounts for Christine's preference for architectural images in the *Mutacion* and the *Cité*; cf. Blanchard 1988, p. 140,

This brings us again to the issue of Christine's knowledge of Latin. Fortunately, the issue is not crucial in the case of topical invention because the art was available not only in ancient and medieval treatises in Latin, but also in Brunetto Latini's *Livre du tresor*. Using the information in it we can see how useful knowledge of the art of topical invention can be for interpreting Christine's own inventions and, more importantly, her evaluation of and arguments for her own opinions.

Bärbel Zühlke has shown that Christine draws on standard topoi to describe herself as well as her father, mother, husband, and children. Christine presents herself, for example, as 'une personne'.[42] Every 'person' has common human attributes such as those mentioned above. Typical for the medieval kind of description, an author chooses from among such attributes those that might best describe what he or she wishes to highlight in a specific person or personification. Christine describes herself in this way. However, unlike Rousseau at the beginning of his *Confessions*, she does not pride herself on a broken mold that would have made her unique, but rather on how closely she resembles her father's mold, despite her failure to make a perfect fit.[43] She states that this deficiency results in part from her intelligence and, more importantly, from her inadequate education because she was a woman, her gender prejudicially depriving her of the opportunity to realize her intellectual potential (*Mutacion*, v. 413–30; *Cité*, pp. 150–52). The description of her education and faculties is thus set by defining topoi: *convictus*, *sexus*, and *habitus*, or the topoi 'way of life', 'sexual gender', and 'character'.[44]

The technique is apparent in Christine's other writings as well. She evokes it in the *Chemin de long estude* using the *aviser–deviser* paradigm, asking herself what properties she will identify in the personification Wisdom, or *Sagesse*, in order to describe her properly.

> Or est il temps que je m'avise
> Comment proprement je devise

1990, pp. 225–29; Desmond 1994, ch. 6; Luff 1999, pp. 380–89, 401–02; Caraffi 2003. The analogy also has a biblical source used by Gerson (Edsall 2000, p. 51). Christine would have known Geoffrey's analogy, either directly from the *Poetria nova*, or from Brunetto Latini's use of Geoffrey's comparison in his *Tresor* (III.17.2.9–18); on Brunetto's use of the *Poetria nova*, see Kelly 1969, pp. 126, 132 and n. 36, 133–34.

[42] Zühlke 1994, pp. 79–80. On the meanings of *personne* in pre-modern times, see Rheinfelder 1928.

[43] 'Sie spezifiziert den Grad ihrer individuellen Ausprägung' (Zühlke 1994, p. 80) [She specifies the degree to which she delineates her individual features].

[44] Zühlke 1994 treats *habitus* (pp. 142, 297 n. 204), *natio* (pp. 187–88), and *sexus* as *virago* (pp. 191–200). On *habitus*, see also Richards 2000b, p. 121; Quillet 2002, p. 686; cf. Fenster 1995, p. 482; Haidu 2004, p. 306. On *sexus*, see Pairet 2002, p. 149. In the *Corps de policie*, Christine seems to understand *habitus* as acquiring a 'seconde nature ... par longue acoustumance de bien ou de mal' (p. 7:8) [second nature ... by long familiarity with good or evil]. Walters 2002a and 2002b treat implicitly *natio* and *patria* as language and country of origin respectively. On these topoi, see Matthew's *Ars versificatoria*, 1:85, 82.

> Les proprietez de sagece,
> Ou toutes vertus a largece
> Puisent et prennent leurs effects
> De tous les cas justement fais.   (*Chemin*, v. 4921–26)
>
> [It is now appropriate for me to construe how I may properly describe Wisdom's properties; all virtues draw abundantly on her, deriving their effects from all actions rightly performed.]

Wisdom is one of the personifications in the debate that closes the *Chemin*. Her words are the case she, like the other personifications, makes in arguing how best to resolve France's problems. Each personification – Wisdom, Wealth, Nobility, and Knighthood – describes an ideal monarch for uniting France and lifting it from its difficulties. Moreover, each proposes a ruler who possesses uniquely the attribute the given speaker personifies: the king should be noble or chivalric, rich or wise. We shall see how Christine herself construes such a king and describes him using topical invention in Chapter 5.

For now, let us consider another instance of original topical invention. Christine follows a traditional medieval plan or code for rewriting a given matter. Such a plan or code is a *gradus*.[45] Here we encounter a striking analogy between some feminist criticism and medieval theories of topical invention on rewriting a conventional description. *Gradus* is analogous to what Sharon Marcus terms a script. She notes that

> we can begin to develop a feminist discourse on rape by displacing the emphasis on what the rape script promotes – male violence against women – and putting into place what the rape script stultifies and excludes – women's will, agency, and capacity for violence.[46]

But scripts, like codes and *gradus*, can be rewritten. 'Ne moremur ubi moram faciunt alii; sed, ubi moram faciunt, transeamus, ubi transeunt, moram faciamus' (*Documentum*, II.3.133)[47] [Let's not dwell there where others did. Rather where they tarry let us pass on, dwelling on what they pass over]. Geoffrey of Vinsauf is more elaborate in the *Poetria nova*:

---

[45] In the *Pastoure* Christine likewise rewrites the *pastourelle*'s traditional rape script, adding the missing steps of the commonplace *gradus amoris* to relate a fantasy tale that, unrealistically, crosses class divisions (Blanchard 1983, pp. 101–03, 141 n. 26). A different script or scenario occurs in other contexts; for example, there is a 'saintly scenario' in the *Trois vertus* (Blumenfeld-Kosinski 2000).

[46] Quoted in Wolfthal 1998, p. 58; cf. Kelly 2005, especially pp. 321–23. Christine too elaborates in the *Cité* on 'women's will, agency, and capacity for violence' in, for example, the cases of Semiramis, the Amazons, and Judith. For similar use of 'script' in describing anger, see White 1998, especially p. 146; White is implicitly treating *gradus irae*. Cf. Cheyette and Chickering 2005, pp. 78–79.

[47] On the background in Horace and in medieval commentaries, see the twelfth-century *Materia* Commentary on Horace's *Art of Poetry* (pp. 353–54 on v. 128–33) which inspired these lines; see also Friis-Jensen 1995.

> Quod minus est supple, quod plus abrade, quod hirtum
> Come, quod obscurum declara, quod vitiosum
> Emenda. Curis istis sunt omnia sana.   (*Poetria nova*, v. 1758–60)
>
> [Amplify what is slight, prune what is redundant, groom what is shaggy, clarify what is obscure, correct what is faulty. Every aspect of the work will be sound because of your careful efforts. (Nims, p. 79)]

This, in medieval terms, is the kind of rewriting Marcus proposes: 'clarify what is obscure' by 'displacing the emphasis'. Such 'selective quotation'[48] is a characteristic feature of Christine's art of invention.

To adopt Marcus's term, from the perspective of topical invention, every action has a script. There is, for example, a *gradus amoris* for falling in love and a *gradus aetatum* for aging, each of which contains topoi or 'places' common to the phenomena they 'script'.[49] Such scripts can be prescribed, as Matthew of Vendôme does for the *gradus amoris*: 'in actuali amoris exercitio precedit intuitus, sequitur concupiscentia, accessus, colloquium, blandimentum, ad ultimum votiva duorum congressio' (*Ars versificatoria*, 4.13) [in the usual course of love seeing comes first, then follow desire, approach, conversation, blandishments, and finally the hoped for union of the two (Galyon, p. 103)]. As an example, Matthew quotes Ovid to explain the probability of sexual intercourse, the last stage in the *gradus amoris*, whether by rape or not: 'A iuvene et cupido credatur reddita virgo?' (*Ars versificatoria*, 1.82) [Can you believe that she was returned a virgin by one both youthful and hot-blooded? (Galyon, p. 49)]. Matthew insists that such scripts must leave no lacunae: 'ut narrationis nulla sit intercisio' (*Ars versificatoria*, 4.13)[50] [so that there is no interruption in the account (Galyon, p. 103)]. Matthew notes how several stages in the youth's *gradus amoris* are missing in this example. But more importantly in Marcus's context, he ignores attributes of the young woman that might show how she responds to her loss of virginity in this way – that is, whether or not she consents to a '*votiva* duorum congressio'. This is the 'place', or *locus* or topos, where rewriting of Ovid such as that suggested by Matthew and Marcus would be appropriate – and where Christine did rewrite.

---

[48] Brown-Grant, trans. *Cité*, pp. xxiii–xxiv, xxx–xxxii. Cf. van der Helm 2004, p. 93, on Christine's description of Semiramis: 'Belangrijk hierbij is: wat laat Christine weg van wat Boccaccio schreef en wat voegt zij er vervolgens aan toe?' [Important in this matter is: what does Christine leave out of what Boccaccio related and what does she subsequently add to it?]

[49] On the *gradus amoris*, see Friedman 1965; on the *gradus aetatum*, Burrows 1986 and Dove 1986.

[50] He notes in the same place an Ovidian example in which two of the stages are missing.

Opinion and Christine's rewriting of common places

Christine can rewrite because a *gradus amoris* presupposes a number of stages, or 'places', that are conventional in relating the progress of lovemaking from first impressions to consummation. It usually includes the five stages, although the precise number is not important – Matthew lists six in the passage quoted above. The common places in a *gradus amoris* are common because they describe the usual course of love, good or bad, including seduction and casual lovemaking as well as sincere affection and marriage. More important is the way in which each stage in the progression is defined or described. That is to say that each stage is a topos or 'place' common to love's progress and, as a common place, subject to interpretation and invention. The author draws out the topos's potential in a specific context. Such 'extraction' gives expression to opinion. Thus, Christine implicitly corrects the Ovidian example used by Matthew to include the effect on and response of the virgin in a society in which loss of virginity is a serious result of rape, both during the act and in its effect on the victim afterwards.[51] This would be an obvious instance of a rewriter dwelling on what her predecessors passed over.

The prescription to abbreviate what is lengthy and amplify what is brief may be perfunctory in classroom exercises. However, it is important to remember the analogies between this stage and learning a foreign language. In a given lesson (or stage of learning), the pupil stresses one grammatical principle such as the subjunctive rather than another such as the indicative, stringing together sentences that illustrate the subjunctive mode. Gradually the pupil becomes aware of when a subjunctive may properly and effectively be used. Similarly, Matthew's and Geoffrey's prescriptions lead beyond the classroom exercise. They actually teach a technique for revising or correcting a subject matter so as to express a new conception of it.[52] That is, they teach the writer how to express a new view of or opinion on a given subject matter.

Matthew of Vendôme offers the simplest scheme. The author considering where to dwell and what to pass over might ask him- or herself the following questions about the proposed script: 'Quis, quid, ubi, quibus auxiliis, cur, quomodo, quando' (*Ars versificatoria*, 1.116) [Who, what, where, with what aid, why, when, in what matter (Galyon, p. 61)]. This scheme for invention is 'an extractive operation'.[53] It admits, of course, variants, just as those for love and the ages of life do. It is easily remembered, even if not in the same words, as D. W. Robertson, Jr., noted in discussing its use by confessors in analyzing sin and determining penance, as it were 'on the spot'.[54] Indeed, as a reader reflecting critically on Ovid's line about the fate of a virgin left alone with a 'hot-blooded youth', Christine might well ask about the virgin: *quis?* For,

---

[51] Wolfthal 1998, p. 67.
[52] On revision and correction, cf. as well Matthew's *Ars versificatoria*, 4.
[53] Copeland 1991, p. 160; see pp. 64–76, 160–65.
[54] Robertson 1946; Gründel 1963; cf. M. Zink 1985, pp. 14–16, 20–21.

although the hot-blooded young man preserves his attributes intact, the maiden no longer has any feature, the single one attributed to her – virginity – having been lost. Prior to intercourse, she is analogous to Gerson's Chastity in the *Rose* debate: a virgin, 'la tres belle, la tres pure' [very beautiful and pure]. But this comparison raises another feature of the query *quis?* Does the virgin desire or not desire, like Gerson's Chastity, what the young man does? Could she too be a *iuvenis cupida*?[55] It is not obvious in Matthew's context that the virgin 'onques ne daigna neiz panser aucune villainne ordure' (*Débat*, p. 60:34–36) [never deigned to think of such vile filth]. Only the context can tell whether she is chaste or libidinous.

This example would have been more explicit to those of Matthew's pupils who knew the context of the line Matthew lifted from Ovid's *Heroides* (V, v. 129). There it is part of Oenone's diatribe addressed to Paris because he jilted her for that 'cow' (v. 117–118, 124), Helen. But Helen was no virgin at the time Paris abducted her. As Ovid's Oenone (here quoting Cassandra) describes Helen, she is the willing object of male passion, an example of 'the woman wants to be raped' commonplace: 'quae totiens rapta est, praebuit ipsa rapi' (v. 132) [yet she who has been so often *ravished* has surely lent herself to *ravishment*], a reference to Helen's having been abducted more than once.[56] Through Oenone, Ovid describes Helen as a *iuvenis cupida*. But she tells a story different from the one Matthew's excerpt might suggest. As Matthew points out,

> si in eodem exemplo incidat attributorum diversitas, referendum est non ad effectum sermonis, sed ad affectum sermocinantis: verba etenim notanda sunt ex sensu ex quo fiunt, non ex sensu quem faciunt.
> (*Ars versificatoria*, 1:115)[57]

> [If, moreover, a diversity of attributes occurs in the same description, *they are to be read according to the speaker's feelings, not according to the mere meaning of the words.* For words are to be understood on the basis of the sense in which they are used, not merely on the basis of the sense they make. (Galyon, p. 61)]

---

[55] Kelly 1995a, p. 39. We cannot, in the context of topical invention, exclude the virgin who wants to lose her virginity – Briseida, for example, not as Christine represents her (*Othea*, 84), but as a loving woman in Benoît de Sainte-Maure's *Troie* (Kelly 1995b). Christine knew about Briseida, if not from Ovid's *Heroides*, then from its French adaptation in the *Histoire ancienne jusqu'à César*; see Campbell 1924, pp. 83, 91; Willard 1981b; Parussa, ed., *Othea*, p. 444.

[56] Helen herself implies as much when she suggests ravishment as the best way to conciliate her desire with her reputation in *Heroides*, XVII, v. 187–88: 'utilis interdum est ipsis iniuria passis./ sic certe felix esse coacta forem' [Wrong sometimes brings gain even to those themselves who suffer it. In this way, surely I could have been compelled to happiness]; see Demats 1973, pp. 94–95.

[57] Similarly, *Tresor*, III.3.4, where the speaker is advised to use language appropriate to the way he or she construes the case. This is an issue in the *Rose* debate when evaluating Reason's use of words like *couilles* and *reliques* and Amant's reaction to them.

Ovid's Oenone is jilted and jealous.

Did Christine know this passage in Ovid's *Heroides*?[58] This raises anew the issue of her knowledge of Latin and her reading of works written in that language. She knew Oenone's plight. Lorete relates her story briefly in the *Dit de la pastoure* in an effort to discourage Marote's love for her nobleman (v. 1324–41); the example is appropriate because Oenone too was a shepherdess and, therefore, of lower social standing than her princely lover.[59] In putting the story into Lorete's mouth Christine realizes the moral profit commentators traditionally identified in, or read into, Ovid's *Heroides*.[60] In any case, the contents of Ovid's succinct reference to Helen are found in another work Christine did know: the second redaction of the *Histoire ancienne jusqu'à César*. Christine used this redaction in the *Mutacion de Fortune*.[61] Unlike the first redaction, this redaction inserts French adaptations of some of the *Heroides*, including Oenone's letter (she is Cenona in the *Histoire*),[62] which is inserted after Paris ravished Helen and brought her to Troy.[63]

Christine probably knew this redaction of the *Histoire ancienne* in London BL Royal 20 D.I., which was in the Louvre in 1380.[64] The following excerpt adapts the passage referred to above as follows:[65]

> Il fait ore bien a croire que iouene iouuencel et chault rendist belle damoiselle pucelle quand il la tenist en sa poeste; yce ne croirai ie car ie scay bien que amours montent quant les 'ij' parties sont d'un acort et say bien que pues monter. Et se tu dis: elle nen pot mes se len li fist force, ie te respont: vne se contregarde d'estre rauie et ceste est souuent rauie pour quoy nous pouons sauoir que elle se fait rauir de sa volente.   (Fol. 49 v°, b)

> [It is now well to think that a hot young man would return a beautiful damsel as a virgin when he had her in his power, but I don't believe it, for I know what love can accomplish when the two are in accord and I know what it can lead to. And you claim that she had no defense when she was raped, but

---

[58] Christine rewrites Helen's story as well; see below, p. 59. This example illustrates description in a context common in Christine. It is not possible to know whether she actually read Ovid's *Heroides* or knew them only through their vernacular versions in the *Histoire ancienne jusqu'à César*. However, she appears to have rewritten Oenone's story in the version told by Lorete in the *Pastoure*, v. 1324–1421; see Benkov 2002, pp. 70–72. On the reception of Ovid's work in Christine's time, see Ruhe 1975, pp. 286–94. On its extensive copying in the Middle Ages, especially in the fifteenth century, see Dörrie 1960, especially pp. 118–24.

[59] See Perugi 1998, p. 7.
[60] Minnis 1991, p. 25.
[61] Campbell 1924, p. 87; Solente, ed., *Mutacion*, vol. 1, pp. lxvi–lxvii.
[62] Jung 1996, pp. 507–08.
[63] Jung 1996, p. 513.
[64] Jung 1996, p. 505.
[65] I am grateful to Keith Busby, who made a copy of the second redaction's version of Oenone's letter for me using Paris BNF fr. 301, 'manuscrit copié sur le manuscrit BL Royal 20 D.I.; contenu identique' (Jung 1996, p. 552); see also Avril 1969, pp. 300–14.

> I answer that one protects oneself from being abducted. And since this woman is often abducted, we can conclude that she arranges willingly her abductions.]

The *Histoire ancienne* adaptation is wordier than Ovid's lapidary Latin. Nonetheless, it contains the aspersions on Helen's character that Christine deletes entirely from her version in the *Pastoure* in order to stress the inequality in Marote's amorous relation and in this way to turn the shepherdess away from her nobleman. I shall return to this example in Chapter 4.

However, on the level of classroom instruction like that provided by Matthew of Vendôme and Geoffrey of Vinsauf,[66] more will be required than perfunctory answers to the obvious topical questions *quis? quid?* etc. This is where one considers not Oenone's reaction but Ovid's intention in presenting her in the way he does. For example, although one learns what questions to ask, which features of a given subject matter should the questions address? Our two sources among the arts of poetry offer similar advice. Geoffrey of Vinsauf summarizes the topoi as follows:

> Si bene dicta notes et rebus verba coaptes,
> Sic proprie dices. Si mentio namque sit orta
> Forte rei, sexus, aetatis, conditionis,
> Eventus, si forte loci vel temporis:[67] haec est
> Debita proprietas, quam vult res, sexus, et aetas,[68]
> Conditio, eventus, tempus, locus. Ista venustas
> Est electa, quia bene cum determino totum
> Termino sub tali forma.   (*Poetria nova*, v. 1842–49)[69]

> [If you heed the directives carefully and suit words to content,
> you will speak with precise appropriateness in this way. If
> mention has perhaps arisen of an object, sex, age, condition,
> event, place, or time, it is regard for its distinctive quality that
> the object, sex, age, condition, event, time, or place claims as
> its due. Felicity in this matter is an admirable thing, for when I
> make an apt use of qualifying words [*determino*] I give the
> whole theme a finished completeness [*termino*]. (Nims, p. 82)]

Matthew of Vendôme identifies slightly different topoi from Geoffrey's: 'attributa persone undecim: nomen, natura, convictus, fortuna, habitus, studium, affectio, consilium, casus, facta, orationes' (*Ars versificatoria*, 1:77) and 'attributa negotio novem: summa facti, causa facti, ante rem, cum re, post rem,

---

[66] See other examples in Kelly 1999a, pp. 100–02.
[67] On these topoi, see Kelly 1991, pp. 71–78. Cf. Cecchetti 1991, pp. 8–21.
[68] On this correction, see Sedgwick 1927, p. 339.
[69] See Nims, trans., *Poetria nova*, p. 108 n. 1843.

facultas faciendi, qualitas facti, tempus, locus' (*Ars versificatoria*, 1:94)[70] [eleven personal attributes: name, nature, way of life, fortune, character, goals, appetites, judgment, luck, exploits, and eloquence (Galyon, p. 48) – and nine attributes of the action: the gist of the action, the cause of the action, the action preceding the action described, the action accompanying the said action, the action following the said action, the ease with which it was done, the quality of the action, the time, and the place (Galyon, p. 55)]. Matthew defines and illustrates each topos, in some cases with sub-categories. For example, he locates the quote on Ovid's *iuvenis cupidus* under *natura*. According to Matthew, the *natura* topos and its varieties 'sumuntur a natione vel a patria vel ab etate vel a cognatione vel a sexu' (*Ars versificatoria*, 1.82)[71] [are a result of *native language*, native land, age, family, or sex (Galyon, p. 49)]. Matthew illustrates his instruction with our line from Ovid: 'ubi dicitur *a iuvene* argumentum est a natura, ubi dicitur *a cupido* argumentum est ab affectione; et similiter in multis exemplis. Unde exempla ad mentem exemplificantis debent retorqueri' (1.115) [where the line says 'youthful', we have an attribute based upon *the common place* nature; where it says 'hot-blooded', we have an attribute based upon *the common place* disposition. And it is similar in many instances. Thus an example ought *to be turned to express the mind of the author of the example* (Galyon, p. 61)]. In a totally different context, Christine applies topical invention as Matthew and Brunetto Latini describe it to rewrite Helen as victim in both *Othea* (43, 68) and the *Cité des dames* (p. 406).[72]

Liliane Dulac has implicitly suggested how the art of topical invention is used in Christine's and Boccaccio's versions of Semiramis. Their accounts 'ne sont pas essentiellement des récits. Ils sont subordonnés à la construction des personnages: en général les éléments narratifs, les événements ou actions illus-

---

[70] Matthew draws his topoi from Cicero's *De inventione* (Faral 1924, pp. 77–78). Christine could find them, drawn from the same source, in Brunetto Latini's *Tresor*, III.52–53; Brunetto's French terms for persons are *non, nature* (including *malles ou femiele, païs, vile, lignie, cors* or *corage*), *norreture, fortune, habis, estude, volentés, conseil, cheoite, oevre*, and *dit*; and, for action, *some; achoison; apareil*, or *devant, sur*, and *aprés le fait; pooir; maniere; tens* and *saisons*; and *lieux*. *Vile* probably reflects Italian political units; *vile*, as *cité*, is the locus for the *Cité des dames*.

[71] On *locus a loco*, see Ribémont 1995, whose definition of the topos and its articulation fits my usage here: 'une matrice originelle à partir de laquelle la génération spatiale pourra avoir lieu' (p. 245); Christine for her part 'puise dans le monde encyclopédique ce dont elle a besoin pour son propre discours' (p. 257); on *locus a loco* and *a materia*, see also Pratt 1994, p. 62; Brown-Grant 1999a, pp. 150–51; and (implicitly) on *locus a sexu*, Brown-Grant 2000a. Cf. Cerquiglini 1994, pp. 80–82; Kottenhof 1994, pp. 45–46. Lechat 2002, p. 518, recognizes a number of the topoi in the description of Charles V and his family members in *Charles V*; he also notes their 'enumerative' character, resembling instruction in the arts of poetry and prose. However, he does not make the connection between Christine's practice of topical invention and the instruction in those treatises.

[72] Reno 1980, pp. 275–76. In the *Epistre Dieu* (v. 604–16) Christine argues that Eve did not deceive Adam, but was, like him, deceived by Satan, and that she followed Satan's counsel in good faith. Satan's role is analogous to that of seducers who take advantage of women. Christine also likens deceived men to women in the *Rose* debate; see p. 96.

trent et explicitent le portrait.'[73] For example, Christine's version of Semiramis's life in the *Cité des dames* illustrates the art of topical invention; rewritten she resembles the other women admitted to the *City of Ladies* insofar as 'elles deviennent aussi admirables qu'émouvantes, une fois écarté le masque repoussant que leur avait infligé les calomnies masculines'.[74] This conforms to the medieval tendency to use topical invention for praise or blame (see Chapter 5).

Such topical invention is also evident in Christine's description of herself in the *Mutacion de Fortune*. As we have seen, Matthew defines *natio* as native language, *patria* as country of origin. Christine describes herself as a French-language author of Italian birth.[75] Her age (*aetas*) defines the parameters of her love life; thus, Christine's marriage to Etienne de Castel when she was fifteen introduces ten years of happiness cruelly terminated by widowhood at twenty-five. Her family (*cognatio*) is foregrounded when she describes the virtues she inherited from her father, together with the difficulty she had in realizing their potential because of her gender (*sexus*).[76] Disturbing has been the identification of her mother as Nature, not her actual mother – a modification analogous to that of the omission of features in the description of the maiden in Ovid's lines,[77] where topoi express thought while setting aside features that do not support the opinion being expressed. This is the 'filter' by which Christine rewrites and reconfigures traditional material, including the figure of the mother.[78]

Topical invention, then, is a kind of interrogation typical in argument. It does not require that topoi be applied in the systematic, rigid way suggested by the medieval arts of poetry and prose. Reading masterpieces was also part of the writer's formation. Thus, another critical model for topical invention whom Christine knew, Boethius contributed both to medieval ideas on such topoi[79] and illustrated their original use in a work all the disputants in the *Rose* debate were familiar with: his *Consolation of Philosophy*.[80]

---

[73] Dulac 1978, p. 317; see González Doreste and Del Mar Plaza Picón 2002–03. Cf. Trachsler 2000, pp. 9–31; Orbán 2004; van der Helm 2004. For additional examples of Christine's interest in Semiramis, see *CB* 92, v. 27–29; *R* 14, v. 10; *AB* 11, v. 17–18.

[74] Dulac 1991b, p. 36.

[75] For example, *Mutacion*, v. 157–68; *Chemin*, v. 6292–98; *Advision*, III.iii.8–9, 50–51. Cf. Brownlee 1995a.

[76] Cf. Zühlke 1994, pp. 7–8, 12, 45.

[77] Brownlee 1991, p. 44, notes that in Christine's allegory, Nature appears as her mother, while Fortune functions as mother of her male self. Nature and Fortune are topoi; see *Ars versificatoria*, §§1.79–82, 1.84. Matthew distinguishes between *fortuna*, as one's fate in life, and *casus* as its more transitory twists (§1.89–90) – for example, the death of Christine's husband.

[78] See Altmann 1996, p. 390.

[79] In the *De differentiis topicis*; see Robertson 1946, pp. 11–12; Gründel 1963, pp. 30–32.

[80] The *Laborintus* names the *Consolation* as a model for writing (in Faral 1924, p. 361, v. 681–82). Boethius is cited not infrequently in the arts of poetry and prose to illustrate

In the *Consolation*, Philosophy poses 'a few small questions' ('pauculis rogationibus', *De consolatione*, I Pr. vi.1)[81] at the end of Book One so as to determine how far Boethius's understanding extends and where it fails him. In what follows, I have inserted the topical questions after Philosophy's questions; they serve as rhetorical equivalents to the philosophical queries. Note as well that the questions ask for Boethius's opinion. First, 'Huncine ... mundum temerariis agi fortuitusque casibus putas an ullum credis ei regimen inesse rationis?' (*quomodo?* 'in what manner?') [do you think ... that this world is subject to random chance, or do you believe that it is governed by some rational principle?], a question Boethius answers satisfactorily. Next Philosophy asks: 'Dic mihi, quoniam deo mundum regi non ambigis, quibus etiam gubernaculis regatur aduertis?' (*quibus auxiliis?* 'with what aid?') [Tell me, since you have no doubt that the world is ruled by God, do you know *how* it is governed?]. Boethius cannot answer this question, nor the next: 'meministine quis sit rerum finis quoue totius naturae tendat intentio?' (*cur?* 'why?') [do you remember what the end, or goal, of all things is – the goal toward which all nature is directed?]. He is unable to recall what he once knew. With the next question he is more successful: 'Atqui scis unde cuncta processerint' (*quis?* 'who?') [Do you know where all things come from?], a question to which God is the answer. Philosophy expresses astonishment that Boethius knows the origin of all things but not their end. Then pushing on: 'hominemne te esse meministi?' (*quis?* 'who?') [do you remember that you are a man?]. To his virtual 'Of course', she goes on to inquire: 'Quid igitur homo sit poterisne proferre?' (*quid?* 'what?') [Then, what is a man? Can you give me a definition?], only to receive a partial answer. Philosophy is interrogating her pupil as D. W. Robertson, Jr., has shown that a medieval confessor might. She diagnoses Boethius's malady and offers a cure as a kind of penance. Like Amant in the debate with Reason, Boethius the prisoner is defective in the use of the four 'virtues' Christine identified as typical of her own mental abilities: *consideracion*, *discrecion*, *retentive*, and *memoire*. In the *Advision*, Part Three, Christine too fails to use these powers of thought and memory until corrected by Philosophy.

Philosophy's interrogation conforms to the procedure that both Christine and her opponents refer to as *esplucher*, that is, the analysis of opinion alluded to earlier.[82] In the *Rose* debate, each side attacks its opponents' opinions about the romance by direct or indirect questions. For example, Gerson, using apostrophe, interrogates Jean de Meun himself:

> Qui est plus tost empris ou enflanmé au feu de vilains plaisirs que sunt les cuers humains? Pour quoy donques souffloies tu ce feu puant par les vens de toute parole legiere et par l'auctorité de ta persone et ton exemple? Se tu

diverse features of composition.
[81] For the ensuing questions, see *De consolatione*, I Pr. vi (and Green, trans., pp. 18–19).
[82] See p. 48.

ne doubtoies alors Dieu et sa vanjance, que ne te faisoit sage et avisé la pugnicion qui fu prise d'Ovide? (*Débat*, p. 67:212–17)

[Who is more afflicted or inflamed by the fire of vile pleasures than we are in our hearts? Why then did you blow up this fetid flame with the winds of all your frivolous language and with the authority of your personal example? If you didn't then fear God and His vengeance, why did the punishment administered to Ovid not make you sensible and prudent?]

Gerson is castigating a virtual sinner or penitent for past sins. Unlike Pierre Col, Gerson identifies the *Rose*'s Fol Amoureux with Jean de Meun.[83] Christine too uses the procedure of topical interrogation effectively ('Qui sont fames? Qui sont elles?'), and then goes on to answer her own questions with a startling identification: 'si sont elles vos meres, vos suers, vos filles, vos fammes et vos amies; elles sont vous meesmes et vous mesmes elles' (*Débat*, p. 139:775, 781–83)[84] [Who are women? Who are they? They are your mothers and sisters, your daughters and wives and dear ones. They are identical with you yourself and you with them].

Topical questions such as these focus on specific places in an opponent's argument that the questioner calls into doubt and seeks to overthrow or undermine by, as it were, restating them. They lead to a sequence of argument and counter-argument. For example, using the *quid?* circumstance, Gerson first qualifies Jean's disciples – 'quelle ignorance est celle ycy, o biaux amis' (*Débat*, p. 70:289) [what ignorance is this, my fine friends?] – then, *quis?* to identify Jean with Fol Amoureux in the *Rose*, before generalizing on the misfortunes such persons have produced in the world. Who caused the fall of Troy and the death of so many fine warriors? Who exiled Tarquin? Who deceives innocent maidens and nuns? Who forgets God and the saints? Who ignores family duties? Who provokes civil strife and violence? 'C'est par fol amoureulx' (*Débat*, p. 71:313) [It's the work of Fol Amoureux] – it's the work of Jean de Meun.

Generally, then, the *Rose* debate elicits topical questions such as who? what? where? when? how? and why? appropriate to analysis, or *esplucher*, in rhetorical debate. Such questions are not merely rhetorical in today's common conception of the device. Being cogent, they demand or suggest answers.[85] The variety of questions that appear in medieval philosophical, moral, and other writings suggests that the topical script can be easily rehearsed and adapted, with

---

[83] Contrast Gerson, pp. 67:227–68:231, 70:294–97, and 78:488–89. Pierre Col contests the identification (p. 92:110–11), while Christine seems ambiguous on it (p. 130:495–96).

[84] I return to this identification of Jean's disciples with women in Chapter 3.

[85] Robertson identified other instances in which the topical questions resurface, independently, even in modern times (Robertson 1946, p. 14 n. 41). I found another example in a Dutch newspaper: 'Wie met wie, waar, wanneer, hoe vaak, en inwelke staat, zijn te topische vragen die iedere nieuwsjager ... kan beantwoorden' (Boerdam 1997) [Who with whom, where, when, how often, and in what circumstances are the topical questions that everyone in pursuit of news can ... answer].

'discretion' and 'consideration', from memory without becoming a rigid stereotype. However, as Robertson also notes, the best known formula today, that quoted by Matthew – 'Quis, quid, ubi, quibus auxiliis, cur, quomodo, quando' (*Ars versificatoria*, 1.116)[86] – was widespread, probably because its meter, the Latin dactylic hexameter, made it easy to remember.

According to medieval textbooks, the choice of answers to topical questions produces different kinds of discourse,[87] with more or less stereotypical answers to the questions. Gender (*sexus*) and family (*cognatio*) are two such prominent topoi in medieval writing. Their articulation can play against or with convention, eliciting strikingly original, even controversial answers. Thus, the invention of the circumstances that define Christine's life in the *Mutacion* harbors problems in the gender and family topoi. As noted above, Christine identifies what today we call her biological father, but not her biological mother. Nature is her mother (*Mutacion*, v. 339–68).[88] Moreover, her transition to widowhood is described allegorically as a change not only in social order from wife to widow but also, more strikingly, in gender from woman to man. With these changes, Christine's account becomes controversial, at least for modern scholarship. By excluding her biological mother in identifying her parents, does she not anticipate her own rejection of her gender in order to assume tasks traditionally assigned to men, in the event that of *chef de famille*? Christine's characterization of her mother is not far removed from Matthew of Vendôme's failure to articulate the virgin's reactions to her 'hot-blooded youth'. Here, in Christine scholarship, we encounter critical matters of opinion.[89]

Opinion becomes verisimilar when description conforms to common beliefs and expectations. According to Matthew of Vendôme, for example, Cicero describes the luxurious beauty of Sicily to justify his argument on Verres's licentiousness in that setting.[90]

> Cum Verrem redargueret de adulterio in Sicilia perpetrato, descripsit multipharias illius regionis delicias ..., ut, audita loci venustate, coniecturale

---

[86] See as well *Tresor*, III.45.

[87] Schnell 1998b; Nagel 2000.

[88] Her mother functions as an interruption or disturbance of her thought in the *Cité* (p. 40; *Chemin*, v. 6393–98); cf. the *Advision*, I.i.4–7, which serves as a continuation of the interrupted *Chemin* when Christine returns to sleep and dreams. On the mother figure in Christine's writings, see Lorcin 1989; Blumenfeld-Kosinski 1990, pp. 285–89; Quilligan 1991, *passim*; Tarnowski 1994; Callahan 2000; Dziedzic 2002. Ribémont 2000 discusses the ideal or exemplary mother in Christine's writings, but not Christine herself as mother or Christine's own mother. On Christine's family, see Wandruszka 2000; cf. also Arden 2002 and the perceptive article by Lorcin 2002.

[89] On her father's agreement with her views on the education of women, and her mother's differing opinion. Her mother held her daughter back, according to the *Cité*; on this matter, see Willard 1984, p. 33; Quilligan 1991, pp. 134–39; Cerquiglini 1993, pp. 35–36.

[90] See Thoss 1972, pp. 36–43.

esset argumentum[91] Verrem in loco[92] tante pulchritudinis sibi a Cicerone deputatum licentius commisisse adulterium. (*Ars versificatoria*, 1:110)

[When Cicero refuted Verres's defense against the charge of *illicit sexual conduct* in Sicily, he described the many attractions of that country ... so that when his *judges* understood *how lovely the country was*, they would consider Verres, who *gave in to lust* in the midst of such beauty, to have more unbridled lusts than Cicero had imputed to him. (Galyon, p. 59)]

We might say people would be more likely to believe a person guilty of sexual misconduct if he or she was on a cruise, especially if we go on to describe at some length the features of the ship that would facilitate or even promote such conduct. Of course, we do not know how Verres responded to this hypothetical argument. If we did, we might find a debate analogous to that about the *Rose*. Here, again, opinion is at issue: is the *Rose* licentious? does it incite to sexual misconduct, which is Christine's opinion, or does it dissuade such conduct, as Jean de Meun's 'disciples' contend? Topical description, as we have defined it here, is an important feature in advancing one's opinion in such debate.

To put the issue in perspective as well as to anticipate Christine's views on love and lovemaking, let us look at the *Rose* debate in its current context, contrasting it with some medieval opinions in order to recover something of the urgency of the issues for the disputants. Many of the *Rose*'s readers today do not consider sexual intercourse outside marriage a vice or sin. Rather many focus on free will, responsibility, consent, and sexual orientation. In critiquing the conclusion of the *Rose* today, moreover, debate often turns on the rape of the rose. Rape is generally condemned by the *Rose*'s readers today, and some modern critics of the *Rose* have claimed that the lover rapes the young woman the rose represents. Does the text support this interpretation? That is, does the work's sexual climax describe *votiva duorum congressio* or not? That is the issue, and here opinions diverge.[93] If Amant does not rape the rose, then the quality of his seduction, and the woman's response to it, is the issue. But this reading of the *Rose* reflects modern consensus, not medieval opinion. Here again we confront our current uncertainty regarding responses to sexuality in earlier times that Haasse reminds us of. Medieval morality might condemn consensual, even conjugal lovemaking if not practiced for procreation. It is noteworthy in this analysis that no one in the *Rose* debate raises the issue of rape; its, and Jean de Meun's, presumed licentiousness sufficed to quicken controversy around 1400.

---

[91] *Coniecturale argumentum* here refers to a verisimilar description and its implications.

[92] On *locus a loco*, see *Ars versificatoria*, 1:109.

[93] Bel Acueil protests, but consents (*Rose*, v. 21702–12); see Kelly 1995a, pp. 9–10, 34, 71–73. Jean's *Rose* is a fiction; one can evaluate only his text and its implications as allegory.

Euhemerism

Topical description is important in Christine's use of euhemerism. Euhemerism is the search for historical explanations of myths that permitted Christian authors to use them in religious, moral, and literary compositions. Moreover, the practice was compatible with topical invention when an author rewrote a source, as we have seen Christine do, by changing or rewriting common places. If 'the traditional deities were merely earthly rulers, whom the gratitude or adulation of their subjects had raised to a place in heaven',[94] then replacing deified features with appropriate human features was an uncomplicated descriptive task. Christine first uses it in the *Epistre Othea* to praise or blame exemplary conduct. She actually explains the practice, citing Fulgentius as authority, in the *Chemin de long estude* (v. 5243–62).[95]

There were problems in appreciating this mode in the Middle Ages. One such problem was the use of pagan examples. Gabriella Parussa notes the strict distinction Christine makes in the *Epistre Othea* between pagan examples and thinkers in the gloss on chivalry, on the one hand, and, on the other, the Christian examples and thinkers in the allegory on spirituality.[96] Likewise problematic, in the *Cité des dames*, Christine includes women whose lives are immoral by her own standards, especially their love lives. How convincing to the thoughtful reader in the Middle Ages can goddesses such as Minerva and Ceres be, or passionate lovers such as Dido and Medea, all admitted to the City of Ladies? Why are Venus and Briseida excluded?

To answer the first question, one must recall that for Christine and her contemporaries, euhemerizing Greek and Roman myths was standard methodology.[97] Pagan myths were thought to arise from human actions that could be evaluated. Minerva invented the Greek alphabet, arithmetic, weaving, olive oil, military equipment, and musical instruments, activities and objects associated with her divinity in ancient religion (*Othea*, 13–14; *Cité*, pp. 170–74); similarly, Ceres invented agriculture, making it possible to gather humans together in civilized, settled communities (*Othea*, 24; *Cité*, pp. 174–76).[98] These women's achievements were so remarkable that statues were erected in their honor, leading to their deification, as Christine argues in the *Chemin de long estude* when referring to Fulgentius (v. 5243; see also *Advision*, II.vii.50). Beneath the surface of these fables, Christine discerned a historical and moral truth that was

---

[94] Seznec 1953, p. 12.

[95] In the *Cité*, Christine explains Minerva (pp. 170, 174), Ceres (p. 176), and Isis (p. 178) as euhemerized mortals. Euhemerism served her purposes since these women's achievements were so spectacular that monuments were erected in their honor, which led to their identification with divinities. Cf. *Policie*, p. 55:22–32, on Julius Caesar's deification.

[96] Parussa, ed., *Othea*, pp. 14–15.

[97] Cooke 1927; Seznec 1953, especially Book One; Jung 1971, especially pp. 57–64; Zühlke 1994, pp. 180–84.

[98] See Kellogg 1990. In the *Advision*, Opinion teaches Adam and Eve some of these skills (II.iii.15–18).

still valid. Even as a 'lie', the fables retained their moral and spiritual authority: 'se tel ne fu, bien pot estre semblable' (*Othea*, p. 196, v. 57; cf. p. 503, v. 47) [if it didn't happen that way, it could still be analogous to what did happen]. In this way, such fables became credible illustrations of an opinion, especially because, in Christine's time, many women actually practiced the arts she says that they invented according to the *Cité*.[99] The fables earn Christine's approval because they correct false opinion on the impotence of women in the arts and sciences by illustrating the actual and, perhaps more importantly, the potential achievements of exceptional individuals. Ultimately, Christine's goal is to use fable or falsehood to teach a valid moral lesson (*Othea*, p. 199, ll. 82–84).

But what about Medea and Dido? In *Charles V*, Christine declines to treat unworthy features of the king's life and character. Similarly, the *Cité des dames* includes only virtuous women, that is, those whose moral strength explains their accomplishments. Thus, just as vices and errors are deleted from Charles V's biography, so in Christine's city 'n'abitent fors toutes dames de renommee et femmes dignes de loz, car a celles ou vertue ne sera trouvee les murs de nostre cité seront forclos' (*Cité*, p. 54) [will dwell none but all renowned ladies and praiseworthy women, for those deficient in virtue will be shut out of our city's walls]. The process of describing virtue in women can be as selective as for Charles V and his family. Perhaps more astonishingly, the *Cité*'s portrait of Medea reports her skill in the arts, including the necromancy with which she aided Jason, but there is no mention of the infanticide,[100] only of her falling in love (*Cité*, pp. 162–64, 380–82; cf. *Othea*, 58). Such selectivity is not hypocritical on Christine's part. She is adapting exemplary material to moral ends using the art of topical invention.[101] Such selective topical description serves as the topical invention of historical women for the purpose of presenting exemplary models. If some like Briseida and Heloise are excluded, silence regarding their careers condemns their lives that exemplify vice in, for example, the *Epistre Othea*. By contrast, the turnabout in the life of the former prostitute Affre shows how the immoral may become moral and even saintly (*Cité*, pp. 491–93).

The principal difference, then, between *Charles V* and the *Cité des dames*, both epideictic treatises, turns on common public opinion regarding the object of praise. The intended audience for *Charles V* includes Christine's patrons as well as French readers in general, mostly nobility, who can be assumed to regard her encomium favorably; indeed, her patron, Philippe the Bold, duke of

---

[99] Plebani 2003, pp. 49–50.

[100] Which Christine knew (*Mutacion*, v. 14765–86). On this and Christine's original depiction of Medea, see Morse 1996; Caraffi 2000. On an analogous, open contrast between the good Semiramis and the incestuous Semiramis, see van der Helm 2004, pp. 93–96; and between the good Dido and Dido victim of passion, see Fenster 2000, pp. 471–73. Dido does not appear in *Othea*. Infanticide for a good cause is acceptable to Christine; for example, mothers offer their children to martyrdom in the *Cité*, pp. 472–74.

[101] Cf. Blumenfeld-Kosinski 1994, pp. 718–19.

Burgundy, commissioned the work as an encomium. Furthermore, by Christine's standards, there appears to be little in Charles V's life that is blameworthy.[102] By contrast, the *Cité des dames* was written to correct the false opinion, widespread among men and even women, that women are naturally inferior and morally blameworthy. It certainly attracted attention; the *Cité* was more widely disseminated and translated than *Charles V*.[103] Following her approach in the treatise on Charles, in the *Cité* Christine uses selective topical invention in order to counter misogynist invective. To do so, she euhemerizes, providing an array of exemplary women, positive examples in contexts such as government, learning, moral and social responsibility, and faith. In this respect, her encomiastic description of these women is analogous to that of Charles V.

Rhetorical hypothesis and Christine's changing opinions

Christine de Pizan's mastery of rhetorical tools to promote and evaluate opinions is illustrated by her use of another factor in topical invention, the rhetorical hypothesis. Hypothesis in rhetoric has a technical meaning that distinguishes it from a thesis. A thesis states a general opinion, such as to take a lover is wrong (a thesis Christine accepts).[104] When the thesis is applied to an individual it becomes a hypothesis.[105] Topical invention colors the individual so that, as an example, he or she supports a given thesis in a verisimilar way.[106] For example, in the *Mutacion*, Christine attributes the loss of her husband to Fortune and interprets it as bad fortune. The thesis that fortune alternates between good and bad becomes a hypothesis when her own life illustrates it. If Fortune changes Christine's happy marriage into an unhappy widowhood, it follows that she is the victim of Fortune. Both thesis and hypothesis, in debate, support opinion.

But the description of Lady Opinion shows that personal or subjective opinions can change. In the *Advision*, for example, Christine's opinion on her misfortunes changes, not haphazardly, but as an intellectual *dépassement*, part

---

[102] Solente, ed., *Charles V*, vol. 1, pp. lxxxiv–lxxxvi.

[103] *Charles V* survives in six medieval manuscripts but in no medieval translations (Kennedy 1984, p. 103). There are twenty-seven manuscripts or fragments of manuscripts for the *Cité* as well as translations into Flemish and English (Kennedy 1984, pp. 93–94; see also Curnow, ed., pp. 300–589; Caraffi, ed., pp. 514–15). There is a Portuguese translation of its sequel, the *Trois vertus*; see Willard and Hicks, ed., *Trois vertus*, p. xvi.

[104] Further examples of such theses are found in Isidore's opinions discussed above, pp. 32–33.

[105] Lausberg 1973, §§68–78; cf. *Tresor*, III.2.6 (Messelaar 1963 does not clarify this terminological distinction). Since Christine believed in astrology (Willard 1980), a judgment regarding character based on a person's horoscope was, for her, a valid hypothesis. In the *Corps de policie*, p. 41, she explains how, by virtuous conduct, one can resist astrological influences.

[106] On these *colores operum*, see Matthew's *Ars versificatoria*, 1.46; he borrows the term from Horace; see Munari, ed., p. 63 n. 46.

of her 'effort constant pour se maîtriser, s'élever, s'améliorer'.[107] She learns in the *Advision* that she was not a victim of Fortune but of Opinion.[108] Lady Opinion makes the case for this view, as argued earlier, and Lady Philosophy confirms Opinion's opinion by reinterpreting Christine's autobiography in Boethian terms in Part Three of the *Advision*. There Christine comes to see the loss of her husband as a kind of good because it opened up to her the scholarly life she chose to follow.[109] Opinion is a kind of topos susceptible of diverse amplifications, each of which may be true, false, or uncertain – that is to say, more or less probable or improbable. The opinion that fortune causes her unhappiness and the opinion that opinion does so are two theses that raise the question: which, fortune or opinion, is the true cause of Christine's unhappiness? That is the issue. In the Boethian context of the *Advision*, Christine's very unhappiness becomes untenable. To her, her own life is a hypothesis illustrating the power of opinion and how opinions may be corrected.

For Christine, love is an especially slippery topic when it comes to opinions. She knew this from her own experience. In the *Advision*, she denies the opinion that she took a lover after her husband's death (III.vi.135–55; cf. vii.2–4). Because there is no tangible evidence for such an affair the accusation becomes slander, that is, false opinion, reflecting misogynist views about widows. 'Qui mesdit par opinion se puet aucunement fonder sur aucune apparence *ou couleur* qui lui appert comme il lui semble de ce que il dit' (*Trois vertus*, p. 148:37–39; my emphasis) [slander is sometimes based on opinion because of some feature *or color* that seems to conform to what is said]. We recall that 'color' as shade distinguishes one opinion from another in Christine's description of Lady Opinion.

Life is, metaphorically, a 'champ de bataille' (*Advision*, III.xx.33); one must be well armed when engaging in combat on the fields of human endeavor in which clashing opinions are as rife as they are diverse – shifting and colored as the description of Lady Opinion illustrates. But it is also important to ascertain whether the reason one goes to battle is valid. Love too can be described as a kind of war. The *Roman de la rose* illustrates this on its literal level[110] by portraying conflict between personifications in a tournament thinly veiling a potential rape (*Rose*, v. 15038–104, 15273–628, 20674–780). But is it a just war? Hardly, according to Christine de Pizan, for whom the *Rose* is an unacceptable guide for young men and young women. Its seductive landscape, like Verres's Sicily, promotes lust. That is why she claims that Jean's disciples would not let their daughters read the romance, despite their opinion that it turns readers away from sensuality, not towards it (*Débat*, p. 15:111–16).

---

[107] Poirion 1965, p. 254.
[108] Brown-Grant 1999a, pp. 109–10; Dulac 1998b, pp. 80–82. Semple 1998a shows how her views on aesthetics and action evolve.
[109] *Advision*, III.xviii.22–30; see Zühlke 1994, pp. 201–03.
[110] Baumgartner 2001.

A major fault with the *Rose*, in Christine's opinion, is its one-sided picture of seduction, or even of any allurement or love quest, whether well-intentioned or not. Specifically, she argues that Jean, in proposing to 'descripre entierement amours ... ne la deust mettre si extreme a une seule fin, voire fin si deshonnestement touchee' (*Débat*, p. 130:474–76) [describe love fully ought not to have shown it so radically fixed on a single goal, indeed, on a goal treated in such a gross way]. The hypothesis one defends requires both positive and negative examples – a good Dido and a bad Briseida. To Christine's mind, Jean's topoi are marked too plainly on one side of love's spectrum. As a result, the *Rose* does not condemn lust, as its disciples claim; it fosters it. The *gradus amoris* is not in dispute here, but its epideictic mode is. Blame as well as praise, invective and panegyric may be appropriate in the rhetoric of love, depending on the kind of love depicted. Of course, there is Reason's long plea to abstain from foolish love; but, to Christine, Reason's language makes her duplicitous.[111] One sees how faith (Christine's moral condemnation of lust), reason (the alleged one-sided argument Jean advances), and personal experience (Christine's response to offensive language) inform her opinion of the *Rose* while shaping her condemnation of the poem.

However, since opinion on the *Rose* does not include articles of faith (*Débat*, p. 149:1115–18), Christine chose rewriting in order to correct the poem's *gradus amoris*. In doing so, we can expect her to remove the allegedly one-sided vision of the romance by a fuller description of love, whether 'pure' or erotic. By such inventive rewriting, Christine attempts to persuade her audience to favor her thesis: what she deems true opinion on love and lovemaking – true because supported by reasonable evaluation of what typically transpires in such love. She exemplifies her opinion in part by her own experience prior to widowhood; yet even when conjugal affection is more a duty than a willing impulse, it must be adhered to, even in bad marriages (*Trois vertus*, pp. 54:71–55:87; cf. *Débat*, pp. 139:803–140:812). Of course, in Christine's world, divorce for spousal cruelty was not an option. There was flight, but how would that have improved an abused wife's lot around 1400?[112]

---

[111] In the *Rose* debate Christine condemns Reason because of her language, although, in the *Deux amants*, she expresses approval of the rest of Reason's argument. One or two words uttered by Reason near the end of her episode make all the difference to Christine.

[112] Cf. Rossiaud 1988, pp. 41–49; cf. Solterer 1995, pp. 157–58.

Allegory and opinion

In the diptych formed by the *Chemin de long estude* and the *Advision Cristine*, Christine uses the allegorical mode to describe herself in quest of truth in a world dominated by multifarious, often misleading, debatable, and conflicting opinions. She states at the beginning of the *Chemin* that her pilgrimage, as she calls it, began under the guidance of the Sibyl; however, her journey is not complete when the poem ends. She stands at the midpoint of her life and, as it were, of her two-part work (cf. *Advision*, I.i.2–10). In the *Advision*, therefore, she perseveres in the clerkly role she assumes at the end of the *Chemin*. As 'antigraphe de ses aventures' (*Advision*, I.v.12),[113] she implicitly assumes the role of amanuensis in Alain de Lille's sense in the *Anticlaudianus* when he refers to himself with the synecdoche *calamus*, or pen, and as prophet.[114] As scribe, Christine states in her gloss of the *Advision* that

> tout ce qui est contenu es dis chappitres ensuivant, se a droit sont regardez, sont concurrans et acordans aux dis des prophectes sur les temps a venir avec lesquelz s'acorde la saincte Escripture. (*Advision*, p. 10:279–81)
>
> [everything contained in the following chapters, if one reads them rightly, will be found to be in harmony and agreement with the words of the prophets concerning the future, and they agree with Scripture.]

Terre's complaint in the *Chemin* is rewritten in the *Advision* as a *planctus Franciae*, a synecdoche consistent with the prominence of the French court in the *Chemin* and with that of France herself, renamed Libera[115] in the first part of the *Advision*, on national chaos. Warfare and other kinds of violence that prevail among the French are evoked in Libera's summary of the history of France as a sequence of Fortune's mutations.

Of course, since Christine is writing an allegory, much is not as it seems on the literal level. Polysemous dream is thought, as she suggests in the treatise's gloss (*Advision*, p. 3:4–12). For example, Christine glosses the grotesque figure of Chaos, a personification drawn from allegorical poetry, as 'confusion, qui encore assez est au monde' (p. 3:23–24)[116] [disorder that is still

---

[113] Cf. p. 6:140; on this term, see Reno and Dulac, ed., *Advision*, p. 147 n. V/11–VI/11; Laennec 1993.
[114] Cf. Meier 1979.
[115] Dulac 1998b, p. 84.
[116] 'Désordre' is the meaning proposed by Reno and Dulac, ed., *Advision*, p. 216 s.v. Christine's literal definition of chaos as 'la masse que Dieu fourma, dont il trey ciel et terre et toutes choses', p. 3:22–23 [the mass that God formed, from which he drew forth heaven and earth and all things], recalls Bernardus Silvestris's *Cosmographia* (Blumenfeld-Kosinski 1995, pp. 174–75). The principal difference between them is that Bernardus's chaos is eternal. The connotation of chaos as shame (*Robert*, p. 473) also fits Christine's moral and social context in the *Chemin* and *Advision*. On Aquinas's connotation of *chaos* in Christine, see Richards 2003, p. 44.

widespread in the world]. In fact, chaos as 'confusion' is apparent at the beginning of each of the *Advision*'s three parts. The personification of the gargantuan, all-devouring Chaos fed by Nature adumbrates Libera's complaint about the desolation wrought on her kingdom following Charles V's untimely death, as well as the erroneous opinions prevailing in religion and philosophy in Part Two and Christine's mistaken construe of her own life in Part Three. Each part thereby identifies one of the three allegorical levels on which Christine suggests reading chaos in the *Advision*: 'la fiction de cestui livre se puet alegorisier triblement, c'est assavoir assimiller au monde general, qui est la terre, aussi a homme simgulier et puis au royaume de France' (*Advision*, p. 6:111–13) [this book's fiction can be allegorized on three levels. That is, it can apply to the world at large, which is the earth, and to the individual, as well as to the kingdom of France]. But Christine does not claim that these are the only contexts in which her work can be read. Rather she invites her readers to do what allegory presumes: dream on, as it were, that is, think on allegorically in order to find meaning in and thus extract true opinion from her fictions about the world, the self, France, and other suitable subjects. She appeals for subtle reading.

Her allegory is therefore complex, multi-layered, and open-ended. In each part of the *Advision*, Christine, as *antigraphe*, records the words of, respectively, Libera, Lady Opinion, and Lady Philosophy–Theology, as well as a Christine figure who represents the author. Each of the three parts begins in chaos. The actual chaos of human life, from birth to death, is analogous to Libera's amplification and application of the theme by describing the rebellion, pestilence, and death, madness and wars civil and among nations, that characterize recent French history. The second part evokes the chaos of religion occasioned by heresies and the schism, and that of philosophies whose diversity mirrors the rent robe of Boethius's Philosophy; the end reverts briefly to current political torment. Finally, Christine's own confusion is the matter of her complaint to Lady Philosophy, again an adaptation of the Boethian model to her personal circumstances and to her faith. Thus, each part of the *Advision* functions as an allegory of the two other parts.[117]

> Christine offers, chapter by chapter, a three-tiered interpretation of the first thirteen chapters of the *Avision* as they relate to (1) 'the world in general, which is the earth,' (2) man alone, and finally (3) the kingdom of France (f. 3a). Thus, for example, the figure of Chaos in the first chapter can be seen as representing the whole world, the individual human being, and the kingdom of France (ff. 1b-d). In similar fashion, the sixth chapter, which begins the complaint of the 'dame couronnee' (France), can be taken as (1) the world's

---

[117] Brown-Grant 1999a, pp. 97–100, focuses on the political context for Christine's 'mirror of princes'. Christine was probably influenced by Gerson's sermon, *Vivat rex* (Reno and Dulac, ed., *Advision*, pp. xiv n. 16, and xxi–xxiv; Dulac 1998b, p. 83). On Gerson's influence on Christine, see also Edsall 2000.

lamentation over the fall from the golden age, (2) the individual soul's lament over its fall from grace, and (3) the historical complaint the figure of France delivers to Christine (ff. 3d–4c).[118]

Importantly, Christine's allegory is not based on exact equations of two levels of meaning. Rather, the context within which the reader or audience reflects and forms individual opinions opens up her allegory to multiple, even unique, personal meanings. 'As already noted, the preface begins with the statement that its purpose is to "open the way" for the reader who might want to explore the full richness of the work.'[119] The interest and beauty of the *Advision* lie in its interpretative potential.

Christine is using the poetic mode. 'En telle parolle dicte par poisie puet avoir mains entendemens, et lors est la poisie belle et soubtille quant elle puet servir a plusieurs ententes et que on la puet prendre a divers propos' (*Advision*, p. 3:9–12) [Language as poetry can have many meanings; poetry is beautiful and subtle when it can carry several meanings and be interpreted in diverse ways]. Christine Reno convincingly shows that, although Christine de Pizan wrote her 'preface' to explain only part of the *Advision*'s first part, she actually uses it 'to draw the reader ... into the work in a process of reflective analysis'.[120] This is truly 'subtle reading'.[121] Christine gives expression to opinions on a variety of subjects, while eliciting readers' thoughts in other contexts that her descriptions might suggest.

Thus, the implications of the *Advision*'s allegories go beyond this particular treatise. What Christine sets out is a program for reading the poetic mode. Like the *Epistula Can Grande* attributed to Dante on how to read the *Divine Comedy*, her program of 'subtle reading' is suitable to all parts of the work and, indeed, to other works that she wrote in the poetic mode. This suggests how men can read the *Cité des dames* with profit and how women can benefit from reading works addressed to men like the *Epistre Othea* and *Charles V*. Such reading implies the principle that we may term *mutatis mutandis*. The king's virtues extolled in *Charles V* are important, *mutatis mutandis*, for Louis de Guyenne in the *Livre de la paix* and for the princess in the *Trois vertus*, just as the admonitions addressed to her are, *mutatis mutandis*, valid in the lives of other women in the various social orders beneath her, from countesses and duchesses to peasants and prostitutes. The mutable features of unique individuals are topoi that characterize each individual and his or her experiences without eliminating

---

[118] Reno 1992b, p. 220. On biography and autobiography in Christine's poetics, see Blumenfeld-Kosinski 2001.

[119] Reno 1992b, p. 221; see also Brown-Grant 1992; Paupert 2002b, pp. 512–18; Dulac and Reno 2003; cf. Walters 2002a, p. 245, and 2002b, pp. 153–67. See Hicks 1995a, p. 238, on 'l'isotopie entre affaires d'état et affaires de famille' in the *Epître à la reine*; and Krueger 2003 on the multiple allegorical readings of 'treasure' in the *Trois vertus*.

[120] Reno 1992b, p. 221.

[121] On subtlety in allegory, see Huot 1993b.

him or her from the class to which each belongs and by which he or she is evaluated.

> C'est nostre entente que tout ce que recordé avons aux aultres dames, tant es vertus comme ou gouvernement de vivre, en ce qui puet a chascune femme apertenir, de quelque estat que elle soit, soit aussi bien dit pour les unes que pour les autres, si en puet chascune prendre telle piece qu'elle voit qui lui apertient. (*Trois vertus*, p. 171:15–20)[122]
>
> [We wish that everything we have set out for some ladies be applied as well to every woman, whatever her social standing, whether it treats virtue or how she leads her life; in this way each woman can take whatever part seems to fit her circumstances.]

Similarly,

> se aucune goute ou miete en puet cheoir sur les hommes, ne la vueillent pas par despris escourre ne gicter la aval; car bonne doctrine se puet comparer au bon et loyal ami, lequel quant il ne puiet aidier, au moins ne nuit il pas. (*Trois vertus* p. 166:30–34)
>
> [if some drop or crumb happens to fall to men, let them not scornfully reject it or toss it aside. A good lesson can be likened to a good and faithful friend. If he doesn't help, at least he does no harm.]

'Voilà une acrobatie qui vise à la neutralité et, partant, à une conception des vertus et des vices enfin a-sexuée.'[123] Each treatise in the poetic mode allows the reader to read beyond explicit contexts in order to find broader and other meanings that the work might suggest. Such subtle reading is analogous to the way medieval authors read and rewrite by topical invention, mentally rewriting, as it were, by personal interpretation and critical reflection. Such reading is also more individual insofar as one reader will exemplify topoi differently from other readers – for example, the topos *sexus* in the case of male and female readers, or the topoi *fortuna* and *casus* in the case of princesses, widows, and prostitutes.

This topical and allegorical potential of the medieval poetic mode, including literal and allegorical reading, reflection, and rewriting, is characteristic of the art since the High Middle Ages. Its best known vernacular illustration is Marie de France's reference to subtle reading in the Prologue to her *Lais* in order to draw out a source's *surplus de san*.[124] But it also raises a problem that thrusts us once again into the realm of opinion. For the open-ended character of poetic allegory 'does not indicate Christine is limitlessly generous with her readers,

---

[122] An analogous social hierarchy structures the *Corps de policie*.
[123] Angeli 2002, p. 121, and 2003, p. 68. See also Morse 1996, pp. 96, 218, on gender-neutral virtue and vice in Christine's examples.
[124] Kelly 1992, pp. 110–14.

inviting them to interpret her text as they will',[125] We see this in the way Christine presents and corrects her own opinions in the *Advision* and elsewhere.

Self-correction and change of opinion

Lady Opinion recalls Christine's attribution of her personal misfortunes in the *Mutacion* to Fortune herself. Opinion corrects her, arguing that she, Opinion, is the first and primary cause of those misfortunes. The argument is striking. First, it means that Christine's life is not unfortunate; that is a false opinion. The transformation in Christine's life related in the *Mutacion* came about through her husband's unexpected death and her ensuing material losses, a view perfectly consistent with traditional views of Fortune's interventions. In the context of Boethius's views on Fortune, however, Christine has lost nothing. She only thinks she has. That is, she holds an opinion about what happened to her, and that opinion makes her unhappy. Lady Opinion corrects her error. Then, using discretion and *entendement de raison*, Philosophy sets her pupil straight on this matter in Part Three of the *Advision*. In the second part, Opinion is merely claiming to be a first cause, not an explanation of what happened to Christine. Lady Opinion is defending a thesis. Philosophy prescribes harsher medicine by turning Opinion's thesis into a hypothesis. She shows Christine that her husband's death made possible her self-realization as a *fille d'escole* (*Advision*, III.xviii.22–32). A life free for study, introspection, and writing is hardly a misfortune for a person like Christine. Accordingly, she corrects her opinion and changes her life.[126] She now realizes that the opinion that she experienced misfortune is the source of her grief, not Fortune herself, who has no power over those who do not cling to her false goods, even when the false good is a good husband.[127]

This change in opinion is supported by Christine's faith. Theology reminds her of this, leading to rational introspection that leads to a just appreciation of her own experience. In the allegorical mode of the *Advision*, Christine's new understanding of her experience is applicable not only in her own life, but also in explaining the woes of France and the confusion of religious and philosophical opinions that confound good order in the nation and in human thought.[128]

---

[125] Tarnowski 2000, p. 111.

[126] Brown-Grant 2002, pp. 42–43.

[127] Tarnowski 1994, p. 125. Boethius's family circumstances were different: as he wrote in prison, his father, chaste wife, and children were still alive and well (*De consolatione*, II Pr. iv.5–8). However, Christine did draw consolation elsewhere from her chaste daughter's decision to become a nun, and her son's successes in English and French courts. Cf. Brown-Grant 1999a, pp. 116–18.

[128] Richards 1994.

As argued above, there are three areas in which opinions flourish according to the *Advision*: France, the world, and the personal life. The *Advision* also proposes three criteria for judging opinion: *loy, raison,* and *vray sentement*.[129] These sets of three gloss one another allegorically. For example, France's rise from chaos in Part One mirrors Christine's own ascension to truth in Part Three. Keeping such 'effets de miroir' in mind as well as an eye on the common places she chooses to emphasize, I propose to examine in the next three chapters Christine's opinions in the light of these three criteria. This order corresponds to Christine's own program of reading. In that program, one reads the literal text simultaneously on one or more allegorical levels, each level corresponding to a different context. Yet the reader should not ignore the other explicit or implicit contexts that overlap with the one chosen. Thus, like *Charles V*, the *Advision*

> is more than an intellectual biography or a humanistic quest for literary immortality,[130] but it also instructs the reader on how to read metaphorically, underscoring that the metaphor connects 'the political salvation of France, the moral salvation of the individual, and the salvation of humanity in general'.[131]

This is the poetic mode Christine prefers and that she says is natural to her at the moment she begins her most productive period, from about 1400 to 1410. It is a reflective mode appropriate to the expression and critique of personal and general opinions; that is, it encourages rational thought on personal, moral, social, political, and philosophical or theological issues in her times. It is open to changing opinions by rereading in new contexts. Although my analysis tends to take apart what is so carefully meshed in the *Advision*, it will, I believe, still be possible to set out the diverse facets of Christine's thought on opinion in a coherent, yet clearer whole in the conclusion on subjectivity and truth.

The next three chapters have another rationale as well. In the *Advision*, Christine treats opinion of three different kinds: opinions on which there is general agreement in her intended audience; opinions on which there are opposing views; and opinions that most people reject. We have seen Christine attack the prevalent opinion in her times that fortune causes human misery. In the following three chapters we shall see how she treats, and changes her opinions on, misogyny, noble or chivalric love (commonly called courtly love), and self-interest and the nation. On misogyny, she opposes common opinion. On love, she must confront confusion and human mutability. Finally, anticipating general agreement that Charles V was a good king who ruled France

---

[129] These correspond approximately to the religion, theoretical philosophy, and practical philosophy that Echtermann and Nagel 2000, pp. 503 and 509–10, perceive in, respectively, Justice, Raison, and Rectitude in the *Cité* and the *Trois vertus*.

[130] Although that 'quest' is also present in Christine's view of her work; see, for example, the *Chemin* and the *Trois vertus*, pp. 225:23–226:33.

[131] Forhan 2002, p. 149; quote from Brown-Grant 1992, p. 96.

well, she reinterprets self-interest as enlightened self-interest that can save the nation as it did under Charles V. In all these issues, Christine champions what she calls in the *Rose* debate opinion as 'certainne science' (*Débat*, p. 131:511), to which is opposed 'oppinion volomptaire' (p. 131:532) or 'folle oppinion' (p. 123:256–57).[132]

---

[132] Cf. Dulac 1991a. Note also Christine's distinction between 'oppinion de gent' (*Débat*, p. 124:286), or 'popular opinions', and the opinions of the high-born and learned (p. 146:993–98). Christine's opinions still reflect some prejudices of her time. Like the Vieil Horace in Corneille's play, she believed that 'C'est aux rois, c'est aux grands, c'est aux esprits bien faits / A voir la vertu plaine en ses moindres effets' (*Horace*, v. 1717–18). Of course, the king must 'look' – that is, use consideration and discretion to decide on what actions are virtuous. Cf. von Moos 2002, pp. 16–17.

3
Misogyny, Introspection, and Radical Opinion

> DIEU LE PERE
> Nous prendrons
> Ceste coste et l'edifirons
> De char et d'ame intellective,
> Et elle raisonnable et vive
> Sera femme bien denommee ...
>
> ADAM
> ... cest os la de mes os yssi
> Et la char de ma char aussi;
> Virago la dy par raison.[1]

One can best study Christine de Pizan's use and evaluation of opinion at those critical moments when she changes her mind. There are four principal instances of such changes in her writings. Taken separately, they fall within the context of the three kinds of opinion treated in what follows: opinions generally received that she contests, treated in this chapter on misogyny; controversial opinions, analyzed in Chapter 4 on noble love; and, finally, generally accepted opinions that Christine shares, discussed in Chapter 5 on the king and national self-interest. The fourth change, treated in the preceding chapters, is the major breakthrough in her world view, inspired by Boethius and Aquinas and described in the *Advision*, as a result of which opinion replaces fortune as first cause of human calamities and crises. Although no one seems to have considered this change before her, it is the foundation for the three other changes that we shall now be investigating. Together these four changes are critical in Christine's 'schooling' – that is, in her quest for truth using the intellectual equipment Nature gave her as well as the learning and experience that she acquired during her eventful, albeit studious and somewhat reclusive life.

---

[1] *Passion*, v. 596–600, 608–10: *God the Father*: 'We will take this rib and build it up with flesh and an intelligent soul; both reasonable and living, she will be properly called a woman.' *Adam*: 'This bone is of my bone, as this flesh is of my flesh; I rightly name her a virago.'

A major quandary

Surely Christine's most striking and dramatic change of opinion is that related at the beginning of the *Cité des dames* (pp. 40–50). This episode shows vividly how reading and reader response reveal *vray sentement*; such reading experience can be as cogent as that encountered in the 'real world'. In this well-known episode, Christine undergoes a paradigm shift in thought. Seeking diversion from more demanding studies, she opens a book recommended as light reading.[2] The book is Matheolus's *Lamentations*. While reading this poem relating a 'bigamist'[3] former priest's misogynist, misogamist diatribes, Christine wonders whether women are indeed inferior human beings because of the depraved morality, physical weakness, and inborn deformities such writings attribute to them. Christine confronts, in both her reading and her dealings with others, the conflict between misogynist authority redolent of the faith she does not doubt and her own feelings that contradict that authority. She expresses the quandary as follows:

> Mais nonobstant que pour chose que je y peusse congnoistre tant longuement y sceusse viser et esplucher, je ne apperceusse ne congneusse tieulx jugemens estre vraye encontre les natureulz meurs et condicions femmenines, j'arguoye fort contre les femmes, disant que trop fort seroit que tant de si renommez hommes, si sollempnelz clercs de tant hault et grant entendement, si clervoyans en toutes choses comme il semble que ceulx fussent, en eussent parlé mençongieusement. (*Cité*, p. 42)

> [But despite anything I might have known or examined and analyzed over a very long time, I could not perceive or recognize any truth in such judgments made against the natural mores and condition of women. Nevertheless, I persisted in arguing vehemently against women, claiming that it would be highly unlikely that so many renowned men, such serious clerics of so lofty and great understanding, so perceptive in all things – so it seemed that they were – would have erred.]

These words are not to be taken lightly in Christine's intellectual climate. She confronts here grounds for valid authority in matters of opinion dating back to Aristotle: 'ce qui est admis par tous ou par la plupart ou par les sages, et parmi ceux-ci, soit par tous, soit par la plupart, soit par les plus illustres et respostables'.[4]

---

[2] On the value of such diversion, see *Policie*, p. 99:10–22.

[3] 'Bigamist' in the sense of a man who marries a widow (cf. Gauvard 1991, p. 591 n. 73). Perhaps the fact that Christine was a widow herself made Matheolus's satire more personally repugnant. On the problematic features of reading this work in Jean Le Fèvre's translation of the misogynist *Lamentations* alongside his philogynist *Livre de Leesce*, see Blumenfeld-Kosinski 1994; Pratt 1994, 2002b.

[4] Von Moos 2002, p. 17; cf. von Moos 1988, pp. 326–27.

She is moved to question one of the oldest and most venerable foundations of authority in the Western scholastic tradition.[5]

Initially, Christine sides with the learned men and traditional authority, accepting misogyny as a valid opinion: 'ainsi m'en rapportoye plus au jugement d'autruy que a ce que moy mesmes en sentoye et savoye' (*Cité*, p. 44) [thus, I relied more on the judgment of others than on what I myself felt and knew].[6] Her initial submission to authority is not so scandalous as it might seem today. Christine learns from authorities. To question them might seem to be presumption, or *cuidier*, even rebellion. It could lead to heresy, a frightening prospect in the fifteenth century. Thus, in order to understand better her own alleged depravity, she begins a two-pronged process of introspection and of inquiry among women friends. Her quandary arises when misogynist opinions such as those expressed in the *Lamentations* and elsewhere (including the *Roman de la rose*) conflict with her own failure to discover natural depravity in herself or in many other women.[7]

Here we have a true conflict of opinion stemming from disparity between authority and experience.[8] The problem was especially acute in the Middle Ages when authority as *loy* both divine and secular was grounded in faith and, therefore, prevailed over individual experience when it opposed that authority. Indeed, even women submitted to misogynist authority, as Christine herself does at first, and as her own mother, more representative of her gender at the turn of the fifteenth century,[9] did in opposing the interests of her daughter in deference to woman's conventional role (*Cité*, p. 316). For these reasons, Christine's conflict with authority was no doubt all the more deeply felt and troubling to her.

Opinion and *sentement*: the problem

How did Christine de Pizan authorize her own *sentement* vis-à-vis established authority?[10] Since opinion, as she uses the word, has no authority apart from that which individual conviction, reason, and/or experience give it, the individual's

---

[5] See P. Ptassek, 'Endoxa', in *HWR*, vol. 2, cols. 1134–38. Christine may have known this tradition through her reading of John of Salisbury's *Policraticus*, III.5, 58–60, or its French translation, *Policratique*, III.5, 29.

[6] On what follows, see Nouvet 1996, pp. 280–81; Forhan 2002, pp. 54–56. On the repetitiveness in the misogynist tradition, see Vincent-Cassy 1986; Bloch 1991, pp. 3–4.

[7] Cf. M. Zink 1985, p. 12: 'Tout part du donné sensible, et l'idée qui le dépasse, ou à plus forte raison qui s'oppose à lui, est sentie comme un paradoxe.'

[8] Haidu 2004, pp. 305–09. On the interplay between reading and personal experience in Christine's writings, see Ribémont 2002b.

[9] See Gauvard 1991, p. 324.

[10] See Jacqueline Cerquiglini in Poirion 1983b, p. 286. However, tradition also offered some inspiration and authority for Christine's critique of misogyny in the rhetorical tradition of topical rewriting (Blamires 1997).

evaluation of personal opinion requires his or her weighing experience, thought, and feelings both personal and as professed by others.[11] The last group includes literary examples. Beginning with the troubadours, as shown above, love poets (or the voices that speak for them) claim to be sincere – they speak, sing and write *de sentement*.[12] It is therefore a striking innovation on Christine's part when she insists – and insist she does[13] – that her love poems are not written *de sentement*. This personal view represents a kind of subjectivity. If for Christine 'subjectivity ... results from a break with convention',[14] what she means here is that her 'true feelings' lie elsewhere and, therefore, that the sentiments and experiences expressed in her love poems are indeed not her own.[15] Besides her interest in subjects she deems more important than love and lovemaking, Christine's lack of amorous or erotic *sentement* is also evident in her response in the *Advision* to accusations of her alleged affairs, accusations to which the writing of the love poems may have, or could have, given some credence.

One of the main reasons Christine rejected even ideal love was misogyny. Like Matheolus's *Lamentations*, the *Roman de la rose*'s literal narrative contains many misogynist passages that support, as well as actions that conform to, this prejudice. Christine feels herself to be a victim of the prejudice, most notably in the *Cité*. Obvious belittling of her opinion by Jean's disciples[16] may also have caused her to relive experiences of ill treatment as a widow after her husband's death (*Advision*, III.vi.33–228). Yet medieval misogyny in her time relied on authorities which she recognized, especially those which gave expression to her faith, such as the Bible, interpretations of the Bible, and the writings of Church fathers. Eve too was a powerful example. Christine had therefore to confront formidable odds if she wished to question misogynist opinion, carrying out a virtually Copernican revolution against broad, almost universal majority opinion.

The issues are clear. Are women naturally or by creation physically, intellectually, and morally weaker, more reprehensible than men, and, therefore, inferior to them? Christine's response is grounded in part on *vray sentement* – her own feelings.[17] The debate is not frivolous; a stand-off like that in the *Rose* debate is not acceptable when misogyny is at issue. Now she must convince the whole world, as it were, that her personal feelings about women are valid.

---

[11] On the possibilities and problems of personal experience in Christine's time and in modern legal controversy, see Case 1998. On the relation between experience and memory, see Zimmermann 1993, pp. 44–47.

[12] See Cropp 1975, pp. 129–30, 253–74; Kelly 1978, pp. 245–55.

[13] This is a leitmotif in all her works on love; see Chapter 4.

[14] Richards 1998a, p. 10; cf. Quilligan 1991, pp. 16–17; Semple 1998b, pp. 109–12; Adams 2002; Pratt 2002a.

[15] Pinet 1927, pp. 220–21, makes a distinction between subjective untruth in the poems and objective truth held by the author.

[16] Willard 1984, p. 77.

[17] Walters 1996, pp. 131–32; Schnell 1998b, pp. 300–03; cf. *Débat*, p. 55:248–50.

To do so, she turns to the 'figurations diverses que prennent les relations entre hommes et femmes dans la littérature'.[18] As *antigraphe*, she will record the 'commandments' of divine Wisdom (*Advision*, pp. 6:140–7:142)[19] in order to show that misogyny contributes not to greater virtue but rather to a general moral decline[20] in all spheres of human activity (cf. *AB* 6).

In spite of the deference Christine shows for learned opinion, she does have some consolation, not unlike that which Aristotle offers her in Part Two of the *Advision* on First Causes. As Aristotle demonstrated in treating first causes and as Reason reminds her again in the *Cité*, authorities can err; even Aristotle erred on occasion, as another authority, Augustine, shows (*Cité*, p. 48).[21] If authorities such as these have differing opinions, may not others disagree with them too? On most philosophical opinions Aristotle's own prevail in Christine's mind, not only because he corrects the explanations advanced by other philosophers, but also because he provides a rational account of the Material Cause that Christine presents as *vraie opinion*.

Misogyny was a different matter. There were precious few Aristotles or Gersons[22] to speak in support of her feelings or to argue for her worth as a human being. Aristotle's misogyny compounded her dilemma because he was among the learned whose opinions she hesitated to doubt.[23] Against misogyny, a generally received opinion among authoritative men, Christine voices her own dissenting opinion based on her feeling that she and other women are not naturally inferior or depraved as misogynists claim. The 'crown' of her intelligence, she asserts in the *Mutacion*, is constrained only by prejudice against educating women. Given her awareness of her own feelings in response to such opinion, it is not surprising that the *Cité*'s Reason argues for the evidence of experience over against received opinion. Reason, the first of the three new authorities to address Christine's dilemma, seeks to liberate[24] her from that ignorance or lack of self-knowledge that makes her reject 'ce que tu ne scez de certaine science, et ajoustes foy a ce que tu ne scez ne vois ne congnois autrement fors par pluralité d'opinions estranges' (*Cité*, p. 46) [what you do not know by certain knowledge, while giving credence to what you neither

---

[18] Zimmermann 1995, p. 343.

[19] This passage is found in Christine's Gloss to the *Advision*. In the treatise itself, the word refers to her service of a 'dame couronnee' who personifies Libera or France; Christine proposes to record France's 'aventures' as well as 'oroisons et chançons' about them (*Advision*, I.v.12–14). The earlier version of the *Advision* used the term 'philographe' for 'antigraphe' (*Advision*, p. 16, var. 12).

[20] Kottenhoff 1994, pp. 66 n. 120, 80–82.

[21] Cf. Rivera Garretas 2003, p. 90.

[22] On Gerson's rejection of a love for fear of sinning, see Huizinga 1997, p. 204. His conduct conforms to Christine's advice in the *Enseignemens*, 76, to distance oneself if one wishes to escape love's domination.

[23] See Green 1998, pp. 154–58.

[24] Libera is the name for France in the *Advision*; it is not, conversely, inappropriate to apply it, allegorically, to Christine herself as she frees herself from misogynist oppression.

know nor see nor perceive other than in the light of multiple opinions that you do not share]. Reason is here directing Christine in the process of forming an opinion, the *aviser* process referred to above (*Cité*, p. 48; cf. 'viser et esplucher', p. 42). Reason is arguing eloquently; allegorically, Christine is using *entendement de raison* to validate personal experience. Indeed, Christine is the agent for such understanding, in both senses of *entendement* as *entendre*: she listens closely, which produces consideration, and she comprehends what she hears using discretion.

Christine's intellectual virtues in the *Cité des dames*

The intervention of Reason and her sisters, Rectitude and Justice, is in part an act of consolation. Like their predecessor, Boethius's Philosophy, they console Christine by exploring an important moral issue – in the *Cité*'s case, the moral issue of misogyny. The three personifications constitute a kind of trinity in which each personifies an aspect of the same notion: 'entre nous .iij. dames que tu vois cy sommes comme une mesmes chose ne ne pourrions l'une sans l'autre' (*Cité*, p. 62)[25] [we three ladies you see here are, as it were, one and the same; we could do nothing apart from one another]. In sequence, they advance a line of reasoning from beginning through middle to a conclusion. To *aviser* is thereby to *viser*, or aim at a goal that one reaches by *esplucher* (*Cité*, p. 42), an operation also apparent in the *Advision* when Christine considers Boethius's *Consolation* (see above, pp. 60–62). In the *Cité*, Christine parses the latter's Philosophy as Reason, Rectitude, and Justice. But both model and adaptation illustrate rational direction of thought towards a just end that also consoles. The result is *deviser*, or the description of the City of Ladies that corrects misogynist opinion and protects good women from its effects. Here the writer's *deviser* inspires the reader's *aviser*.

Studies of the *Cité* have focused on the examples of illustrious and exceptional women. Although *per se* important, these examples belong to a larger argumentative framework, or *arenge* (*Cité*, pp. 150, 378). That is to say that the *Cité* is primarily a series of discussions between Christine and each of the three personifications. In these discussions of issues in misogyny Christine expresses her doubts, raising questions the personifications answer while elucidating the answers by relating the lives of women that exemplify the points

---

[25] Hicks 1988, p. 339 n. 19, points out that they are subsumed under Prudence in the *Trois vertus*. Cf. a similar array of virtues forming a whole in Chartier's *Esperance*, Prose X, ll. 82–85: 'Car lez bontés et lez vertus ne sont jamaiz discordans ne derrogans ensemble, ainçoys consonent et acordent bien avecquez bien, et verité avecques verité' [For the goods and virtues are never in disagreement or in conflict with one another; rather good is in harmony and agreement with good, as virtue is with virtue].

made in the answer (*deviser*).²⁶ Thus, two *modi tractandi* dominate the *Cité*'s composition: the *modus probativus et improbativus* in the discussions that argue for women's virtues and against their assumed moral depravity, and the *modus exemplorum positivus*, which illustrates virtues and vices with examples. The two modes reveal another important feature of the treatise. The City of Ladies admits only virtuous women. But the *Cité des dames* includes in its discussion allusions to women who are not virtuous by Christine's standards; it also includes men who, as misogynists, are in error or whose lives exemplify vices imputed to women (*Cité*, pp. 66–76, 274–76, 334–44).²⁷

During the discussions, the intellectual virtues that Christine also names in the *Mutacion* come into play: *consideracion*, *discrecion*, *retentive*, and *memoire*. Since the personified ladies are projections of Christine's own thought, their thought processes correspond to her own. For example, in answering Christine's query regarding women's prudence, Reason notes that God granted the ability to think rationally to both men and women: 'c'est voir que Dieux ... a donné a entendement de femme assez apprehensive ²⁸ de toutes choses entendibles concevoir et congnoistre et retenir' (*Cité*, p. 194) [it's true that God made woman's understanding sharp enough to apprehend, know, and remember all that can be grasped]. Such *entendement* relies on reason as *entendement de raison*. Reason, for example, refers to Christine's 'entendement qui me sache veoir' (p. 52) [understanding able to perceive me], as does Justice: 'sain entendement qui me veult croire' (p. 60) [sane understanding willing to heed my words]. *Entendement* is the agent that will do Reason's job: 'Pren la pioche de ton entendement et fouys fort' (p. 64) [Take up the spade of your understanding and dig vigorously]. We recall that *esplucher* includes not only eliminating what is not needed or, here, what is erroneous, but also finding solid grounds for investigation. In this way, Christine's *Cité* arises from her consideration, discretion, and recall of what she has learned and experienced.

To change received opinion on misogyny, Christine had to reconsider fundamental articles of her faith as the Church taught it. Especially crucial was the issue of Eve's responsibility for original sin. In the *Epistre au dieu d'amour*, she questions the traditional interpretation by proposing another occasionally heard, but less damning reading; both the man and the woman cooperated in the sin.²⁹ Some morally corrupt women whom Christine mentions elsewhere

---

²⁶ Cf. González Doreste and Del Mar Plaza Picón 2002–03, p. 329. See also Trachsler 2000, pp. 305–06, on the 'encadrement' of the *Cité des dames*.

²⁷ Cf. Richards 2000b, pp. 124–26.

²⁸ This is a noun, as at *Cité*, p. 150: misogynists believe that 'entendement de femme est de petite apprehensive' [woman's understanding is scarcely able to grasp ideas].

²⁹ *Epistre Dieu*, v. 604–16; cf. *Cité*, p. 78, where Eve is lauded in language reminiscent of Aelred de Rievaulx's description of her creation from Adam's rib and, therefore, her destiny as companion: 'elle devoit estre coste lui comme compaigne' [she was meant to be alongside him as a companion]. On this passage, see Blumenfeld-Kosinski 1995, pp. 171–72; Kelly 1995a, pp. 58–60; cf. Walters 1989, p. 9; Brown-Grant 2003, pp. 88–94; Fenster 2005, p. 64. Did Christine know Aelred, perhaps in Jean de Meun's lost translation catalogued in

are excluded from the City of Ladies. Eve[30] and Briseida (cf. *Othea*, 84), and, perhaps, Heloise.[31] But, using the art of selective topical description discussed above, Christine also rewrites some biographies. She allows for the moral failures of Semiramis, Dido, and Medea when they are offset by virtuous conduct in other respects.[32] As mentioned earlier, Medea is read *in malo* as lover (*Cité*, pp. 380–82), but *in bono* as artist (pp. 162–64), because of which she is admitted into the City.[33] In this way Christine adapts models for rewriting she found in Petrarch and Boccaccio,[34] eliminating the chaff but keeping the grain. Rereading her source-authors for the *Cité*, Christine rewrites them *in bono* as the lives of illustrious women; specifically, she selects topoi misogynist sources ignore and in which she can invent positive descriptions. The device is analogous to her recommendation in the same work to read Jean de Meun and Matheolus as antiphrasis, 'quelque fust leur entente es lieux ou ilz blasment les femmes' (*Cité*, p. 48) [whatever their intentions may have been in the misogynist passages].[35] Similarly, Christine herself adapts Ovidian fables as moral lessons in *Othea*. If all these works literally represent women's potential to do wrong, Christine's rereading and rewriting by antiphrasis and allegory show their capacity to do good. In this way philogynist hyperbole confronts misogynist hyperbole. The *Cité*'s *modus tractandi* is analogous as encomium to that which we find in *Charles V* for the king and his family. As we shall see in Chapter 5, which compares the *Cité* and *Charles V* as epideictic, they are not so much biographies that record what happened as, more importantly, moral treatises showing what is possible if a person realizes his or her virtuous potential. The epideictic mode that emphasizes men's virtues but ignores vices

---

the royal library in her times (Delisle 1907, vol. 2, p. 67, item 379)? Eve does not appear in *Othea*; see Fenster 1995.

[30] She is named in treating original sin (*Cité*, pp. 78–80), but does not appear in the City itself. On Christine's subtle rewriting of Eve's role in original sin, see also Reno and Dulac, ed., *Advision*, p. 164 n. III/13–14.

[31] Richards 1993, pp. 140–43. Cf. *Enseignemens*, 44, 55.

[32] Walters 1989, pp. 8–9; Quilligan 1991, pp. 69–85, 171–77; Morse 1996, pp. 230–36; Caraffi 1998, pp. 71–75. Similar 'filtering' occurs in the 'Lay mortel' that closes the *Cent Ballades d'amant et de dame*; see Altmann 1996, pp. 389–91. Luff 1999, p. 401, likens such rewriting to shaping the stones that go into building the City of Ladies. On Christine's rewriting of Helen in *Othea*, see Reno 1980, pp. 275–76; on her rewriting of the Judgment of Paris using diverse sources and in different contexts, see Ehrhart 1990; on Dido, see Desmond 1994. See as well *Epistre Dieu*, v. 437–44 (Medea) and 445–60 (Dido); *CB* 83, v. 18–22 (Medea).

[33] Christine ignores here the infanticide that she reports in the *Mutacion*, v. 14774–86; cf. Morse 1996, pp. 97–102; Thompson 1999. For analogous 'metamorphoses' of Arachne, see Wisman 1997, pp. 145–47.

[34] McLeod 1991, pp. 125–36; Walters 1994; Brown-Grant 1995; Caraffi 2002; González Doreste and Del Mar Plaza Picón 2002–03. It is common in medieval fiction to adapt the literal level to a different allegorical meaning; see the discussion of the phenomenon in Heitmann 1963.

[35] Is this not close to what Jean's 'disciples' proposed for reading the *Rose*?

in *Charles V* is equally valid when rewriting the lives of illustrious women in the *Cité des dames*.

Christine uses antiphrasis in the traditional way, expressing the opposite of a literal statement, 'si comme on diroit tel est mauvais, c'est a dire que il est bon' (*Cité*, p. 48) [as if one were to say a given person is bad, meaning that he is good]. This is an important change, given the fact that she does not propose such a *modus tractandi* for obviously misogynist, but literal works such as Ovid's *Ars amatoria*, Cecco d'Ascoli's *Acerba*, or the anonymous *Du secret des femmes* (*Cité*, pp. 74–78).[36]

The women portrayed in the *Cité* are exceptional, not average or typical. Their opposition to, even defiance of, imposed ideas and expectations may well convince readers of some women's potential in war,[37] learning, and sanctity. But Christine's women do so at a cost. They perpetrate violence, deceive by hiding their identity, and suffer imprisonment, physical or mental violence, and martyrdom. Yet they succeed. They do so because they have fortitude. They are *femmes fortes* or viragos, hardly a negative term in Christine's vocabulary, because they realize stereotypical male virtues while preserving stereotypical female virtues.[38] Not all women possess such 'virility'. In Christine's opinion, the natural woman is 'simple, quoye et honneste' (*Cité*, p. 68) or 'quoye, rassise et en cremeur' (*Cité*, p. 80)[39] [honest, reserved, and honorable ... reserved, calm, and fearful]. If such women do not inspire imitation, they do foster an individual sense of personal worth and potential.

---

[36] However, Christine could discriminate (see Margolis 1986, pp. 362–63, on *esplucher*). In the *Cité* (pp. 74–76) she condemns Cecco's misogyny and heresy but in the *Mutacion* (v. 4655–62) she approves his condemnation of rebellion and violence, both treated subjects in his *Acerba*; see Curnow, ed., *Cité*, p. 1048 n. 26a. The Lady, a moderating voice in *Deux amants*, lauds Reason's criticism of foolish love in the *Rose* (v. 958–77). On Christine's use of Ovid, see Brownlee 1990, pp. 162–73; on her use of Jean Le Fèvre's *Leesce*, see Pratt 1994, pp. 61–64. These choices illustrate *esplucher* as discretion.

[37] On heroism in Christine's women, see Ballet-Lynn 1991.

[38] McLeod 1991, pp. 123–24. Perhaps the androgynous character of Christine as virago explains her reluctance to present herself as exemplary (Zühlke 1994, pp. 45–47, 191–200). Christine claims in the *Mutacion* that she differs from men only by her sexual gender (v. 393–400).

[39] Cf. *Trois vertus*, p. 111:46–47. Christine turns to these women at the end of the *Cité*, pp. 496–98, where she recommends the same qualities that she evokes at the beginning of the *Cité*, pp. 68, 80. She uses some of these or analogous attributes to describe the sibyl in the *Chemin*, v. 458–74 ('honneste et sage', 'rassise', 'simplement atournee', 'honorable', 'Quoye', 'maistrece de tous ses sens'). It is noteworthy that magnanimity produces analogous traits in men: 'paisible, debonnaire, souef, rassis, doulx, et reposé' (*Paix*, p. 103) [peaceful, gentle, mild, calm, agreeable, and deliberative]. Cf. Fenster 2002.

The misogynist's *vray sentement*

A crux in the confrontation of *vray sentement* with opinion is the misogynist's *vray sentement*. How do we evaluate the man's opinion when he truly feels that women are abhorrent or depraved?[40] Or, more to the point here, how may we distinguish between Christine's opinion of her worth and the misogynist's opinion of her inferiority if both are based on *vray sentement*? Although the answers may seem obvious enough today, their implications for the validity and limits of *vray sentement* are important and, therefore, deserve review here. We must therefore consider not only the solution to the problem, but also the implications of the issues for the authority of Christine's own feelings and experience.

Several explanations have been offered to account for misogynists' feelings towards women. Simon Gaunt has argued that some medieval misogyny can be accounted for by the feelings of homosexual men.[41] His argument is credible up to a point, although it would be difficult today to determine how widespread or conscious the phenomenon may have been at any time in the Middle Ages, including Christine's. Moreover, the religious opprobrium attached to homosexuality as a sin may have kept some from realizing their own sexual orientation with the result that they 'sublimated' it as misogyny. But does that necessarily lead to homosexual scorn for women? Gaunt's argument stands nonetheless as an illustration of how some writers' *vray sentement* may support misogyny. More noteworthy, perhaps, is that by dint of being virtuous one may also become a misogynist,[42] for example, through the education of monks. Finally, Christine offers another explanation for misogyny, using Jean de Meun as an illustration.

> Et vraiement puis que en general ainsy toutes les blasme, je ne tiengnnes que onques fust acointé ne hantast fame honorable, mais par plusseurs paillairdes et fames dissolues hanter – comme sont celles qui ou vilain vice de luxure trop conmunement s'abandonnent –, cuida ou faigny savoir que toutes femmes telles fussent; car d'autres n'avoit cognoissance. (*Débat*, p. 55:215–21)[43]

[And in truth since he blames all women in general, I don't believe he ever met or frequented an honorable woman; rather by frequenting a number of loose, dissolute women, like those who abandon themselves too freely to the villainous vice of lust, he assumed or pretended to know that all women are like them. For he never knew any other kind.]

---

[40] Cf. Richards 1996, p. 98: 'Clerkly misogyny, *based on male subjectivity*, had given rise to the abuses Christine attempted to address' (my emphasis). Cf. Blamires 1997, pp. 40–42, 47–48.
[41] Gaunt 1995, pp. 79–81.
[42] Hicks 1988, pp. 331–32.
[43] See also *Débat*, pp. 18:215–24, 130:495–96; *Othea*, v. 321–40.

In cases such as these, the *vray sentement* of misogynists who have not known good women opposes the *vray sentement* of some women.[44] Such men frequent only women who are excluded from the *Cité des dames*, women like the young Vieille in the *Roman de la rose*.

But the stakes are even higher. It is one thing to disagree regarding the morality of the *Roman de la rose*. Failure to bridge the gap between opposing views in the *Rose* debate merely leaves unresolved issues. If Christine can burn her copy of the romance, Jean's disciples can treasure theirs (*Débat*, pp. 21:317–22:329). But when the social and moral status of half the population is at issue, *vray sentement* leads to specific restrictions being imposed on the weaker by the more powerful. Christine's writings illustrate this injustice in her own life and in the fates of other women, setting out the threats they expose themselves to when they are not prudent or are simply victims.

There is therefore a crucial difference between misogyny in real life and in fiction. In the *Rose* debate, for example, there may be strong feelings, but they are about an essentially external object, since the *Roman de la rose* is not a feature of either Pierre Col's or Christine de Pizan's nature. Each can therefore take it or leave it as, in Boethian terms, an external good or evil. But in misogyny, as Christine frames the issue, her being a woman is a part of her nature, whereas it is not of Pierre Col's. She can therefore claim an authority he lacks: 'de tant comme voirement suis femme, plus puis tesmoingnier en ceste partie que cellui qui n'en a l'experience, ains parle par devinailles et d'aventure' (*Débat*, p. 19:255–58)[45] [inasmuch as I am indeed a woman, I am better able to bear witness on this matter than he who does not know what it is to be a woman, but rather speaks about them by guessing or by hit and miss]. This is the obvious counter to the misogynist's *vray sentement*. Christine's *vray sentement* is true because it is her own feeling as a woman about herself and other women. The misogynist lacks the self-knowledge of Christine's women. The same holds for Pierre Col and all the others in the *Rose* debate, with respect to misogyny, because they are not women.[46] Since correcting misogynist feelings based on a woman's *vray sentement* – *vray* because it is truly felt about herself – is imperative, Christine needed to know herself and other good women in order to present themselves to men.

What is the self? Christine may have thought of the soul, the properties of which include the God-given virtues and faculties discussed in Chapter 1. It

---

[44] Christine sought the views of other women on the claims of misogyny: 'semblablement discutoye des autres femmes que j'ay hantees ... qui de leur grace m'ont dit de leurs privetez et estroictes pensees' (*Cité*, p. 42) [I discussed these matters with other women I frequented, who graciously confided in me their personal circumstances and private thoughts].

[45] See as well the epigraph to Chapter 6 and *Débat*, pp. 19:255–58, 55:248–50; Case 1998; Blumenfeld-Kosinski 1994, pp. 712–13.

[46] Although Gontier Col's wife's views are rarely noted, they are compatible with Christine's (Rossiaud 1986, p. 156).

seems likely that she also thought of herself as a persona, that is, as a type.[47] As such, the persona has human similarities and differences that distinguish types. Her description of women based on social status in the *Trois vertus* illustrates this.[48] However, Christine's distinctions among persons refer not so much to individual differences, but to types distinguishable by features such as those identified in Chapter 2's discussion of the topoi of persons. Clearly important in the matter of misogyny is the topos *sexus*, or 'gender'. Although Pierre Col and Christine de Pizan are both representative of the human person, each is distinct in gender. Pierre Col can speak from experience only as a man. Christine de Pizan can speak *de sentement* only as a woman. Although Col can have *vray sentement* about women, he cannot, quite literally, feel what it is like to be a woman, any more, it must be added, than Christine can feel what a man feels – unless, of course, she leads a man's life, as suggested by the gender change in the *Mutacion*. However, it is doubtful that many men in her audience would have agreed to assume women's traditional roles. But both can listen to thoughts and observe actions that would influence opinions about good or bad men and women; Christine writes for such audiences. Their opinions are corroborated or corrected by *esplucher* using reason, observation, and reflection.

The writings Christine criticizes in the *Cité* illustrate gender distinctions in the way they are interpreted. As noted above, her response to reading the *Rose* and, more importantly, Matheolus is different from that in reading treatises such as Ovid's *Ars amatoria*, Cecco d'Ascoli's *Acerba*, or the anonymous *De secretis mulierum*. The latter are straightforward proponents of misogynist opinions. Works like the *Rose* and Matheolus's *Lamentations* are, as Christine herself notes, written 'en maniere de trufferie' (*Cité*, p. 42). The *Rose* can be read as antiphrasis; Matheolus's poem is a kind of farce mocking the misogynist, antimatrimonial, but 'bigamist' cleric lamenting his own conjugal or sexual woes.[49]

Christine began reading Matheolus because someone recommended it as light-hearted, amusing *trufferie*; she opened the book seeking relaxation from her more demanding studies. This is how a man might read it. Her experience was not the same, obviously. There is a divide here between the *vray sentement* of men laughing at a stereotypical man they do not identify with and that of a woman who finds the same man's outbursts characteristic of authoritative stereotypes through the ages,[50] and perhaps especially offensive to her as a

---

[47] Zühlke 1994, p. 45; cf. Rheinfelder 1928.

[48] Lorcin 1995. The *Corps de policie* divides all human beings in much the same way, from the king to commoners.

[49] Cf. 'la truffe' (*Cité*, p. 46; on this mode, see as well pp. 154, 230, 236, 366, 368); Christine uses 'fanfelues' (p. 50) in an analogous way. The word seems to have a broad semantic range. For example, there are permissible 'truffe[s] a rire' among women (*Trois vertus*, p. 94:98; cf. *Policie*, p. 4:32–35).

[50] Pratt 1994, p. 66 n. 35; cf. Kelly 1995a, pp. 152–58.

widow. Where men seem to have read the foolish bigamist and his outrageous outbursts as we might Arnolphe's in Molière's *Ecole des femmes*,[51] Christine was offended by Matheolus's diatribes as women have been offended by Molière's *Femmes savantes*.

What did Christine expect in reading a work described as *trufferie*? She obviously expected to be amused. She could appreciate farce even when it represented marriage. Two of her ballades illustrate the farcical mode. *AB* 8, for example, evokes a complacent husband who allows his wife to indulge her desires, including those an *ami* might satisfy.[52] *CB* 78 mocks the jealous husband: 'Hé! Qu'il dessert bien qu'on le face coux / Le baboïn' (v. 15–16)[53] [Ah! He certainly deserved being cuckolded, that baboon!]. In another context, she reports as farcical alchemists' attempts to make gold from excrement or old shoes (*Advision*, II.xviii.53–76). But when Ovid, Jean de Meun, and Matheolus show the spouse who would abuse even an innocent wife or when they relate an immoral seduction, *trufferie* becomes what Christine terms *goliardise et deshonnesteté* (*Débat*, p. 51:81–82), that is, vice that exceeds the bounds of amusing farce and becomes morally reprehensible.[54]

The validity of *vray sentement* depends in part, then, on self-knowledge. This is important. But, if humans can err, even regarding their own feelings and themselves, will her own 'true' feelings pass honest, rational scrutiny? How can one determine the validity of one's feelings and thus their approximation to true opinion? These are questions Christine confronts in the *Cité des dames*.

To answer them requires introspection. This means scrutinizing the evidence of one's own feelings in Reason's mirror, measuring them against experience, knowledge, and authority. Then Rectitude can emerge and Justice prevail. The process is represented and carefully set out by the three ladies who personify Christine's thought. The standards are evident in the mirror of Reason, the plumb line of Rectitude, and the measuring cup of Justice. Reason's mirror permits the observer to see his or her own qualities and defects as well as virtues and vices. Using Reason's mirror, 'les exances, qualitez, proportions et mesures de toutes choses sont congneues ne sans lui riens ne peut estre bien faict' (*Cité*, p. 52) [the essences, qualities, proportions, and measurements of

---

[51] But there was also criticism and debate about Molière's play which is dealt with in his two short plays, *La Critique de l'Ecole des femmes* and *L'Impromptu de Versailles*.

[52] The permissive husband reappears in the twelfth Joy in the *Quinze joies de mariage*. Is his wife the kind of woman Christine thought Jean de Meun frequented?

[53] The type is omnipresent in the *Quinze joies*.

[54] Elsewhere in the *Rose* debate Christine speaks of 'goliardises et deshonnestetés' (p. 14:84–85) as being far worse than 'maniere de jolie nouvelle' (p. 20:275); such *truffes* are written only for pleasure, not profit; cf. Minnis 1991, pp. 23–31. According to *Prouverbes*, 86: 'Tourner a truffe aucune foiz injure / En certain temps est scens' [Sometimes turning injury to a joke is reasonable on appropriate occasions]. In the *Advision*, III.vi.173–77, Christine relates treating as 'trufe' the jokes she was victim of while trying to settle her financial estate after her husband's death.

all things are known; without it nothing can be done well]. This is self-knowledge. The emphasis on measurement carries over to Rectitude's plumb line[55] and Justice's measuring cup. Introspection is a just and exact evaluation of one's feelings. Only after such introspection and evaluation can a *sentement* be said to be *vray*. At that moment it becomes a true opinion – as long as nothing emerges to correct or change it.

Christine allows for error in judgment while providing a method to correct such error. Ideally, the result will be, or seem to be, rational, right, and just. If it does not, further introspection and correction become necessary. As observed in Chapter 2, Christine corrects her own opinions about her life in the *Advision*. Her *vray sentement* when she became a widow was that she was the victim of Fortune. Therefore, she wrote the *Mutacion* to show how she, like all humankind throughout history,[56] was held in thrall by Fortune. The *Advision*'s correction shows that Opinion actually determines the misfortunes that Christine attributed to Fortune in the *Mutacion*. In the *Cité*'s description, moreover, Christine quickly[57] corrects her initial submission to the opinions of authoritative misogynists; she clearly expects them to do the same. She recognizes the virtue she knew in herself by introspection as a true good in the Boethian sense. She could also illustrate her sentiments by exemplary women whose crowning glory is the Virgin Mary. In a way she achieved what Nimrod failed to do with the Tower of Babel, not by aiming to usurp God by building upwards to Heaven, but by bringing Heaven to earth in the person and virtues of the Virgin Mary, queen of the City of Ladies.[58]

'Natural' women in the *Livre des trois vertus*

Let us now turn to the book Christine wrote for 'natural' women. Here we confront anew opinions whose credibility can be appreciated only by bearing in mind the issues Hella Haasse raises in the epigraph quoted at the beginning of this book. According to the *Livre des trois vertus*, as noted earlier, the 'natural' woman is *simple, coye, honneste, rassise*, and *en cremeur*, or should be because such virtues shield her from misogynists' blame. This treatise differs from the *Cité* in part because it is more hortatory than epideictic, and in part because it is more practical,[59] broadening the scope of the *Cité* to include

---

[55] On Christine's Rectitude, see Richards 2002.

[56] The exception is God's chosen people as long as they conform to His will; see *Mutacion*, v. 8238–44, 8415–42.

[57] This is obviously a dramatic moment, which Christine crystallizes in the episode in which she reads Matheolus. Her works show that she had been confronting misogyny well before she wrote the episode or first read Matheolus.

[58] Christ, Christine's namesake according to the *Mutacion* (v. 371–78), came to earth to save by becoming a man; cf. McLeod 1991, p. 133: 'Although the city of ladies ultimately derives its authority from God, its significance is earthly.'

[59] Willard 1981c; Brown-Grant 1999b, pp. 17–18; Lacarra Lanz 2001.

women, good and bad, from all levels of society.⁶⁰ A virtual *sermo ad status feminarum*, the *Trois vertus* incorporates the traditional hierarchy of *oratores*, *bellatores*, and *laboratores* in the *Cité*, introducing a horizontal awareness of social status among the *laboratores* and the *bellatores* in town and country.⁶¹ Christine even presents women as *oratores* who chose the active life as well as those who follow the path of contemplation.⁶² She still contrasts women as either remarkably good or remarkably bad;⁶³ the latter include those who are denied entrance into the City of Ladies, and whom, like 'ordes pierres broçonneuses et noires' (*Cité*, p. 68) [foul, coarse, and blackish stones], she removes from its grounds.⁶⁴ But, perhaps like Dido and Medea, they are also redeemable in the *Trois vertus*.

The primary virtue of the natural woman is chastity, a virtue that is confirmed in the public eye as honor and in the woman's own mind by a good conscience. Chastity is the source of moral strength.⁶⁵ The word refers not only to sexual abstinence; it is also evident as sobriety in dress and conduct. It pleases God while preserving honor in the world's eyes. Like Judith who slew Holophernes, the chaste woman is the *virago* or *femme forte* whom Christine promotes in all her writings when speaking of good women. But such fortitude can also manifest itself in fearful women, or 'craintives' (*Trois vertus*, p. 218:73).⁶⁶ Chaste women, fearing harm to their person from unchaste men, are able to confront misogyny because chastity is honorable, honor being public esteem

---

⁶⁰ Nagel 2000, pp. 115–17.

⁶¹ Bornstein 1981.

⁶² As writer, Christine illustrates a type of *orator* in the active sphere. Cf. Corti 1983, p. 155: 'La classification des femmes laïques reflète le même schéma: on part des nobles pour arriver aux femmes *pauperes in villis* et enfin aux *mulieres meretrices*.' Corti is referring to Humbert de Romans's *De eruditione praedicatorum*, but her words fit grosso modo the array of orders in both the *Trois vertus* and the *Corps de policie*.

⁶³ As in the contrast between Jean Le Fèvre's *Matheolus* and his *Livre de leesce*. At the beginning of the *Cité* she may refer to a manuscript containing both these works because, as she states, it allegedly 'parloit a la reverence des femmes' (*Cité*, p. 40) [spoke well of women], a statement that could apply only to the *Leesce* (Curnow, ed., *Cité*, p. 1037 n. 1).

⁶⁴ Morally, these stones are analogous to the 'man' Chrétien de Troyes describes as herdsman in *Yvain*: 'Uns vilains qui resambloit mor' (v. 286) [a villein resembling a blackamoor]. As late as the seventeenth century La Bruyère describes such persons as 'livides et tout brûlés de soleil' (*Caractères*, 'De l'homme', §128). Nobility are white-complexioned, as are the virtuous. On the relation between physical appearance and virtue as it applies to Christine herself, see Chapter 1, pp. 21–22.

⁶⁵ *Cité*, especially in the section on chaste women, pp. 318–26, 500–02; *Trois vertus*, pp. 168:98–169:126, 215:1–218:75. See Reno 1981; Willard 1981a, p. 159; Brown-Grant 2002, pp. 47–52; and, in general, Bugge 1975.

⁶⁶ On this word as an anagram for Christine, see Schilperoort 1936, pp. 81, 83; Cerquiglini, ed., *CBAD*, pp. 22–23; Nouvet 1996; Altmann 1999, p. 238; Tarnowski 2003, pp. 184, 196 ns. 8–9. It is perhaps not inappropriate to recall that Fear was strong enough to halt the advances of Amant in the *Roman de la rose* (v. 15580–99); Chastity by herself was not so strong, as the *Rose*'s denouement suggests.

that leaves the woman on the moral pedestal on which Christine implies that she naturally belongs. I shall return to this moral pedestal below.

But first I would like to consider how honor, as Christine understands this quality, can be vouchsafed, especially in the light of the authoritative and emotional misogyny that asserts woman's natural propensity to moral perversity. Here the good woman with the virtues that Christine recommends must confront misogynist opinions that range from firm conviction to suspicion.[67] To such minds the good woman is unnatural.

Christine's solution is, as suggested above, conscience. *Vray sentement* and her faith validate conscience and assure the individual that she is innocent of the wrongs imputed to her by misogynists.[68] Since Christine emphasizes sobriety and chastity, her conscience is informed by the morality of her faith (*Trois vertus*, pp. 43–47). But her conception of conscience is not purely reductive; that is, conscience is not unreflective imposition of rules. Probing one's conscience can be an investigative process, 'se tu espuluches bien ta conscience' (*Trois vertus*, p. 127:123–24) [if you carefully probe your conscience]. By such sifting and winnowing, one comes to understand the virtues the chaste woman seeks to acquire. For example, she will understand humility: 'qui vouldrait bien espuluchier et cueillir les louenges de ceste vertu d'umilité, ce que la Saincte Escripture en dit seroit si comme une droicte abisme' (*Trois vertus*, p. 167:70–73) [whoever wishes to probe thoroughly and garner the praises of that virtue called humility would find in Holy Scripture, as it were, a truly bottomless source of knowledge]. The *Trois vertus* is itself an 'abyss' of examples on how to probe one's conscience in the light of divine wisdom and worldly prudence (p. 41:3–9; cf. pp. 121–23).

Humility brings us to woman's natural moral pedestal, as mentioned above. In the *Trois vertus* Christine insists on humility in aristocrats whose only real claim to nobility is, she asserts more than once, outstanding virtue, not blood (p. 163:75–96).[69] By the same token, she devotes most of her treatment of

---

[67] For example in the following passages in the *Trois vertus* in which she describes specific false opinions or 'abusions': a princess should not perform charitable visits to the unfortunate (p. 39:66–71); reputation is synonymous with honor (pp. 41:11–16, 76:55–57); gossip (p. 74:55); women cannot manage their affairs (p. 82:46–48); suspicions about amorous liaisons (p. 113:93–94; cf. pp. 113:106, 132:58, 182:126, 193:125); love makes one happy or a man brave (pp. 115:141–116:171); one can hide love (pp. 118:221 and 239, 119:245); slander (p. 126:88–89; cf. pp. 143–48, 217:49–52); a woman should cultivate a wide range of relations at court (p. 130:7–9); presuming oneself worthy out of envy and pride (p. 134:20–23; cf. pp. 136:9–11, 159:51–54, 161:26–29); the opinions of men presumed to be wise (p. 151:57–58; cf. p. 202:46–51); blood, not virtue, confers nobility (p. 163:75–96); opinion cannot deceive (p. 164:105–06); poor judgment (p. 179:39); bad reputation (p. 192:111); and, finally, opinion contrary to established truth (p. 214:71–72).

[68] The reliance on conscience as consolation is no doubt modeled in part on Boethius's self-justification. On conscience as a defense against envy, see *Trois vertus*, p. 137:38–40.

[69] This is an opinion Christine shared with the *Rose*'s Reason and Nature (v. 6538–62, 18577–88). Christine's authority is Saint Augustine (*Trois vertus*, p. 163:83–86); she also found the idea in Boethius's *Consolation*, III Pr. 6.7–9 and Met 6 (*Policie*, pp. 74–75) and

women's virtues to the princess and, just beneath the princess, women of high nobility because – *noblesse oblige* – the virtues that constitute their nobility should make them exemplary. The term 'betters' is appropriate, and the noble woman (and man), as a 'better', should live up to higher standards imposed by virtue, as these apply both to their soul – *sapience* – and to their human body – *prudence mondaine*.[70] These are virtues that their 'inferiors' can emulate, but can rarely achieve, nor can they be expected to.

It follows that the social hierarchy allows for adaptations. For example, pregnancy outside marriage or from adultery is a greater sin in a princess than in her lady-in-waiting. For example, in Chrétien's *Yvain*, it would be a greater fault in Laudine than in Lunete. Accordingly, Christine approves of what she calls the 'juste ypocrisie' (*Trois vertus*, p. 68:58) of the *demoiselle de cour*[71] who, learning that her mistress is

> grosse sans estre mariee, – si la conforta ... et elle meismes, afin que quant l'enfant venoit qu'elle peust dire que il fust sien, fist entendre qu'elle estoit grosse; et par celle voye la sauva de mort et garda de deshonneur. Et telz choses faire ... n'est pas mal, mais tres grant charité.
> (*Trois vertus*, p. 129:169–76)
>
> [pregnant but not married, consoled her; moreover, she professed that she herself was pregnant so that she could claim to be the child's mother when it was born. In this way she saved her mistress from death and dishonor. Acting in this way is not wrong, but very charitable.]

Such charity accounts for the greater leniency Christine advises in judging the lower social orders in, for example, meeting religious duties (*Trois vertus*, pp. 207:14–17, 218:12–219:34). God made *laboratores* less responsible for their actions and character.[72] Similarly, 'le servant qui moins reçoit de guerredons de son seigneur moins est obligié a son service' (*Cité*, p. 46) [the servant who receives less recompense from his lord is less obliged to serve him]. In the final analysis, Christine is more concerned with these women's honor than their bodies. This is consistent with her conviction in matters of faith which take precedence over social opinion where opinions differ and are, consequently, debatable (*Trois vertus*, p. 49:52–64).

---

in Brunetto Latini's *Tresor* (II.63.15, 102.2). On the distinction between humility as a moral virtue defined by biblical and ecclesiastical tradition and humility in the noble person, see (with examples from Froissart's *Chroniques*) Picoche 1976, pp. 72–77; on the changes in the word's semantic range since the Middle Ages, see Picoche 1978.

[70] There is an even higher standard: the saintliness of those who choose the contemplative life (*Trois vertus*, pp. 22–25; cf. Blumenfeld-Kosinski 2000).

[71] See Lorcin 1988, pp. 364–65.

[72] The line of reasoning is consistent with Christine's own distinction between her perfect, God-given virtues, and the imperfect body Nature fashioned to hold them, hindering their full realization.

Christine also argues that conscience prescribes the wife's duties in protecting her husband, even when such actions border on imitating Griselda, a 'forte femme en vertu' (*Cité*, p. 346; cf. pp. 346–56) [woman whose virtue is fortitude]. Even 'aux princepces et dames ou autres tenues en tel servage Prudence ne puet donner autre enseignement – et si n'est il pas petit – ne mais prendre en pacience et faire tousjours bien a leur pouoir, et obeir pour avoir paix' (*Trois vertus*, p. 81:27–31) [to the princesses, ladies, and other women held in such bondage Prudence can teach no other lesson – and it is a not insignificant lesson – than to bear up patiently, ever acting as best they can and obediently in order to have peace]. Writing in her fifteenth-century world,[73] Christine counsels such prudence because there is no escape from a bad marriage unless the husband dies: 'il faut que tu muires et vives avec lui, quel qu'il soit' (*Trois vertus*, p. 55:86–87) [you have to live and die with him, no matter what his character may be]. No wonder that so many widows chose not to remarry, although, if young, they were obliged to follow the wishes of their parents in making the decision (*Trois vertus*, pp. 188–96). Christine too chose not to remarry, despite the fact that remarriage might have relieved her financial and other difficulties.[74] Indeed, virgins and widows are the most enterprising, independent, and numerous women in the *Cité des dames*.[75]

Communication of *vray sentement* across gender boundaries

The communication of *vray sentement* must confront a stark distinction, mentioned earlier, between male and female gender and, more specifically, the distinct experiences of each gender.[76] In the *Cité*, Christine says that she consulted other women in order to gauge her own reaction to misogyny. In spite of her views on gender distinctions, Christine claims in the *Mutacion* that she changed her gender upon becoming a widow. Since she is not making a pre-modern case for sex change, what does such a mutation imply regarding the *vray sentement* of a man or a woman? Does Christine de Pizan acquire the *vray sentement* of men through her mutation? And, correspondingly, can a man

---

[73] Cf. Lorcin 1988.

[74] By remarrying, Christine would also have run the risk of enduring the indignities of a charivari, a custom she hardly would wish to experience. On widows and charivari, see Gauvard 1991, pp. 590–93; Crane 2002, pp. 143–45. Christine did not know the contemplative life, 'dont il me poise' (*Cité*, p. 23:34) [which I regret]. She may have turned to it at the end of her life after taking refuge in Poissy; see Dulac 1998a. For Christine's views on the widow and widowhood, see Brownlee 1995b.

[75] Dulac 1991; Plebani 2003, p. 49.

[76] Christine's changing image of her metamorphoses in the context of the gender topos anticipates, but is not identical with, recent transformations in feminist thought on the issue of essentialism. On this 'essentialist' feature of Christine's thought on gender, see Quilligan 1991, pp. 6, 16 *et passim*; Chance 1996; cf. Richards 1996, pp. 101–12.

undergo such a transformation in experience and himself acquire *vray sentement* regarding women's experience?

Christine began her career by writing 'd'autrui sentement' (*Advision*, III. vii.24–25) in her *Cent Ballades*. But these are poems about mostly literal love, a subject she came to regard as unworthy of serious attention. When the woman becomes a virago, she becomes 'celle qui a vertu et force d'omme' (*Cité*, p. 210) [a woman who has a man's virtue and fortitude].[77] Such character shows prudence: 'femme forte, c'est a dire, prudente' (*Cité*, p. 198)[78] [a woman of fortitude, that is, one who is prudent]. But this transformation is still expressed on the literal level.

How can she, as a woman and even as a virago, understand the feelings of others, and, more specifically, of men? The answer, she discovered, is furnished by the allegories of poets. Such a poetics is aptly illustrated by the allegorical gender changes described in the *Mutacion* (v. 1025–158). Ulysses's men change into pigs; Tiresias becomes a woman and then returns to being a man; finally, a daughter, Yplis, becomes a son.[79] These are poetic allegories, but they do not exemplify understanding *vray sentement* across gender lines. Such changes in the poetic mode do offer, however, a means to transfer, allegorically, the experience of one gender to another. The surface text describes a change in sexual gender and office – the woman becomes a man, the crew-member or passenger becomes a pilot.

An eloquent, and thus rhetorically effective passage in the *Rose* debate deserves attention here because its clarifies Christine's two-pronged approach to misogynist opinion – two-pronged in the sense that she distinguishes between her own treatises addressed to men, such as her contributions to the *Rose* debate and the *Epistre Othea*, and those addressed to women such as the *Trois vertus* and Sebile de Monthault's admonition inserted there from the *Duc des vrais amants*. Addressing men in the *Rose* debate, she exclaims 'Qui sont fames?' and then goes on to answer her own question, as quoted earlier: 'si sont elles vos meres, vos suers, vos filles, vos fammes et vos amies; elles sont vous meesmes e vous mesmes elles' (*Débat*, p. 139:775, 781–83) [Who are women? ... They are your mothers, sisters, daughters, wives, and women friends; they are you yourselves and you yourselves are they]. What does this explicit attention to gender mean?[80]

---

[77] The idea comes from her reading of Solomon's *Proverbs* (*Cité*, pp. 198–200), doubtless one of the 'proverbes estranges' that fascinated her. On Christine's changing views on the 'virility' of such women, see Angeli 2003.

[78] To be prudent is 'avoir avis et regart sur les choses que on veult emprendre, comment ilz pourront estre terminees' (*Cité*, p. 202) [to consider in the tasks one wishes to undertake how they may be brought to a conclusion]; see also *Trois vertus*, pp. 191:95–192:96.

[79] See Pairet 2002, pp. 161–64. Christine also alludes to the Ceyx and Alcyone myth; on this metamorphosis in the context of Christine's poetics, see Blumenfeld-Kosinski 1997, pp. 178–87.

[80] On a similarly problematic change of grammatical gender in the *Rose*, see Kelly 1995a, p. 25.

First, let us consider the redefinition of gender in the *Mutacion*. Here, gender is defined in terms of roles. A man is one who captains a ship or heads a family. In assuming this role on the death of her husband, Christine becomes a man in order to repair the ship of her family that had foundered on the rocks after the loss of its pilot. Allegorically, then, Christine becomes a man. She has to adopt the male role because her husband has died. The role, in other words, determines and explains her allegorical metamorphosis.

Likewise, Christine uses allegorical metamorphosis in the *Rose* debate. There, the question, 'Qui sont fames?' arises during the discussion of Jean de Meun's and Ovid's alleged argument that it is better to deceive than to be deceived. In their works, the victims of deception are women. In the context of the role one plays, Christine redefines men and women not by gender but on moral grounds: all seducers are men and all the seduced are women, whatever their actual gender. It follows that, if her reading of Jean de Meun is correct, his 'disciples' have been seduced and deceived by their 'master'. This distinction between the deceivers and the deceived fits Jean's own description of the Great Deceiver, Faux Semblant, who includes men and women in his catalogue of deceivers.

> Car s'i font el que il ne dient,
> certainement il vos conchient,
> quelconques robes que il aient,
> de quelconques estat qu'il saient,
> soit clers, soit lais, soit hon, soit fame,
> sires, serjanz, baiasse ou dame. (*Rose*, v. 11047–52)

> [For if their actions do not correspond to their words, they do indeed make an ass of you, whatever dress they may don, whatever their status in life – religious or secular, be they man or woman, lord or servant, maid or lady.]

This passage is obviously a rhetorical tirade. But that does not mean it is insignificant. Rhetorical exclamations such as this must be verisimilar to be convincing. They may also be striking or astonishing in order to gain attention, and, as a result, bring out a new idea or point of view.[81]

In allegory, Christine discovered a way to communicate *vray sentement* to, as it were, aliens – a woman telling her feelings as a woman to men who cannot share her feelings as a woman would. Allegorically, she redefines the two literally different types, man and woman, as another type both can belong to. Just as Christine comes to know the man's feelings as head of a household when her husband dies, men like Jean de Meun's disciples may come to understand better woman's feelings about seduction or deceit if they become victims of seduction or deceit themselves. Jean de Meun seduces his 'disciples'.

---

[81] Enders 1999.

Validation of *vray sentement*

Vray sentement remains tricky and slippery. It is notoriously difficult to discern or evaluate the *sentement d'autrui* even when it is sincere. Feelings can deceive, as misogynists show and Christine recognized. Furthermore, *sentement* can fluctuate or change, just as the opinions it supports do. Christine was not always sure of her own feelings. At the beginning of the *Cité* she hesitates between accepting and rejecting misogyny. Let us examine Christine's approach to the problem of *vray sentement*. Then we can, in conclusion, explore her poetic response to misogyny.

First, how can one validate one's own feelings vis-à-vis learned authority? When Christine confronts this quandary at the beginning of the *Cité*, she feels that authoritative misogynist allegations do not fit her knowledge of herself. Still, she hesitates, doubting her own feelings when confronted with the weight of learned authorities on the subject. By drawing arguments and examples from the same authorities, however, she succeeds in turning their own evidence against them. She does this by amplifying topoi different from theirs that, importantly, fit her own *sentement*. We have observed such rewriting in discussing the rape script in Chapter 2. In the *Cité*, Christine proceeds in a similar fashion. For example, she does not exclude the prostitute Leonce from the City of Ladies; rather, she rewrites the prostitute as a learned woman who stood up to Theophrastus (*Cité*, p. 160).[82]

By accumulating examples of such positive rewriting, Christine overcomes her doubts through 'exaggeration'. *Exaggeratio*, in rhetorical terminology, 'piles on' evidence. By focusing only on those topoi that can be made to support opinions she espouses, she accumulates verisimilar evidence for her feeling that women can be virtuous, while evoking analogous feelings in her readers.[83] Such one-sided evidence is hyperbole – that is, exaggeration not meant to deceive. The result in the *Cité* is a philogyny as extreme as the misogyny it opposes. Such exaggeration restores balance. Women, like men, can be good or bad. The *Cité* acknowledges this by admitting only the former within its walls. Hence, some outsiders will fit the misogynists' stereotypes as Christine understands them – for example, the dissolute women she believed Jean de Meun frequented (*Débat*, pp. 18:215–21).[84]

---

[82] A form of self-defense as well, since Jean de Montreuil likened Christine to Leonce (*Débat*, p. 42:8–10); see Quilligan 1991, pp. 168–69; Richards 1996, p. 128 n. 18. Christine rewrites Leonce as she does other traditional feminine villains as a learned woman (Caraffi 1998, p. 79 n. 8); she retorts indirectly by likening Pierre Col to Heloise, a *meretrix* (*Débat*, p. 146:1015–18; see Richards 1993, p. 142).

[83] On this sense of *exaggeratio*, see Kelly 1992, p. 50. Christine's accumulation of such examples is also related to *frequentatio*, or multiplication of diverse examples under one heading (Faral 1924, p. 67).

[84] 'Jehan de Meung ne senti onques que fu honourable amoureux' (*Débat*, p. 130:495–96) [Jean de Meun never knew what an honorable lover was].

Although such dissolute women are absent in the *Cité*, they do appear in some of Christine's other works, notably Briseida in the *Epistre Othea* and Eve in the *Advision*. By restoring this balance, she confirms her *vray sentement* of women's worth. In another hyperbole, she asserts that bad women are not natural, but that such women are a minority (*Cité*, p. 256).[85] Her opinion is valid in debate because her sense of her own worth is founded on her virtue as she and her faith understand that virtue: *simple*, *coye*, *honneste*, *rassise*, and, most individually, *fille d'escole* (cf. *Débat*, pp. 147:1043–149:1093). To be sure, this is still an opinion. But the evidence of her religion, her reasoning, and her experience is in harmony with it. Thus, they support her conviction that her opinions regarding misogyny and women's potential for virtue are valid.

The gender change in the *Mutacion* may also reflect Christine's doubts at that time regarding her worth as a woman. The *Cité* refers to those doubts as part of her experience in reading Matheolus. The *Advision* ascribes them to opinion, albeit a false opinion uninformed by Boethian distinctions between true and false goods.[86] In the same treatise she learns to rely on her own virtues, the very qualities she possesses naturally as true goods. These virtues enable her to confront fortune and her false opinion of its power.

Faith, reason, and misogyny

Two additional features of Christine's thought are important in validating her correction of misogyny: faith and reason. One cannot doubt the profound sincerity of Christine de Pizan's faith, a faith that inspired her religious writings in verse and prose and her moral convictions. It supported her belief in the divine right of kings, in the superiority of the noble order,[87] and in the fundamental unity of the Church. Yet faith did not preclude differences of opinion. Schism itself illustrates the diverse, often erroneous opinions of the faithful. In reference to Aristotle on God's alleged envy, Christine rejects the opinion because envy in God is impossible (*Charles V*, vol. 2, pp. 174–75); in the same work, she faults the pride of someone who mocked the gods because he thought

---

[85] She admits that they have had less opportunity to do wrong because of misogynist prejudice (*Cité*, pp. 80, 256). She also confesses that in her youth, childishness turned her away from serious study (*Advision*, III.viii.12–17; cf. *Chemin*, v. 1122–24); but this happens to young men too.

[86] The false goods include family members she relied on until her widowhood. Boethius's family, intact at the time he wrote, was a consolation for him (*De consolatione*, II Pr. iv.5–9). Christine as widow had only her mother, her daughter and one or two sons, all of whom she was responsible for; see Callahan 2000, pp. 487, 489, based on *Advision*, pp. 121–23. She seems to have received no support from her brothers in Italy, or from her husband's family, two sources of support she evokes, without reference to herself, in the *Trois vertus* (see pp. 82–90, 188–93); she merely recalls a conversation she had with her father-in-law (p. 19:161–65; cf. p. 84:50–52).

[87] Forhan 2002, pp. 84–87.

he was more powerful than they (vol. 1, pp. 78–79). The same overweening pride characterizes those nobles who believe all things are permissible to them (vol. 1, pp. 17–18). It is also the source of rebellion in the people.[88]

Christine's ultimate authority in these and all matters is Scripture. Her opinion on a debate among theologians illustrates this. At issue was whether Christ left anything of his body after ascending to heaven. She sides with those theologians who accept that, for example, His blood, hair, nails, and such could well have remained here below as relics. But there is a proviso: 'sauve toutes raisons d'Escripture Sainte ou theologie' (*Charles V*, vol. 1, p. 96)[89] [subject to the correction of Holy Scripture or theology]. Faith is the ultimate authority in matters of opinion, and theology is the voice of faith. It finds a voice in, for example, Gerson's Eloquence Theologienne. Christine's faith was so strong that she accepted contemporary miracles.[90] For example, she believed reports of levitation by a saintly woman (*Charles V*, vol. 2, p. 67). This view is congruent with her acceptance of the miracles recounted in Book Three of the *Cité*. In this work too, faith bolsters true opinion, even though the same ecclesiastical authorities that she drew her examples from promulgated misogyny. To deal with this conundrum, Christine turns to reason.

Christine's opinions are not founded on faith alone. Reason is her principal arbiter. As she advises her son, 'Prudence aprent l'omme a vivre en raison, / La ou elle est eureuse est la maison' (*Prouverbes*, 2) [Prudence teaches to live by following Reason; that home is happy where she dwells]. Skill in debate is important and effective rhetoric is crucial in rational debate about opinions. Although in the *Rose* debate, reasons, reasoning, and evidence for reasoning differ widely and sharply, Christine admires a well-presented case (*arenge*). Elsewhere, she extols Charles V as a master speaker and rhetorician: 'sa belle parleure tant ordennée et par si belle arrenge, sanz aucune superfluité de parole' (*Charles V*, vol. 1, p. 49)[91] [his beautiful, well ordered speech so beautifully arranged, without any superfluity in language]. Charles's eloquence and virtues made him a virtual reincarnation of the ideal orator, the *vir bonus dicendi peritus*.

The same rhetorical standard obtains in the *Cité*. Two features of Christine's *arenge* there are important. First is the opinion on misogyny. Did God actually make women as vile as men claim? How can Christine explain her own self-doubts in this matter? Reason, Rectitude, and Justice appear and offer answers, complete with examples. Conforming to the answers the three personifications

---

[88] Sigal 2002, pp. 819–21.

[89] The example is a good illustration of Christine's religious mentality. As in the *Chemin*, she refuses to rise too high on the Ladder of Speculation.

[90] To put her views on miracles into perspective, it is noteworthy that Blaise Pascal planned to use them in the seventeenth century as proof of the Christian religion; see his *Pensées*, §§211, 333, 419–51.

[91] See above, pp. 24–25. Cf. *Charles V*, vol. 1, pp. 59–60, and vol. 2, pp. 34, 116–17, 120. On Louis d'Orléans's eloquence, see vol. 1, pp. 173–74. Christine emphasizes anew the importance of the ruler's eloquence in *Policie*, pp. 43–46, and *Paix*, pp. 165–71.

give, Christine relies on *consideracion* and *discrecion*; the examples bring Christine's memory into play. This is *esplucher* (*Cité*, p. 42). Reason explains that, although Christine is a woman, God's gifts to her are sufficient to resolve issues of opinion. This is because God bestowed on women understanding sufficient to construe, know, and retain all that is comprehensible (*Cité*, p. 194). Native genius, or 'sens naturel', and learning, or 'science acquise' (p. 196), permit all human beings to use their understanding to deal with the society into which they are born and to lead moral lives.[92] By bringing her reasoning into line with morality, Christine reconciles her reasoning with faith.

To be sure, Christine de Pizan allows for differences between men and women in the *Cité*. For example, women are physically weaker than men (*Cité*, pp. 102–04, 152). They are less gifted for courtroom argument since God has assigned them different tasks (pp. 92–94). There are anomalies or exceptions among the women Christine describes in the *Cité*. She demonstrates this by a variety of the *translatio imperii et studii* commonplace, with the corollary familiar from Chrétien de Troyes as the translation of *chevalerie* and *clergie*.[93] The first book of the *Cité* relating her discussion with Reason recounts the accomplishments of women who have governed and conquered, including those who actually fought in armed, even hand-to-hand, combat; she then concludes Book One by relating the achievements of women who contributed to knowledge and learning, and helped to preserve learned traditions. Such deviations from the norm do not question the norm; rather they show the potential realized by exceptional individuals. Thus, the deviations are praiseworthy because exceptional women prove that no woman, by her feminine nature alone, is made inferior to men. Both genders encompass an array of statuses (in the medieval sense of social orders) from the lowest villeins to the higher nobility and saints. Natural physical features take on varying form; Joan of Arc, a shepherdess, became a conquering warrior, although the shepherdess in the *Dit de la pastoure* cannot change her status nor become a wife to a nobleman or, it appears, anyone else.

An analogy with Christine's depiction of Charles V proves illuminating. Criticized for not participating in person as vigorously as a monarch should in the wars of his time, although a man, Christine notes that he was not physically strong – implicitly, he was no Semiramis. This explains, Christine argues, his

---

[92] Reason leaves open the question of which is better, native genius or learning: 'sur ceste proposicion pevent estre fondees maintes opinions desquelles pevent sourdre assez de questions' (*Cité*, p. 196) [on this issue many opinions may be based that give rise to numerous questions]. The issue is not pertinent to the building of the City of Ladies and, therefore, the issue of woman's intelligence (*Cité*, p. 198).

[93] Christine enunciates the principle in *Chemin* as *translatio imperii* in the Trojan lineage (v. 3525–80), and a *translatio studii iuris* which has become uncertain in her time (v. 6211–18). The principle of *translatio studii* is also suggested in her account of Charlemagne's alleged transfer of the university from Rome to Paris (*Chemin*, v. 5905–12). Walters 1989 places Christine's *Epistre au dieu d'amours* in a *translatio studii* that includes Guillaume de Lorris and Jean de Meun.

limited participation in French wars (*Charles V*, vol. 1, pp. 48–49).⁹⁴ As with many women, the weakness is natural, that is, imposed by Nature when fashioning the body. It follows that weakness does not reduce women's intelligence any more than physical weakness does that of Charles V. Since intelligence may even make up for physical weakness (*Cité*, p. 152), women may overcome relative physical weakness as the king did, and some woman may equal or surpass some men in traditional male roles. To convince those of doubtful or contrary opinion, therefore, the *Cité des dames* relates the achievements of historical women in activities commonly reserved for men: government, arms, science, and learning. Their accomplishments vouch for the truth of Christine's opinions; the compelling evidence speaks directly to reason, the faculty that is to be swayed by laudable examples that refute false opinions – in this case, the errors of misogyny. In effect, Christine is following the poetic prescription to dwell on what has been passed over while rejecting what is commonplace. But this does not alter her view that the office assigned to woman in the household must take precedence for most women.⁹⁵

Christine develops her original opinions on misogyny by grounding her thought on faith and reason. Her first step is to acknowledge that God created men and women not as unequal but as in some ways different from one another. Using reason and, more importantly, *entendement de raison*, she reviews evidence for misogyny, refuting it in the light of her self-knowledge and history. In the *Cité*, Christine expresses her *vray sentement* as both feelings and experience. Women are physically weaker; therefore, they are not always suitable for the physically demanding roles men assume (*Cité*, pp. 102–04). Furthermore, their more passive, submissive nature disinclines them to assume active public roles, notably as lawyers (*Cité*, pp. 92–94). They are less warlike and, as daughters, are generally more honorable and caring towards parents and relatives (*Cité*, pp. 238–42). They are also more constant lovers, although Christine cautions against trying to prove it outside of marriage (*Cité*, pp. 374–404).

These opinions establish certain norms. Nevertheless, every norm has its deviations; it fluctuates between 'what should be' and 'what is'.⁹⁶ When called upon to act, or given the opportunity to do so, some women of great virtue realize an exceptional potential or gift despite 'natural' weaknesses – for example, Joan of Arc and many of the martyrs in Book Three of the *Cité des dames*. In Christine's opinion their virtues are more effective than mere physical

---

⁹⁴ That the king should not expose himself to danger is a principle Christine elaborates on in the *Fais d'armes*.

⁹⁵ This is the much discussed conservative Christine defending woman's place in the home rather than in public affairs which she commits to men: 'Il souffist qu'elles facent le commun office a quoy sont establies' (*Cité*, p. 152) [It is enough if women exercise the common role which was assigned to them]. Christine, thus, did not entirely reject her mother's emphasis on the woman's place in the household.

⁹⁶ Schnell 1998a, pp. 772–74.

strength. Virtues, after all, enhance the virtuous person's capacity to wage war, govern, resolve legal disputes, and lead a good life. The examples in the *Cité* muster an array of historical evidence, from euhemerized myth to chronicles. Her model is Boccaccio, whose method lends authority to her own opinions and the art used to illustrate them.[97] More specifically, this poetic mode permits her to adapt unflattering or contrary evidence by using conventional ways of rewriting like those discussed in Chapter 2. We have seen this in the cases of Medea and Dido. It is also evident in more truly historical examples like Semiramis's incestuous marriage to her son, which Christine excuses as early custom and false religious beliefs. Christine allows for moral progress (*Cité*, p. 108).[98]

The *Cité*'s Book One also treats women who have excelled in the arts. Again the array of examples is broad, extending from practitioners of necromancy through those who excelled in the liberal arts and the mechanical arts. Each of these women is a 'femme forte' (*Cité*, p. 198) because

> Elle a avironné ses rains de force en la constance de solicitude, et ses bras sont endurcis en continuelle bonne oeuvre. Et pourtant la lumiere de son labour ne sera ja estainte, quelque temps tenebreux qu'il face. Elle s'embesogne meismes es fortes choses et, avec ce, ne desprise pas les femenins ouvrages, ains elle meismes y met les dois.   (*Cité*, p. 200)

> [She girded her loins with fortitude by dint of constant solicitude. Her arms grow hard by constant good works. Yet the radiance of her labors will never be obscured no matter how dark the times may be. She toils even in the midst of difficult trials and, at the same time, does not scorn womanly tasks, but rather takes up these tasks on her own initiative.]

Prudence unites all the figures in Book One of the *Cité*,[99] for Prudence is foresight in conceiving, planning, and executing tasks; Reason is her guide (*Cité*, pp. 194–200; *Prouverbes*, 2).[100]

These examples show that Christine distinguishes between two kinds of virtue in women. One kind is physical strength, which God in His disposition of creation assigned as a norm to men; the other is moral strength, which He

---

[97] On her original, not slavish imitation of Boccaccio and, perhaps, Petrarch, see Brown-Grant 1995.

[98] Quilligan 1991, p. 81, refers to Christine's 'dismissal of the salvo against mother/son incest', using anthropological evidence for 'such a scandalous move on Christine's part'. This seems to make too much of Christine's explaining Semiramis's conduct as being natural because she did not know divine law.

[99] All the exemplary women in Book One, from Amazons and rulers to scholars and housewives, manifest prudence. This virtue more than any other permits entrance into the City of Ladies. Prudence mondainne is the principal counselor in the *Trois vertus*. Cf. Alain de Lille's *Anticlaudianus*, where Prudence is also named Phronesis and Sapientia, and has direct access to divine truths; his Prudence is perhaps more akin to those who follow the contemplative life as Christine describes it in the *Trois vertus*.

[100] Forhan 2002, pp. 100–08.

assigned to women (*Cité*, pp. 102–04). Women who practice the latter virtue actually succeed even in the activities God allotted to men. These *femmes fortes* realize, like Artemisia, virtues that also comprise the epideictic description of Charles V: *vertu, sagece de meurs, chevalerie, prudence,* and *hardiece* (*Cité*, p. 136). Likewise, Book One is an array informed by exceptions to the misogynist norm. Christine is herself such an exception. Like the examples she lauds in Book One, she is exceptional in both senses of the word: outstanding and unique. Using her mental qualities bestowed by God, Christine overcame her 'natural' physical limitations by virtue in both her thought and her life.

Reason is a critical factor in realizing virtue. In the *Cité*, Reason corrects human error, directing those in error towards truth. To do so she uses an allegorical mirror so that anyone who looks into it can know his or her duty by rational means. This mirror is also a source of self-knowledge by introspection (*Cité*, p. 52). The reader too learns how to measure up in God's scheme of things by comparing herself – and himself – to the illustrious figures that make up the City of Ladies. Accordingly, Reason functions as an intellectual faculty that leads to understanding. Christine's own 'exceptionality' is consistent with the mirroring process since she is endowed with the virtues that allow her to perform a unique task in rehabilitating society, like many of the women in the *Cité*. In this way, she establishes her credentials for penning the treatises on government that she wrote between 1405 and 1418 before withdrawing to Poissy, and into silence, until 1429 or 1430, when she composed her last poem, on Joan of Arc.

This rational, reflective process punctuated by examples for forming correct or true opinions obtains in Books Two and Three of the *Cité des dames* as well. Thus, each personification who engages Christine displays an ever more differentiated array of exemplary good women. In Book Two, Rectitude catalogues wise women, beginning with the sibyls and continuing with other women who prophesied.[101] There follow those who showed great devotion to husbands, including older husbands, and to parents. Rectitude goes on to show that women can be trusted with secrets (a rebuttal to the *Rose*) and can give wise counsel. Finally, she shows how their courage has been beneficial, and how their learning has contributed to better morals, including chastity even among beautiful women, constancy in love, and largess. Rejecting misogyny promotes the commonweal.

The *Cité*'s array of good women is constructed by first articulating a misogynist opinion, then countering it with examples that support the opposite opinion. The hyperbolic descriptions of *femmes fortes* are contrasted with men who illustrate the alleged defects of women, with the moderating admission that not all women are perfect. Christine considers only *preudes femmes* in the

---

[101] Cf. Blumenfeld-Kosinski 1995.

Cité des dames. The *Trois vertus* sets out the conduct necessary in contemporary terms for attaining that 'goodness'.[102]

Rectitude voices another factor in Christine's analysis of opinion. Going beyond distinguishing good from evil, Reason's office, Rectitude admonishes all to do good and uphold the truth; in doing so, they will defend those who suffer or are wronged (*Cité*, pp. 58–60). Rectitude sets the standards of good and evil, recognizing the good, punishing the evil, and restraining all who would do wrong. Rectitude's office is reflected in the more discriminating display of exemplary women, including a sharp distinction between women who are good and those who are bad. As we have noted, the poetic mode and topical invention permit Christine to glide over traditional defects in order to focus on virtuous features.[103]

Justice, the last personification through whom Christine refracts her opinions on misogyny, is a stern taskmaster: 'Je ne flechis nulle part, car je n'ay amy ne ennemi ne escalourgiant[104] voulenté. Pitié ne me convaint ne cruauté ne me meut' (*Cité*, p. 60) [I bend nowhere, nor do I have friend, enemy, or mutable will. Pity does not persuade nor does cruelty move me]. Justice corrects and distributes favors according to truth founded on faith; for Christine, therefore, such justice is entirely certain. Justice's examples represent the 'heights' – the 'combles' – of the City to which the Virgin Mary descends as sovereign over saints and martyrs, a queen beneath whom good women find their place,[105] just as the French do beneath their king. The royal family that concludes Book Two finds itself positioned beneath a heavenly host of martyrs.

Justice, 'fille de Dieu', receives a measuring cup from God (*Cité*, pp. 60–62). She measures all things according to divine standards, bringing those of 'sain entendement' to correct themselves and to do unto others as they would have others do unto them (*Cité*, p. 60). Other measurements exist among humans, but these measurements can be unjust. They measure, as Justice puts it, 'soubz ombre de moy' (*Cité*, p. 62) [in my shadow]. Like Lady Opinion, an 'ombre' of truth, these other, human measures fluctuate as much as the league in Rabelais's France, where the distance it measures in one part of the country differs from that used in other regions (*Pantagruel*, p. 268). Only Lady Justice's measurements are constant and, because confirmed by faith, unimpeachable. The sovereignty of Mary confirms this standard as absolute and inflexible.

Exemplifying Justice herself, the Virgin Mary admits all good women into her city. These include 'toute dame honorable', all 'qui amez gloire, vertu et loz' (*Cité*, p. 496) [every honorable lady ... you who love glory, virtue, and renown]. All women are exhorted to emulate the virtuous women she praises.

---

[102] See Guarinos 1998.

[103] Cf. Lemaire 1994, pp. 134–40.

[104] This changing color of will mirrors the colors of opinion as she changes her mind. See Curnow, ed., *Cité*, p. 1135.

[105] Cf. the *XV Joies* in which Christine prays to the Virgin to grant that she might 'vivre a ton bon exemple' (v. 32) [live in accordance with your good example].

In a final peroration, Christine calls on wives, maidens, widows and 'toutes femmes – soient grandes, moyennes ou petites' (p. 500), to resist 'prejudices' (p. 502).

Christine's peroration has a broader sub-text that vouchsafes its universal validity: men too can learn from the *Cité* since they too must learn to eschew false opinion and turn to virtue.[106] How this is done is set out in two treatises that promote virtue by showing how to educate young persons for the virtuous life. The *Trois vertus* addresses women, the *Epistre Othea* men. They illustrate what Rüdiger Schnell terms different discourses whose discrepancies derive from the norms they propose to different audiences living in the real world.[107] But both works bolster resolve and strengthen virtue by praising it, its adherents, and its effects.

The three ladies, Reason, Rectitude, and Justice, who give voice to Christine's attack on misogyny are not distinct from one another.[108] As we have seen, they are 'une mesmes chose', constituting stages in evaluating opinion.[109] Reason disposes; Rectitude arranges and applies; and Justice deriving from God and faith completes the task. Furthermore, they interface with the three criteria for getting at true opinion: reason, *vray sentement*, and religion. In the *Cité des dames*, Christine begins with *vray sentement*: her emotional, heartfelt response to misogyny and her consternation when authorities express misogynist opinions that contrast with her own experience and that of other women. She turns to Reason corroborated by Rectitude and Justice to resolve her intellectual, moral, social, and personal quandary. The same learned tradition that fostered misogyny reveals its own errors in the examples she culls from historical and other documentary evidence. As a continuation of the *Cité*, the *Trois vertus* completes her vision in practical terms. Beginning where the *Cité* leaves off, with princesses and queens, it concludes with prostitutes, embracing thereby women of all social classes while advising them to be good and true to their nature.[110] The descending social hierarchy of the *Trois vertus* mirrors the ascending hierarchy illustrated by the construction of the City of Ladies while providing the practical application of the morality idealized in the allegorical treatise's euhemerism and historical vignettes.[111]

Christine's religion is once again the final arbiter. She promotes humility, patience, long-suffering, submission, and prudence.[112] These are virtues men

---

[106] *Cité*, pp. 254, 314, 334–44, 374–76.

[107] See Schnell 1998a, p. 777, and 1998b.

[108] Christine links them as critical thought in the *Livre de la paix* to show how 'droit justice et raison' justify a just war; see Van Hemelryck 2000, p. 687.

[109] Cerquiglini 1994, pp. 91–95; Kottenhoff 1994, pp. 66–75.

[110] See Dudash 2003, pp. 811–15.

[111] Is Christine adapting Dante's inside-out world that projects the heavenly hierarchies in *Paradiso*? Note too that 'à mesure que l'on descend l'échelle sociale, le cercle des récepteurs ciblé s'élargit aussi par rapport au sexe' while 'gender differences' diminish (Brandenberger 2002, p. 139).

[112] Boulton 2003. Philosophy promotes patience as virtue in *Advision*, III.xxii.

can practice too.[113] With virtue based on prudence, reason, rectitude, and justice, the social order can be restored and maintained.[114] This political philosophy comprised, therefore, the art of living well in the kingdom of France. 'Tu es politique', she says to Philosophy in the *Advision*, 'car tu aprens a bien vivre, car nulle cité n'est mieulx gardee que par le fondement et lian de foy et de ferme concorde a amer le bien commun qui est tres vray et tres souverain' (*Advision*, III.xxvii.24–27)[115] [You are good government, for you teach how to live well; this is because no city is better preserved than by the foundation and bond of faith and firm accord to love the commonweal that is very true and sovereign]. Combating misogyny is one way to maintain a rational and just social order.

---

[113] Cf. Kottenhoff 1994, pp. 74–75. On men in the *Cité*, see Richards 2000b, pp. 124–26.

[114] Willard 1992, pp. 28–29; Forhan 1992, pp. 40–67; Brown-Grant 1992, p. 101.

[115] See Dulac 1992a, p. 130.

4
Love, Reason, and Debatable Opinion

> Car en amor a maint degré:
> Al comencier est debonaire;
> Le gent blandist por mix atraire;
> Et puis, quant il est ore et leus,
> Reset bien mostrer de ses jeus.[1]   (*Ille*, v. 921–25)

In her early writings Christine de Pizan saw a defense against misogyny and a hope for the commonweal in noble love. Good lovers are a bulwark against misogynist defamation in both the *Epistre au dieu d'amours* and the *Dit de la rose*. Yet, as with misogyny, a change of mind occurred in her opinion about such love, albeit the change took place over a somewhat longer time. The change was also related to her views on misogyny and her search for effective ways of combating that prejudice.[2] As Christine's views evolved, she perceived more clearly that not *la donna*, but *l'amor'è mobile*. This awareness began to emerge in her early lyric cycles. The change was complete by the *Duc des vrais amants*, the *Dit de la pastoure*, and the *Cent Ballades d'amant et de dame*. Henceforth, not love, but virtue alone, as Boethius and her religion understood it, offered protection against misogyny. Although early on Christine counted virtue among the defining features of noble love, virtue later became antithetical to even 'pure' love. We can follow her change of opinion on love more circumstantially than with misogyny, since it emerges as her opinion evolves, not as a sudden, dramatic paradigm shift like that recounted in the *Cité des dames*.

All of Christine's love poems, from the most positive early compositions to the pessimistic Dits that she wrote after them, evoke, in whole or in part, the pattern suggested in the epigraph to this chapter. Love has wonderful beginnings. It lures its followers on in the hope of bliss and chivalric deeds. But, as time passes, love becomes unstable.

---

[1] For love has many a stage. At the start it is ennobling, flattering people the better to attract them; but then, at the right time and place, it knows very well how to play its tricks.

[2] See Hauck 1995, pp. 228–34.

> Au commencier m'as le cuer aluchié,
> Par moy donner assés de tes soulas;
> Mais quant tu l'as fermement atachié,
> Adonc de ses plaisirs despouillié l'as.   (*CB*, 40, v. 9–12)³

> [At the outset you lured me on by granting me great solace, but when you had me firmly attached to you, you deprived me of all love's pleasures.]

Here is an opinion falsified by experience and mutable Fortune. Such instability leads to a conflict between virtue and love, a conflict that Christine at first sought to resolve by promoting a chaste love as an incentive to chivalric virtue which, in turn, would defend women. This is a traditional medieval commonplace.⁴ But the attempt failed. She accordingly changed her mind, coming out firmly as opposed to any love not sanctioned by marriage.

Christine's changing opinion on love

In the *Rose* debate, Christine de Pizan distinguishes between the kind of love illustrated in Jean's poem and that practiced by some of her contemporaries.

> Je croy que plusseurs ont amey loyaument et parfaitement qui onques n'y couchierent, ne onques ne deseurent ne furent deceu, de qui estoit principale entencion que leurs meurs en vaucissent mieulx, – et pour celle amour devenoyent vaillans et bien renommés, et tant que en leur viellesce ilz louoient Dieu qu'ilz avoient esté amoureux.   (*Débat*, p. 129:458–64)⁵

> [I believe that a number of men have loved with perfect constancy without ever consummating their love, nor did they ever deceive or be deceived. Their principal purpose in loving was to enhance their worth. Their love made them valiant and renowned, so much so in fact that in their old age they praised God for having been lovers.]

---

³ See also *CB* 40, v. 13–16; 44, v. 8–21; 63.

⁴ The belief that love makes one a better knight was widespread in the fifteenth century (Szkilnik 2003; cf. Stanesco 1988). Some of Christine's early poems celebrate chivalric love; see *AB* 29–31 (and the note, pp. 305–06), 33, 52; *EAB* 9. In the *Advision*, she criticizes extravagant exploits wherein, for example, knights fight for their beloved without adequate armor (II.xix.27–32). Her words recall the extravagant vows of Boort and others in the Prose *Lancelot*: a knight will joust with one foot on his horse's neck, another will not take lodging before defeating six knights, still another will not lie naked with a maiden before defeating three knights, and so on – including Agricol li Bials Parliers who will fight wearing only his shirt and the shift and wimple of his beloved (*Lancelot*, xlviii.5–12). Christine condemns all such undertakings as vain in the *Fais d'armes*, p. 199; cf. p. 201.

⁵ Jaeger 1999, p. 121, refers to this passage. For an illuminating discussion of such 'chaste love', see his chapter 5, which also contains an analysis of the *Duc des vrais amants* (pp. 202–04).

As late as 1402, she still upholds this ideal in addressing

> Dames amoureuses,
> Qui de tout bien sont desireuses,
> J'entens de l'amour ou n'a vice,
> Mal, villenie, ne malice;
> Car quiconques le die ou non,
> En bonne amour n'a se bien non. (*Dit Rose*, v. 613–18)
>
> [Loving ladies who desire everything good; I mean love that harbors no vice, evil, villainy, or malice. For, whether one believes it or not, there is only good in good love.]

The *Roman de la rose*'s illustration of lovemaking contrasts with the *amor purus* Christine extols in these lines. Not, of course, the dubious *amor purus* Andreas Capellanus recommends, where lovers bed down in the nude but avoid sexual intercourse (*De amore*, p. 212).[6] Christine's ideal lovers eschew sexual intercourse. She names some such lovers, notably, Bertrand Du Guesclin and Jean de Werchin, seneschal of Hainaut (*Débat*, p. 129:464–67).[7] Moreover, she upholds this view in the three poems composed during the time the *Rose* debate was also occupying her. Her chivalric love is platonic; it leads to moral excellence, valor, and fame (*Dit Rose*, v. 2–8, 215–17, 309–10).[8] It is not deceptive, a point she stresses in the *Epistre au dieu d'amours* (v. 67–90). Such love is also distinct from lust, or the *luxure* she condemns among knights in the *Chemin de long estude* (v. 4368–74, 5523–46).[9]

This is the kind of love the Duke aspires to in the *Duc des vrais amants*. In this poem, the lovers embrace and kiss, but are fully clothed; they always rendezvous with a witness. There is no suggestion that their love is ever consummated. This is the kind of love Christine admired in Du Guesclin. But

---

[6] See Monson 2005, especially pp. 305–14.

[7] Hicks, ed., *Débat*, pp. 224–25 ns. 129/465; Willard 1990b. Christine names other chivalric lovers in the *Epistre Dieu*, v. 223–58; the *Deux amants*, v. 1560–1704 (the latter again includes Du Guesclin, v. 1569–85); *Trois jugemens*, v. 6–10; *Poissy*, v. 2070–75. She addresses the *Dit de la rose* to noble, chivalric lovers and to honorable *damoiselles* who are loved (v. 1–12, 613–18). Their love 'conduit / Ceulz qui du bien faire sont duit' (v. 309–10) [guides those who have learned good conduct]. On Christine's rewriting of the *Rose* in these early works, see Brownlee 1992.

[8] Perhaps Christine had in mind the ideal kind of love that Machaut extols in some of his poems, most notably the *Remede de Fortune*. In particular, Machaut's adaptation of Boethius's notion of virtue to virtuous love may have especially appealed to her (see Kelly 1978, ch. 6). Like Machaut's lover, the princess in the *Duc* wants 'souffisance' in love (p. 142:21). Such love anticipates the two kinds of chivalry evoked in *Othea*, a distinction Tuve links to that between heavenly and terrestrial chivalry in the *Queste del saint graal* (Tuve 1966, pp. 51–55); there are some such loves in the Prose *Lancelot* (Hahn 1988, pp. 136–43). Thomas Aquinas too distinguishes between *amor amicitiae* and *amor concupiscentiae* (De Gendt 1999, p. 192; cf. Schnell 1985, pp. 54–57). Cf. Christine's *Enseignemens*, 80.

[9] On chivalric *luxure*, see as well *Policie*, pp. 35, 50–51, 80–81, 107–08.

by the time she wrote the *Duc des vrais amants*, Christine's opinion on such love had radically changed. The Duke's love does not make him a better knight; suspicions of betrayal are quickened in both partners as time passes; life drags on and love becomes a tale of misery. As Sebile de Monthault warns the Duke's beloved in words that contradict Christine's views on Du Guesclin's love as depicted in the *Rose* debate,

> ne vous fiez es vaines pensees que plusieurs joennes femmes ont qui se donnent a croire que ce n'est point de mal d'amer par amours, mais qu'il n'y ait villenie ...[10], et que on en vit plus liement, et que de ce faire on fait un homme devenir vaillant et renommé a tousjours mais. Ha! ma chiere dame, il va tout autrement! (*Duc*, p. 173:74–80)
>
> [don't trust the vain ideas of some young women who fall into the error of thinking that there is no wrong in a courtly love, provided it is free of baseness ..., and that it makes for a happier life while making the man valiant and renowned forever more. Ah! My dear lady, things turn out quite differently!]

The Duke in this Dit is no Du Guesclin, although he tries to be one. It is impossible to be such a lover because, for Christine at the time she wrote the *Duc des vrais amants*, 'l'amour est un état aliénant'.[11] Perhaps this radical change of opinion explains the absence of the *Dit de la rose* in her collected works after 1402. Its defense of good love as a source of chivalric valor is incompatible with Sebile de Monthault's categorical rejection of such love.[12]

How did Christine come to this radical change of opinion?

Signs of change appear in her early counsel on the good life in the *Epistre Othea* and the *Enseignemens moraux*. In the former treatise, Christine condemns sexual intercourse outside marriage because it leads to infidelity, as with Briseida (*Othea*, 84; see also 7, 58). Although sincere love may be possible (*Othea*, 47), she prefers abstinence (43:21–30, 56, 58). These opinions are not incompatible with the kind of love Christine admired in Du Guesclin. Yet the dangers of even such ideal love are real, requiring constant care and vigilance on the lovers' part. These concerns finally outweigh any advantages in good love. Discovery leads to shame or mockery (*Othea*, 56); silence becomes obligatory (62), leaving the pair prey to suspicions and grief. Rather than inspiring prowess, love may actually produce *recreantise* (*Othea*, 73). 'Make love, not war' was not Christine's motto (see *Othea*, 75). Analogous views are

---

[10] Christine's euphemism for sexual intercourse in the *Duc*; see v. 2742–47, p. 182:7–8, v. 3326–27 (cf. 'oultrage', v. 2202); as well as in the *Cité*, p. 332, and the *Trois vertus*, p. 113:87. Cf. *Epistre Dieu*, v. 75.

[11] Dulac 1973, p. 227; see in general pp. 227–28.

[12] Willard 1981a; Laidlaw 1986, p. 56; Fenster, ed., *Epistre Dieu*, pp. 17–18, 21. The *Epistre au dieu d'amour* survives in all but one of Christine's manuscripts; however, its case against misogyny is compatible with the *Cité des dames* whereas the *Dit de la rose*'s encomium of noble love is not compatible with Sebile de Monthault's invective.

expressed in the *Enseignemens* she wrote for her son, Jean de Castel (*Enseignemens*, 44, 47, 76, 80). Besides warning him against misogynist speech (*Enseignemens*, 38, 77), her counsels also focus on marriage and the choice of a wife (51, 55, 91, 94); in *Othea*, 20, she recommends that the choice of a life's partner should be suitable in rank and status.[13]

In the *Duc des vrais amants*, what I shall designate as 'Du Guesclin love' does not bring happiness, nor does it make the Duke a better knight. One can never know what is transpiring in another person, even a loved one, nor can one ever be sure of the longevity or the constancy of amorous feelings, no matter how sincere they may have been at first. To be sure, the *Epistre Othea* puts matters in a more positive light.

> Nous devons par especial eschever: jugement sus autrui, premierement car nous ne savons de quel courage sont les choses faites, lesquelles condampner c'est grant presomcion, si le devons interpreter en la meilleure partie; secondement car nous ne sommes pas certains quieulx seront ceulx qui a present sont bons ou mauvais. (*Othea*, 73:47–53)
>
> [We must especially eschew judging others, first, because we don't know what feelings motivate actions that it is presumptuous to condemn arbitrarily; we should rather interpret positively; and second, because we are unsure what kind of persons they will be who are now good or bad.]

But in love it is dangerous to look on the bright side. Lurking beneath these admonitions to refrain from judging by appearances is the threat that appearances may, in fact, not deceive and that something improper is indeed going on. Uncertainty gives rise to gossip, doubts, lovers' quarrels and, finally, end-of-love stories such as those Christine relates in the *Duc des vrais amants*, the *Dit de la pastoure*, and the *Cent Ballades d'amant et de dame*. The mutability of love and lovers, both men and women,[14] brings Christine from her conception of a good, Du Guesclin kind of love in the *Rose* debate to the emphatic condemnation of all extramarital loves that she puts in the mouth of Sebile de Monthault, a condemnation she reinforces by copying it into the *Trois vertus*. Regardless of the sincerity of the lovers, the real world is inhabited by Jasons and Briseidas. In love, nothing is sure; there is only instability, and honor is at stake.

---

[13] These views anticipate the problem of the lovers' widely different social status in the *Dit de la pastoure*. See too *Débat*, p. 129:449–55, where Christine opposes such unequal relationships.

[14] Examples appear in her early poems. For example, the man who leaves a beloved *damoiselle* for a more noble *dame* in the *Trois jugemens*, and the initially receptive lady in the *Dit de Poissy* who abruptly rebuffs a man when he declares his love.

Extramarital love in Christine's early poems

Christine wrote favorably about chivalric love, notably in her praise of Du Guesclin's chivalric love in the *Rose* debate and in other works written around 1400, such as the *Epistre au dieu d'amours*, the *Dit de la rose*, some debate poems, and some early lyrics. As Joël Blanchard remarks on the *Pastoure*,

> le texte donne à voir une dernière fois l'image qui cristallise ce que fut un temps le fantasme de la bergère, et peut-être aussi celui de Christine, celle d'une courtoisie régénérée. Image déjà éteinte, isolée dans cette fin de texte et qui évoque irrésistiblement la fin du fantasme, l'épuisement du désir, le dernier éclat qu'il a donné à voir.[15]

Christine's early lyrics illustrate that 'fantasy', revealing by contrast the change in her opinion on ideal love that culminates in the words of Sebile de Monthault and the shepherdess Lorete.[16] Two of her early examples deserve special attention: a young, apparently unmarried damsel ('damoisele')[17] in Christine's first lyric cycle, the *Cent Ballades*, and the poems on her own love, including her marriage and widowhood, in the ballades that precede the damsel's cycle and in Book One of the *Mutacion de Fortune*.

The *Cent Ballades* is not a continuous narrative like some of Christine's Dits or the *Cent Ballades d'amant et de dame*. Yet many have noticed incipient narrative sequences in this and other collections of ballades and rondeaux she wrote.[18] Kenneth Varty grouped some of them on this principle in his anthology of Christine's lyrics as 'A Woman's Story' and 'A Man's Story'.[19] They are, as it were, excerpts from a variety of interlaced stories, where the change of voice is obvious to the attentive reader perceiving that now a man, now a woman is speaking, or that a 'Christine voice' has thrust itself into a sequence; sometimes an anonymous Dame speaks, at other times a Damoiselle. Now, the commonplace *gradus amoris* motif always permitted the attentive audience of medieval courtly love lyric not only to locate which stage in that scheme the poem represents – sight, speech, touch, and so on – but also how the poet amplifies a given topical stage or 'place' in a specific poem.[20] In the *Cent Ballades*, the section following the midpoint (*CB*, 50–90) represents a display case of diverse love situations variously fitted into the *gradus amoris* scheme; all these poems illustrate common places in the topical scheme of the

---

[15] Blanchard 1983, p. 116.

[16] Willard 1987. Their voices silence the positive recommendation of such love by the lady who, at the approximate midpoint of the *Deux amants*, evokes a middle ground between dark despair and youthful optimism.

[17] See *CB* 41, v. 17–18, and 42, v. 21.

[18] Willard 1987 refers to ballades 21–43 and 87; see also Laidlaw 1998a, p. 63, and 2004, pp. 38–39, 43–44. For other examples, see Laidlaw 1998b, pp. 122–25.

[19] *Anthology*, pp. 11–42.

[20] Laidlaw 1998a, pp. 68–69.

commonplace *gradus amoris*, each poem articulating a particular version of the distinct common places or stages it exemplifies. This is not new. Beginning with the earliest troubadours and *trouvères*, audiences could recognize and evaluate subtleties in form and content like those Christine articulates in the *Cent Ballades*.[21] Laidlaw has described such audiences for Christine as follows:

> The audience to which Christine de Pizan's *Cent balades* were addressed understood the ballade form and appreciated the subtleties of which it was capable. Experience had attuned their ears; to coin a phrase, they were well versed. Their knowledge of poetic practice would enable them to distinguish – more readily than a modern reader can – those poems that conformed to standard patterns and those that showed some degree of innovation or virtuosity. They were, moreover, aware of the recent changes in poetic practice and fashion.[22]

One such change was the gradual emergence of lyric sequences or cycles of lyrics recounting all or part of a 'story'.[23] Christine's elaboration of complete and incomplete narrative cycles is, then, congruent with her adaptation of the so-called fixed forms after their liberation from musical or melodic patterns.[24] Both Dits and romances inserted lyrics in order to amplify on the narrative potential of lyrics that were written well before the Dits or other narratives into which they were inserted or, more accurately perhaps, around which the narrative was wrapped.[25] One might even conjecture that Christine's changing opinion on the possibility of ideal love led her to the single narrative sequence where, in her opinion, only one denouement was possible: the literal or figurative death of the loved one and of the love itself.[26]

---

[21] Kelly 2000; cf. Pickens 2000, pp. 218–19.
[22] Laidlaw 1998a, p. 62.
[23] Kelly 1978, pp. 5–6; Hauck 1995.
[24] Cf. Altmann 1996.
[25] Kelly 1999a, pp. 222–24; for an example, see Kelly 1978, pp. 212–18, on René d'Anjou's *Cuers d'amours espris*.
[26] Cf. Adams 2002. On death as a motif in the *gradus* or *finis amoris*, see Kelly 1978, ch. 8; Ribémont 1991; Cerquiglini 1993b, pp. 55–56. The survivor's grief may be, as it were, short-lived; the narrator in Chartier's *Livre des quatre dames* stops grieving when a new love begins (Laidlaw, ed., *Chartier Works*, p. 33). But the apo koinu principle remains intact in the *Belle dame sans merci* and for the first woman in the *Livre des quatre dames*, since we do not learn for certain whether or not the lovers died, although in the case of the *Belle dame sans merci*, Chartier wants us to believe it possible; see v. 781–84 in *Chartier Works*, p. 359. It is taken for granted by Baudet Herenc, *Accusations against the Belle Dame sans mercy*, v. 157–60, in *Quarrel*. This colors variously the deaths at the end of Christine's poems – the death of love implied by the real or metaphorical death of the lover as the end of love. The *Belle dame* also influenced an original adaptation of the Narcissus story in a late medieval *Narcisus*; see v. 571–80, 1268–69, and Van Gijsen 1998, pp. 165–71. *Narcisus*, v. 808–19, suggests that Echo is punished because she had rejected *sans mercy* a good love prior to meeting Narcissus.

Apart from the *Dit de la pastoure*, the affairs Christine relates involve very noble women, identified as damsels, ladies, or even princesses. Perhaps this is in part because of her choice of patrons.[27] The role of hierarchy is nonetheless similar to that in the *Trois vertus* and the *Cité*, where the princess is the principal exemplar because her conduct was expected to be more upright than that of women of lower social status. *Noblesse oblige* (see *CB*, 96). Interestingly in this respect, the woman of the first ballade cycle in the *Cent Ballades* seems to be unmarried. She is never referred to as a *dame*.

Two ballades suggest that she is a *damoiselle*. The title *damoiselle* first appears when she begins to suspect that her lover has fallen in love with another: 'il n'est damoiselle / Ne nulle autre, ce sçay certainement, / Qui jamais jour l'aime plus loiaument' (*CB*, 41, v. 17–19) [there is no damsel nor any other woman, I know for sure, who will ever love him more constantly]. *CB* 42 is even more explicit. In a dream, Morpheus 'trop me desconforte / Quant il me dit qu'une autre damoiselle / Tient mon ami' (v. 20–22) [greatly distresses me when he tells me that another damoiselle holds my beloved]. If the dream is true – and it is certainly a possibility in the fictional world Christine portrays – then the circumstances attendant on an adulterous love must be modified to fit an unmarried noblewoman's affair. In *CB* 46 she considers a new love after her former lover has proven unfaithful. Although in *CB* 48 she swears off all love, in *CB* 49 a suitor appears despite her rejection of love. Will a new *gradus amoris* cycle begin? The narrative line follows that for the other cycles and the Dits – it is a conventional *gradus amoris* followed by a *deminutio* including separation, decline, suspicion, and termination. However, in the case of the unwed damsel of Christine's *Cent Ballades*, the 'mortal' denouements that play on the love–death commonplace of traditional courtly lyric are missing. Being unmarried seems to offer a return to life. Of course, at the time Christine was writing the *Cent Ballades*, she was still promoting 'pure love' like that she attributes to Du Guesclin in the *Rose* debate. However that may be, the maiden's freedom in the *Cent Ballades* will be firmly suppressed in the *Livre des trois vertus*.

This is a crux in interpretation of Christine's opinion. Her fixed-form cycles, like those by many other contemporary authors, have in the past been viewed as a combination of brief, coherent sequences interrupted or terminated by different subjects. This is apparent in the topical variety of *CB* 51–89. More recently, however, some scholars have offered a different perspective by pointing out larger or broader, albeit 'fluid', coherence in the arrangement of the *Cent Ballades*.[28] They identify two major narrative cycles in the first half of the collection, the one devoted to Christine's grief because of her husband's death, and the other to the woman's affair and its unhappy ending discussed above. This first half ends at *CB* 50, a midpoint at which Christine restates the

---

[27] Poirion 1965, pp. 245–46.
[28] Willard 1981d, pp. 169–73; Laidlaw 1994; Altmann 1995; Laidlaw 1998a.

disclaimer in *CB* 1: she as author neither shares nor seeks to share the feelings she writes about. In her case, no new love is possible. 'Je chante par couverture' (*V* 1, v. 1) she assures us elsewhere (*V* 15; *R* 7, v. 8–9; cf. *R* 11); this becomes a leitmotif in her later Dits opposing such love.[29]

Other features open the *Cent Ballades* to yet another reading that enriches our appreciation of the work, but does not require our favoring one interpretation over the other. First, as we have seen, there is no evidence that the women speaking in the narrative sequence following the poems on Christine's marriage and widowhood is a lady, or *dame*, and therefore married.[30] Furthermore, we might ask if Christine's denial of amorous involvement was meant to include the poems of grief about her widowhood. To be sure, this is a possible interpretation of their content. But it is also possible to read these poems in, as it were, *ordo artificialis*: the account of a love that ended not through inconstancy, infidelity, or indifference, but because of the lover's death – in Christine's case, the death of her husband. A lover's threatened, impending, or actual death was commonplace in amorous poetry by troubadours and romancers. Yet, as the Belle Dame sans mercy opines,

> Si gracïeuse maladie
> Ne met gaires de gens a mort,
> Mais il siet bien que l'on le die
> Pour plus tost actraire confort.   (*Chartier Works*, v. 265–68)[31]
>
> [Such a gentle malady is rarely mortal, but it behooves one to say so in order to bring comfort.]

The death of a beloved became a more credible commonplace during the Hundred Years War and at the time that Christine was writing. After the disastrous defeat at Nicopolis in 1396, Christine evoked imprisonment and death in the *Dit de Poissy*. Death is a factor not only in the courtly love register of the *Dit de Poissy* and Chartier's poems; it emerges outside the courtly register of her love poems, as in consolatory writings such as the *Epistre de la Prison de vie humaine*.

In the *Belle dame sans mercy* Chartier leaves open the possibility that the disconsolate lover did indeed die (v. 783–84). The narrator in his *Livre des quatre dames* announces that his own first love died, as happened to one of the four ladies. But he overcame his grief and found a new love. He advises all

---

[29] The boundary between poetic play and underlying seriousness is a major feature of Christine's lyric poetry; see the illuminating discussion of this aspect of poetics in Johnson 1990, ch. 2.

[30] This contrasts with the voice after *CB* 50, described as that of a Dame (*CB* 51, v. 3). A *damoiselle* also figures in the third 'case' in the *Trois jugemens* (v. 1278–79); her lover forsakes her for a more noble *dame* (v. 1331).

[31] Critics seem more convinced of the woman's death after the 'lay mortel' that closes the *Cent Ballades d'amant et de dame*.

four ladies to seek comfort in hope, all of which suggests a period of grief followed by a return to a new life and, perhaps, a new love like that which opened to the damsel of the *Cent Ballades*.[32] Written in the wake of Agincourt, Chartier underscored the four causes arising from that battle: death, imprisonment, missing in action, and cowardly flight. Similarly, the *Cent Ballades* was being written when the battle of Nicopolis occurred. That great French disaster was certainly on readers' minds who recalled experiences similar to those in the *Quatre dames*. Christine further evokes these battles in other collections.[33] Yet, the *Cent Ballades' damoiselle* might recover from such grief, a factor suggesting the work's cyclicity referred to above. Those who would deny the distinction between *dame* and *damoiselle* that divides the sequence before *CB* 50 and after could still envisage a woman whose first lover died. But if the second lover proved unfaithful or inconstant, she could have married and then discovered a new love. Why not? Chartier says he acquired a new love in the *Livre des quatre dames*. And, like Chartier, Christine, and the courtly tradition, knew that love changes and that new loves are not impossible.

In the last ten poems of the *Cent Ballades*, Christine turns away not only from love poetry but also from her widowhood and sorrow. This last sequence opens with a 'balade poetique' that seems to rewrite Jean de Meun's example of Venus and Adonis.[34] However, in Christine's poem Adonis is not dead, as in the *Rose*, but only threatened by Mars, the god of war and Venus's other lover. Juno, the goddess of marriage, can save him, not Venus.[35] Christine had been reading Boethius and Aristotle. Boethius taught her that Nature is more powerful than Fortune (*CB* 97). Christine has also learned from Aristotle that the sound mind, granted by Nature, can overcome Fortune. What is such a mind?

> C'est sens et discrecion
> Entendement, consideracion,
> Aristote moult apreuve memoire.   (*CB* 97, v. 21–23)[36]
>
> [It is sense and discretion, understanding, consideration;
> Aristotle very much prizes memory.]

---

[32] The problem of a new love is evident in Christine's *Trois jugemens* and in other such debates (Hauck 1995, p. 244). Once again we find confirmation of lessons taught in Andreas Capellanus (*De amore*, rule 7), suggesting that, for all the satire or irony modern readers have discerned in this treatise, the satire and irony played on a certain reality. Change is also the central issue in the *Trois jugemens*; see Becker 1967, p. 523. On Christine's possible influence on Chartier, see Willard 1981d, p. 178, and 1981e, pp. 84–86.

[33] Becker, 1967, p. 521; Blumenfeld-Kosinski 2002a, 2002b.

[34] See also Laidlaw 2004, pp. 51–53. On this fable in the *Roman de la rose*, see Kelly 1995a, pp. 79–80.

[35] Note her opposition to Jupiter's affairs in *CB* 61, where a 'cow' appears as the unmarried woman.

[36] Roy, ed., *CB*, p. 300, cites Aristotle's *Metaphysics* as source.

Christine is beginning to define the intellectual virtues she describes in the *Mutacion*. In *CB* 98, she lauds 'desir de savoir' (v. 1), Opinion's father in the *Advision*. *CB* 99 grounds her philosophy in faith – 'Si comme il est raison que chescun croie / En un seul Dieu, sanz faire aucune doubte' (v. 1–2) [Just as it is reasonable that everyone believe in only one God, without any doubt] – and her hope for a blissful afterlife.[37] We see here beginning to form the lineaments of the personification Philosophy–Theology in the *Advision*'s Part Three, the personification that corrects the despair and suicidal urges she recalls at the beginning of the *Cent Ballades*[38] and which prepares for the discovery announced in the *Advision* that her good husband was a false good. In the context of her love poems, a good lover is *a fortiori* a false good. The widow Christine refuses to love or marry another man.

Rewriting love

Christine attacks what she deems Jean de Meun's laudation of carnal love (*Débat*, pp. 129:470–130:476) because he failed to show fully what love is and can be. Obviously, the *Rose*'s love, on the surface at least, is vulgar, carnal, and licentious. Correcting the *Roman de la rose* means altering what in Christine's opinion is disreputable in the poem. By correcting she rewrites earlier paradigms in such a way as to replace or supersede them.[39] Christine chooses that option when she describes conjugal love and chivalric love.[40] The latter sort is the love she exemplifies in historical figures like Du Guesclin, Jean de Werchin, and the other honorable lovers she extols in her early poems. In this way, she shows how Jean could have been less one-sided in his presentation of the *gradus amoris*.

But Christine goes even further. First, she distinguishes herself at the outset of all her love poems from the lovers she writes about. Christine will have

---

[37] Christine ends other fixed-form cycles in this way; see *R* 69; *V* 16.

[38] *CB* 5, 6, 8, v. 8–11, 9, 17, v. 12–14; *R* 1, v. 6, 4, v. 3–4 and 11, 7, v. 5–6. In the *Mutacion*, she recalls thoughts of suicide when she learned of her husband's death (v. 1240, 1251–64). Cf. Christine's reference to Hero's suicide after learning of Leander's death 'at sea' in *CB* 3, v. 17–20. Chartier describes a similar movement from suicidal urges to faith in the *Livre de l'espérance*.

[39] Jean himself rewrites Guillaume's version by directing Guillaume de Lorris's poem into a different moral context. For her part, Christine rejects this distinction on the grounds that the two parts are of one piece (*Débat*, p. 141:840–42), but Gerson does not share her opinion (*Débat*, pp. 85:659–86:669); see Kelly 1995a, pp. 32–36.

[40] Stäblein-Harris 1992 suggests how recycling the *Rose*'s vocabulary can alert informed audiences of the changes Christine makes. Others corrected by glossing; for example, Jean Molinet glosses the *Rose* in prose using the antiphrasis that Christine recognized as the way of reading the *Rose* (*Cité*, p. 48). See Tuve 1966, especially pp. 237–84, for a critical assessment of Molinet's imposed allegory; Badel 1980, pp. 122 n. 15, 440–41.

none of this; they relate feelings she neither shares nor approves of.[41] When she writes love poetry, whether in her Dits or in the fixed-form anthologies, Christine proclaims that she does not write *de sentement*, which implies both that she does not love and that she does not share the experiences of the women she writes about. In her earliest collection, the *Cent Ballades*, Christine attributes this to her mourning as widow: 'je n'ay pas sentement ne espace / De faire diz de soulas ne de joye' (*CB* 1, v. 9–10) [I have neither feeling nor time to write poems of solace or joy]. Later, she likens her *Cent Ballades* to the false muses Philosophy rejects (*Advision*, III.vii.13–24).

Does she contradict herself in the last ballade in this cycle? To be sure, she claims that 'Cent balades ay cy escriptes, / Trestoutes de mon sentement' (*CB* 100, v. 1–2) [I have written here a hundred ballades, all of which express my feelings]. I suspect, however, that she does so in the context of the grief expressed in *CB* 17, v. 1–2: 'Se de douloureux sentement / Sont tous mes dis, n'est pas merveille' [if all my poems express grief, it's no wonder]. Christine has no desire to love again (*CB* 19, v. 7–8). No solace or joy tempts her; her feelings ('sentement') are dulled ('arudi') (*CB* 19, v. 19–20). Therefore her love poems express 'd'autrui sentement' (*Duc*, v. 7).[42]

This is a radical departure from a medieval commonplace. Narrators and lyric poets traditionally claim that they write *de sentement*. Indeed, as Machaut puts it, 'Qui de sentement ne fait, / Son ouevre et son chant contrefait' (*Remede*, v. 407–08) [who does not write with feeling fails to compose a good poem or song].[43] Froissart too illustrates the importance of *sentement* in love poetry.[44] When Christine claimed that she did not write *de sentement*, the innovation was surely striking. Yet if the sincerity of her poems as expression of love is lost, she gains by having the power to consider and evaluate with discretion different versions of the *gradus amoris* and its common places. In this way, she gives *sentement* its broader meaning of experience from which one learns. This is the experience of most of the lovers in her love poetry, and it is a sobering experience from which others learn a lesson quite different from that taught by diverse personifications in the *Rose* or even Christine's own poems up to about 1402. Christine as widow not only rejects a new love in her own life, she argues against it in any relationship other than conjugal. Her last love was for her husband, and, as a widow, she remained as true to him as a turtledove (*CB* 14, v. 15–16; *R* 1).

---

[41] Guillaume de Lorris's prologue identifies the *Rose*'s author with the lover in the dream (*Rose*, v. 21–44). Jean names Guillaume in his continuation in a virtual obituary (v. 10496–534), and then introduces himself as Love's servant (v. 10535–44).

[42] Cf. *CB* 50; *CBAD*, v. 1–8. Cf. Paupert 1993; Hauck 1995. Her denial does not preclude drawing on her own experience when she evokes moments of happiness while married or the widow's grief, a grief because of a love-death; see Johnson 1990, p. 96.

[43] Kelly 1978, pp. 245–48; Cerquiglini 1985, pp. 195–97.

[44] Schwarze 2003, ch. 2.

The second innovation that Christine introduces besides not writing *de sentement* is her adaptation of Jean de Meun using the epideictic and invective modes. The former, adumbrated in her criticism of the *Rose*, extols chivalric love. But the *Dit de la rose* is her last work to do so. Thereafter, she rejects even this kind of love by showing the disastrous results of all extra- and premarital love. This is a correction of the more conventional lovers illustrated in the *Cent Ballades* and the *Dit de la rose*. Christine's subsequent love poems go beyond the *gradus amoris* that portrays a happy end to tell what happens after the sequence climaxes.[45] That is, she records a *continuatio amoris* and, indeed, a decline (*deminutio*) and virtual death (*finis*) of love[46] that almost always went unreported in earlier poetry.

Charles V as antiphrasis of the *Rose*'s lover

As we observed in Chapter 2, youth is a hot-blooded, impetuous stage in life. Youth is a stage, moreover, in the commonplace *gradus aetatum* or ages of life script. Christine's laudatory description of the young Charles V recalls her criticism of Jean de Meun's depiction of such a youth and of his failure to show by positive examples what good love is and can be. The king's youth is also Christine's first criticism of the virtuous love she had earlier idealized in Du Guesclin. In her view, we recall, Jean de Meun praises a foolish lover worthy only of vituperation, all the while treating his actions as if they are exemplary and laudatory. To promote good love, one praises virtue. Christine makes Charles V the exemplar of such virtue in love, although not the kind of love illustrated by Du Guesclin. Therefore, Charles V's youth is also Christine's first implicit criticism of the virtuous love she had earlier idealized in Charles's High Constable.

Christine recognizes a natural sequence in the ages of human life. She names six ages after Charles V's birth: infancy (*enfance*), adolescence (*adolescence*), youth (*jeunece*), prime of life (*homme parfait*), maturity (*meureté*), and old age (*envieillis*) (*Charles V*, vol. 1, pp. 32–36).[47] Recalling the language she uses with respect to the virtues in the *Mutacion*, Christine writes that in the prime of life humans realize best the faculties Nature bestows on them. In fully realized maturity this occurs in the fiftieth year when

> cellui, qui est de sain et sage entendement, a soy a ja recueilli les vertus du sentement de clere cognoiscence des choses, qui savables lui pevent estre. Or est temps d'en user par l'admenistracion de raison; or sont faillies les

---

[45] Of course, Jean's examples of lovers foreshadow the same grievous continuation for his dream lovers (Kelly 1995a, pp. 88–89). Cf. Hauck 1995.

[46] Language borrowed from Andreas Capellanus's *De amore*.

[47] Zühlke 1994, pp. 30–31. The king's *gradus aetatum* is cut short when he is forty-four so that he did not actually reach maturity or old age (*Advision*, III.v.7–9).

impetueuses chaleurs, que jeunece souloit procurer, et les superflues voluptez, qui empeschent la liberté des sens. (*Charles V*, vol. 1, p. 33)

[the person of sane and prudent understanding has already gathered in the fruits of experience through clear knowledge of things insofar as he or she can know them. This is the time to use them under Reason's guidance. Now the impetuous fires that Youth stoked have died out, as have the idle passions that are an impediment to the freedom of the senses.]

Such mature persons are both astonished at and grateful for having escaped the perils of youth.[48] The experience acquired in childhood and youth blossoms as prudence, or that discretion that can guide the individual in confronting life's tasks and obstacles.

As a young man, Charles offers Christine the opportunity to amplify on this age and her opinion of the young king's exemplary illustration of it (*Charles V*, vol. 1, pp. 22–36). This amplification offers numerous parallels and contrasts with *gradus amoris* such as those that Jean de Meun describes in the *Roman de la rose*. Christine's treatment of the topoi that make up this script, however, colors them differently in conformity with her opinion as to how the thirteenth-century romance should have been written. Charles V's coronation while he was still a young man motivates Christine's digression on the stage of youth in his *gradus aetatum* (*Charles V*, vol. 1, pp. 23–36). By removing the one-sidedness of Jean's satire, Christine complements the *Rose*'s description of vice-ridden love with an exemplary picture of how one young man passed through this highly charged period in his maturation.[49] Christine corrects Jean de Meun by exemplifying high-born, royal and aristocratic nobility whose lives, as she maintains in the *Trois vertus*, should be models of moral conduct for all their subjects (*Charles V*, vol. 1, pp. 27–28).[50] As prince and then king, Charles V is a model, even in his youth, because he was a virtuous lover. The 'assemblement de jeunece, oisiveté et poissance ensemble' (*Charles V*, vol. 1, p. 27) [combination of youth, idleness, and potency] is all-consuming. Yet the young Charles resisted those debilitating forces on his own rational initiative, which made him praiseworthy and exemplary in Christine's eyes.

Christine evokes the Boethian metaphor of mild and harsh medicine to direct the young person on the right way, allowing, as in Charles's life, 'verdeur de jeunece' to progress towards 'meureté raisonnable' (*Charles V*, vol. 1, p. 30) [green youth ... reasonable maturity]. The, as it were, *vert galant* Prince Hal becomes the wise king, happy to have escaped the perils of youth. Christine's description of the young Charles, modeled on, but a correction of, the *Roman*

---

[48] This idea from Cicero's *De senectute* is also found in Reason's argument in the *Rose*, v. 4467–76. Christine again refers to Charles's virtuous youth in the *Advision*, I.xi.5–8, and *Paix*, p. 74.

[49] See *Prouverbes*, 55. Cf. Mühlethaler 2002, pp. 594–96. On the same age in *Trois vertus*, see Pratt 2002a, pp. 678–80.

[50] See above, pp. 92–93.

de la rose, is a 'gros exemple' (*Charles V*, vol. 1, p. 30) [rough illustration]⁵¹ that reconfigures the image of youth in Jean de Meun so as to make the young man conform to social and moral standards that, in Christine's opinion, ought to prevail. As a counter-example of Fol Amoureux in the *Roman de la rose*, the king is noble and listens to reason; by contrast, Jean's lover has only *vilenie* on his mind.⁵² Charles V is, therefore, an exception to the norm; he is a *puer senex* 'qui meismes en tres jeune aage volt cognoistre les effetz de vertu' (*Charles V*, vol. 1, p. 35)⁵³ [who even in his early youth wished to learn how virtue acts].

Christine goes on to contrast the young king's virtuous inclinations with what we shall call the *vetulus insipiens* who regrets the loss of his youthful desires and potency (*Charles V*, vol. 1, pp. 35–36). This male variety of Jean de Meun's Vieille is prone to misogyny.⁵⁴ Gender is not an issue here, though, since both the *Vetulus* and the Vieille (or *Vetula*) express analogous complaints: the former regrets his loss of potency, the latter the loss of her physical charms. In *Charles V*, the recurrent feminine gender of abstract nouns reinforces the analogy between Christine's *Vetulus* and Jean's Vieille.⁵⁵ Youth is a time of emotional chaos that Reason alone can treat (*Charles V*, vol. 1, pp. 24–25). The 'mouvemens', 'passions', and 'operacions diverses' typical of youth incline the young person to sensuality, which in turn drives him or her towards other, associated vices and away from rational conduct (*Charles V*, vol. 1, p. 22). This 'voye d'oiseuse' seems to lead to a veritable paradise when one is young (p. 25).⁵⁶ Such idle opinions are, however, 'volontaires au contraire de raison'⁵⁷ and 'foles' [willingly oppose reason ... foolish] because they incite to 'foles amours' [foolish love], waste, and, ultimately, a 'vieillece sousfraiteuse' (pp. 25–26) [destitute old age]. The topical outline for foolish love found in the *Roman de la rose* is evident in this argument, but the mode is unambiguously critical. Christine's invective is neither farce nor satire⁵⁸ (the two most common ways

---

⁵¹ On this term for moral illustration, see Meyenberg 1992, pp. 148–49 n. 30; Kelly 1995a, pp. 18–19.

⁵² Cf. the *Dit de la rose* on honorable and villainous nobility (v. 315–98).

⁵³ 'Jeune' seems to refer to Charles's age after his adolescence when he did not manifest such virtuous inclinations; but this is a feature of the young man's life Christine declines to relate in her panegyric biography (*Charles V*, vol. 1, p. 17). She again refers to this change in Charles's character in the *Advision*, I.xi.7–8, and *Paix*, p. 68; cf. Lemaire 1994, p. 91.

⁵⁴ *Cité*, p. 70. Cf. Zühlke 1994, pp. 197–98; Forhan 2002, p. 97.

⁵⁵ Cf. Fenster, ed., *Epistre Dieu*, pp. 17–18.

⁵⁶ This is the burden of Genius's sermon on paradise in the *Rose*. On the scope of such real and misogynist 'idleness' in late medieval opinion, see Vincent-Cassy 1992.

⁵⁷ Cf. this sense of *volontaire* in the *Débat*, p. 84:626–38 (Gerson).

⁵⁸ Christine is following a *gradus amoris* analogous to that in the *Rose*, albeit her moral condemnation in *Charles V* is not through satire but through corrective rewriting. Note as well that she 'feminizes' men like Fol Amoureux, reminding her readers that people generally 'dient que ce ne sont que commeres' (*Charles V*, vol. 1, p. 26) [call these men no better than *commeres*]; Solente translates the word as 'hommes efféminés' (vol. 1, p. 26 n. 1; cf. Blanchard and Quereuil 1999, p. 80; *Robert*, p. 454; Rossiaud 1986, pp. 163–64). Given some of the

the *Roman de la rose* has been read as a moral poem[59]), but moral admonition through exemplification.

Aging for the *Rose*'s Vieille and for Christine

Christine's rejection of love after her husband's death allowed her to contrast herself with Jean's Vieille in the same way she contrasted Charles V and the *Rose*'s Fol Amoureux. The contrast intersects with the analogy referred to above between her *vetulus insipiens* and Jean's Vieille. These oppositions and analogies underscore moral principles in Christine's thought founded on rational guidance while conforming to the method of arriving at true opinion she sets out in the *Advision*. True opinion on moral issues is based on religious teachings, reason, and experience. The social consequences of failure to live by such moral standards derive from false opinions.

Before going on to see how Christine deals with these issues, alternately considering men and women, we may first take a look at the similarities and differences between the fate of Christine the widow and that of the Vieille when her youth faded and her lover abandoned her. After ten years of a good marriage, Christine's husband Etienne de Castel died unexpectedly, leaving his wife to confront the severe trials of widowhood while maintaining their family on her own. The moment of loss is set forth in the shipwreck image and the allegorical gender change in Book One of the *Mutacion*;[60] the tribulations of her widowhood are detailed in Book Three of the *Advision* and a number of lyric poems. Like Christine the wife, the young Vieille is fortunate for a time. But her preferred lover, a *ribaud*, does not marry her. Rather he lives off her earnings from prostitution and pilfering until finally leaving her in old age to live in squalor (*Rose*, v. 14441–507).

Christine reports in the *Advision* that she was accused of having taken a lover after her husband's death, an accusation that, if true, would have aligned her with the Vieille. She emphatically denies the claim (*Advision*, III.vi.138–45).[61]

---

pejorative connotations of *commeres* (as, for example, in the *Quinze joies de mariage*), might one not translate the word as 'busybody lovers'? Fol Amoureux in the *Rose* is a *commere* in this sense. Chartier uses the word to designate cowards who flee battle who are, therefore, unworthy of their love (*Chartier Works*, p. 284, v. 2875). Christine refers to 'commerages' as the actions of unchivalrous knights (*Chemin*, v. 3752–57). Elsewhere she describes such men as 'molz et delicatis comme femmes' (*Policie*, p. 47:29) [sensual and soft like women]. *Commere* is therefore the opposite of virago. Such men were not necessarily unattractive; for example, a woman describes her beloved in *R* 56, v. 5, as 'plus doulz qu'une pucelle' [sweeter than a maiden].

[59] Minnis 2001.

[60] See the same image in *CB* 13; *Advision*, III.vi.33–35, xxii.2–4.

[61] On her sharp condemnation of slanderers, see Schilperoort 1936, pp. 28–29. Contemporary readers may well have taken first-person lyric as self-expression, a good reason for Christine to deny writing *de sentement* (Hauck 1995, p. 219).

This does not preclude her having been the victim of attempted seductions.[62] Even when writing the amorous lyrics her patrons requested, she claims to have no personal interest in such subjects; she writes love poetry only to please others and for compensation.[63] On the personal level, to be sure, her love poems also promote her own moral agenda. By contrast, Jean's Vieille never loses at least vicarious interest in lovemaking, alternately striving for vengeance as she ages and gushing enthusiastically about Amant's physical attractions and sincerity.[64] She is a *vetula insipiens*, the feminine counterpart of impotent old men who cannot accept their impotence.[65]

To deal with such 'old boys and girls', the *Rose* enunciates the principle of *contraires choses* by which one may get at the truth.[66] Christine enunciates the same principle in *Charles V*.

> Pour ce que les differences des choses contraires l'une de l'autre en leur estre sont plus nottoirement cogneues et aperceues ... quant le bien est louez, ce est en vituperacion du mal, aussi, quant le mal est blasmé, ce doit estre à l'augmentacion du bien. (vol. 1, p. 74)
>
> [In order that the essential differences between opposites may be more readily understood and perceived ... good is praised in order to condemn evil, just as, when evil is blamed, it must be in order to promote the good.]

The contrast between Christine's usage and Jean de Meun's is obvious. Whereas Christine seeks to exalt Charles V's virtues and excoriate the vices he shuns, Jean shows lovers interested only in sexual gratification and profit. To realize this two-pronged offensive, Fol Amoureux becomes a gigolo. In his mind, the principle of *contraires choses* is reduced to contrasting young and old *cons* as sources of pleasure and, for the gigolo, profit. For her part, the young Vieille practices prostitution for profit. But with the passage of time, the Vieille ages and becomes a go-between, again for profit. While Christine too contrasts young and old men, *contraires choses*, she lauds the former's virtues while excoriating the latter's tired libido.

Although Reason tells Amant to eschew pursuit of sexual gratification, the Vieille pushes Bel Accueil towards it. As Christine never tires of warning her

---

[62] We might see such experiences behind Lady Loyalty's assertion that she often tested Christine's fidelity (*Dit Rose*, v. 296–98), a fidelity that could only have been to her husband, both before and after his death. Cf. Solente 1974, p. 342.

[63] Poirion 1965, pp. 247–53. At first she also sought diversion by writing love poems as a distraction from sorrow (*Advision*, III.vii.21–24); even Plato, she notes, amused himself by reading Sappho (*Policie*, p. 97:34–38). On her misunderstanding of what Plato read, see Kennedy 1998, pp. 739–40; Cerquiglini 2003, pp. 80–81.

[64] Kelly 1995a, p. 129.

[65] In the *Rose* too, Amant contemplates seducing rich *vieilles* (Kelly 1995a, p. 104); Christine ridicules such women in the *Trois vertus* (p. 193:144–48). See also Fenster, ed., *Epistre Dieu*, pp. 12–13.

[66] Regalado 1981.

readers even in her early poems,[67] love is a dangerous route for women to follow. When read as antiphrasis, that is, by the principle of *contraires choses*, a reason-figure is required for Jean's *Rose*. The Vieille hardly meets such standards.[68] Sebile de Monthault does.

Opinions on chivalric love

The *Rose*'s lovers are not lovers in the style Christine attributes to Du Guesclin. This is her point in the *Rose* debate. How then did she come to reject even this noble, chaste love? Sebile de Monthault provides the answer. This exemplary 'sibyl' is not concerned with the kind of love the *Rose* illustrates. Rather she confronts and counters the very justification of chivalric love that Christine herself expresses in the *Rose* debate and the *Dit de la rose*; that is, she opposes the commonplace that noble love promotes prowess and chivalry. Christine accepted this opinion in her early writings, as we have seen, because at that time she believed that such love would serve to combat misogyny. Her subsequent criticism of this view as false opinion occurs in the contexts of love, eroticism, and the constancy of emotions.

Focusing on gender in the *Epistre au dieu d'amours*, Christine states in well-known lines that misogynist works were not written by women, but by men (v. 407–11). An analogous observation can be made regarding traditional love poetry. Indeed, 'si "je" est "un autre"',[69] the woman reading the largely male-voiced lyric tradition may well want to hear what the *je* has to say when a female voice speaks. Christine supplies that voice in ways heretofore not heard in love poems by women[70] or in *chansons féminines* composed by men.[71] In part reflecting on her own loss on the death of her husband,[72] but, more importantly, on the experience of women whose voice she evokes in her lyric poems, Christine passes from promoting chivalric love like that she admires in Du Guesclin to her categorical rejection of any extramarital love for women, or men, by invariably and irreversibly painting dramatic, tragic, and exemplary conclusions to such loves. Her pictures are bleak for both women and the men even in noble loves like Du Guesclin's. Like that of the lovers Christine criticizes in these writings, her own *vray sentement* changes. This is in part because lovers may deceive. But there is a more profound reason for her radical rejection of the traditional ideal of chivalric love that she lauds in the case of Du Guesclin's

---

[67] *CB* 59, 60, 86, 89; *V* 12; *R* 42; *AB* 28, 43.

[68] See Krueger 1993, pp. 219–23, 232–36. In Christine's view, in the *Rose* debate, as we have seen, Jean's Reason does not meet those standards either.

[69] Poirion 1965, p. 250.

[70] See McWebb 1998; Neumeister 1999; *Trobairitz*; *Songs Women*. For a survey of *'femmes de plume' génétiques, textuelles et virtuelles*, see Tyssens 1992.

[71] Kelly 1978, pp. 5–6.

[72] Poirion 1965, pp. 251–53.

love in the *Rose* debate and promotes in the *Epistre au dieu d'amour* and the *Dit de la rose*. It is the very instability of love itself.[73] Lovers may simply fall out of love, or they may fall in love with someone new. The common place *affectio* or appetite is amplified no longer as constant and chaste, but as inconstant and erotic.

Christine confronts, therefore, two commonplaces of love and lovemaking: erotic pleasure and its consequences – moral, social, and psychological.[74] Her emphasis on the dangers of love for young women and the urgency with which she makes her case in, for example, the *Trois vertus* not only for continence but, more importantly, for radical avoidance of even the appearance of unacceptable social or moral attachments contrast sharply with the exemplary tone of *Charles V*. This is in part because of the emotional damage of a failed love or deception, and in part because of the dire social consequences for the woman found or deemed guilty of incontinence or even frivolity that makes others suspect an extramarital love life.

The charges of alleged immorality are evident in the gossip accusing Christine of having taken a lover during her early widowhood. By all evidence, the threat of being called a slut and the awful consequences for the victims of such slander were very real in the fifteenth century; these consequences included rape. The seducing woman, in contrast, would not jeopardize the seduced man's honor; she might even enhance it in some milieus.[75] As Maureen Dowd effectively overstates the matter in a *New York Times* editorial: 'No man has ever been consumed with fear about being a slut.'[76] This must *a fortiori* be borne in mind in evaluating a fifteenth-century woman author's views on seduction, even when the seducer's sentiments are sincere. Widows, for example, could not only be called sluts, they could be treated like sluts.[77] Jean de Montreuil likens Christine to Leonce, a whore.[78] The belief that such women desired rape was a commonplace justification for rape, and Christine was well aware of this threat.[79] Accordingly, no doubt, Christine describes Leonce only as a philosopher (*Cité*, p. 160),[80] figuratively rehabilitating her in conformity with her counsel to rehabilitate prostitutes in the *Trois vertus*.

---

[73] Perhaps it is noteworthy in this context that Christine even questions her conjugal love in the *Advision* as an impediment to her studious life.

[74] Hauck 1995.

[75] See Fenster 2000; cf. Gauvard 1991, pp. 321–22.

[76] *New York Times*, July 17, 2000. I wish to thank Sandra Ihle for this reference.

[77] Gauvard 1991, pp. 325–26, 338–39; Zimmermann 2002, p. 26. Again the accusations of having a lover are an illustration from Christine's life (see note 142 below); cf. *AB* 6, v. 19–23, on the fate of abandoned widows. The poem is inserted into the *Advision*, III. vi.185–218.

[78] *Débat*, p. 42:5–10; see Walters 1998, p. 160.

[79] For examples in Christine's writings, see *Cité*, pp. 328–34; *Advision*, I.xxv. Cf. in general Gauvard 1991, pp. 330–39. Christine's lessons contrast with what other treatises taught (Roussel 1994, pp. 56–69; Nagel 2000).

[80] See Curnow, ed., *Cité*, p. 1069 n. 87; Cerquiglini 2003, p. 81.

Therefore, in evaluating Christine's counsel, as expressed by Sebile de Monthault, we must not ignore the world she observed around her and described, and for which she wrote.[81] The *Trois vertus* shows that the choices available to any woman were limited; she could expect to become a wife (and, potentially, a widow), a nun, or a prostitute: 'les filles doivent être pures ou publiques'.[82] Little else seems to have been available. Prostitution may have been the only route open to destitute widows whose families could not or would not take them back,[83] along with that of 'fallen' or abused women (cf. *AB* 6, v. 19–27). Therefore, Christine's opinions are not those of a prude divorced from reality.

Nor was she 'frigid'. Her marital bliss is generally received as credible. The ballade evoking the first night of a marriage (*AB* 26) is often cited as a preamble to her poems on her widowhood, although it is actually an isolated subject in the *Autres balades*. Another ballade suggests the pleasures of foreplay, pleasures whose reality and appeal Christine nowhere denies:

> le gracieux tast
> Des doulces mains qui, sanz lait desplaisir,
> Veuillent partout encershier et enquerre.   (*AB* 35, v. 23–25)
>
> [the pleasing touch of gentle hands; without groping, they
> desire to seek out and explore everywhere.]

The ballade containing these lines is also inserted into the *Dit de la pastoure* (v. 1780–82). But Christine approves of such foreplay only within the socially acceptable norms of marriage (as in *AB* 26) because of the dire social or personal consequences for those who do not conform to those norms. This caution regarding the, as it were, 'color' of Christine's opinion on the matter will be illustrated below in poems such as the *Dit de la pastoure*. For now, it will serve as a context for the analysis of the *Trois vertus* and the *Epistre Othea* as treatises on the good life and the place of love and lovemaking in it. In them, Christine has abandoned the essentially platonic notion of chivalric love

---

[81] On violence against women in the Middle Ages, including wives and maidservants, see Willard 1987, p. 171; Dulac 1990; Gauvard 1991, ch. 13; Desmond 2003; Brundage 2000, especially pp. 191–95 on fourteenth-century Paris; and Hanawelt 2000, especially pp. 200 and 208–14 on maidservants.

[82] Rossiaud 1986, p. 160; Gauvard 1991, p. 588. See Rossiaud 1988, pp. 195–204, and Hanawalt 2000, for examples.

[83] There is no record that Christine's Italian relatives, including her brothers, Aghinolfo and Paolo, came to her and her mother's assistance when they became widows (Willard 1984, p. 39; but see p. 165 on the role they may have had in bringing their sister to the attention of the duke of Milan). Her brothers may have been poor themselves (Wandruszka 2000, p. 123). The same is true for her late husband's family with whom Christine was in contact (*Trois vertus*, p. 19:162–63); cf. pp. 84:50–85:64 on the threats to a widow's son if there is strife between families. Fortunately, Christine was resourceful; she had received enough education to be able to support herself and her family by writing and producing manuscripts.

possible among virtuous lovers like Du Guesclin, denying the possibility of such love in Sebile de Monthault's letter in the *Duc* and the *Trois vertus*. All her writings after the *Epistre Othea* and the *Enseignemens* express this opinion.[84] One must note the chronology of the changes in the context of Christine's evolving opinion. Otherwise the lesson to the young man in *Othea* will seem more indulgent than that given the young woman in the *Trois vertus*.

As discussed above, love as Christine presents it mirrors polarized views commonplace in medieval misogyny and phylogeny. Her entrance into the debate on the *Roman de la rose* as well as Jean de Meun's and her agreement regarding the identity of the Fol Amoureux entail a similarly polarized view of what we may term philandry and misandry. In the *Rose* debate, Christine distinguishes between what she deems good and bad women and good and bad men. What is good or bad is determined by her own moral standards, religious faith, and experience. The distinction permits her to laud good men and good women. Since the mode of such writing is hyperbole, it does not confront the complexities of human interaction in love and lovemaking. Yet no kind of human interaction is more complex or fraught with uncertainty than amorous relationships, or more subject to opinion and opinion making; moreover, opinions are conditioned and controlled by the diverse historical circumstances that make the opinion of a fifteenth-century woman like Christine so different from that of most modern women.[85]

Gradus amoris and its varieties

Love poetry relies on rhetoric, the art of conjectural argument, and, therefore, on contrasting, variable, and imprecise opinions. The rhetoric of love brings us back to topical invention, discussed in Chapter 2. The lover, whether sincere or a philanderer, male or female, noble or common, will follow similar stages in pursuing the object of his or her desire. The beloved will do the same. The questions asked, whether directly to the other, or to oneself, or to an intended audience,[86] will rehearse circumstantial queries such as *quis? quid? ubi? quibis auxiliiis? cur? quomodo? quando?* in order to form an opinion about the potential lover and the kind of love he or she seeks or claims to seek.[87] The answers color and distinguish each stage in the *gradus amoris*, suggesting the quality and sincerity of emotion as well as the longevity of that sincerity. The issues are as commonplace in Andreas Capellanus and the *Roman de la rose*

---

[84] Kelly 1994a, pp. 89–97.

[85] The quandary is eloquently expressed in Hella Haasse's rhetorical question in this book's epigraph and sharp debates in modern scholarship on Christine's opinions like those referred to in the Introduction.

[86] On audiences and performance for courtly love poetry, see Kelly 2000.

[87] The proposals and questions in Chartier's *Belle Dame sans merci* illustrate dramatically such repartee.

as in Chrétien de Troyes, Marie de France, the thirteenth-century prose romances, and traditional courtly lyric – and modern novels. Christine herself expresses the same conviction Chrétien does in *Yvain* regarding the sincerity of love in bygone times,[88] a conviction, and thus an opinion, she presumably formed by reading and being influenced by antecedent courtly literature. But regarding her own time, the opinion that ideal chivalric love was feasible with the right person outside of marriage changes radically. We can observe this change in her rewriting of the *gradus amoris* script.

The articulation of the *gradus amoris* script depends on the kind of lovers depicted and how they think, feel, and act. There are four commonplace kinds of love: conjugal, prudent (*fin'amour*), foolish (*fol'amour*), and young. Very much present in Christine's writing is the continuation of the script, or *conservatio amoris*, including *finis amoris*.[89] Although continuation is not usually a part of the *gradus amoris* commonplace in scholarly discussion, it is very much a natural extension of the paradigm and occasionally a topic in courtly narratives.[90] What happens after consummation? They live happily ever after, as in many romances? Infidelity, as in Chrétien's *Lancelot* and the *Roman de la rose*? Or what? Interestingly, Christine applies considerable ingenuity to describing this phase so often idealized in the romance tradition, but almost absent in the lyric tradition except for the occasional alba, a genre that might describe a fleeting love, perhaps a one-night stand.[91]

The principal difficulty in traditional courtly lyric is to distinguish between foolish and prudent love. Given Christine's early views on the desirability or even the feasibility of the latter, the issue colors her poems in significant ways. Foolish love (*amor stultus*) like that in the *Roman de la rose* appears in a few of Christine's lyric pieces.[92] Prudent love (*amor sapiens*) is proclaimed in the Du Guesclin kind of love in the *Epistre au dieu d'amours* and the *Dit de la rose*; it is also the lover's goal in the *Duc des vrais amants*. Conjugal love (*affectio coniugalis*) is described in Book One of the *Mutacion de Fortune*, and several lyric pieces (*CB* 5–20; *R* 1–7; *AB* 26), and, by antithesis, among the *mal-mariées* (*AB* 8) and in unhappy marriages like those evoked in the *Trois vertus* and the *Cité des dames*.

---

[88] See *Epistre Dieu*, v. 23–32; cf. *Yvain*, v. 12–28.

[89] The commonplace *conservatio* and *finis amoris* are treated by Andreas Capellanus (*De amore*, Part Two).

[90] Chrétien treats it in a conjugal context in *Erec* and *Yvain*. There are many varieties in the prose romances (Hahn 1988). Machaut too describes two kinds of love, the one based on desire, the other on hope, terms that he explicates as, respectively, sexual desire and platonic admiration; see Kelly 1978, ch. 6.

[91] The exception proves the rule. For example, the child in the poignant *chanson* attributed to Jacques d'Autun is unique; the poem too is unique because it depicts a *finis amoris* in which the rejected lover is also father of the beloved's child (*Poèmes d'amour*, pp. 133–37).

[92] For example, *CB* 78; *R* 15, 41–44, 46, 51, 55–58; *AB* 8.

These diverse kinds of love – conjugal, prudent, foolish, and young – adapt, in whole or in part and in diverse ways, the common places of the *gradus amoris* commonplace. For, although the model is a commonplace, the descriptions of the places common to it vary, often considerably. That is, they are diversely articulated, or invented, depending on the author's conception of the stage in specific narrative circumstances such as gender, social standing, marital status, and consanguinity.[93] The blueprint or *archetypus* of the *gradus amoris*[94] is a general plan, yet one easily identifiable by anyone, whether author, reader, or audience, who imagines love's stages. Let us now turn to Christine's depiction of a *gradus amoris* that problematizes love such as that she once admired in a Du Guesclin.

Gradus amoris and its sequel in the Duc des vrais amants

Christine de Pizan's most elaborate *gradus amoris* and its constituent topoi are found in the *Duc des vrais amants*. Since she argued in the *Rose* debate that Jean de Meun should have satirized foolish love in a more obvious, balanced manner, I shall be comparing her treatment of the Duke's *gradus amoris* with that of the Fol Amoureux in Jean de Meun's *Rose*. In addition, since Christine took Guillaume de Lorris's part as one with Jean's, I shall include its narrative as part of Jean's poem and its context.[95] The discussion will include comparison of stages or topoi in the *gradus amoris* script as each poem articulates them.

Two features of the *Duc des vrais amants* are crucial in evaluating the opinions it exemplifies. One is Christine's view, expressed in the *Trois vertus*, that the wife should accept her marriage however bad it may be. The other is that the man's disillusion is just as significant as the woman's. Since both features relate to opinions Christine expresses in other works, taken as a whole such opinions form a moral and social context and intertext for the *Duc des vrais amants* narrative.

The *Rose* begins its *gradus amoris* with sight, the *Duc* with *pensers*, an inversion of the commonplace scheme that usually locates thought after sight. In the *Rose*, the young man who becomes Amant wanders aimlessly about until, happening on the Garden of Deduit, he enters its wonderfully joyous world. Soon after, shadowed by the god of Love, he arrives at the fountain of Narcissus, sees the rose, and falls in love. This is a complete surprise to him, a true *coup de foudre*. Passion overwhelms him. Indeed, his first, erotic impulse is to pluck as many rosebuds as he can. It is only after he fixes his attention on a particular bud that the god of Love strikes him through the eyes, turning his passion for

---

[93] Benkov 2002. For example, the lovers in the *Duc* are cousins, an incestuous relationship in Christine's time; curiously, Sebile de Monthault does not refer to this impediment.

[94] On *archetypus* as 'blueprint', see Kelly 1999a, pp. 30–31, 49–51.

[95] She could envisage a context like Guillaume's separate from Jean's, as, for example, in *AB* 9–10.

plucking rosebuds into a love for the one bud he has chosen.[96] By contrast, Christine's Duke is more deliberate and self-conscious. He reflects on, then accepts the commonplace opinion that he must love in order to improve himself (*Duc*, v. 41–82). A Du Guesclin avatar, he seeks a person worthy of his love service; after failing to fall in love with several otherwise attractive women – the *Rose*'s rosebuds – he catches sight of his cousin and his *gradus amoris* progresses (v. 228–304).

The sight stage already shows how each author has differently articulated the topoi sight and thought. Christine's Duke is more self-conscious and prudent than the *Rose*'s lover. Since she argues that the *Rose*'s lover was too exclusively erotic – the hormones of a young man of twenty – she reconfigures the moment of sight to conform to a different kind of love, what we today might call a courtly love and certainly one that follows on reflection and a young knight's desire to improve by following traditional ideas on the beneficial effects of good love. Good love is chivalric because it makes the nobleman a better knight: 'A celle fin qu'a vaillance je tire, / Pourvoyez moy de dame et de maistresse, / Vray dieux d'Amours' (*Duc*, v. 75–77) [so that I may become valiant, give me a lady and mistress, true god of love].[97] This is the chivalric love of a Du Guesclin. In effect, the Duke has already approached an ideal that the *Rose* lover never attains. Neither, however, does the Duke.

The next stage or topos falls between sight and approach; it also returns to thought in the conventional way, that is, as a more focused *pensers* than that which inspired the Duke's search for a suitable love. Andreas defines love as sight followed by great, even excessive thought on and preoccupation with the object of affection. Whatever Andreas's intentions in his treatise, the definition he proposes becomes a commonplace. It reappears in the *Rose* (v. 4347–54), and variants of it are apparent in Christine's writings and elsewhere[98] as thought alternating with sight.

In the *Duc des vrais amants*, a cycle of approach and separation becomes susceptible of diverse developments depending on the narrative setting and action at each stage of the Duke's *gradus amoris* and in conformity with the opinion on love proposed. Guillaume de Lorris anticipates this cyclic movement in the god of Love's instruction on the 'adventures' awaiting Amant, adventures he represents in the encounters between Amant and the rose; Jean de Meun adopts the pattern for two more such encounters that complete the *Rose*'s *gradus amoris*.[99]

---

[96] On these events and the transformation, see Kelly 1978, ch. 4. Jean de Meun has Amant revert to his earlier collecting of rosebuds, or 'sexual sampling', at the end of his continuation (Kelly 1995a, p. 35).

[97] These are the faithful, 'pure' lovers we observed above whose principal goal was to improve themselves (*Débat*, p. 129:460–62). Cf. *Othea*, 47. The Duke will hardly evince the same satisfaction in old age as the Du Guesclin lover does.

[98] See Kelly 1978, pp. 166–67.

[99] See Kelly 1972, pp. 62–65, and 1995a, pp. 33–34, 66–67. For a thorough discussion of this paradigm, see O'Leary 1980.

In Christine's *Duc*, however, a major departure from the *Rose* version of the *gradus amoris* occurs: the exclusion of 'la chose vilaine', or intercourse, as the final stage in the commonplace scheme.[100]

> D'amours je jouÿ
> A mon gré, sans villenie.
> Car qui dira, je lui nie,
> Qu'en nostre amour il eust oncques
> Lait fait ne vilain quelconques.   (*Duc*, v. 3323–27)
>
> [I enjoyed my love to my satisfaction, without villainy. For no matter what any one says, I deny that our love ever included anything ugly or base.[101]]

My interpretation of the love the Duke espouses as virtually platonic needs some clarification. That the love is consummated has been argued on the evidence of these lines:[102]

> Lors ma Dame, ou toute grace
> Maint, tres doulcement m'embrace
> Et plus de cent fois me baise.
> Si demourray en cel aise
> Toute la nuit, et croyez
> Vous, amans qui ce oyez,
> Qu'a mon aise bien estoie!   (*Duc*, v. 2859–65)
>
> [Then my Lady, in whom dwells all that is good, embraces me very sweetly, kissing me a hundred times over. I remained in such delight all night; and you lovers who hear this can rest assured that I was indeed happy!]

But that interpretation of the lovemaking described in those lines is incompatible with a later statement.

> ... tout avez ouÿ,
> Comment d'amours je jouÿ
> Car qui dira, je lui nie,
> Qu'en nostre amour il eust oncques
> Lait fait ne vilain quelconques.   (*Duc*, v. 3322–27)

---

[100] Thus, the *fin'amour* the Duke envisages conforms by and large to the love based on hope, that is, the 'platonic' love promoted by Machaut in a number of his Dits, and most systematically in the *Remede de Fortune*; see note 8 above.

[101] 'Vilain' connotes sexual intercourse in this context in Christine's vocabulary; see p. 110 and n. 10 above.

[102] Brown-Grant 1999a, p. 212. The Duke's love is not the kind Christine castigates in the *Advision*, I.xv.39–58, where Lust seduces Chivalry, making it impotent, although chivalric love does cause the Duke's *recreantise*, as we shall see.

> [You have heard how I took delight in love to my liking, with no illicit or vulgar conduct. For, to whoever says the contrary, I deny that there ever was any offensive or obscene act of any kind.]

Given the precise sense of illicit sexual intercourse that Christine gives to *villenie* in love, there can be no doubt that the Duke is denying such intercourse in his relationship – unless, of course, he is lying. But this would reduce the issue to a banal and, indeed, minor version of 'did they or didn't they?' But it seems to me more important when one recalls Christine's ideas in the *Rose* debate on ideal love of which Du Guesclin is the prime exemplar. Christine is practicing the selectivity appropriate in making exemplary conduct conform to a given model, in this case the Du Guesclin model according to which the lovers never made love. In fictional narrative like the *Duc des vrais amants*, one can follow the fictional moral of the speaker unless there is clear evidence that he or she is lying or in error (for example, when Amant claims constancy in the *Roman de la rose*[103]). That is, the Duke's love conforms to the prudent love Christine admires in the *Rose* debate. The Du Guesclin kind of love rejects consummation, but fosters chivalric prowess (cf. *Débat*, p. 129:455–64). Christine's version of what Andreas terms *amor purus* excludes not only the sexual act but even nudity and isolation. A third person is always present when the Duke and Princess rendezvous. Christine has changed her mind. She is showing that matters turn out bad even in the best of loves, a point Sebile also makes (*Duc*, p. 173:74–85). The Duke's love is not the kind that Christine castigates in the *Advision* (I.xv.39–58), where Lust seduces Chivalry, making it impotent. She is rejecting the ideal, Du Guesclin kind of love she earlier praised, but no longer.

Therefore, the consequences for the Duke are not the same as for Christine's Du Guesclin. To be sure, the Duke and the Princess enjoy clandestine encounters that include other major stages in the *gradus amoris* script: conversation, kissing, and even caressing.[104] Both believe that in this way they preserve their honor, satisfy the emotional demands of their love, keep the affair secret, and inspire the chivalric achievements that justify the Duke's decision to love in the first place. All this is possible, we might say, because, in the language of the *Rose*, the Duke is content with the leaf offered by Bel Accueil; he does not ask for the rosebud (*Rose*, v. 2860–61, 2886–88). The Duke's love is prudent. But, as he learns to his dismay, leaves wither much as roses fade.

For all is not as it was supposed to be. Christine introduces ambiguity and potential warnings from the beginning. At the outset of the so-called tournament

---

[103] Contrast this with the night Meliador and Hermondine spend without intercourse, but with another woman present (*Meliador*, v. 17594–762). Of course, there are differences too: these lovers plan to marry, not engage in adultery.

[104] *Duc*, v. 2676–82, 2859–65, 2886–92, 3095–97.

between personifications of the Lover's attributes and those attributed to the Rose Jean de Meun inserts a hunt metaphor.

> Or antandez, leal amant,
> Que li dieu d'Amors vos amant
> Et doint de voz amors joïr!
> En ce bois ci poez oïr
> Les chiens glatir, s'ous m'antandez,
> Au connin prendre ou vos tandez,
> Et le fuiret, qui sanz faillir
> Le doit fere es raiseauz saillir.
> Notez ce que ci vois disant,
> D'amors avrez art souffisant. (*Rose*, v. 15105–14)

> [Now, faithful lovers, pay attention: may the god of Love advance you and grant that you enjoy your loves. In these woods you can hear the dogs bark, if you get what I mean, after the rabbit you are hunting, and the ferrets will make it spring for sure into the snares. Note what I am telling you and you will possess a sufficient art of love.]

Christine recycles the hunt metaphor, relocating it near the beginning of the *Duc des vrais amants*, when the Duke first sees and falls in love with his cousin. As in Jean de Meun's *Rose*, the commonplace metaphor alerts the reader to the context for the ensuing narrative.

> Fain me prist d'aler chacier
> Et, pour deduit pourchacier,
> Fis aux veneurs levriers prendre,
> Et firons. Lors, sans attendre,
> Entrasmes en un chemin
> Qu'assez souvent je chemin,
> Mais n'eusmes pas moult erré
> Quant un grant chemin ferré
> Nous mena en une voye
> Ou connins assez sçavoye. (*Duc*, v. 95–104)

> [A longing[105] overcame me to go hunting. So, in order to pursue pleasure I had the pickers get the hunting-dogs and ferrets; then, without further ado, we set out on a way I often take. We had not gone far when the main road led us to a way where I knew there were lots of rabbits.]

---

[105] Literally, 'hunger'.

The rabbit hunting metaphor was widely known; its implications for the sexual hunt are unmistakable.[106] Christine has adroitly conjoined two motifs that inform the French courtly tradition: love as a source of chivalric worth and love as sexual hunt. The *Duc*'s conjuncture of these two suggests the instability and ambiguity of even ideal love.

The Duke and the Princess's affair is designed to overcome this problem by excluding the sexual act, or the commonplace consummation of the sexual hunt for *connins*, while maintaining the commonplace that love enhances prowess, and, more specifically in the Duke's case, chivalric worth. This is his goal in seeking a love in the first place; it is also a goal Christine advocates in her early writings. Love is, in other words, the means to that goal, and the end justifies the means in the Duke's mind. Otherwise, the *gradus amoris* is intact even though incomplete, or at least somewhat unconventional.

The *Duc des vrais amants* adopts another disturbing feature from the *Rose*. The Duke has the assistance of his cousin, who functions as an Ami, the *Rose*'s authority on seduction and deception. And there is deception. This cousin, who is also the Princess's cousin, lies to her about the Duke by claiming that he did his best to dissuade the Duke from loving (*Duc*, v. 2149–50), but that the Duke's imminent death from unrequited love obliges him to appeal to her. This lie (see v. 1888–2010) shows the cousin playing the same role as Ami in the *Rose*.[107] For her part, Christine's Princess has an understanding 'Vieille,' who, although not old, does support her mistress's affair (*Duc*, v. 2615–16, 2659–69).

Major differences between the Duke's love and that related in the *Rose* include the fact that the Princess is married to an older man and that she is her lover's cousin. Her honor is in jeopardy. Even if adultery in the strict sense of the word is avoided, her reputation can be damaged if gossip, or Malebouche, assumes his[108] usual role. This is precisely what happens at a time when all seems to be going well. As in the *Rose*, Malebouche begins to prattle after they kiss.

When the Princess's cooperative 'Vieille' must leave her service, she appeals to a former governess to return, fully expecting that her relation to the Duke will continue as before. The former governess is Sebile de Monthault, Dame

---

[106] *AB* 48. See, for example, Schmolke-Hasselmann 1982. On the *double entendre* of 'connys' in medieval erotic language, see Fenster, ed., *Duc*, p. 220 n. 104. In another context, Christine uses it in the *Trois vertus* to show how the clever governess leads her charge into the 'trap' of virtue; see Cerquiglini 1985, p. 122; Dulac 1992b; Nagel 2000, p. 114. This 'seduction' to virtue is evidence for the claim that an image does not always carry the same metaphorical message, although the commonplace traditionally associated with the hunt and capture image may well have intertextual power.

[107] And Pandarus's role in Chaucer's *Troilus and Criseyde*. Thus, the Duke differs from the Du Guesclin of the *Rose* debate who, allegedly, did not deceive nor was he ever deceived (*Débat*, p. 129:459–60).

[108] On Malebouche's masculine gender in the *Rose*, see Kelly 1995a, pp. 108–22.

de la Tour.[109] The echoes of Reason in the *Rose* and the Sibyl in the *Chemin* are obvious. Sebile conjoins the attributes of Reason and those of the Vieille as Guillaume de Lorris represents her; she is a woman whose long life has given her the experience needed to know young love and perceive its schemes and pitfalls. As a sibyl, she is also prophetic.

Sebile's response to the Princess's invitation reveals that the word is out. She herself, although separated from the Princess by some distance, has heard talk of the latter's relation with the Duke. Moreover, she prophesies a decline in their love that will undermine its *conservatio*. Sebile's letter sets out in detail her opinion and prophecies. It is a masterpiece on the power of opinion and its pitfalls.[110] Both the Princess and the Duke believe love can be a good; they think that it can be a source of pleasure while enhancing the knight's prowess and the worth of the lady who inspires his chivalric achievements. Sebile accepts none of this. 'Il va tout autrement' (p. 173:80) [it doesn't turn out that way at all]; such 'foles oppinions' (p. 175:139) are based on false reasoning and *cuidier*, or erroneous opinion (pp. 174:112, 178:215, 234, and 179:243). Christine places in Sebile's mouth the vision of the young princess's love that she describes in the *Trois vertus*.[111] Honor is lost through the *médisance* of servants and others in a position to observe the changes in the Princess's behavior and embroider on it. 'Car poson qu'il n'y ait meffait de corps; si ne le croyent mie ceulx qui seulement orront dire: tele dame est amoureuse' (p. 174:98–99) [Let us suppose that no physical misconduct occurs. Yet those will never believe it if they hear it said that 'such and such a lady is in love']. Sebile therefore counsels a complete turnabout. The Princess must radically correct her opinion and immediately alter her conduct. When she does not, Sebile, implicitly following the advice of the *Trois vertus*, finds a suitable – real or feigned – justification to turn down the Princess's offer: her own daughter is too ill to be left without her mother's care (*Duc*, p. 171:10–12).[112]

A major factor in Sebile's reasoning is the inconstancy of men. This is, of course, another opinion. Its force derives from the vulnerability of women to opinions about love, even when they are innocent and the men are honorable and honest. For example, a widow was considered fair prey in Christine's time because she had no husband, but was no longer a virgin; so was the wife whose husband was absent.[113] The absence of the Princess's husband facilitates their early clandestine meetings. But eschewing the 'chose vilaine' in no way stifles

---

[109] On the relation between the Dame de la Tour and the Dame de la Tour Landry, see De Gendt 1999, pp. 200–06.

[110] Besides her edition, *Duc*, ed. Fenster, pp. 9–12, 19–27, see Fenster 2000, pp. 470–73.

[111] See *Trois vertus*, pp. 96–104, 123–29, and, in the Letter, pp. 109–20.

[112] See *Trois vertus*, pp. 106:69–107:84, 108:103–19.

[113] Rossiaud 1988, pp. 42–43. Christine alludes to these dangers in the *Trois vertus*, pp. 89:69–90:94, 104–09. We recall that marrying a widow is farcical in Matheolus's *Lamentations*.

gossip, as Sebile predicts (*Duc*, v. 1451–58, p. 172:25–27, v. 3359–62).[114] In the *Duc des vrais amants*, a sincere, idealized, adulterous, albeit chaste love turns sour despite its sexual innocence.

Additional causes of the failure emerge in the *Duc*'s *conservatio*, or, more precisely here, the *deminutio* phase of the affair.[115] Difficulties arise when the husband returns, hears the rumors, and imposes greater restrictions on his wife that keep the lovers apart (cf. *CB* 78). Moreover, love does not inspire the Duke's prowess. Reluctant to distance himself from the Lady he loves but cannot visit, he becomes an inactive or *recreant* knight (*Duc*, v. 3352–81).[116] When, finally, he must depart in order to salvage his chivalric reputation, the separation is long and painful. He spends a year campaigning in Spain (v. 3427–29), then ten more years in the Holy Land (v. 3451–53).[117] Alas, 'l'amour, qui sépare et isole, ne peut être que source d'infortune'.[118] Over the years jealousy grows as rumors report infidelities; the fear of no longer being loved runs deep (v. 3464–3504).[119] Communication almost stops so that explanations and justifications become well-nigh impossible. There is no *conservatio amoris*, only a slow, melancholy decline and, finally, end of love.[120] Although the Princess does not suffer the Vieille's fate in the *Roman de la rose*, her lot is hardly enviable. The Duke's constancy forecloses the life of seduction Amant looks forward to in the *Rose*. The *Duc des vrais amants* evokes a chivalric love; it also illustrates a failure not unlike Orpheus's 'qui trop amoit ne se pot tenir de retourner pour s'amie que a regarder desiroit' (*Othea*, 70:29–31) [who loved excessively and could not refrain from returning to his beloved, whom he desired to see].[121]

Given the opinion about chivalric love she expressed in the *Rose* debate, Christine could have related an ideal Du Guesclin love in the *Duc des vrais amants*. But her opinion has obviously changed. Her approval of such love in the *Rose* debate shows signs of changing in the *Epistre Othea*.[122] Christine's new conviction is too firm, and, perhaps, the threat to her own reputation too great, to allow her to go on idealizing chivalric love. Henceforth, Christine wrote only tales of forlorn love like the *Duc des vrais amants*.[123]

---

[114] Willard 1987, p. 168. On the effect of the unwanted return of a husband, see *R* 42.
[115] Cf. *De amore*, pp. 284–90.
[116] Cf. *Othea*, 73, 75; see Brown-Grant 1999a, pp. 69–70.
[117] On travel and separation in some of Christine's lyric cycles, see Altmann 2000.
[118] Dulac 1990, p. 28.
[119] See as well the poems in the small anthology appended to the *Duc*, pp. 198–218.
[120] Cf. Andreas Capellanus's belief that love must either grow or decline, but cannot remain on an even keel (*De amore*, p. 356, rule iv).
[121] Similar statements are found in the *Duc*, v. 3345–58, 3432–49, 3456–59. On diverse readings of the Orpheus myth, including some that support misogyny and misandry, see Heitmann 1963.
[122] See Brown-Grant 1999a, pp. 77–78. Were experiences in Louis d'Orléans's court a partial explanation for this change? See Willard 1984, pp. 51–53.
[123] Cf. Adams 2002; Cerquiglini 2002.

Gradus amoris and its sequels in the *Dit de la pastoure* and the *Cent Ballades d'amant et de dame*

Like the *Duc des vrais amants*, Christine's other poems on love contain narrative sequences that are modeled on a *gradus amoris* as well as a *conservatio* followed by a *deminutio* and *finis amoris*. Thus, the *Dit de la pastoure* and the *Cent Ballades d'amant et de dame* may be viewed as part of a triptych with the *Duc* at the chronological center.[124] In all these Dits, a sad denouement follows separation.

The earlier *Pastoure* relates an *amour disproportionné* as a sentimental, yet apparently platonic, relationship between a knight of high nobility and an unmarried shepherdess.[125] The later *Cent Ballades d'amant et de dame* recounts the affair between a knight of some nobility and a married lady. Is this affair consummated? Christine is not explicit, although the passionate lines in Ballades xxviii–xl might certainly suggest more transpired than in the *Duc des vrais amants* and the *Pastoure*. The *Pastoure* does not relate the *deminutio* as lengthily as the other Dits do. The shepherdess's Prince does not return in the *Pastoure* after leaving for chivalric exploits. Perhaps social inequality made a gradual *finis amoris* less realistic for Christine's fifteenth-century audience.[126] But the *Pastoure* contains a voice also found in the *Duc*. Lorete sets out the errors and dangers of Marote's fancy and fanciful love in language that echoes Sebile de Monthault's admonitions; however, Lorete does not abandon Marote, like Sebile de Monthault but remains faithful, like, *mutatis mutandis*, the damsel in the *Trois vertus* who pretends that a princess's extramarital child is her own.[127]

Unlike the *Pastoure*, where the reader never learns what transpires in the nobleman's mind,[128] the ballade cycle of the *Cent Ballades d'amant et de dame* imitates the *Duc des vrais amants* in allowing both partners to speak. Here the *conservatio* gives way to a *deminutio* marked by growing sorrow as each lover comes to suspect infidelities and betrayals. Separation for honor and reputation is a commonplace motif, although the case against the constancy of the male lover has seemed more convincing to most scholars. To be sure, 'in these multivalent works, for every doubt the ladies dramatize, the texts offer male

---

[124] They are, as a group, also a virtually three-part compilation on failed love. On the chronology, see Willard 1984, pp. 70–71, 150.

[125] On this *Dit* see Blanchard 1983, pp. 93–118; Lefèvre 1988; Paden 1994 and 1996; Smith 1999.

[126] Cf. *Enseignemens*, 87: 'Trop ne te dois humilïer / Ne moult estre familier / A tes serfs' [don't lower yourself too much or be overly familiar with your serfs]. Another incomplete shepherdess's tale is Joan of Arc's, 'Une femme – simple bergiere – / Plus preux qu'onc homs ne fut à Romme!' (*Jehanne*, v. 198–99) [a woman, a guileless shepherdess, worthier than any man ever was in Rome]. But Joan belongs among saints, not lovers, for which there was some precedence.

[127] Blanchard 1983, pp. 108–16; Lorcin 1991, pp. 93–95.

[128] He speaks, but nowhere are we told what he thinks or what world he actually lives in when not with the shepherdess.

voices objecting'. Yet, 'constrained to conceal their love affairs and therefore unable to gain adequate assurances of each other's fidelity through regular communication, Christine's courtly lovers, men and women, suffer constantly the anguish of not being able to gauge their partner's state of mind'.[129] There is no straightforward statement of 'fictional fact' – that is, a statement by the narrator that the one or the other lover is actually guilty of inconstancy or infidelity. In all three works, the *Duc*, the *Pastoure*, and the *Cent Ballades d'amant et de dame*, love changes, but never for the better, a point that Christine seems to make exemplary. The lovers' fault is in consenting to love. The reader must form his or her own opinion about each lover's honesty. Lacking any explicit authorial statement, such opinion will be conjectural.

Christine's opinion that ideal love is impossible rings truer in the light of such exemplary uncertainty. This brings us to an important reason for her changed opinion on chivalric love. No one can know for sure, let alone trust, the *sentement d'autrui*; indeed, no one can even trust his or her own feelings.[130] *Sentement* includes both feelings and experience and Christine's Dits bear this out even in the context of loves far nobler than those depicted by Jean de Meun. The sincerity of reciprocal love in the *Duc des vrais amants* does not preclude doubts and suspicions that arise during long separations; Christine brings this out forcefully in the exchange of lyric pieces appended to the Dit. This mini-cycle illustrates failed attempts to communicate out of separate solitudes, attempts that fail to bridge the abyss between the lover who writes and the *sentement d'autrui*. These poems, meant to communicate sincere feelings, become monologues of distrust.[131]

The dominant motif in all these poems is the suspicion of passionate lovers. Suspicion is a kind of jealousy. Doubts, however superficial or commonplace, surface and are expressed; renewed declarations of constancy allay fears for a time. Then, doubts return. This is the cycle of noble love. Of course, passion itself produces a certain confusion, as when the lady uses language usually reserved for foolish love to describe her rationality prior to the *coup de foudre* that commences her passion. Surrendering to love – 'Pouoir n'ay de m'en oster' (*CBAD*, 22, v. 9) [I lack the power to withdraw from it] – reason submits.

> Cuidoie estre en sens montée
> Plus qu'autre, en greigneur savoir
> Que Salemon; asotée

---

[129] Adams 2003, p. 158. See Almeida Ribeiro 1989, p. 43; Adams 2002, pp. 6–8, and 2003, pp. 154–59.

[130] Christine may have expressed her own feelings *couvertement* if one reads the *Pastoure* as an allegory of a widow's bereavement; see Lefèvre 1988, especially pp. 343–46; and Paden 1994 on the prologue to *Pastoure*, which makes the shepherdess's loss a virtual allegory of Christine's widowhood. We recall that Christine wrote that she contemplated suicide when her husband died.

[131] Cf. Perrand 1999; Willard 1981b.

Bien estoie, a dire voir,
Et qui y aroit pouoir?   (*CBAD*, 22, v. 10–14)¹³²

[I thought myself to be more sensible than any one else, and more knowledgeable than Solomon. But, to tell the truth, I was quite besotted. And who could resist?]

This transmutation of values and traditional hierarchies, in which one's own opinion is falsified by the language used to describe it, is the foundation for the declining communication between the two lovers in this lyric cycle. As their opinions vary, so is the reader him- or herself hard put to evaluate the truth of mutual affirmations and accusations. As with Christine's other Dits, the *Cent Ballades d'amant et de dame* offers a paradigm of failure, an image of how little one knows oneself when in love, how little one knows the beloved, and how difficult it is to communicate feelings convincingly to others. The cycle ends with a 'Lay mortel' (p. 138), or commonplace love death.

The *Cent Ballades d'amant et de dame* reveals Christine's art of writing on controversial subjects and her skill in making crystal clear her 'true opinion' in the face of the lovers' confusion. Even if the *gradus amoris* can be read as sincere for both the lover and the lady,¹³³ its *conservatio* fails. Is the lover vacillating, changing, becoming unfaithful? Which one? We can, of course, read the evidence both ways.¹³⁴ If the man remains faithful, the situation is analogous to that in the *Duc*; if we read him as unfaithful, his love is not even noble, either because he is a false seducer, or because his feelings are unstable. In both cases, *l'amor'è mobile*. In Christine's opinion, also expressed by Sebile de Monthault, *fin'amours* leads to dismay, disarray, shame, misunderstanding, and even death. In this context too, *l'amor'è mobile*.

> Like Opinion of *L'Advision Cristine*, seduction, in the realms of love and reading, in itself is neither good nor bad, but varies according to the quality of what it discovers. It is a prerequisite, a means, a way of acquiring, but its moral dependence upon an initially unknown factor renders it hazardous.¹³⁵

The *Pastoure*, the *Duc*, and the *Cent Ballades d'amant et de dame* seem to begin with sincere love. Yet in all three the *gradus* and *continuatio* go awry without one's being able to identify precisely when the difficulties begin, or whether either lover is modeled on the *Rose*'s characters so redolent of *faux semblant*, although this reading is not altogether impossible for the noblemen in the *Pastoure* and in the *Cent Ballades d'amant et de dame*. Despite the often heard opinion today that these lovers are insincere or unfaithful, the 'operations

---

¹³² Cf. Almeida Ribeiro 1989, pp. 37–38.

¹³³ Adams 2000, pp. 414–16.

¹³⁴ On this critical or apo koinu approach, see Kelly 1994b (on Marie de France) and Kelly 2001 (on the *Rose*). Cf. Friedman 1989, pp. 441–44; Taylor 2002, pp. 849–52.

¹³⁵ Adams 2000, p. 414.

of uncertainty' in these narratives precludes any definitive statement.[136] The reader or audience is left to reflect on the hermeneutic dilemma[137] posed by the diverse explanations outlined above, none of which allows for a happy ending. What all these Dits share with the *Rose* is the abandonment of reason.[138] Reason, we recall, is a fundamental source of true opinion. With Christine, 'l'introduction dans le *dit* d'une signification morale signe également la fin du fantasme et annihile toute virtualité narrative'.[139]

The social significance of love is also a factor in reading these Dits. One consideration that may have loomed large in medieval readers' minds is the fate of the woman whose honor is lost by such affairs. For example, in his informative study of prostitution, Rossiaud notes rape, prostitution, and physical abuse as real threats for women lovers.[140] Such threats no doubt account to some degree for Christine's anxiety when gossip reports that she has taken a lover. Her fear may stem as much from the fact that such gossip about her reputation let men presume the right to victimize a widow of allegedly light morals (cf. *Cité*, pp. 332–34). Most of the women in Christine's Dits and lyric cycles are of very high birth and, thus, relatively safe from all except their own husbands or others of comparable status. The peasant girl in the *Pastoure* risks far more once the powerful lord withdraws from her, from rape to rejection and a life of prostitution. Does the *Trois vertus* not tacitly suggest that the only options available to medieval women are the nunnery, marriage, widowhood, and prostitution?[141]

Love and the widow Christine

None of these specific misfortunes is related by Christine, except occasionally by allusion.[142] Surely contemporary audiences were aware of what might happen to the shepherdess. Still, apart from the *Pastoure*, Christine does not take up loves in the middle or lower social orders where the threat to women was greater and protection less; she refers only occasionally to domestic violence or the lot of servants whom she represents more as a threat to the princess's reputation than as victims of harassment and sexual abuse from their masters, male co-workers, and others. Had Christine related the lives of these men and women, the tale might well have been closer to what Jean de Meun relates in

---

[136] Blanchard 1983, pp. 99, 108; see also Nouvet 1996, p. 293; Adams 2003.
[137] Hauck 1995, p. 253; see pp. 248–59.
[138] Adams 2000, p. 417.
[139] Blanchard 1983, p. 114.
[140] Rossiaud 1988, pp. 41–43.
[141] Cf. Lorcin 1994, pp. 204–05.
[142] Why not? For the same reasons she opposed explicit language in the *Rose*? Or were there deeper fears? On anxiety in Christine's writings, see Laennec 1993; Krueger 1998.

the *Roman de la rose* about the Vieille and Ami, or about the Jealous Husband and his wife.

Christine insists that love poetry holds little interest for her, that she herself is not in love, and that she does not have a lover.[143] However, in the descriptions of her marriage, we find patterns that inform her fictional tales. Her husband died while away from Paris serving the king; the *Cent Ballades* begins with the cycle on her widowhood, a series of poems evoking loss and decline after death.[144] They recall the common places of *deminutio* that we observe in the love poems, but with a redefinition of the principal figures. Yet, despite the reservations Christine expresses in the *Advision*, the written evidence is that her marriage was as happy in its early stages as the adulterous and premarital loves Christine relates in her love poems. Even Christine's sense of mortal grief is not without parallels among the women in these poems.

Widowhood was, of course, a continuation, but not like that for the damsel of the *Cent Ballades*, who could envision a new love, as Christine seems to suggest. But Christine was also aware of the threats that lay in wait for her as an attractive young widow. At the same time she was reading Boethius. From him she learned the real significance of opinion vis-à-vis fortune. She corrected her opinions on the chivalric love that she had admired in Du Guesclin and revised the *gradus amoris* and its continuation in the love poems she wrote thereafter. She tried to turn from the subject[145] to the more serious matters she wanted to study and write about. Among her more serious concerns was France. That is, she turned from lessons of self-interest for women in love to enlightened self-interest for the good of the nation as a whole.

---

[143] McGrady 2000. On the analogy between her attribute as 'clergesse' and her male contemporaries who were clerics, see Attwood 1998, pp. 21–26, and, on writing *de sentement*, pp. 41–51.

[144] See Willard 1984, pp. 39–40; Zühlke 1994, pp. 67–69; Adams 2003, pp. 152–55. Cf. Blanchard 1983, pp. 94–95; Paupert 1993, pp. 1065–66.

[145] Although she never repudiated the early poems she had written (Attwood 1998, p. 29), with the possible exception of the *Dit de la rose* mentioned above.

5

Self-Interest, Common Opinion, and Corrective Encomia

> Un mouvement constant la conduit du fait particulier
> à la matière générale du bon guide, du bon prince.[1]

Christine de Pizan was typical of her times in being unaware of the value of individual psychology. Indeed, psychology and psychiatry, as we know them today, did not exist for her time other than as a physiology based on the humors or on natural or God-given intellectual virtues and faculties like those she describes in her own mind and body.[2] A proper balance of the humors was desirable in humans; such balance was achieved in moral terms, not by psychoanalytical introspection. Hence, when dealing with individual problems, there was a movement towards the more general that might explain and permit evaluation and treatment of the individual's problem.[3] This led Christine to consider individual opinions in the context of moral and political debate. In confronting the chaotic state of French society in the early fifteenth century Christine quite naturally turned to moral generalizations. Her exemplar for analysis was the body politic of which the king was the head by divine right.[4] If the body politic is healthy, its members, as parts of the body, will be sound too; individuals too, as parts of the body's members, would profit when the body politic was in good health. Christine began to probe the causes of France's troubles with this image in mind.

---

[1] Blanchard 1986b, p. 52. Cf. von Moos 1988 p. 504.
[2] Lewis 1964, pp. 152–74. See also Picherit 1994 and 1995; Van Gijsen 1998, pp. 160–63; Brown-Grant, trans., *Cité*, p. xx; Galderisi 2002. Cf. von Moos 2002 on *sensus communis*.
[3] See Blanchard and Mühlethaler 2002, p. 42.
[4] She uses the image of the body politic adapted from John of Salisbury's *Policraticus*; see Forhan 2002, especially pp. 49–65.

France and self-interest

The *Chemin de long estude* relates a quandary analogous to that which we observed in the *Rose* debate. Nobility, Knighthood, Wealth, and Wisdom confront the turmoil of contemporary France before the court of Reason. There is no resolution to their debate in the poem.[5] However, the issue is not merely academic. France was in great trouble at the time Christine wrote. Its difficulties affected the commonweal, including the fate of women and the place of love in human life. The *Chemin* (v. 2861–90) suggests that covetousness is the root of the problem,[6] since different groups place self-interest before the common good. As we shall see, Christine also changed, or at least modified, this opinion, effecting another turnabout in her thought. Instead of condemning self-interest, she encouraged enlightened self-interest. Such enlightenment judges individual, family, or group self-interest as good when contributing to the common good. This reevaluation of the significance and meaning of self-interest is the fourth major change in her thought.[7]

It is a striking change. Christine seems to have been aware of its implications and originality. As noted in my Introduction, she makes her appeal for the commonweal as a *femme passionnee* (*Policie*, p. 1:7). In her usage, this expression is a virtual oxymoron,[8] as the caveat that introduces her statement makes clear: 'Se il est possible que de vice puist naistre vertu, bien me plaist en ceste partie estre passionnee comme femme' (*Policie*, p. 1:6–7) [If it is possible that vice beget virtue, it quite suits me in this matter to be a woman gone mad]. Her 'passion' is a profound desire for virtue precisely because virtue is, for Christine, the source of the common good as much as of individual felicity.

Christine covets virtue, thereby revising Boethius's criticism of false goods, as discussed in Chapter 1. Such goods are not false when they derive from or promote virtue; they are indeed desirable, if not always gained in this life. She discovers another source of virtue in vice in her reflections on self-interest, a vice that La Rochefoucauld will find at the heart of all human endeavor. But, as is often the case in Christine's thought, ideas are *contraires choses* that have morally good and bad connotations, much as opinions have diverse shades of meaning. Enlightened self-interest is good when it is synonymous with virtuous self-interest.

---

[5] On the indecisive conclusion in dream vision poetry, especially poems on political issues, see Marchello-Nizia 1985.

[6] The same conviction is expressed in *Paix*, pp. 78, 97–98, 151–53.

[7] On what follows, see especially Forhan 2002.

[8] Cf. Blanchard and Quereuil 1999, p. 290 s.v. *passionné*: 'incapable de se maîtriser, furieux, emporté'. The 'passions' are always irrational and morally negative in the *Corps de policie*; see p. 9:21. They include anger and hatred (p. 52:9–10).

As time passed, Christine 'wrote more about the plight of France than she did about the plight of women'.[9] But the poetic mode she glosses in the *Advision* permits her readers to recontextualize a received context such that, allegorically, France can represent all of humanity, the plight of women, and Christine's own extraordinary life. Public and private virtues are analogous and interrelated, much as the macrocosm and microcosm are. Saving France, improving women's lot in France, good love – all are matters of self-interest.[10] But they are also interrelated; amelioration in the one domain improves matters in the other. As a kind of synecdoche, the improvement of the parts improves the whole, just as improvement of the whole, France, contributes to more general amelioration in all sectors of society. We have observed such correlations in the autobiographical parallels with history in the *Mutacion* and the *Advision*, works in which Christine moves back and forth between the individual's lot and the nation's fate. It is therefore fitting to conclude this study of Christine's opinions by putting them in their broadest, most general, historical context: France between the death of Charles V and the emergence of Joan of Arc.[11]

Christine's realization in the *Advision* that opinion is a more powerful force than fortune went hand-in-hand with her Boethian view of virtue as an impregnable defense against fortune. Virtue in the king, the queen, and their subjects defends France against her enemies from within and without; Christine thought that Charles V's reign was solid evidence in support of this opinion. In the *Advision*'s first part, she argues that the Boethian model of virtue explains national well-being while its absence leads to misfortune. The more numerous rulers who are victims of fortune are also given over to vices; the most successful kings, including Clovis, Charlemagne, Louis VIII, and Louis IX, illustrate the Boethian ideal.[12] Charles V, the last of the virtuous rulers (*Advision*, I.viii–xi; cf. *Chemin*, v. 5001–46), is her primary exemplar of virtue in the monarch because he brought order to the realm. In the *Corps de policie* and the *Livre de la paix*, she is still lauding his reign. But the king is a model of the virtue available to all men and women who eschew vices in order to excel in learning and government, love and marriage, war and the contemplative life. Christine praises and promotes virtue because it serves moral, social, political, and individual good throughout society.

Moreover, as she shows in the debate that concludes the *Chemin de long estude*, fractured self-interest splits the realm into contending rivalries like those that were undermining French society during her adult life. Rivalries were

---

[9] Gottlieb 1985, p. 348; cf. Willard, ed., *Paix*, pp. 15–16; Lemaire 1994, p. 438; Blumenfeld-Kosinski 1999.

[10] See *Paix*, pp. 173–76; Solterer 1995, p. 164. In the *Cité*, p. 332, and *Policie*, p. 27:4–5, Christine notes the increased incidence of rape in times of war; cf. Ramsay 2002.

[11] For overviews of the historical calamities of these years, see Huizinga 1997; Schnerb 2001; for society, see Gauvard 1991.

[12] Cf. Nabert 1997. Nabert finds Clovis named only in *Charles V* (p. 231); however, he also appears in the *Advision*'s gloss (p. 8:212–15). In the treatise itself, Christine alludes to him as 'le·V$^{e\cdot}$ filz' (I.viii.13–15; see Reno and Dulac, ed., pp. 149–50 n. VIII(13)).

everywhere, among princely families and popes and between town and gown as well as within social groups; rebellions exploded intermittently in town and countryside (*Advision*, II.xvii).[13] In the *Chemin* debate, she depicts the self-interest of personified social groups as each argues that a ruler should be chosen from its midst as the best solution to France's problems. Wealth, Nobility, Wisdom, and Knighthood put partial self-interests before the enlightened self-interest of the whole nation; each speaker is of the opinion (*Chemin*, v. 3164) that the best king will come from its order. Rather than attack self-interest as such, Christine argues that self-interest requires the union of all these powers under a sovereign who rules in the interest of all. She continues to uphold this opinion in her later treatises.

> Le bon prince ... doit voloir que de ses subgez chascun face en paix l'office en quoy Dieu l'a establi, les nobles ce qu'ilz doivent faire, le clergié entende aux sciences et au service divin, les marchans a leurs marchandises, les gens de mestier a leurs ouvraiges, les laboureurs au cultivement des terres, et ainsi chascun en son degré vive par bonne policie. (*Policie*, pp. 16:37–17:2)[14]

> [The good prince must want each of his subjects to fulfill peacefully the office to which God has assigned him or her: the nobles in their assigned role, the clerical class applying itself to the sciences and to divine service, merchants to business, tradesmen to their works, farmers to cultivating lands. In this way let each person live in good order on his or her social level.]

Such enlightened self-interest promotes the common good and individual prosperity because each group diligently fulfills its assigned tasks in the body politic, uniting society and nation under the good prince, much as in Charles V's reign. This is the essence of Wisdom's recommendation in the *Chemin*: the king should be noble, chivalric, and wise – a reincarnation, as it were, of Charles V; as such, he will use the nation's wealth for the common good. But Christine's proposal failed because self-interest remained divided, finally tearing the nation apart. After the English and the Burgundian massacres in Paris in 1418 Christine fled to Poissy.[15]

Enlightened self-interest

Christine's two major epideictic works, the *Fais et bonnes meurs de Charles V* and the *Cité des dames*, focus on men or women whose virtues make them

---

[13] See Dudash 2003, pp. 821–23, 826–29.

[14] See also *Policie*, p. 40:1–6. As we have seen, Christine relates social unity to the commonplace image of the body politic allegorically interpreted as the head representing the king and the lower parts of the body the corresponding social groups, from nobility to common people (*Policie*, pp. 91–92; cf. ed. Kennedy, pp. xxxv–xxxvi.). Cf. Dudash 2003.

[15] Leppig 1992, pp. 143–44; McKinley 1992.

praiseworthy. Other works of a more practical nature set out an agenda for realizing this goal; they include the *Corps de policie* and the *Livre de la paix*. These and analogous writings apply the same moral standards to both sexes.[16] All treat matters of opinion supported by examples that praise or correct real or potential conduct, whether in private life, historical events, or government. The goal in all these writings is the common good.

Christine de Pizan does not forget the menace of misogyny. Sylvia Nagel notes that, for Christine, upholding the commonweal also protects women.[17] Thus, Christine not infrequently emphasizes the sexual gender of her examples in order to contextualize her argument and to take practical account of the social constraints of her times. To do so, she describes the topos *sexus* in order to laud or criticize different representations of each gender according to her standards, standards she adapted to social status and social norms. This is to say that, although the standards are the same for both men and women, social circumstances, especially misogyny, the social status to which women belong, and social orders, require different, yet complementary approaches and lessons. Accordingly, the virtue of both men and women is the object of Christine's praise, just as vice earns her invective. Nevertheless, various devices, notably topical abbreviations, glossing over, or even silence, may downplay actual vices or defects in order to amplify on virtues.[18] The examples she uses derive their authority from their verisimilitude and cogency, not from their historical or documentary validity.

Christine's reevaluation of self-interest in her historical writings represents a long, anguished, and sometimes perplexed process.[19] It can recall the medieval commonplace, as the eleventh-century life of Saint Alexis puts it, that

> Bons fut li secles al tens ancïenur,
> Quer feit i ert e iustise ed amur;
> S'i ert creance, dunt or n'i at nul prut.
> Tut est müez, perdut ad sa colur:
> Ja mais n'iert tel cum fut as anceisurs.   (*Alexis*, v. 1–5)[20]

> [Good was life here below in bygone days, for then there was faith, justice, and love, as well as belief – nothing worthwhile is left of that now. All has changed and lost its quality. It will never again be as it was among our ancestors.]

---

[16] Brown-Grant 1995 and 2002. Cf. Richards 1994, p. 27: 'the members of the City of Ladies will typologically represent all of humanity'; and Richards 1996.

[17] Nagel 2000, p. 116.

[18] Malosse 2000. Dissimulation is a feature of Faux Semblant that Christine seems to admire in Jean's description of this personification; see p. 13 n. 29, above. Elsewhere she notes instances in which such dissimulation is good; see, for example, p. 93, on the governess in the *Trois vertus* who hides her mistress's unwanted pregnancy by claiming to be mother of the child.

[19] See Blanchard 1986b; Blumenfeld-Kosinski 2003; Ribémont 2003.

[20] Cf. Brown-Grant 1993, pp. 211–16.

However, Christine does not envision a prehistoric Golden Age,[21] nor evoke a prelapsarian Eden. Her Golden Age is the reign of Charles V.

Storms came rolling across France after the king's death. Here too, Christine's life mirrors larger French reality. About the time the king died, so did her father and husband;[22] Louis d'Orléans was murdered, Charles the VI's madness waxed and waned, and the kingdom fell apart as invasions from abroad and internal strife engulfed France. As she looked back to the reign of Charles V, Christine saw his glory grounded on the very virtues she extols in her writings. After his death, virtue began to cede to self-interest.[23] France's tribulations continued, calamity following on calamity. In the *Chemin de long estude*, Christine names no new ruler capable of uniting *bellatores*, *oratores*, and *laboratores* in a strong, functional nation, no doubt in part because the mad king Charles VI still wore the crown. The schismatic Church offered little hope. There must have seemed as if there could be no salvation for France when Christine took refuge in the convent in Poissy in 1418.

Caught between reason and emotion, Christine's opinion on France's fate also fluctuated during these years. Hope did shine from time to time. First, it emerged in the person of the Dauphin, Louis de Guyenne, for whom she wrote the *Corps de policie* and the *Livre de la paix*. With him she hoped that, once crowned, he would restore the virtues and successes of his grandfather. But the Dauphin died before ascending the throne. Still later, almost as if to add an example to the *Cité des dames*, hope returned in a certainly unexpected, and therefore seemingly miraculous way: Joan of Arc, the peasant girl from Domremy, was nearing Paris after victory at Orléans and the coronation of Charles VII in Rheims.

In order to write her treatises on good government, Christine faced a number of problems. The early death of Charles V was followed by the madness of Charles VI shortly after he assumed authority under initially auspicious circumstances. She appealed to Charles VI's queen in the *Epistre à la reine*, but the appeal was ineffective. Military defeats at Nicopolis and, later, Agincourt, and violent, chaotic infighting within the royal family, including the murder of Louis d'Orléans and, later, of Jean sans Peur, signaled the monarchy's failure to wield the scepter effectively. The appeal to virtue that was so strong in *Charles V* fell on deaf ears.[24] Nothing seemed effective in uniting the opposing self-interests.

Fully convinced that action was required, Christine changed tack. To her emphasis on virtue as a noble incentive, she added the very self-interest that seemed so baleful under Charles VI.[25] 'In a fragile world, the only safety can

---

[21] Brown-Grant 1988; cf. Ribémont 2002a.

[22] All of Christine's male relatives in France died before she did, including one anonymous son in childhood and her other son, Jean de Castel, about 1425.

[23] Forhan 2002, p. 109. Cf. Blanchard 1986a, pp. 427–28; Dulac 1992a, pp. 133–34.

[24] Lemaire 1994, pp. 136–40.

[25] On what follows, see Forhan 2002, pp. 100–09, 124–25, 162–64.

be found in prudence, the prudence of self-interest.'[26] Prudence showed that self-interest was essential to the commonweal (*Chemin*, v. 4457–60, 5113–14, 5488–92). The kind of unity, counsel, and cooperation she sought under the king in the *Chemin* was in the interest of all. Unfortunately, even such appeals to enlightened self-interest failed to impede the deepening national and moral quagmire of narrow self-interest. Then, suddenly, the very religion Christine withdrew into in 1418, rent as it was by the ongoing schism, became the source of unexpected salvation with the emergence of Joan of Arc. What better confirmation of her faith and virtue than the Maid of Orléans? Did Christine de Pizan experience a renewal of faith and ultimately a general change of opinion from despair to hope before she closed her eyes for the last time? Did she die still confident that 'n'y a si forte / Resistance qui à l'assault / De la Pucelle ne soit morte' (*Jehanne*, v. 406–08) [no resistance is strong enough to survive when attacked by the Maid of Orléans]? Or did she lay her pen down upon learning of Joan's capture and, perhaps, martyrdom? Whatever the answers to these questions, she obviously saw France's fate as hanging in the balance of Providence, which works best, in Christine's opinion, when enlightened self-interest unites the different French factions into one force (as during Charles V's and Joan of Arc's early successes). Providence is more powerful than either fortune or opinion.

Fortune and counsel

As we have seen, Christine began her reflection on historical change in the *Mutacion de fortune*. Typical of fifteenth-century historical writing, the poem's structure and content are mostly determined by chronology. After relating her own alternately fortunate and unfortunate life, Christine describes Fortune's castle in contemporary terms[27] before setting out a lengthy chronicle of Fortune's role in history from the Tower of Babel down to her own times. Every event reported, from biblical to modern times, conforms to the conventional image of fortune. As repetitive history,[28] fortune is a constant force in human affairs, ever raising and lowering the mighty and their empires. Escape occurs only if Providence intervenes, as in parts of Jewish history (*Mutacion*, v. 8241–44,

---

[26] Forhan 2002, p. 163. Prudence is a fundamental virtue that Christine promotes in the lost *Livre de prudence*, the *Corps de policie*, and the *Livre de la paix*; see Delogu 2005, pp. 51–53. For its place in human thought, see above, pp. 42, 120.

[27] On the place of this description in the *Mutacion*, see Brownlee 1991. The description of Fortune's castle is an instance of *ordo artificialis* in that it sums up contemporary moral history and is, therefore, a conclusion to the chronological chronicle of the other great kingdoms in this poem's third part. Christine would have known this principle of natural and artificial order from Brunetto Latini's *Tresor*, III.xi (Kelly 1969, pp. 131–32).

[28] On repetitive history, see Stierle 1972, pp. 183–85.

8416–42).²⁹ Virtue can be effective too. Charles V's knowledge and prudence gave him the foresight and intelligence ('providence' and 'avis') needed to overcome France's enemies (*Mutacion*, v. 23539–44). Of course, Providence operates only for the virtuous.

Both the *Mutacion*'s autobiographical first part and its chronological world history in the third part portray the passage of time as the unremitting, often dreary turn of Fortune's Wheel in human affairs. The same cycle is implicit in the description of Fortune's castle in the middle section, since the description applies to all times and places. This image of fortune in history is so commonplace in Christine's time as to require no further discussion here, were it not for her correction of it in the *Advision*. As we have seen in Chapters 1 and 2, Christine changed her mind in that treatise, arguing that not Fortune, but Opinion is the source of her own and history's problems. Her authority for this correction, Boethius, justifies her reliance on virtue as an escape from Fortune's uncertainties. It also prepares for Christine's reevaluation of self-interest.

How do Christine's opinions on self-interest fit into these parameters? As shown earlier, Christine adopted the Boethian opinion that believing in Fortune's dominance in human affairs actually opens the door for Fortune to act in those affairs, whereas virtue provides the means to escape from Fortune's dominion. In reviewing history, this meant identifying and praising those whose virtue successfully overcame the woes of their times. For Christine, the archetype of such virtue is the good king, a case made in the *Chemin de long estude*, where covetousness and envy,³⁰ both aspects of self-interest, can be overcome by returning to virtue under a wise and just king.

Having modified her earlier opinion that Fortune is the primary cause of her own woes, Christine turned to reviewing the same assumption about France's calamities. Conflicting opinions may lead to rational debate or to irrational war. In the *Chemin de long estude*, Christine, descending from the firmament, stops in the sphere of the air where a debate among self-interested forces in society takes place. The debate begins with a complaint probably modeled on Nature's complaints in Alain de Lille's *De planctu Naturae*³¹ and the *Rose*, except that Christine rewrites the *planctus Naturae* in these two works as a *planctus Terrae*.³² Terre's complaint focuses less on individual morality than on social morality. She appeals to Reason to act against the self-serving covetousness rampant in society because it leads to the war and destruction that tear France apart. To depict this state of affairs, Christine adopts the commonplace image

---

²⁹ Cf. Beer 1992, pp. 127–28, who treats providential history as distinct from history dominated by fortune.

³⁰ On these vices in the *Chemin*, see especially v. 3033–50, 3151–65, 4589–602, 5913–20.

³¹ Christine cites the *De planctu* in the *Chemin*, v. 5207–08. Gerson refers to it in the *Débat*, p. 80:526–28.

³² Dulac 1998b, pp. 84–86. The *planctus Terrae* anticipates the *planctus Liberae* alias *Franciae* in the *Advision*. On the *planctus* in Christine's time, see Gauvard 1995, pp. 109–10, and Slerca 1998.

of man, also found in the *De planctu Naturae* and *Roman de la rose*, as the sole unnatural creature in God's universe.

> A toute riens son devoir
> Voy faire, fors a homme lige,
> De paradis hoir, s'il ne tient
> A lui. Car bestes mues font
> Leur devoir, comme il appartient,
> Et les hommes si se deffont.   (*Chemin*, v. 2669–74)

> [I see everything do its duty except our liegeman, heir to Paradise, insofar as he alone is responsible. For mute beasts do their duty, as is proper, while men do not.]

The ensuing clash of opinions[33] pits Nobility, Knighthood, Wisdom, and Wealth against one another. Each personification blames one of the others for the nation's wrongs while offering herself as a solution; the very narrowing of criticism to only one personification shows each speaker's failure to view the entire picture of the nation and its troubles. This is indeed narrow self-interest. Even Reason, the judge of the debate, is not without fault. In a striking response to Reason's return to her tower (as she does in the *Rose*), Wisdom notes that by returning there, Reason abdicates responsibility[34] and fails to do her duty:

> Dieux, ma dame, comment
> Me blasmez vous dont n'ay retrait
> Le monde du mal ou il trait?
> Et comment l'en peusse retraire,
> Sanz vous qui ça vous voltes traire
> Pour ce que les mondains entendre
> Ne vous vouloient, n'a bien tendre?   (*Chemin*, v. 2994–3000)

> [In God's name, my lady, how can you blame me for not having lifted the world out of the evil it draws towards? How could I do so without you, you who chose to withdraw up here because no one on earth wanted to hear you or strive for good?]

Without Reason, Wisdom is ineffective and peace on earth impossible. Reason must blame herself for her willful absence.[35] By the same token, each of the personifications in the debate can be faulted for thinking only of herself rather than the common good.

---

[33] See *Chemin*, v. 3164, 3451; cf. also *avis*, v. 3261, and *cuidier*, v. 3273. Christine contrasts these two varieties of opinion again in *Prouverbes*, 17–18. On Libera's criticism of such partiality in the *Advision*, see Brown-Grant 1999a, pp. 115–16.

[34] On this correction of the *Rose*, see Willard 1984, p. 106; cf. Adams 2000, p. 423.

[35] Food for thought among discerning readers of Reason's abandonment of Amant in the *Rose*.

Reason does not respond directly to Wisdom. Indeed, none of the debaters responds to the various wrongs or failings imputed to them. Christine seems to imply that, wherever the fault may lie, united action is needed.

> Or sus doncques! Ce dit Raison,
> De ceste chose nous tayson.
> Ce qui est fait ne peut deffaire,
> Mais penson s'il se pourra faire
> Qu'aultrement le monde arreé
> Puist estre qui est desreé.   (*Chemin*, v. 3009–14)
>
> ['Let's get busy then!' exclaims Reason. 'Let's say no more on the present topic. What's done cannot be undone. Let's see whether we can find a way to bring this disorderly world back into order.']

By shifting the debate from mutual vituperation, Reason appeals for common effort. Each personification argues that a representative of the group she personifies can best govern the world and direct it towards universal peace and good order. Nobility recommends a person of the highest nobility – the Holy Roman Emperor because his lineage extends back to Troy.[36] Knighthood recommends a knight, whereas Wealth proposes a rich man whose largess will bring peace and good order to the world.[37] Finally, Wisdom prefers a wise and learned ruler who, like Solomon, will uphold justice equitably. These 'local' certainties ignore the broader national need for consensus; they are subjective, but unenlightened. What is needed, Christine seems to imply, is someone possessing all these qualities.

Yet the centrifugal movement of debate and accusation precludes unity, according to Wisdom. Reason acts on that opinion, resolving the debate and unifying action. The centripetal movement she initiates brings the conflicting opinions together and, accordingly, into perspective. As variously personified shades of opinion, all four personifications identify, each in its partial view, elements necessary in the agency that will govern the world. But unity is required.[38] The agency for such a 'rainbow coalition' of the diversely colored opinions is

> a strong ruler in a centralized kingdom advised by a panel of experts ... Anything that would tend to further fragment the monarchy and the country could be viewed as an evil to be avoided ... Christine preferred an interlocking

---

[36] Christine may have had in mind the French claim to the Imperial throne; see Beaune 1985, p. 50, and *Jehanne*, where she expresses the opinion that the recently crowned Charles VII 'doit estre empereur' (v. 128) [should be emperor].

[37] Wealth's opinion recalls the largess economy described in Jean Renart's *Guillaume de Dole*; see M. Zink 1979, p. 21.

[38] Forhan 1996, pp. 72–78.

interdependence of social groupings that could intercede with each other as needed.[39]

Under such a king, narrow self-interest becomes mutual self-interest uniting the four social groups in a common purpose. Such enlightened self-interest works for all. The body politic is again in good health.

The political issues are, therefore, analogous to moral issues evoked in the *Rose* debate and to philosophical issues in the debates that color diverse opinions in the *Advision*. In the *Chemin* debate, Reason identifies the king as a central figure because he derives his authority first and foremost from God.[40] Thus, the debate in the *Chemin* is a road map to a solution, although it does not resolve the issues. All must turn to the sovereign French court (*Chemin*, v. 6258–68) for what Wealth calls the 'sentence diffinitive' (v. 3841). Maistre Avis, a masculine Opinion (v. 6227), agrees (v. 6219–25). Using *discrecion* (v. 6225), all urge the court to 'les parties en accort / Mettre par loyale sentence' (v. 6274–75) [bring the parties together in loyal agreement]. The hypothesis of the *Chemin* is that the French court can unite the contending parties in the debate under a wise king who can restore peace (*Chemin*, v. 6336–45). Although the *Chemin* shows Reason returning to earth from her tower, no decision is reported that actually resolves the problems that plague the French nation.[41] Only a virtuous king can do that.

Maistre Avis voices Christine's opinion that the united French court can accomplish the task of restoring peace because all cooperate. The one figure not specifically identified who would bring all this about and personify national unity in his person, is, of course, the actual king. Unfortunately, it is not the deceased Charles V le Sage, but the king the poem is dedicated to, Charles VI the Mad (*Chemin*, v. 9–12).[42] This is no doubt the source of Christine's dilemma. It prevents the articulation of a definitive opinion, a possibility marked by the interruption of her dream when her mother knocks at the door to awaken her daughter (v. 6394–98). That knock suggests that Christine found no solution in the depressing reality of a mad king's court.

Awakening traditionally ends allegorical dreams inconclusively.[43] The audience is left to sort matters out more or less individually or through discussion, as is the case with the conclusion of the *Roman de la rose*,[44] or to await a pronouncement from a patron on the work's import, as in Christine's own debate poems:

---

[39] Forhan 2002, p. 99.
[40] Krynen 1981.
[41] This is typical in open-ended debate poetry. As in her address to the queen in the *Rose* debate, Christine appeals to a king for decisive action in the *Chemin*.
[42] See Hicks, trans., *Charles V*, p. 16; cf. her gloss to the *Advision*, p. 10:268–71. Did Christine have Louis d'Orléans in mind? See Ouy and Reno 2000; Dudash 2003, p. 816.
[43] In Christine's case, 'la mère interrompt' (Dziedzik 2002, p. 497). On reawakening, see Cerquiglini 1993c; Maddox 2000, ch. 3.
[44] Kelly 1995a, p. 151.

Quoiqu'on en appelle au jugement du dédicataire, le débat reste éternellement ouvert, le lecteur n'aura pas de réponse; il n'y en a pas, pour une raison au moins: la souffrance n'est pas dans la cause de l'affliction proprement dite mais dans la perception et l'appréciation de cette cause.[45]

Nothing has been resolved at the end of the *Chemin*. This is what we might expect, given 'the dysfunctional state of contemporary France'.[46] Christine must return to sleep and to dreaming in order to continue. The return takes place in the *Advision Cristine*, a work in which dreaming works as a metaphor for thought (*Advision*, p. 3:17). Not surprisingly, her first encounter there is with Chaos caused by unenlightened self-interest. In her personal life, Christine thinks her way from chaos through uncertain opinion to the virtuous life.[47] For the nation, she turns to the life of Charles V as a personal and national exemplar.

Charles V, epideixis, and opinion

What kind of king can unite France? Christine finds the answer to this question in the person and reign of Charles V. The composition of the biography of Charles V, as description, relies on the art of topical invention in the panegyric mode and on the *aviser–deviser* paradigm. Christine identifies attributes of Charles that made him admirable and successful (*aviser*) and then describes them for her readers (*deviser*). This provided a model of kingship that could be communicated to subsequent kings and dauphins as a guide (*aviser*).

Christine's life of Charles V is *Herrscherlob* or panegyric royal biography. Panegyric, or epideixis, has a place as demonstrative oratory alongside judicial and deliberative oratory (*Tresor*, III.2.8–11).[48] As praise or blame, epideixis is common in medieval historiography.[49] A ceremonial mode, it was often little more than a kind of scholastic exercise for festive moments. But it also served to exemplify (*Tresor*, III.13.10–11). This is Christine's purpose in *Charles V*. Accordingly, she describes a virtuous prince in order to set an exemplary standard for noble thought and action that can be beneficial for France and, thus, promote the commonweal.[50] More specifically, in order to laud the deceased king, Christine describes his virtues in order to show how beneficial they were in the king's pursuit of national unity. Nobility and Knighthood as

---

[45] Chareyron 2002, p. 244.
[46] Cropp 2002, p. 302.
[47] Cf. Brucker 2001.
[48] Curtius 1954, chs. 8, 9, and 10. For background, see Momigliano 1971; Pernot 1993; Malosse 2000. Christine distinguishes between such laudation, or *louange*, and flattery, or *blandice* (*Charles V*, vol. 1, pp. 180–85); see Blanchard 1986b, p. 48, and 1986c, pp. 44–46.
[49] Kleinschmidt 1974; Mühlethaler 2002.
[50] See Dulac 1994; Zimmermann 1994; Brown-Grant 1995, on panegyric in the *Cité des dames*.

well as the Rich and the Wise can unite by emulating those virtues. In this way, panegyric promotes enlightened self-interest.

Praise of Charles's virtues and promotion of those virtues in his successors requires panegyric in historical writing, especially biography, and in treatises on good government. Charles V exemplifies sovereignty in all Christine's political works, from *Charles V* to the *Livre de la paix*. Her acceptance of the duke of Burgundy's commission to write a laudatory biography of Charles V[51] differs from the usual commission to write love poetry; in this treatise, Christine truly writes *de sentement* because her opinions conform to her new goal to write in order to promote the commonweal.

According to the *Corps de policie*, renewal will come through the union of chivalry, clergy, and people. The same opinion prevails in the *Livre de la paix*, where Christine reviews once again the virtues she finds in Charles V, encouraging his grandson, Louis de Guyenne, for whom she wrote the treatise, to emulate them. Charles's queen, Jeanne de Bourbon, serves as an analogous example of royal virtues for women in the *Trois vertus*. In both the *Cité des dames* and the *Trois vertus* past achievements confirm contemporary instruction on virtue.[52]

In order to write about Charles V, Christine also relies on the faculties Nature bestows on her in the *Mutacion*.[53] In the following passage one discerns them anew, although in slightly different language. Christine beseeches God to grant her eloquence, clear thought, and understanding so that she can elucidate what she draws from memory: 'euvre mes levres, enlumines ma pensée, et mon entendement esclaires à celle fin que m'ignorance n'encombre mes sens à expliquer les choses conceues en ma memoire' (*Charles V*, vol. 1, p. 4) [open my lips, illuminate my mind, enlighten my understanding so that ignorance may not encumber my mind in explaining matters conceived in my memory]. These words echo her reliance on faith, reason, and *vray sentement* in finding and expressing true opinion. Opinion is hardly problematic for her in *Charles V*. Christine found the king's life virtuous and, therefore, praiseworthy. Her patron, the duke of Burgundy, agreed. Who in France would have disagreed?

As in most of Christine's other writings,[54] *Charles V* contains three parts. However, it is not compiled in the same way as the third part of her *Mutacion*. It is a compilation,[55] but not a strictly chronological compilation. Each part describes how Charles V incarnates a specific virtue in an exemplary manner.

---

[51] See the analogous representation of herself in *Paix*, pp. 60, 63–64.

[52] Willard 1984, pp. 122–23. See also *Charles V*, vol. 1, pp. 53–57; *Trois vertus*, p. 47:12–17.

[53] This poem moved Philippe of Burgundy to invite her to write *Charles V* (vol. 1, pp. 6–7).

[54] See Solente, ed., *Charles V*, vol. 1, p. xxx (to which add the *Mutacion*). On Christine's coherent use of tripartite divisions, see Blanchard and Mühlethaler 2002, pp. 21–23.

[55] 'Ceste petite compillacion par moy traittiée' (vol. 2, p. 193; cf. vol. 1, p. 7) [this brief compilation I drew up].

That is, Christine's account of the king's life describes an 'abstract' king,[56] one identified by those topoi that she chooses to extol by description and definition. She also calls *Charles V* a 'traittié' (*Charles V*, vol. 1, pp. 7, 8). As we have seen, 'treatise' in Christine's time refers to two modes: the *modus tractatus* and the *modus tractandi*.[57] As *tractatus*, *Charles V* has three parts. Each part is amplified using specific ways of treating, or of *tractandi*, notably praise and blame as panegyric and invective.[58] Christine treats 'noblece de courage' in Part One, 'chevalerie' in Part Two, and 'sagece' in Part Three (*Charles V*, vol. 1, p. 9) – three of the ideas that, personified, debate before Reason in the *Chemin de long estude*.[59] It is also noteworthy that *Charles V* adds Christine's own experiences,[60] including what she herself witnessed,[61] thereby reviving and adapting the traditional medieval preference for eye-witness accounts in historical writing.

Charles V is a virtual mirror for princes,[62] analogous to the kind of mirror Peter von Moos describes in John of Salisbury's *Policraticus*, a work Christine knew.[63] The biography shows what an exemplary prince does that is praiseworthy and exemplary. Charles's life and virtues constitute an *exemplum*, and are part of an inductive procedure.[64] This is because an example contains topoi.[65] Such topoi or common places in examples have a potential for interpretative amplification. Indeed, the same material may permit an opposition (*contraires choses*) that allows reading the example *in utramque partem*. In *Charles V*, such antiphrasis permits both praise of the king's virtues and invective addressed to the vices he resisted in himself and his realm (vol. 1, p. 6).

That Charles V possessed the three virtues Christine emphasizes – nobility, chivalry, and wisdom – she does not doubt. Although a darker side in the king's life and family is hinted at, she argues that the epideictic mode does not allow her to treat it. She thus declines to describe unspecified defects in Charles's

---

[56] Kantorowicz 1957, p. xvii. The abstract person is analogous to the person endowed by God with perfect gifts, but gifts whose power depends on the body they are located in; see above, pp. 21–22. Ethical constraint is the only limit on the abstract king's absolute power (Parussa 1996, pp. 132–33). Christine shows the same purpose in *Othea*, written (or copied) for various princes, any one of whom might have ascended the throne (Parussa, ed., *Othea*, pp. 81–86).

[57] See above, pp. 7–8.

[58] On the originality of *Charles V*'s composition, see Blanchard 1990; on invective in her writings and those of her contemporaries, see Blanchard 1986c.

[59] Wealth is not a virtue in *Charles V*; as we have seen, this personification is excoriated in the *Chemin*.

[60] Blanchard 1990, pp. 218, 203–12; Blanchard 1993, pp. 222–26.

[61] Blanchard 1990, p. 216.

[62] Krynen 1981, pp. 64–65; Blanchard and Mühlethaler 2002, ch. 1, especially pp. 18–26.

[63] In the original and/or in the French translation by Jean Foulechat; see *Charles V*, vol. 2, p. 44; von Moos 1988, pp. 142–43 and n. 1106; Forhan 1992, 2002; Quillet 2002.

[64] Von Moos 1988, pp. 188–208.

[65] On *locus ab exemplo*, see von Moos 1988, pp. 427–34.

life and character. Christine is quite clear on this intention,[66] stating not infrequently that, for example, 'le texte de mon livre si n'est que en louant les vertus, et parler des vices seroit hors de mon propos né' (*Charles V*, vol. 1, p. 182) [my book is written only in praise of virtues; treating vices would not fit my intention]. Invective is reserved for those who exemplify the vices and defects opposed to Charles's virtues. True opinion qualifies the king for such praise. Such selection and deletion of material is characteristic of the topical invention of *gradus* scripts (see Chapter 2). In *Charles V* Christine uses the technique to set out an array of royal virtues.[67]

What in Christine's life qualifies her to treat virtue? She describes herself as of noble birth through her Italian family and ancestry; she names herself 'Filz[68] de noble homme et renommé' (*Mutacion*, v. 171) [son of a noble, renowned man]. That she describes herself as of moderate beauty suggests that she accepted her limitations and place beneath the princesses and other ladies of the *Cité* and the *Trois vertus*. More specifically, in the Prologue to *Charles V* Christine also discusses her qualifications for the task of writing panegyric history. She depicts herself as a 'femme soubz les tenebres d'ignorance', but 'douée de don de Dieu et nature en tant comme desir se peut estendre en amour d'estude' (vol. 1, p. 5) [woman in the shadow of ignorance endowed by God and nature insofar as desire can go with the love of study]. *Ignorance*, but also *desir de savoir* – these are Lady Opinion's parents in the *Advision*.

Accordingly, opinion as she defines it in the *Advision* is the context for her inquiry into Charles V's virtues: the opinion here is that the king was an exemplary, praiseworthy monarch. In the *Chemin de long estude*, Reason entrusts Christine with the task of admonishing the court because of her 'meurs', 'inclinacion', and 'affeccion' (v. 6307–08). These topoi – *habitus*, *studium*, and *affectus* – identify and authorize the *fille d'escolle*'s intervention as Reason's voice, the school being that of the Sibyl herself (cf. 'de nostre escolle ancelle', v. 6294).[69] By a studious, retired lifestyle, Christine sought to overcome her deficiencies and achieve a virtuous, praiseworthy life. This goal strengthens her resolve to pursue her task. Being virtuous, she knows virtue *de sentement*. There are rewards too; each virtue will also give her renown lasting long after her life is over (*Advision*, II.xxii.63–71, III.x.38–44). Virtue bestows renown because the virtuous person is praiseworthy (*Cité*, p. 54). The same holds for the nation and its king (*Advision*, I.iv.2–13). These are the qualities Christine brought to the composition of her panegyric on Charles's virtues.

---

[66] Solente, ed., *Charles V*, vol. 1, pp. lxxxiii–lxxxv; Willard 1984, p. 125.
[67] Vol. 1, pp. 180–84, 189–92, 198–99. This conforms to her tendency in the *Cité* to adapt her mini-biographies to her moralizing intentions; see above, pp. 66, 84.
[68] 'Leçon donnée par tous les mss.' (Solente, ed., v. 171 var.) Cf. Holderness 2002.
[69] On the various images of the sibyl in Christine's writings, see Fenster 2003.

Laudation for Christine de Pizan does not support pride or vanity,[70] although this vice, common among the royalty and aristocracy she wrote for, did not go unnoticed. She believed that such pride stems from a false opinion as to the source of nobility.[71] True nobility is founded on virtue. 'Gentillesce vraye n'est autre chose / Fors le vaissel ou vertu se repose' (*Prouverbes*, 41; cf. 39) [True nobility is nothing more than the vessel in which virtue rests].[72] Christine does not hesitate to correct those who are of the opinion that blood or birth suffices to make the person noble. Partly to correct this opinion she later pens her political treatises on France, peace, and the national welfare.[73]

Christine lauds Charles V's virtues to the extent that she can identify and illustrate them on the basis of her own experience as well as the reports of reliable witnesses and her own reading (*Charles V*, vol. 1, p. 9). She focuses on his virtue since, as her reading of Boethius shows, virtue is the best defense against fortune. The approach is entirely conventional and consistent with her views elsewhere. In Christine's thought, political and moral issues are intertwined.[74] Indeed, Charity Cannon Willard has noted that Christine's praise of Charles V links a moral, pedagogic intent to the context of the *translatio imperii* commonplace.[75] As suggested by this commonplace, the renown of exemplary lives that panegyric biography preserves for posterity makes possible the virtual rebirth or, more precisely perhaps, reincarnation of virtues in other persons.[76] In Christine's use of this image, one perceives her anxiety about France's fate after Charles V's passing and her fear that the *imperium* will pass to another kingdom.

---

[70] Tarnowski 1998, pp. 153–55, 157–58. Pride is an immoral and false opinion according to Brunetto Latini's *Tresor*; see Messelaar 1963, pp. 41, 161, 343, 377.

[71] *Chemin*, v. 4119–40 (with Boethius as authority), 4209–26; *Policie*, pp. 74–75; *Paix*, pp. 146, 177. The *Livre de la paix* also states that nobility arose from original equality (p. 128). See as well *Trois vertus*, p. 162:72–96 (cf. p. 133:86–99, on 'grandeur bien seant a femme' [grandeur most fitting in a woman]). Christine describes her own nobility as deriving from her virtues; see *Advision*, III.xvii.23–24, and, more generally, all of section xvii.

[72] By glossing over Charles's faults or weaknesses, Christine can magnify his virtues. For example, she redefines Charles's failure to participate actively in his wars, a feature that she evaluates positively as prudence (*Fais d'armes*, pp. 21–23); see also Lemaire 1994, pp. 88–90; Willard 1998, pp. 5–7; Delogu 2005, pp. 48–50. Christine also appears to gloss over certain excesses in Charles's adolescence, limiting herself to condemning those who permit them in princes under their supervision (vol. 1, pp. 17–18). Her counsel on wise supervisors parallels that given for the upbringing of princesses in the *Trois vertus*.

[73] Quillet 2002.

[74] See Parussa, ed., *Othea*, p. 81.

[75] Willard 1984, p. 105; see also Zumthor 1972, p. 25; Richards 1992, pp. 76–77; Walters 1998; Quillet 2002, p. 690; Walters 2003a, 2003b.

[76] Willard 1984, ch. 6. On Joinville's *Vie de Saint Louis* as model for Christine's *Charles V*, see Angeli 2000, pp. 431 n. 14 and 432 n. 18; Mühlethaler 2002, pp. 599–600; on John of Salisbury's influence, see Forhan 2002; Quillet 2002.

Biography as description: praiseworthy features in Charles V's life

Choice of material for inclusion in Christine's panegyric occurred prior to writing, when she considered the evidence provided her on Charles's deeds and mores (*aviser*). The method is analogous to that which she uses in perusing Valerius Maximus's *Facta et dicta memorabilia* for material that delineates more sharply the exemplary features of Charles's life and character that she chooses to praise. Valerius Maximus, a compiler of anecdotes carefully arranged by topics, was read and used by authors like Christine in search of historical examples.[77] Given what one is looking for, the reader mines the Roman compiler's treasure of examples much as we might read collections of maxims by La Rochefoucauld or Pascal,[78] seeking inspiration or impetus for our own thought (*Policie*, pp. 22–23).

> Lis voulentiers belles hystoires
> Quant tu porras, car les nottoires
> Exemples sont souvent valables
> Et font gent devenir savables.   (*Enseignemens*, 36)

[Read willingly fine histories when you can, for their noteworthy examples are often valid; they make people more knowledgeable.]

Ideally, the reader interrogates the examples for circumstances susceptible of elucidation in support of a given opinion.[79] Medieval biography thus links contemporary life with ancient examples that the contemporary individual, as I have suggested, reincarnates.[80] The abstract king emerges through the affinities between his virtue and actions and those illustrated in Valerius Maximus's examples as well as in other such sources. He reappears in virtuous monarchs like Charles V. By this process, Christine compiles a biography as florilegium.

> Ay cueilli fleurectes souefves et belles ou champs des escriptures ..., lesquelles dictes fleurectes sont yssues des germes entre les autres nobles plantes de . vij. principaulx racines de vertu dont la premiere et de laquelles les autres naissent et viennent a nom de prudence.   (*Paix*, p. 64)[81]

[I have gathered a few small, yet fragrant and beautiful flowers from the fields of letters; the aforementioned little flowers issued among the other noble plants from seeds of the seven principal roots of virtue, the first of which, and the one from which the others spring and derive, is called prudence.]

---

[77] Cf. Lechat 2000 on Christine's use of French translations of Valerius Maximus.
[78] Cf. von Moos 1988, pp. 135–37; McLeod 1991, pp. 113–14.
[79] See Zühlke 1994, pp. 120–21, on this process.
[80] Cf. Stierle 1972.
[81] Cf. *Charles V*, vol. 1, pp. 9–10.

While reading her sources, Christine implicitly asks standard topical questions such as *quis? quid?* etc. She selects 'places' or topoi in her *matière*, in this case, the life of Charles V, suitable for planting the seeds gathered from her reading, seeds that flower as specific arguments or examples. Choice from sources depends on how well an example lends itself, or can be fashioned to lend itself, to illustrating, in Charles V's case, that virtuous king discerned in Christine's mind.[82] Such examples exemplify Charles V's life and virtues.

Christine is not looking for the individual Charles V. Her art illustrates what von Moos terms 'Entindividualisierung' – Charles is, as it were, 'deindividualized' in order to represent an ideal, in this case, the ideal king.[83] The ideal king she abstracts from her evidence will be exemplary and praiseworthy. Accordingly, *Charles V* does not relate Charles's life in full detail. For such details, Christine refers her readers to the *Chroniques de France* whenever they wish for more information on events she relates only briefly or leaves out, especially the unfavorable material mentioned above that she claims to be unsuitable in epideictic history. Even 'innocent' history can be out of place. For example, towards the end of the biography she refers to an attempt to poison the king. After a brief summary, she cuts short her account in this way:

> Les causes pour quoy cest esploit fu fait, et pour qui, et à quel instigacion tel trayson machynoient, je me passe, pour ce que moult ne touche à ma matiere, et qui plus en vouldra savoir, trouver le pourra assez près de la fin, où les *Croniques de France* traittent du dit roy Charles, après le trespassement de la ditte royne Jehanne de Bourbon.   (vol. 2, p. 139)[84]

> [I pass over the causes for this exploit, and why and at whose instigation such a betrayal was planned, because these matters are not especially germane to my subject; those who wish to know more can find it near the end of the *Chroniques de France* where they treat King Charles after the death of his queen, Jeanne de Bourbon.]

According to this passage, the topoi *cur?* and *quis?* or *causa* and *persona* are excluded because the answers are not germane to praise of the king. Christine refers the curious reader to the *Grandes Chroniques*. Those who consulted them there would learn the names of those who instigated the plot and their reasons.[85]

---

[82] Cf. Geoffrey of Vinsauf's *status archetypus* (*Poetria nova*, v. 47–48); on this term, see Kelly 1991, pp. 37–38, 64–68, and Kelly 1999a, pp. 30–31 *et passim*. Christine would have known the principle from Brunetto Latini's *Tresor* (Kelly 1969, p. 126; see above, p. 51 n. 41).
[83] See von Moos 1988, p. 102; Skemp 1996.
[84] Cf. *Charles V*, vol. 1, pp. 15–16, 198–99; vol. 2, p. 139.
[85] See Reno 1992a, p. 179.

Order in Charles V's character and conduct

An orderly array of virtues translates into a virtuous life. In the case of the king, the virtues he embodies determine how he acts. Being a virtuous king, his acts translate into good government and good governance. Ultimately society and the individual profit. Whenever Christine evokes Charles V, the king's character and actions exemplify good order in any realm in which virtues and governance are in harmony.

Each of the three parts of *Charles V*, on, respectively, nobility, chivalry, and wisdom, illustrates an array of virtues in Charles V's person.[86] Charles's family is described under nobility, his royal vocation under chivalry, and his mind under wisdom. Each feature is also linked to historical evidence; each part begins with a brief look into the distant past. Part One traces the king's ancestry back to Troy.[87] Part Two describes the origins of chivalry. Finally, Part Three apostrophizes the deceased king as God's vassal because he received the gift of wisdom from God. Each part also uses definitions and descriptions. The definitions include not only a definition of the principal virtue treated in each part, but also a definition of its constituent virtues or 'properties'. The descriptions constitute a *norma vivendi* or 'exemplarisches Vorbild'[88] – that is to say, they illustrate the virtues in action both in Charles's own life and in the lives of his predecessors and contemporaries. The latter serve as virtuous or, by contrast, as vice-ridden illustrations.

As we have shown in Chapter 4, Charles's life has a topical chronology based on a commonplace *gradus aetatum*. Christine's version of the ages of life scheme focuses on youth, prime of life, and maturity. Each age is a topos insofar as each is described so as to elucidate the conduct of the good king at that stage in his life. In this way, she shows that Charles's life was one of good order.[89] The order manifests features of nobility as an array of guiding principles. For example, in Part One she treats 'prudence et sagece', 'justice', 'benigneté et clemence', 'humilité', 'liberalité et sage largece', 'chasteté', 'sobrieté', 'verité', 'charité', 'devocion', and 'mesure'.[90] These virtues explain the king's achievements[91] while defining Charles's virtuous life. Since his virtues are the foundation for his good government, their orderly description is what Christine wants her readers to perceive and appreciate and, ultimately, emulate.

The *gradus aetatum* also shows that the biography in Part One of *Charles V* is not merely a chronological account of the events that shaped the king's life.

---

[86] Dulac 1988.
[87] Note the importance of this ancestry in the *Chemin*, v. 3525–636.
[88] Kleinschmidt 1974, p. 42.
[89] Le Brun-Gouanvic 2001a, pp. 52–55.
[90] See Christine's table of contents, vol. 1, pp. 3–4.
[91] Kleinschmidt 1974, p. 86.

It is a description of the virtues appropriate to each age.[92] Like most such descriptions, the virtues are chosen because they are attributes characteristic of the ideal or 'abstract' person – in this case, the king. Moreover, as Eric Hicks puts it in his translation of *Charles V*, they show 'l'équivalence entre la personne du roi et celle de la France'.[93] As such, the king's 'person' is also a personification. The chronological order of the king's life and the virtues that make that life one of good order do not require *biographie événementielle*:

> Grant narracion faire n'est mie neccessaire ne au propos singulier où je vueil tendre, qui n'est fors seulement trattier de ce qui touchera ses vertus et estat en sages et bonnes meurs, et autres particularitez, lesquelles assez sont sceues par le commun ordre du noble estat roial de France, ne seroient fors prolixitez non neccessaires. (*Charles V*, vol. 1, pp. 15–16)
>
> [Lengthy narrative is neither necessary nor appropriate given my specific intention to treat only his virtues and manner in prudent good conduct; other details that are familiar in the normal conduct of the king of France would be unnecessary verbiage.]

The *fais* related in *Charles V* are, therefore, not events. They are examples of the *bonnes meurs* proper to the good king. As such, Charles's biography is analogous to that not only of ancient heroes and heroines, but of the gods and goddesses euhemerized and allegorized in *Othea* and the *Cité*. By his virtues Charles even adumbrates the saint, a figure whose panegyric informs and defines the *vita* genre in general.

To advance her encomiastic project Christine relies not only on praise, but also on its contrary, blame. As she herself puts it, 'quant le bien est louez, ce est en vituperacion du mal, aussi, quant le mal est blasmé, il doit estre à l'augmentacion du bien' (*Charles V*, vol. 1, p. 74) [the good is praised in order to condemn evil; similarly, faulting evil should enhance the good]. Here too, contraries explain one another. For example, the misfortunes of France prior to Charles's coronation enlightened the young king regarding what, by contrast, would be good for the nation; he could then form a correct opinion regarding the virtues necessary in a monarch who wants to restore the realm. By such discernment, he

> fu enluminé de clere cognoiscence, qui vraiement lui discerna le cler du trouble, le bel du lait, le bien du mal, par laquelle fu inspirez à droitte voie de salut, en deboutant les jeuneces aveuglées par flos d'ignorance. (*Charles V*, vol. 1, pp. 20–21)

---

[92] Christine adumbrates the same scheme in treating youth in the *Corps de policie*; see pp. 3–12, 58–62.

[93] Hicks, trans., *Charles V*, p. 24. Dispensing justice aligns the king with God (Gauvard 1988, pp. 321–23).

[was enlightened by clear understanding so that he could distinguish what was clear from what was obscure, what was beautiful from what was ugly, good from evil; in this way he was inspired to follow the right path to salvation while casting aside youthful acts that are blinded by the waves of ignorance.]

Charles's reflections illustrate the consideration and discretion that Christine names in the *Mutacion*. By his *sens*, *prudence*, and *avis* the king restored the kingdom of France and repulsed its enemies (*Mutacion*, v. 23538–44). Later, in addressing the dauphin Louis de Guyenne in the *Corps de policie* and the *Livre de la paix*, Christine encourages him to cultivate the same virtues so that, like his grandfather, France may recover its former majesty and grandeur. These ideal exemplars give virtually objective validity to Christine's opinions on good government.

Good order in government and governance

Christine's account of Charles V's life shows his successors how a king should live and rule 'en rigle de vie ordonée' (*Charles V*, vol. 1, p. 43; see pp. 39–58)[94] [following a rule of well-ordered conduct]. Order is the key concept. Order, as government, is also public order. Hence the emphasis on ceremony in, for example, the lengthy description – almost forty-five pages in Solente's edition – of the state visit of the Holy Roman Emperor, Charles IV (vol. 2, pp. 89–132).[95] On this occasion, both king and emperor do what kings and emperors are supposed to do in a well-regulated, orderly life. Seen in this light, this most circumstantial account of an event in Charles's life acquires significance beyond mere on-the-spot reporting of a state visit.[96] It proclaims his majesty.[97]

Since Christine's art of description is valid for the king, it is equally valid in praising good and noble women. Therefore, the *Cité des dames* follows an analogous program for its panegyric. As discussed earlier, Christine admits into the City only virtuous, noble women, excluding all women who do not meet high moral standards.[98] Such women are exemplars and, like virtuous kings,

[94] Christine returns to Charles V's exemplary virtues in subsequent treatises; see, for example, *Policie*, pp. 45–47, and *Paix*, pp. 67–72, 100, 108–12, 138–42, 158–62.

[95] Christine refers to this state visit again in *Paix*, pp. 161–62, where it illustrates Charles's discretion in practicing largess (Dulac 1988, p. 132).

[96] Autrand 1995; cf. Dulac 1991a, pp. 117–18. Such order befits a king. On the spectacle of order in Christine's time, see Le Brun-Gouanvic 2001b; Delogu 2005, pp. 43–45. Cf. as well the illuminating explanation of *solempne* in Lewis 1942, p. 17.

[97] Krynen 1981, pp. 129–36; Lemaire 1994, pp. 101–02; Strubel 2000; Blanchard and Mühlethaler 2002, pp. 18–20.

[98] Examples of excluded, or at least unmentioned, women who are named in other writings are Briseida and Heloise. Others who fell in love irrationally – Dido, Medea, and Thisbe – are recuperated as rulers or princesses, but their example as lovers is rejected (*Cité*, pp. 374–408, especially p. 404, where she claims that love always ends 'à leur grant prejudice

tend to look alike despite their diverse careers. The government of the City derives from the Virgin Mary, queen of the City and supreme exemplar of the virtues Christine admires and exemplifies in its inhabitants.[99] The standards are the same in *Charles V*; France is governed by the king, but that governance also includes his family, the French nobility, and, indeed, all of France that falls under Charles's rule. This is the body politic. In the *Cité* too, the female side of the royal family is admitted at the end of Book Two.

But the *Cité des dames* is also different. There is no general prejudice against Charles V in early fifteenth-century France. But, as we have seen in Chapter 3, laudation in the *Cité* serves the purpose of correcting widespread misogynist opinion among men and even among some women. Praising exemplary women corrects a prejudice by showing their virtues and accomplishments, and encouraging women to emulate them as best they can and in the place God has assigned them.[100] Such women, by their virtues, benefit themselves, their families, and their countries. Similarly, praise of a deceased king is meant to foster in France and its magnates the virtues that make such a king successful. Virtue is a source of power that unites the two panegyric works. By overcoming partial self-interest, such subjects come together to promote the general welfare and the common self-interest, both in the City of Ladies and the kingdom of France.

Order structures both *Charles V* and the *Cité*. Both use the three-part division common in Christine's writings.[101] We have seen how *Charles V*'s *ordo tractatus* treats three constituents of Charles's virtue: his nobility, chivalry, and wisdom. The *Cité* uses the literal city image of her allegory to structure its own tripartite division. The first part lays the foundations, the second raises the walls, and the last covers with roofs and towers – the 'combles' that mark the highest nobility among its inhabitants. Here too, virtuous nobility, knighthood, and wisdom characterize the City's inhabitants, just as they function as personifications in the council of Reason in the *Chemin de long estude*.

Another feature of *Charles V* that helps us evaluate Christine's panegyric in the *Cité* is the notion of the king's two bodies, an idea that has also been applied to descriptions of the queen's two bodies.[102] Although the notion of two bodies is not explicit before it is set out for early modern kings in England, it is adumbrated by medieval portrait description and, more pertinently, in Christine's discussion of the perfect gifts God bestows on human beings and

---

et grief en corps, en biens et en honneur et a l'ame' [being prejudicial and grievous to body, possessions, and honor, and to the soul]). Men reading the *Cité* might reach the same conclusion from reflecting on the loves of Lancelot, Gauvain, and Perceval in the prose romances.

[99] As queen, the encomium of the Virgin Mary places her in the context of praise of the queen or princess; cf. Latzke 1979.

[100] Christine's art conforms to, but adapts, panegyric as practiced by other medieval authors; see Brown-Grant 1995.

[101] Solente, ed., *Charles V*, vol. 1, p. 9 and n. 1.

[102] Latzke 1979.

their corporal impediments to full realization of those gifts. I would like to apply these points to exemplary panegyric, and then relate them to the process of forming and defending opinion in the panegyric mode, by setting out an array of virtues and vices that are exemplified in the historical narrative.

The conventional medieval description of ideal beauty is a well-known stereotype. In its fullest form it details corporal, vestmental, and intellectual features of the person the author idealizes.[103] The stereotype was so common by the early thirteenth century that Geoffrey of Vinsauf, a master of stereotypes, considered it hackneyed (*Poetria nova*, v. 622–23). By Christine's time it sufficed to suggest such corporal excellence, fit the body into dress suitable in the context of sumptuary laws, and pass on to the virtues that such a physical, usually noble, subject shows forth. The array of virtues – nobility, chivalry, and wisdom, as well as their components – defines the three-part division of *Charles V* as well as the different virtues and qualities discussed in the three-part construction of the City of Ladies treated in sequence by, respectively, the virtues Reason, Rectitude, and Justice.[104]

In the *Cité*, the body occupied by the virtuous and exemplary persons must be beautiful.[105] The beautiful body is a fitting receptacle for the God-given qualities or virtues the exemplary figures realize. Allegorically, Christine represents this by first removing bad material, the dross of misogyny and evil women; then she constructs solid foundations, strong walls, and the 'combles' that give access to the Virgin Mary as she descends Christ-like from above to reign here below. In this way, the City of Ladies preserves good order, both by a hierarchy that mirrors France's social orders and by the illustrations of its virtues in a well-ordered society. The perfectly beautiful body in a person whose dress identifies his or her social standing illustrates a suitable receptacle, fashioned by Nature and adorned by human arts, for God's gifts. In traditional narrative, the gifts manifest themselves in the way the person conducts him- or herself. That conduct reveals whether the person is praiseworthy or blameworthy, constituting in this way an exemplary argument for praise or blame. Divergence from work to work reflects diverse opinions. A well-known medieval example of such diversity is Lancelot's love, praised in Chrétien de Troyes's *Chevalier de la charrette*, but found blameworthy in the Prose *Lancelot*'s retelling of that source. Christine rewrites her sources for the *Cité* in similar ways. She even virtually rewrites the *Roman de la rose* and Matheolus's *Lamentations* by

---

[103] See Faral 1924, pp. 79–81; Brinkmann 1979, pp. 54–58; Cizek 1994, pp. 134–36. A good study of French examples from the twelfth century is found in Colby 1965. The detailed stereotype is found in Christine's works as well as the more abstract pattern illustrated by descriptions in Matthew of Vendôme's *Ars versificatoria*, 1.49–74. For Christine, see Chapter 1, n. 57.

[104] Virtue is taken here in the sense defined for Latin and Old French in *Robert*, pp. 2240–41: 'toute espèce de qualité est de mérite masculin'. Christine extends their usage to women's qualities and merits in *femmes fortes* or viragos.

[105] Cf. the remark about Elizabeth I attributed to Sir Philip Sydney: 'she was a queen and therefore beautiful' (Collinson 2004, p. 9).

suggesting that they be read as antiphrasis, a suggestion she follows in the works examined in Chapter 4 that selectively rewrite parts of the *Roman de la rose*.

This brings us to a crux in Christine's opinion about nobility. She adopts the clerical commonplace on the relative merits of nobility by birth or blood and nobility by virtue. Traditionally, nobility by birth is a birthright bestowed by Fortune.[106] Physically, Nature endows the person with a body fit to receive the virtues God bestows in their perfection and that the noble man and woman is best equipped to realize. However, noble blood is insufficient if the blueblood fails to 'tendre à haultes choses, amer bonnes meurs et conduire ses fais par prudence' (*Charles V*, vol. 1, p. 10) [strive after noble goals, value moral conduct, and act with prudence]. This reinforces Christine's opinion that 'Gentillesce vraye n'est autre chose / Fors le vaissel ou vertu se repose' (*Prouverbes*, 41) [True nobility is nothing other than the vessel in which virtue rests]. It also accounts for the higher standards she sets for princesses in the *Trois vertus*, while excusing less exemplary conduct in the lower social orders (see above, p. 93). It also explains why villainy in the noble person is more reprehensible than among members of lower orders: the villainous villein is less reprehensible than the villainous aristocrat. Failure to realize God-given virtues in a body well endowed to receive them is a grave violation of God's ordered world and therefore especially blameworthy in nobles. Charles V and the ladies in the *Cité* illustrate the realization of those virtues and, by doing so, they put their noble bodies to noble use. To Christine's mind, such bodies deserve praise. In hortatory treatises like *Othea* and the *Trois vertus*, she urges her noble readers to emulate their noble antecedents. Enlightened self-interest supports virtue by unifying the country; in its absence, violence and strife grow among the nation's powers. Charles V is an especially powerful example. That is why Christine holds him up for emulation to Louis de Guyenne in the *Corps de policie* and the *Livre de la paix*.

Charles V illustrates the virtues of a good king. In the context of Christine's religion, these virtues are desirable in all human beings. If we apply the gradualistic pattern set out in the *Trois vertus* and the *Corps de policie*, Charles V's model virtues radiate throughout his kingdom. All can follow his noble example, or at least strive to do so, as Christine shows for poor or working women who can imitate the princess of the *Trois vertus* without being expected to equal the virtue the princess's nobility makes possible (*Policie*, p. 38:32–35). Ultimately both treatises unite men and women in a great moral enterprise that, Christine believes, France is especially endowed to promote, as the conclusion of the

---

[106] In the *Anticlaudianus* (I, v. 47–54), Alain de Lille describes Nobility as distinct from the other virtues, being endowed by Fortune and Nature, not by God. In the *Rose*, Noblesse finds a place in Love's army (v. 10421). Brunetto Latini grounds nobility only on virtues put into practice (*Tresor*, II.114.3–4), which is analogous to Christine's opinion regarding true nobility.

Chemin argues. The union finds its most splendid representation in the enterprise of the peasant Joan in serving Charles VII.[107]

Joan of Arc, a providential woman

The *Ditié de Jehanne d'Arc* conjoins praise of the new king Charles VII and Joan of Arc, the woman who made his coronation possible.[108] In this, her last work, Christine calls anew on the French to unite behind their king,[109] who is, she believes, in power thanks to Providence. Providence rules over Fortune because God holds sway over all (another instance of the ongoing influence of Boethius on her world view and in conformity with her views on Providence she expresses in the *Mutacion*).[110] Providence supports virtuous rulers who do God's will. The *Mutacion de Fortune* illustrates the dire consequences for those who are anointed, but turn to vice, as did the Hebrews from time to time (v. 8415–36).[111] Charles V did the opposite (v. 23535–44). However, Charles VI's madness and the nobility's disunity and strife stood in the way of such unity. Likewise, the ill-fated career of Louis de Guyenne, another royal hope who died too soon, also proved to be an impediment to the realization of national unity. Christine's view of Joan's emergence in the Hundred Years War relies on Providence. Religion's role in human government and history produces a sense of right that is providential, and that can almost be called patriotic. Epideictic oratory in *Jehanne d'Arc* addresses a France Christine finally saw coming together as before under Charles V, and in ways foreshadowed and promoted as early as the *Chemin* and *Advision*.

Christine's last poem also brings together all the elements for identifying true opinion. Providence at work for the glory of France and its king seemed obvious in Joan of Arc's miraculous ascent (*Jehanne*, v. 81).[112]

> Qui vit doncques chose avenir
> Plus hors de toute opinion
> (Qui à noter et souvenir
> Fait bien en toute region),
> Que France (de qui mention

---

[107] On Christine's disappointed hope that Isabeau de Bavière might save France, see Brown-Grant 1993, pp. 216–23; Parussa 1996, pp. 140–42.

[108] See Kennedy and Varty, ed., *Jehanne*, pp. 9–10, 13. On Christine's place in the elaboration of a 'literary image' of Joan of Arc, see Fraioli 1981.

[109] Charles VII and Joan of Arc mirror her earlier model, Charles V and Du Guesclin; on the latter, see *Paix*, p. 111, where Du Guesclin illustrates Charles's fortitude. She inserts him and others under the category of the 'omme fort' (pp. 109–10), a mirror of the *femme forte* she evokes in the *Cité des dames*. Du Guesclin no longer exemplifies chivalric love.

[110] Arnaville 1998. Philosophy in the *Advision* points out that Providence, not Fortune as in the *Mutacion*, caused Christine's misfortunes (Brown-Grant 1999a, p. 117).

[111] On Christine and Jewish history, see Beer 1992, pp. 127–28; Margolis 1992.

[112] Brown-Grant 1999b, pp. 19–24.

> On faisoit que jus ert ruée)
> Soit, par divine mission,
> Du mal en si grant bien muée. (*Jehanne*, v. 73–80)
>
> [Did anyone, then, see anything quite so extraordinary come to pass (something that is well worth noting and remembering in every region), namely, that France (about whom it was said she had been cast down) should see her fortunes change, by divine command, from evil to such great good. (ed. Kennedy and Varty, p. 42)]

Drawing on the evidence of prophecy,[113] of Joan's accomplishments in spite of seemingly insurmountable obstacles, and of exemplary saviors of their people in the past, both men and women, Christine makes the case for the role of Providence in Joan's career and France's history, an argument founded on faith insofar as, at the time of writing, Joan's career was still in the making.[114] Christine's deep sense – her *vrai sentement* – of Joan's divine mission inspires her to call on the French to unite behind Joan, under God and their king, for the sake of peace and national unity. In a sense, Joan of Arc is closest not only to the king, but also to the queen of the City of Ladies. As Mary was chosen to realize providential history,[115] Joan of Arc was chosen to embrace, it seemed, all of France in her enterprise. Accordingly, in *Jehanne d'Arc*, Christine summons all of France, and all the nation's social orders, to unite under the Maid of Orléans, the king, and God in order to expel the invaders and subdue the rebellious.

Yet the *Ditié de Jehanne d'Arc* is an incomplete biography. Did Christine intend, as in many of her other writings, to compose a three-part panegyric on Joan of Arc as she moved providentially towards triumph? This is, of course, only speculation. But there is an analogy in the composition of the *Livre de la paix*.[116] Louis de Guyenne participated in the negotiations that led to the ill-fated treaty of Auxerre between the duke of Berry and Jean sans Peur in August 1412. This treaty inspired the composition of the *Livre de la paix*. But Christine lay down her pen after completing the first part because the treaty came apart during the Caboche rebellion in Paris in the spring of 1413. The suppression of the rebellion permitted her to take up her pen again and complete the two remaining parts of the *Livre de la paix* by September 1413.

No such turn of events permitted the continuation of the *Ditié de Jehanne d'Arc*. Christine fell silent after reporting Joan's march on Paris, dying shortly thereafter. In the silence of Poissy she was finally overwhelmed by the chaos through which she passed her life. Christine may have, sadly, seen chaos unfold

---

[113] See Brown-Grant 1999b, pp. 20–21; cf. Nichols 1992, pp. 66–76.
[114] Kosta-Théfaine 1998.
[115] See the illuminating comparison between Mary and Joan in Brown-Grant 1999b, pp. 23–24.
[116] See Willard, ed., *Paix*, pp. 22–25, and the *Paix* itself, p. 57.

anew in the fate of France she thought Louis de Guyenne and, then, Joan of Arc might turn around. Whether Christine died before or after Joan's capture and execution would make little difference. Her whole adult life, from the death of her husband to her own death, was spent in the worst years of France's *herfsttij der middeleeuwen*. It was also that awful experience of social and moral chaos that made her opinions unique and memorable, and rewarded her in a way confirming Lady Opinion's promise of renown.

6
Opinion and Subjectivity[1]

> Vraiement je ne pouroie d'aucune chose respondre si proprement come de mon propre fait: si puis en ceste partie tesmoingnier verité de certainne science.
> (*Débat*, p. 148:1067–70)[2]

Christine de Pizan's *œuvre* is complex and can be perplexing today. As Lady Opinion explains, the *Advision* itself

> sera de plusieurs tesmoingnee diversement. Les ungs sur le langaige donront leur sentence en plusieurs manieres: diront qu'il n'est pas bien elegant, les autres que la composicion des materes est estrange. Et ceulx qui l'entendront en diront bien. (*Advision*, II.xxii.59–63)
>
> [will be variously evaluated. Some will give various opinions on its language. They will say it isn't elegant; others will say that the composition of its subject matter is strange. And those who understand it will speak well of it.]

Such diverse readings reveal both centrifugal and centripetal thrusts in the treatise's allegory. On account of its centrifugal qualities, made possible by allegory, the *Advision* moves out from the literal towards diverse explicit and potential allegorical meanings. The centripetal features realized through the intricate interrelations and mirror effects of that same allegory hold the work together in ways set out both in the Phillipps manuscript gloss to the *Advision* and in the links Christine establishes between it and her other works.[3] These diverse connections link her own opinions and those of her readers. As noted

---

[1] What follows on subjectivity is indebted to M. Zink 1985 and a number of articles in *Mittelalterbilder* and *Musique* influenced by Zink's book. Crucial points in my analysis contain specific references to them. See also Wolfzettel 1984; Angeli 1993; Atwood 1998; Luff 1999, pp. 364–65, 400; Zimmermann 2002, pp. 64–65. Kay 1990 complements Zink, although her time frame does not extend to the early fifteenth century.

[2] In truth I could answer regarding myself more accurately than on anything else; here I can bear witness to truth with certain knowledge.

[3] Cf. Armand Strubel in Poirion 1983b, p. 266: 'Chez Christine de Pizan, la pratique allégorique est inséparable de la problématique subjective dans l'*Avision* et dans la *Mutation de Fortune* ...: quête du "je" unificateur parmi les fragments dispersés du "moi" allégorique.'

above, the *Advision* progresses from the most general context, the nation France, to the most individual and personal, Christine herself; at the same time, as allegory the treatise opens up to individual and personal contexts that diverse readers may bring to their reading of the treatise. In all of this Christine's own life and opinions remain central.

Christine the anomaly

Christine is an anomaly in her time.[4] Her conception of opinion and its importance in human life and her manner of dealing with opinions are unique in French literature before Montaigne.[5] But her thought and opinion making also differ from Montaigne's. Her faith gives her confidence in the medieval world view. She may have doubts, but she is not a sceptic. When she admits ignorance or lack of learning, it is by and large to show herself as victim of various misconceptions and errors that violated her world view. By study and writing, she strives to overcome her handicaps while correcting misconceptions and errors that, in her language, become false opinions. Fortune, misogyny, covetousness, envy, injustice, self-interest, vainglory, dishonorable or inhumane conduct – these are the objects of her study, her opinions, and her criticism.

Christine was an anomaly in her time because, as a woman cleric, or *clergesse*, she stood alone outside of and denied entrance to schools; yet she wrote authoritative works to educate the learned and unlearned alike. Moreover, she grounded her opinions, and those of others she accepted or rejected, partly on her own experience, or what she calls 'mon propre fait'. Religion was a firm foundation, the only one that seems to have remained constant to the end when she died at Poissy. But reason also permitted her to progress with a clear mind and good conscience in her quest for truth. Her opinions were based on experience, but not just on her own experience of the world around her and on her feelings about that experience; she diligently tested and evaluated her feelings and experience using faith, reason, and a wide-ranging reading program.

Christine's discovery of the importance of opinion reflects a problem that others have discerned in important authors from the thirteenth to the fifteenth century: anomaly and contingency in human experience.[6] In the major issues on which she confronts opinion – fortune, misogyny, love, and national strife – problems arise because, by confronting opinions, Christine disturbs traditional

---

[4] Morse 1996, p. 235.

[5] For instances of the word *opinion* in Montaigne's writings, see Leake 1981, pp. 891–93.

[6] M. Zink 1985, pp. 75–79, 120–25. More recently, anomaly and contingency have been studied in other late medieval writings; see notably von Graevenitz and Marquard 1998; Vincensini 1999 (on *Paris et Vienne*); Heller-Roazen 2003 (on the *Rose*); Schwarze 2003 (on Froissart's *œuvre*); Kelly 2004.

opinions and disrupts her own chosen path to the good life: the life of the scholar, itself an anomaly for women in her time. As a scholar, Christine studied past writings in order to learn from them, while testing their opinions with her own thought and experience. In doing so, she discovered something about herself. Like the very scholars she admired, she too could err. In particular, when she confronts their learning about women with her own knowledge and experience, she cannot reconcile what she reads with her experience. This quandary is the source of the *Cité des dames*.

Love is another problem, especially the chivalric kind that she admires and even promotes in her early writings, all the while protesting that, since her widowhood, she does not share the feelings of the lovers she describes. Then experience and reason bring her to change her mind. She adopts a more categorical position: chivalric love is impossible and should be avoided at all costs. Even when love is noble, as in the *Duc des vrais amants*, word spreads about and honor is lost, especially the woman's. Happy marriage too is uncertain. The death of her husband taught her so, as did the experiences of the wives she alludes to here and there and the large number of widows who chose not to remarry. The abused or unloved wife and the widow are figures that haunt Christine's views on marriage and love.

Historical contingencies produce anomalies that test even Christine's faith. As in other disappointments she experienced, Charles V, king of France who ruled by divine right, died early. Charles VI followed him and, although ruling by divine right, went mad and the kingdom crumbled around him. Yet Providence did not remove the mad king and provide for a worthy successor such as Louis de Guyenne. The queen, Isabeau of Bavaria, hardly embodied the virtues of Jeanne de Bourbon. And Joan of Arc? We do not know whether Christine came to know her misfortunes. However, given all these calamities, she might well have wondered where divine justice had gone, as sins prevented France from emerging from chaos. Had Justice removed herself as Reason did in the *Roman de la rose* and the *Chemin de long estude*? The normative order fell into chaos because of anomalies in that order such as Charles VI's madness and contingencies such as strife and rebellion within and among the Church, the nobility, and the people.

As the epigraph to this chapter shows, paramount evidence for Christine's opinions remained her own experience. It is no wonder then that, although the *Advision* begins with France's chaos, it passes through erroneous opinions in religion and philosophy to conclude with her own erroneous opinions about the life she deems unfortunate, opinions that require all the wisdom of Philosophy and, ultimately, of Theology to restore faith and understanding to her mind.

There is true anxiety in Christine's experience. Her sense of being alone and threatened is omnipresent.[7] *Creintis* is an anagram of her name; *seulete* is its

---

[7] Ribémont 2002a, pp. 744–45.

distinguishing property. Her anxiety is summed up most insistently in her well-known poem on the death of her husband: 'Seulete suy.' Yet, she insists, 'et seulete vueil estre' (*CB* 11)[8] [I am all alone ... and alone I want to be]. In her solitude, she acquired greater intellectual and social experience, including perhaps that derived from female friendships, although she wrote very little about them.[9] She chose a life of seclusion so that she could pursue her own introspection and studies: 'Seulete suy en ma chambre enserree' [All alone I am enclosed in my room].[10]

Christine's subjectivity

In that 'room of her own', Christine discovered subjectivity as Michel Zink defines it: 'le point de vue d'une conscience' and, more specifically, 'le produit d'une conscience particulière'.[11] He distinguishes such subjectivity from more modern self-expression. We find the medieval kind of subjectivity in Christine de Pizan's writings on opinion. Indeed, her expression of opinion, *de sentement* and based on 'mon propre fait' in opposition to received intellectual and sentimental world views, illustrates the emergence of the subjectivity that Zink delineates in the early and late periods of medieval French literature.

Christine's subjectivity is evident in the reading experience with which the *Cité des dames* begins. In that episode Christine confronts a paradox: the divergence between the received authority of learned misogyny and her sense of her own worth. Her self-knowledge, and the concurrent opinion of other women she consulted, introduced an anomaly into the authoritative world view on women's essence and status. In Zink's context, the anomaly was a paradox arising from the contingencies of a moment, the moment Christine chose to relax by reading a lighter, purportedly amusing work in praise of women: Matheolus's *Lamentations*.[12] Christine's initial response was amazement: 'Ha! Dieux, comment peut cecy estre?' (*Cité*, p. 44) [Oh Lord, how can this be?]. For an answer she turned to introspection. Such introspection had its model in the confessionals.[13] Christine questioned herself in an analogous way, as we have seen. In doing so, she explored dispassionately and rationally her own physical and intellectual features, comparing the properties misogynists assign to her with her own reading of herself and of traditional authorities. In effect, she reevaluated, as in a confession, her own person and conduct, comparing,

---

[8] On this ballade, see Lorcin 2002; Adams 2003, pp. 149–50. On the theme of *seulette* in Christine's writings, in both positive and negative contexts, see Cerquiglini 1988b, pp. 241–44; Paupert 1993, pp. 1066–67.

[9] Lorcin 1991, 2002.

[10] See Brown-Grant, trans., *Cité*, pp. xvi–xvii.

[11] M. Zink 1985, p. 8.

[12] 'Tout part du donné sensible, et l'idée qui le dépasse, ou à plus forte raison qui s'oppose à lui, est sentie comme un paradoxe' (M. Zink 1985, p. 12).

[13] M. Zink 1985, p. 14.

as in topical invention, her reading of women's topoi with those offered by learned misogyny.

Self-examination revealed limitations, both as a woman and as a human being, including limitations imposed by Nature and by society. Her assigned role, as the *Mutacion* shows, was to marry, have children, and maintain a household while her husband acquired the wherewithal to support the family. Then came widowhood and the need to assume the roles of her deceased husband, roles for which neither her upbringing nor her husband had prepared her. She was young and inexperienced. The trials she met were nearly overwhelming. She survived by relying on her intelligence and willpower. That is, she began to discover qualities in herself that corrected misogynist stereotypes.

Zink's description of the place of the allegorical mode in medieval subjectivity fits Christine's experience and thinking between the death of Etienne de Castel and the composition of the *Advision*. This allegorical work, composed

> à travers un regard et un point de vue, ceux du narrateur ... est une perception, c'est-à-dire une organisation cohérente et significative des impressions et des sensations éprouvées par une conscience qui les interprète et les associe en fonction de ses tendances psychiques, de ses schémas intellectuels, de ses souvenirs.[14]

Christine's penchant for the allegorical mode – what she terms the poetic mode – is mirrored in Zink's words. Her thought conjoins personal experience with rational analysis informed by consideration, discretion, memory, and recall. The result is understanding, or *entendement de raison*. Her writing, a quest for certainty in expression of opinion, becomes in this way 'le reflet d'une vérité dans une conscience'.[15]

'L'auteur s'affirme.'[16] Christine's gloss on the *Advision* and her account of how she came to write the *Cité des dames* confirm this. As we have seen, this virtually paradigmatic confrontation of a woman's experience with learned tradition was an anomaly in her time. Anomalies of this kind could be dangerous; they caused many to slip or appear to slip into heresy, as she well knew (*Advision*, II.v.30–42). Yet she persevered in the effort by aligning her thought not only with reason but also with her faith.

The task was not easy. The invention of her singular opinion on woman's worth, for example, follows on anguished internal debate. The *Cité* demonstrates by rational argument, supported by examples, the 'organisation cohérente et significative des impressions et des sensations éprouvées par une conscience

---

[14] M. Zink 1985, p. 166. Cf. Angeli 1993, p. 48; cf. Hauck 1995, pp. 221–22; Romagnoli 2000.

[15] M. Zink 1985, p. 166.

[16] M. Zink 1985, p. 29; see also Willard 1981b; Blanchard 1988, p. 154; Dulac 1991a; Brownlee 2000; Kellogg 2003, pp. 140–41.

qui les interprète et les associe', resulting in 'le point de vue de sa subjectivité'.[17] By projecting herself into the examples she cites in the *Cité* and elsewhere, Christine made them conform to her own thought and experience.[18] This was her art of original topical invention.

Zink goes on to locate subjectivity in a specific time and place. In the *Cité*, a specific moment 'dans le déroulement de sa propre vie'[19] arose from a concatenation of contingencies: the end of the day, Christine's desire for relaxed reading, her mother's call to dinner, and the return the next day to a new, unexpectedly disturbing read. The paradox Christine confronted while reading Matheolus 'est le produit de sa situation particulière et contingente'.[20] Such contingencies were the impetus for the opinion making and opinion changing we have observed in the preceding chapters.

The poetic subject

Contingency and anomaly characterize the fictional subjects Christine describes in many of her poems. In the *Rose* debate she defends a virtually platonic idealization of chivalric love that she admires in distinguished knights like Du Guesclin. The early poems she wrote in the allegorical mode – the *Epistre au dieu d'amours* and the *Dit de la rose* – were composed in the context of the Du Guesclin kind of love. However, after further consideration, she changed her mind about chivalric love. The change is strikingly apparent in the categorical language of Sebile de Monthault. The chaste love of a Du Guesclin is the kind Christine describes in the *Duc des vrais amants* and the *Dit de la pastoure*. But in these Dits, the illustration is not allegorical. 'A l'absolu de l'amour succèdent de petites histoires d'amour enracinées dans les circonstances de la vie.'[21] Both plots detail, in exemplary, yet 'real' time and space, the contingencies that threaten even ideal love in human experience.

Christine's experience and observations that reveal contingency recall the rhetorical *circumstantiae*, notably *ubi? quando?* She found that such topoi are subject to the contingencies of real life and human experience. For example, there is a good old age that is wise and a bad old age that is dissolute; similarly, *oiseuse* can be valuable in the intellectual life but immoral if it leads to lust. To covet is a sin, but coveting virtue is good.[22] In Christine's Dits, her opinion of ideal love is influenced by the way she comes to view these circumstances.

---

[17] M. Zink 1985, p. 106.
[18] Cf. Altmann 1996, p. 390.
[19] M. Zink 1985, p. 106.
[20] M. Zink 1985, p. 121; cf. pp. 22, 142.
[21] M. Zink 1985, p. 22.
[22] On old age, see *Policie*, pp. 34–35, 61; on *oiseuse*, pp. 53–54, 99; on *couvoitise*, pp. 82–83. These examples of discretion emerge in the *Rose* debate, and, indeed, in Christine's discriminating reading of different parts of Jean de Meun's romance.

Hence the contrast between the Duke's perception of his love as a source of chivalric prowess, a perception that conforms to Christine's earlier notion of Du Guesclin love, and Sebile de Monthault's opinion that such love destroys the woman's and man's honor, reputation, and happiness. The *Duc*'s plot recounts the failure of chivalric love, because the knight fails to act as a knight should (*recreantise*) and because, absent from the beloved, doubts and jealousy eat away like a cancer at the lovers' feelings, finally destroying the faith each has in the other's constancy. The denouement in both the *Duc* and the *Pastoure*, where love is platonic, as well as in the apparently consummated love of the *Cent Ballades d'amant et de dame*, is the same. The love is ideal; it is also unworkable because of the contingencies of life. In Christine's world view only virtue can overcome such contingencies. Virtue does not allow for much lovemaking, at least outside marriage. Time passes, circumstances change, doubts arise and with them jealousy. Love dies, while dishonor persists. Virtue in love is possible only in marriage, if one is lucky, since marriage too can be a false good.

These loves, even the platonic ones, are illicit in fifteenth-century opinion. That is, whether adulterous or pre-conjugal, they violate the social order and the place of marriage and status in the moral order. To be sure, there is the problematic cycle of loves in Christine's early poems, some of which are tragic, but others of which allow for change in premarital lovers. Such change moves these poems into the context found in Andreas Capellanus's *De amore*. For example, after two years of widowhood one may honorably take a lover within a courtly love ethic. Chartier and Oton de Grandson allow for such change as the problem of death becomes not just a lover's love-death, but a death like that of Christine's husband, an experience repeated later for Charles d'Orléans. Or in war.[23] In the *Cent Ballades* infidelity allows for the deceived partner to begin a new love after prudent delay. Subsequently, Christine's own experience and observations led her to reject this solution for herself, a rejection she discovered among most widows. She remained adamant.

Courtly love poetry before Christine's time fostered subjectivity as 'the elaboration of a first-person (subject) position in the rhetoric of courtly poetry'.[24] The subject was stylized and might, indeed, shift from one type of love to another, or result in the fragmentation of the subject that is still evident in the poetry of Charles d'Orléans.[25] Audiences too may define how the subject seeks to portray him- or herself;[26] or, more specifically, a patron will, ostensibly, have

---

[23] Kelly 1978, ch. 8.
[24] Kay 1990, p. 1.
[25] Kelly 1978, pp. 207–09, 214; see Kay 1990, ch. 2.
[26] Audience being either the implied audience or audiences in the poem, or 'real-world' audiences, and the way the subject addresses it or them. See Kelly 1978, pp. 248–52; Paradis 1990, pp. 128–31; Kelly 2000.

the last word.²⁷ But it is also likely that 'to convince is ... less important, in literature, than to explore'.²⁸ The sincerity of such a subject will depend on the skill with which the author sets out the poetic character and makes the representation credible. The description mirrors the rhetoric of courtship and seduction. It is also the topical invention of stand-up comedy perfected by poets like Rutebeuf:²⁹ the performance acts out the role the poet assumes. Such role-playing is possible in, for example, public readings like those illustrated in medieval manuscripts prepared in Christine's time.³⁰ This model fits courtly lyric performances as well.

All such 'subjects' are rhetorical constructs. The opinions they express postulate a kind of subject the audience may find credible, but only insofar as it fits or plays on recognizable stereotypes. There is nonetheless movement towards an autobiographical subject, even if that subject is fictitious.³¹ The opinions such subjects express are analogous to those in *jeux-partis* and other debate poems in which the challenger states the issue, but the challenged chooses the opinion he or she will defend. Like stand-up comedy, the views expressed fit a role assumed for the implied or selected audience.

For example, in Thibaut de Champagne's *jeu-parti*, 'Baudoÿn, il sunt dui amant' (*Chansons*, 37), Thibaut proposes a debate on the relative worth of courtesy and beauty as sources of love. Baudouin opts for courtesy, so Thibaut, in spite of his admitted *embonpoint* elsewhere (*Chansons*, 47, v. 11, 18), defends beauty. There is no more reason to suppose that the two debaters actually hold the opinion each defends than that Raoul de Houdenc personally sides with Baudouin's view when the same issue arises and is followed to an exemplary conclusion in *Meraugis de Portlesguez*.³² In most medieval debate poetry, '*Pro* and *contra*, *sic* and *non* could exist ... side by side and did not necessarily have to be resolved',³³ except, of course, in the minds of audiences and readers.

In Guillaume de Machaut's Judgment poems, the *Jugement dou roy de Behaigne* and the *Jugement dou roy de Navarre*, Dits Christine may have known, we find the same author writing in defense of contradictory opinions. Who suffers more is the question, a woman whose beloved has died or a man

---

²⁷ Kelly 1999c. One did write an answer: Jean de Werchin in his *Songe de la barge*; see Willard 1990b, pp. 598–600. There is an 'inconclusiveness' about many such debates that suggests 'an "aesthetics of irresolution"' that Christine shared with her contemporaries (Cayley 2003).
²⁸ Shapley 1970, p. 34; cf. Blumenfeld-Kosinski 1994, p. 707.
²⁹ M. Zink 1985, p. 63; see Regalado 1970, ch. 4.
³⁰ See Becker 1967, pp. 521, 522–23. Huot 1987 discusses the manuscript as performance.
³¹ M. Zink 1985, pp. 47–75; Kay 1990, pp. 145–61; cf. Wolfzettel 1984, pp. 392–97.
³² Fernández Vuelta 1990.
³³ Blumenfeld-Kosinski 1994, p. 707.

whose beloved loves another?[34] The issue may have seemed more urgent in the fourteenth century. The plague was raging (the *Navarre* begins in the midst of the plague) and death in battle was becoming a topic of growing importance as the Hundred Years War ground on and other military disasters like the battle of Nicopolis occurred.[35] Machaut's changed point of view has a certain personal foundation through his experience of the plague and his reading. In the *Navarre* he supports the kind of 'Boethian courtly love' he set out in the *Remede de Fortune*. Ironically, his Machaut figure defends the view espoused in the *Behaigne*, a view the author cannot be expressing *de sentement* because of his conflicting opinion in the later Judgment poem. This provides a certain comic mode in what is basically a philosophical reevaluation of what noble love should be.

This is a model for Christine's own revised opinion and feelings about ideal love. However, in Christine's examples the singularity of her opinion is striking; it rings autobiographically true. Seeking the conventional but finding the anomaly is not comedy in her case.[36] In the *Cent Ballades*, as we have seen, she declares at the outset that she does not write *de sentement* because she is not herself in love, a radical departure from the traditional posture in love poetry, even love poetry by women.[37] When, in the last ballade of this collection, she states that she is writing *de sentement*, her feeling is more in accordance with the views on the moral and philosophical issues of the final poems than those on love.

The problems of courtly love and misogyny disappear from Christine's writing after the *Cent Ballades d'amant et de dame*. More intractable was the problem of France during the dark years between the death of Charles V and the emergence of Joan of Arc. No doubt the downfall of the kingdom made impossible any reevaluation of opinion on misogyny or love. There was a growing urgency, a sense of social responsibility going beyond personal crises, the idealization of love, and even women's issues.[38] Christine's appeal for reform, for unity under the king and rational governance, became ineffective as she watched France sink deeper into chaos. In her late writings, she turns to religious consolation. Then, Christine seems to have fallen silent.

Uncertain and fearful, 'at the end of her life, Christine de Pizan seems finally to have united historical fact and literary posture ... by retiring to a monastery'.[39]

---

[34] On this debate, see Kelly 1978, pp. 137–44. Cf. Mulder 1978, pp. 37–41; Cerquiglini 1985, pp. 63–75.

[35] Machaut evokes the plague in the *Jugement dou roy de Navarre* and Christine the defeat of Nicopolis in the *Dit de Poissy*.

[36] On Christine's sense of humor, see Fenster 1992.

[37] See Altmann 1999, pp. 221–27; *Songs Women*, especially pp. 35–44.

[38] Zimmermann 1991, p. 215. Cf. Hicks 1988, pp. 328–29.

[39] Attwood 1998, p. 171.

> Je, Christine, qui ay plouré
> XI ans en abbaye close,
> Où j'ay tousjours puis demouré
> Que Charles (c'est estrange chose!),
> Le filz du roy, se dire l'ose,
> S'en fouÿ de Paris de tire,
> Par la traïson là enclose,
> Ou à prime me prens à rire.   (*Jehanne*, v. 1–8)
>
> [I, Christine, who have wept for eleven years in a walled abbey where I have lived ever since Charles (how strange this is!) the King's son – dare I say it? – fled in haste from Paris, I who have lived enclosed there on account of the treachery, now, for the first time, begin to laugh. (Kennedy and Varty, *Jehanne*, p. 41)]

Civil war, the English invasion, and Agincourt left her no security outside the convent of Poissy.[40]

The anomaly of the Dauphin's flight – that 'estrange chose' (v. 4) – signaled the surrender of the French crown to an English king. Yet, eleven years later another 'estrange chose' occurred.[41] Joan of Arc, certainly an anomaly, renewed Christine's hope and the faith she took with her into Poissy. At long last France might indeed recover a good king and unite under God. These are her last words.

Autobiography

The 'autobiographical assumption'[42] has returned to recent criticism, largely, I think, because of renewed interest in the writing and lives of women as authors and patrons.[43] To be sure, the assumption is still colored by prejudices and assumptions prevalent at the time early writers wrote, and may be influenced by contingencies we can never understand or even know, as the epigraph to this book suggests. In Froissart's *Meliador*, a damsel's objection to the love evoked in a particular poem – 'onques n'amai par tel art' (*Meliador*, v. 20354)[44] [I never loved in that way] – anticipates Christine's own reaction to court poetry

---

[40] Kennedy and Varty, ed., *Jehanne*, pp. 60–61.

[41] On *estrange*, we recall that the *Advision*, according to Lady Opinion, will strike readers because its 'composicion des materes est estrange' (II.xxii.62). Blanchard and Quereuil 1999, p. 160, translate the word as 'étrange, bizarre'.

[42] Kay 1990, p. 4; cf. M. Zink's criticism of Zumthor's 'formalism' (1985, pp. 47–48). See also Cerquiglini 1988b. Even Christine's pious verse has a personal referent (Gros 1990).

[43] It also permits analyses of the prejudices, intentions, and ignorance perceived in male authors writing about women, including those who criticize misogyny and defend women; see Blumenfeld-Kosinski 1994; Pratt 2002b.

[44] See in general Kelly 1978, pp. 248–52.

and courtly love, as it does that of the Belle Dame sans mercy and her avatars. In Christine's case, the objection rings true because of her categorical stands on misogyny and love. She also realized how unique her views were. That is, unlike the *Meliador* damsel who does love, but not in the way the song sets out, Christine, like Chartier's Belle Dame sans mercy, loves not at all and will not.

Yet something new emerges in Christine's autobiographical persona. Indeed, one of the most remarkable results of the autobiographical assumption in her case is the close correlation between her life as she reports it and the experiences of the Christine character in her writing. As discussed earlier, for example in the *Chemin de long estude*, 'Christine' flies through the air surveying all regions of the world; she then rises up through the heavens to a very high point near the edge of the geocentric universe. We know, of course, that Christine the author did none of this literally. Yet we also know that the image of her voyage reflects her actual education, first by reading historical works – her horizontal journey – and then by studying the philosophers – her ascendancy through the universe. No other medieval French writer of her time offers more material in support of the autobiographical assumption, at least in the traditional sense by which one reads an author's experience in his or her fictional character's 'adventures'. The 'Machaut' in the *Voir-dit* and the 'Froissart' of the latter's love poems do not lend themselves to the kind of autobiographical reading associated with nineteenth-century readings of their works. Charles d'Orléans recedes into silence about his life, although his poems seem to be convincing expressions of his *vrays sentiments*.[45] Villon the author is a mystery.

Christine's reasoned consideration of her own experience, consideration that leads her to discriminating conclusions that conflict with tradition and received learning, inspires her to contemplate and evaluate the nature and problems of opinion when she confronts it in her reading.[46] In doing so, she contributes something truly original to literary experience: a reflection on the uses and personal evaluation of opinion. Although many of her opinions, especially on religion and monarchy, are representative of her times, the *Advision* shows her looking towards a future that, with Rousseau, would defend individual opinions against traditional learning and contemporary political correctness.[47] In both cases, the author grounds individual opinion on reason and experience, Christine's two sources for *certainne science*. *Seulete* in her own time, Christine stood alone against the traditional medieval view of personal existence as being defined only by social status, where 'l'individu n'existe plus socialement ni culturellement, il n'existe qu'au niveau physique'.[48] It is striking that Christine

---

[45] Kelly 1978, pp. 222–29.

[46] Brownlee 2005.

[47] Cf. Tarnowski 2003. See, for example, Christine's proud claim to future fame, placed in the mouth of Lady Opinion: *Advision*, II.xxii.63–71.

[48] Corti 1983, p. 149.

de Pizan saw herself as a person apart while devoting so much of her writing to integrating her compatriots, male and female, into an orderly society morally defensible.[49]

---

[49] Cf. Forhan 1996, p. 70, who defines Christine's individualism as 'an awareness of personal uniqueness within a society, from belonging to that society and acceptance of one's role'. These words reflect the conceptual diptych illustrated by the *Cité des dames* vis-à-vis the *Livre des trois vertus*.

Bibliography

Primary texts

AB	Christine de Pizan. *Autres balades*. In *Œuvres poétiques de Christine de Pisan*. Ed. Maurice Roy. SATF. Paris: Firmin Didot, 1886. Vol. 1, pp. 207–69.
Advision	Christine de Pizan. *Le Livre de l'Advision Cristine*. Ed. Christine Reno and Liliane Dulac. Etudes Christiniennes, 4. Paris: Champion, 2001.
	———. *Lavision-Christine: Introduction and Text*. Ed. Sister Mary Louis Towner. Diss. The Catholic University of America. Washington, DC: The Catholic University of America, 1932.
Alexis	*La Vie de saint Alexis*. Ed. Christopher Storey. TLF, 148. Geneva: Droz, Paris: Minard, 1968.
Anthology	Christine de Pizan. *Christine de Pisan's Ballades, Rondeaux, and Virelais: An Anthology*. Ed. Kenneth Varty. Leicester: Leicester University Press, 1965.
Anticlaudianus	Alain de Lille. *Anticlaudianus*. Ed. R. Bossuat. Textes philosophiques du moyen âge, 1. Paris: Vrin, 1955.
Ars versificatoria	Matthew of Vendôme. *Ars versificatoria*. In Vol. 3: *Mathei Vindocinensis opera*. Ed. Franco Munari. Storia e Letteratura, 171. Rome: Storia e Letteratura, 1988.
	———. *The Art of Versification*. Trans. Aubrey E. Galyon. Ames, IA: Iowa State University Press, 1980.
Balades	Eustache Deschamps. *Œuvres complètes*. Ed. Le Marquis de Queux de Saint-Hilaire. SATF. Paris: Firmin Didot, 1889. Vol. 6.
Caractères	La Bruyère. *Les Caractères ou les mœurs du siècle*. In his *Œuvres complètes*. Ed. Julien Benda. Bibliothèque de la Pléiade, 23. Paris: Gallimard, 1951, pp. 59–478.
CB	Christine de Pizan. *Cent balades*. In *Œuvres poétiques de Christine de Pisan*. Ed. Maurice Roy. SATF. Paris: Firmin Didot, 1886. Vol. 1, pp. 1–99.
CBAD	Christine de Pizan. *Cent Ballades d'amant et de dame*. Ed. Jacqueline Cerquiglini. 10/18: Bibliothèque médiévale. Paris: Union Générale d'Editions, 1982.

Chansons	Thibaut de Champagne, roi de Navarre. *Les Chansons*. Ed. A. Wallensköld. SATF. Paris: Champion, 1925.
Charles V	Christine de Pizan. *Le Livre des fais et bonnes meurs du sage roy Charles V*. Ed. S. Solente. Société de l'Histoire de France. 2 vols. Paris: Champion, 1936–40.
	——. *Le Livre des faits et bonnes mœurs du roi Charles V le Sage*. Trans. Eric Hicks and Thérèse Moreau. Moyen Age. Paris: Stock, 1997.
Chartier Works	Alain Chartier. *The Poetical Works*. Ed. J. C. Laidlaw. Cambridge: Cambridge University Press, 1974.
Chemin	Christine de Pizan. *Le Chemin de longue étude*. Ed. Andrea Tarnowski. Livre de Poche: Lettres Gothiques. Paris: Librarie Générale Française, 2000.
	——. *Le Livre du Chemin de long estude*. Ed. Robert Püschel. Berlin, 1887; Geneva: Slatkine Reprints, 1974.
Cité	Christine de Pizan. *La Città delle dame*. Ed. Patrizia Caraffi and Earl Jeffrey Richards. Biblioteca Medievale, 2. Milan, Trento: Luni, 1997.
	——. 'The *Livre de la Cité des dames* of Christine de Pisan: A Critical Edition.' Ed. Maureen Cheney Curnow. Diss. Vanderbilt University, 1975.
	——. *The Book of the City of Ladies*. Trans. Rosalind Brown-Grant. Penguin Classics. London: Penguin Books, 1999.
De amore	Andreas Capellanus. *Trattato d'amore: Andreae Capellani regii Francorum 'De amore' libri tres. Testo latino del sec. XII con due traduzioni toscane inedite del sec. XIV*. Ed. Salvatore Battaglia. Rome: Perrella, 1947.
Débat	*Le Débat sur le Roman de la Rose: édition critique, introduction, traductions, notes*. Ed. and trans. Eric Hicks. Bibliothèque du XVe siècle, 43. Paris: Champion, 1977.
De consolatione	Boethius. *Philosophiae consolatio*. Ed. Ludovicus Bieler. Corpus Christianorum: series latina, 94. Turnhout: Brepols, 1984.
	——. *The Consolation of Philosophy*. Trans. Richard Green. The Library of Liberal Arts. Indianapolis: Bobbs-Merrill, 1962.
Deux amants	Christine de Pizan. *Le Livre du Debat de deux amans*. In *The Love Debate Poems*. Ed. Barbara K. Altmann. Gainesville: University Press of Florida, 1998, pp. 81–152.
Distinctiones	Alain de Lille. *Distinctiones dictionum theologicalium*. In *Patrologia latina*. Ed. J.-P. Migne. Paris: Migne, 1855. Vol. 210.
Dit Rose	Christine de Pizan. *Dit de la rose*. In *Poems of Cupid, God of Love*. Ed. Thelma S. Fenster and Mary Carpenter Erler. Leiden, New York, Copenhagen, Cologne: Brill, 1990, pp. 91–131.
Divine Comedy	Dante Alighieri. *La Divina Commedia*. Ed. C. H. Grandgent. Rev. ed. Boston: Heath, 1933.

Documentum	Geoffrey of Vinsauf. *Documentum de modo et arte dictandi et versificandi*. In Edmond Faral. *Les Arts poétiques du XIIe et du XIIIe siècle: recherches et documents sur la technique littéraire du moyen âge*. Bibliothèque de l'Ecole des Hautes Etudes, 238. Paris: Champion, 1924, pp. 263–320.
Duc	Christine de Pizan. *Le Livre du Duc des vrais amans*. Ed. Thelma S. Fenster. Medieval and Renaissance Texts and Studies, 124. Binghamton, NY: Medieval and Renaissance Texts and Studies, 1995.
EAB	Christine de Pizan. *Encore aultres balades*. In *Œuvres poétiques de Christine de Pisan*. Ed. Maurice Roy. SATF. Paris: Firmin Didot, 1886. Vol. 1, pp. 271–79.
Enseignemens	*Les Enseignemens moraux*. In *Œuvres poétiques de Christine de Pisan*. Ed. Maurice Roy. SATF. Paris: Firmin Didot, 1896. Vol. 3, pp. 27–44.
Epistre Dieu	Christine de Pizan. *Epistre au dieu d'amours*. In *Poems of Cupid, God of Love*. Ed. Thelma S. Fenster and Mary Carpenter Erler. Leiden, New York, Copenhagen, Cologne: Brill, 1990, pp. 33–89.
Epistre Morel	Christine de Pizan. 'L'*Epistre a Eustace Morel* de Christine de Pizan.' Ed. Jean-François Kosta-Théfaine. *Moyen Français*, 38 (1997), 79–91.
Epistre Prison	Christine de Pizan. *Epistre de la Prison de vie humaine*. Ed. Angus J. Kennedy. Glasgow: French Department, University of Glasgow, 1984.
Epistre Reine	Christine de Pizan. 'Christine de Pisan's *Epistre à la reine*.' Ed. Angus J. Kennedy. *Revue des langues romanes*, 92 (1988), 253–64.
Espérance	Alain Chartier. *Le Livre de l'espérance*. Ed. François Rouy. Bibliothèque du XVe siècle, 51. Paris: Champion, 1989.
Essais	Michel de Montaigne. *Essais*. In his *Œuvres complètes*. Ed. Albert Thibaudet and Maurice Rat. Bibliothèque de la Pléiade, 14. Paris: Gallimard, 1962, pp. 1–1097.
Etymologiae	Isidore of Seville. *Etymologiarum sive originum libri XX*. Ed. W. M. Lindsay. 2 vols. Oxford: Clarendon Press, 1911.
Expositio	Thomas Aquinas. *In duodecim libros Metaphysicorum Aristotelis expositio*. Ed. M.-R. Cathala and Raymundo M. Spiazzo. Turin, Rome: Marietti, 1964.
Fais d'armes	Christine de Pizan. *The Book of Deeds of Arms and of Chivalry*. Trans. Sumner Willard; ed. Charity Cannon Willard. University Park, PA: Pennsylvania State University Press, 1999.
Heroides	Ovid. *Heroides and Amores*. Ed. and trans. Grant Showerman. 2nd ed. rev. G. P. Goold. Loeb Classical Library. Cambridge, MA: Harvard University Press, London: Heinemann, 1986.

Horace	Pierre Corneille. *Horace*. In his *Théâtre complet*. Ed. Maurice Rat. Classiques Garnier. Paris: Garnier, 1960. Vol. 1, pp. 655–718.
Ille	Gautier d'Arras. *Ille et Galeron*. Ed. Yves Lefèvre. CFMA, 109. Paris: Champion, 1988.
Jehanne	Christine de Pizan. *Ditié de Jehanne d'Arc*. Ed. Angus J. Kennedy and Kenneth Varty. Medium Aevum Monographs, n.s. 9. Oxford: Society for the Study of Mediaeval Languages and Literature, 1977.
Lancelot	*Lancelot*. Ed. Alexandre Micha. 9 vols. TLF, 247, 249, 262, 278, 283, 286, 288, 307, 315. Paris, Geneva: Droz, 1978–83.
Materia Commentary	'Anonymi cuiusdam "Glose in Poetriam Horatii".' In 'The *Ars Poetica* in Twelfth-Century France: The Horace of Matthew of Vendôme, Geoffrey of Vinsauf, and John of Garland.' Ed. Karsten Friis-Jensen. *Cahiers de l'Institut du Moyen-Age grec et latin, Université de Copenhague*, 60 (1990), 335–84.
Meliador	Jean Froissart. *Meliador*. Ed. Auguste Longnon. SATF. 3 vols. Paris: Firmin Didot, 1895–99.
Mutacion	Christine de Pizan. *Le Livre de la Mutacion de Fortune*. Ed. Suzanne Solente. 4 vols. SATF. Paris: Picard, 1959–66.
Narcisus	'Das mittelfranzösische Narcissusspiel (L'istoire de Narcisus et de Echo).' Ed. Alfons Hilka. *Zeitschrift für romanische Philologie*, 56 (1936), 275–321.
Othea	Christine de Pizan. *Epistre Othea*. Ed. Gabriella Parussa. TLF, 517. Geneva: Droz, 1999.
Paix	Christine de Pizan. *The 'Livre de la paix'*. Ed. Charity Cannon Willard. The Hague: Mouton, 1958.
Pantagruel	Rabelais. *Œuvres complètes*. Ed. Jacques Boulenger; rev. Lucien Scheler. Bibliothèque de la Pléiade, 15. Paris: Gallimard, 1955.
Passion	Arnould Greban. *Le Mystère de la Passion*. Ed. Gaston Paris and Gaston Raynaud. Paris: Vieweg, 1878.
Pastoure	Christine de Pizan. *Le Dit de la pastoure*. In *Œuvres poétiques de Christine de Pisan*. Ed. Maurice Roy. SATF. Paris: Firmin Didot, 1891. Vol. 2, pp. 223–94.
Pensées	Blaise Pascal. *Pensées: édition établie d'après la copie de référence de Gilberte Pascal*. Ed. Philippe Sellier. Paris: Classiques Garnier Multimédia, 1999.
Poèmes d'amour	*Poèmes d'amour des XIIe et XIIIe siècles*. Ed. Emmanuèle Baumgartner and Françoise Ferrand. 10/18: Bibliothèque Médiévale. Paris: Union Générale d'Editions, 1983.
Poetria nova	Geoffrey of Vinsauf. *Poetria nova*. In Edmond Faral. *Les Arts poétiques du XIIe et du XIIIe siècle: recherches et documents sur la technique littéraire du moyen âge*. Bibliothèque de l'Ecole des Hautes Etudes, 238. Paris: Champion, 1924, pp. 194–262.

	———. *Poetria Nova of Geoffrey of Vinsauf*. Trans. Margaret F. Nims. Toronto: Pontifical Institute of Mediaeval Studies, 1967.
Poissy	Christine de Pizan. *Le Livre du Dit de Poissy*. In *The Love Debate Poems*. Ed. Barbara K. Altmann. Gainesville: University Press of Florida, 1998, pp. 203–74.
Policie	Christine de Pizan. *Le Livre du Corps de policie*. Ed. Angus J. Kennedy. Etudes christiniennes, 1. Paris: Champion, 1998.
Policraticus	John of Salisbury. *Policraticus I–IV*. Ed. K. S. B. Keats-Rohan. Corpus Christianorum: continuatio mediaevalis, 118. Turnhout: Brepols, 1993.
Policratique	Denis Foulechat. *Le Policratique de Jean de Salisbury (1372): livres I–III*. Ed. Charles Brucker. Publications romanes et françaises, 209. Geneva: Droz, 1994.
Prouverbes	*Prouverbes moraulx*. In *Œuvres poétiques de Christine de Pisan*. Ed. Maurice Roy. SATF. Paris: Firmin Didot, 1896. Vol. 3, pp. 45–57.
Quadrilogue	Alain Chartier. *Le Quadrilogue invectif*. Ed. E. Droz. CFMA, 32. Paris: Champion, 1950.
Quarrel	*Alain Chartier: The Quarrel of the Belle dame sans mercy*. Ed. and trans. Joan E. McRae. Routledge Medieval Texts. New York, London: Routledge, 2004.
Quatre dames	Alain Chartier. *Le Livre des quatre dames*. In *Chartier Works*, pp. 196–304.
Quinze joies	*Les .xv. Joies de mariage*. Ed. Jean Rychner. TLF, 100. Geneva: Droz, Paris: Minard, 1967.
R	Christine de Pizan. *Rondeaux*. In *Œuvres poétiques de Christine de Pisan*. Ed. Maurice Roy. SATF. Paris: Firmin Didot, 1886. Vol. 1, pp. 147–85.
Remede	Guillaume de Machaut. *Remede de Fortune*. In his *Le Jugement du roy de Behaigne and Remede de Fortune*. Ed. James I. Wimsatt and William W. Kibler; music ed. Rebecca A. Baltzer. The Chaucer Library. Athens, GA, London: University of Georgia Press, 1988, pp. 167–407.
Rose	Guillaume de Lorris and Jean de Meun. *Le Roman de la rose*. Ed. Félix Lecoy. CFMA, 92, 95, 98. Paris: Champion, 1965–70.
Songs Women	*Songs of the Women Trouvères*. Ed. and trans. Eglal Doss-Quinby, Joan Tasker Grimbert, Wendy Pfeffer, and Elizabeth Aubrey. New Haven, London: Yale University Press, 2001.
Testament	Jean de Meun. *Le Testament Maistre Jehan de Meun: un caso letterario*. Ed. Silvia Buzzetti. Scrittura e scrittori: serie monografica, 4. Alessandria: dell'Orso, 1989.
Tresor	Brunetto Latini. *Li Livres dou tresor*. Ed. Francis J. Carmody. Berkeley, 1948; repr. Geneva: Slatkine, 1998.

Trobairitz	*Trobairitz: der Beitrag der Frau in der altokzitanischen höfischen Lyrik. Edition des Gesamtkorpus.* Ed. Angelica Rieger. Beihefte zur Zeitschrift für romanische Philologie, 233. Tübingen: Niemeyer, 1991.
Trois jugemens	Christine de Pizan. *Le Livre des Trois jugemens.* In *The Love Debate Poems.* Ed. Barbara K. Altmann. Gainesville: University Press of Florida, 1998, pp. 153–202.
Trois vertus	Christine de Pizan. *Le Livre des trois vertus.* Ed. Charity Cannon Willard and Eric Hicks. Bibliothèque du XVe siècle, 50. Paris: Champion, 1989.
V	Christine de Pizan. *Virelays.* In *Œuvres poétiques de Christine de Pisan.* Ed. Maurice Roy. SATF. Paris: Firmin Didot, 1886. Vol. 1, pp. 101–18.
XV Joies	Christine de Pizan. *Les XV Joies nostre Dame.* In *Œuvres poétiques de Christine de Pisan.* Ed. Maurice Roy. SATF. Paris: Firmin Didot, 1896. Vol. 3, pp. 11–14.
Yvain	Chrétien de Troyes. *Le Chevalier au lion ou le Roman d'Yvain.* Ed. David F. Hult. Lettres Gothiques. Paris: Librairie Générale Française, 1994.

Secondary sources

Adams, Tracy 2000. 'Deceptive Lovers: Christine de Pizan and the Problem of Interpretation.' In *Au champ*, pp. 413–24.

—— 2002. '*Eros* or *Anteros*? Christine de Pizan's Economies of Desire.' In *Contexts*, pp. 1–15.

—— 2003. 'Love as Metaphor in Christine de Pizan's Ballade Cycles.' In *Casebook*, pp. 149–65.

Allen, Judson Boyce 1982. *The Ethical Poetic of the Later Middle Ages: A Decorum of Convenient Distinction.* Toronto, Buffalo, London: University of Toronto Press.

Almeida Ribeiro, Cristina 1989. 'Les *Cent Ballades d'amant et de dame* et la tentation du roman par lettres.' *Ariana*, 7, 33–48.

Altmann, Barbara K. 1995. 'L'art de l'autoportrait littéraire dans les *Cent Ballades* de Christine de Pizan.' In *Femme de lettres*, pp. 327–36.

—— 1996. 'Last Words: Reflections on a "Lay Mortel" and the Poetics of Lyric Sequences.' *French Studies*, 50, 385–99; reprinted in *Christine Lyric*, pp. 83–102.

—— 1999. '"Trop peu en sçay": The Reluctant Narrator in Christine de Pizan's Works on Love.' In *Chaucer's Contemporaries*, pp. 217–49.

—— 2000. 'Through the Byways of Lyric and Narrative: The *Voiage d'oultremer* in the Ballade Cycles of Christine de Pizan.' In *Christine 2000*, pp. 49–64, 303–06.

Angeli, Giovanna 1993. 'Christine de Pizan: fantasmagorie del soggetto.' In *Controfigure d'autore: scritture autobiografiche nella letteratura francese.* Ed. Fausta Garavini. Temi e discussioni. Bologna: Il Mulino, pp. 19–54.

—— 1996. '*Fortuna adversa*, Saturne et Villon.' In *Le Moyen Age dans la modernité: mélanges offerts à Roger Dragonetti*. Ed. Jean R. Scheidegger, with Sabine Girardet and Eric Hicks. Nouvelle Bibliothèque du moyen âge, 39. Paris: Champion, pp. 21–32.
—— 2000. 'Charité et pauvreté chez Christine de Pizan.' In *Au champ*, pp. 425–38.
—— 2002. 'Encore sur Boccace et Christine de Pizan: remarques sur le *De mulieribus claris* et le *Livre de la cité des Dames* ("Plourer, parler, filer mist Dieu en femme" I, 10).' *Le Moyen français*, 50, 115–25.
—— 2003. 'Christine de Pizan e il tramonto del cuore virile.' In *Città*, pp. 59–69.
Arden, Heather M. 1993. *The Roman de la rose: An Annotated Bibliography*. Garland Medieval Bibliographies, 8. New York, London: Garland.
—— 1997. 'Women's History and the Rhetoric of Persuasion in Christine de Pizan's *Cité des dames*.' *Moyen Français*, 39–40–41, 7–17.
—— 2002. 'Her Mother's Daughter: Empowerment and Maternity in the Works of Christine de Pizan.' In *Contexts*, pp. 31–41.
Arnaville, Teddy 1988. 'Structuration personnelle du *Ditié de Jehanne d'Arc* (1429).' *Revue des langues romanes*, 92, 287–93.
Attwood, Catherine 1998. *Dynamic Dichotomy: The Poetic 'I' in Fourteenth- and Fifteenth-Century French Lyric Poetry*. Faux Titre, 149. Amsterdam, Atlanta: Rodopi.
Auerbach, Erich 1958. *Literatursprache und Publikum in der lateinischen Spätantike und im Mittelalter*. Bern: Francke.
Autrand, Françoise 1995. 'Mémoire et cérémonial: la visite de l'empereur Charles IV à Paris en 1378 d'après les *Grandes Chroniques de France* et Christine de Pizan.' In *Femme de lettres*, pp. 91–103.
Avril, F. 1969. 'Trois manuscrits napolitains des collections de Charles V et de Jean de Berry.' *Bibliothèque de l'Ecole des chartes*, 127, 291–328.
Badel, Pierre-Yves 1980. *Le Roman de la rose au XIVe siècle: étude de la réception de l'œuvre*. Publications romanes et françaises, 153. Geneva: Droz.
Ballet-Lynn, Thérèse 1991. 'L'Héroïsme féminin chez Christine de Pizan.' *Trivium*, 26, 81–88.
Baumgartner, Emmanuèle 2001. '"Batailles que li con esmurent" (*Roman de la rose*, v. 13894): de la banalisation du mythe antique dans l'œuvre de Jean de Meun.' In *Riens ne m'est seur*, pp. 69–79.
Beaune, Colette 1985. *Naissance de la nation France*. Bibliothèque des Histoires. Paris: Gallimard.
Becker, Philipp August 1967. 'Christine de Pizan.' In his *Zur romanischen Literaturgeschichte: Ausgewählte Studien und Aufsätze*. Munich: Francke, pp. 511–40.
Beer, Jeanette M. A. 1992. 'Stylistic Conventions in *Le Livre de la mutacion de Fortune*.' In *Reinterpreting Christine*, pp. 124–36.
Benkov, Edith 2002. 'Unmanning Hercules: Myth and Gender in the *Dit de la pastoure*.' In *Contexts*, pp. 65–74.
Blamires, Alcuin 1997. *The Case for Women in Medieval Culture*. Oxford: Clarendon Press.
Blanchard, Joël 1983. *La Pastorale en France aux XIVe et XVe siècles: recherches*

sur les structures de l'imaginaire médiéval. Bibliothèque du XVe siècle, 45. Paris: Champion.

—— 1985. 'Artefact littéraire et problématisation morale au XVe siècle.' *Le Moyen Français*, 17, 7–47.

—— 1986a. 'Christine de Pizan: les raisons de l'histoire.' *Moyen Age*, 42, 417–36.

—— 1986b. 'L'Entrée du poète dans le champ politique au XVe siècle.' *Annales*, 41, 43–61.

—— 1986c. '"Vox poetica, vox politica": l'entrée du poète dans le champ politique au XVe siècle.' In *Etudes littéraires sur le XVe siècle: actes du Ve Colloque International sur le Moyen Français, Milan, 6–8 mai 1985 – Vol. III*. Contributi del 'Centro Studi sulla letteratura medio-francese', 5. Scienze filologiche e letteratura, 31. Milan: Vita e Pensiero: Pubblicazioni della Università Cattolica del Sacro Cuore, pp. 39–51.

—— 1988. 'Compilation et légitimation au XVe siècle.' *Poétique*, 74, 139–57.

—— 1990. 'Christine de Pizan: tradition, expérience et traduction.' *Romania*, 111, 200–35.

—— 1993. 'Christine de Pizan: une laïque au pays des clercs.' In *Hommage Dufournet*, pp. 215–26.

Blanchard, Joël, and Jean-Claude Mühlethaler 2002. *Ecriture et pouvoir à l'aube des temps modernes*. Perspectives littéraires. Paris: Presses Universitaires de France.

Blanchard, Joël, and Michel Quereuil 1999. *Lexique de Christine de Pizan*. Matériaux pour le *Dictionnaire du Moyen Français (DMF)*, 5. [Paris:] Klincksieck.

Bloch, R. Howard 1991. *Medieval Misogyny and the Invention of Western Romantic Love*. Chicago, London: University of Chicago Press.

Blumenfeld-Kosinski, Renate 1990. 'Christine de Pizan and the Misogynistic Tradition.' *Romanic Review*, 81, 279–92.

—— 1994. 'Jean le Fèvre's *Livre de Leesce*: Praise or Blame of Women?' *Speculum*, 69, 705–25.

—— 1995. 'Das Konzept von Frau und Mann bei Hildegard von Bingen und Christine de Pizan.' In *Tiefe des Gotteswissens–Schönheit der Sprachgestalt bei Hildegard von Bingen. Internationales Symposium in der Katholischen Akademie Rabanus Maurus, Wiesbaden-Naurod, vom 9. bis 12. September 1994*. Ed. Margot Schmidt. Mystik in Geschichte und Gegenwart: Texte und Untersuchungen. Abteilung I: Christliche Mystik, 10. Stuttgart-Bad Cannstatt: frommann-holzboog, pp. 167–79.

—— 1997. *Reading Myth: Classical Mythology and Its Interpretations in Medieval French Literature*. Figurae. Stanford, CA: Stanford University Press.

—— 1999. '"Enemies Within/Enemies Without": Threats to the Body Politic in Christine de Pizan.' *Medievalia et Humanistica*, n.s. 26, 1–15.

—— 2000. 'Saintly Scenarios in Christine de Pizan's *Livre des trois vertus*.' *Mediaeval Studies*, 62, 255–92.

—— 2001. 'Christine de Pizan et l'(auto)biographie féminine.' *Mélanges de l'Ecole française de Rome: Italie et Méditerranée*, 113:1, 17–28.

—— 2002a. 'Alain Chartier and the Crisis in France: Courtly and Clerical Responses.' In *Courtly Literature*, pp. 211–20.

—— 2002b. 'Two Responses to Agincourt: Alain Chartier's *Livre des quatre dames*

and Christine de Pizan's *Epistre de la prison de vie humaine.*' In *Contexts*, pp. 75–85.
—— 2003. 'Christine de Pizan and the Political Life in Late Medieval France.' In *Casebook*, pp. 9–24.
Boerdam, Jaap 1997. 'Het Primaat van de intimiteit.' *NRC Handelsblad*, October 18.
Bornstein, Diane 1981. 'The Ideal of the Lady of the Manor as Reflected in Christine de Pizan's *Livre des trois vertus*.' In *Ideals*, pp. 117–28.
Boulton, Maureen 2003. '"Nous deffens de feu, ... de pestilence, de guerres": Christine de Pizan's Religious Works.' In *Casebook*, pp. 215–28.
Brandenberger, Tobias 2002. 'La réception portugaise de Christine de Pizan: un nouveau contexte.' In *Contexts*, pp. 129–40.
Brinkmann, Hennig 1979. *Zu Wesen und Form mittelalterlicher Dichtung*. Darmstadt: Wissenschaftliche Buchgesellschaft, Tübingen: Niemeyer.
Brown-Grant, Rosalind 1988. 'Décadence ou progrès? Christine de Pizan, Boccace et la question de "l'âge d'or".' *Revue des langues romanes*, 92, 295–306.
—— 1992. '*L'Avision Christine*: Autobiographical Narrative or Mirror for Princes?' In *Politics*, pp. 95–111.
—— 1993. 'Les Exilées du pouvoir? Christine de Pizan et la femme devant la crise du Moyen Âge finissant.' In *Apogée*, pp. 211–23.
—— 1995. '*Des hommes et des femmes illustres*: modalités narratives et transformations génériques chez Pétrarque, Boccace et Christine de Pizan.' In *Femme de lettres*, pp. 469–80.
—— 1999a. *Christine de Pizan and the Moral Defence of Women: Reading beyond Gender*. Cambridge Studies in Medieval Literature, 40. Cambridge: Cambridge University Press.
—— 1999b. '"Hee! Quel Honneur au Femenin Sexe!" Female Heroism in Christine de Pizan's *Ditié de Jehanne d'Arc*.' In *Writers and Heroines: Essays on Women in French Literature*. Ed. Shirley Jones Day. Bern: P. Lang, pp. 15–30.
—— 2000a. 'Christine de Pizan: Feminist Linguist *avant la lettre*?' In *Christine 2000*, pp. 65–76, 306–07.
—— 2000b. 'A New Context for Reading the "Querelle de la *Rose*": Christine de Pizan and Medieval Literary Theory.' In *Au champ*, pp. 581–95.
—— 2002. 'Mirroring the Court: Clerkly Advice to Noble Men and Women in the Works of Philippe de Mézières and Christine de Pizan.' In *Courtly Literature*, pp. 39–53.
—— 2003. 'Christine de Pizan as a Defender of Women.' In *Casebook*, pp. 81–100.
Brownlee, Kevin 1990. 'Ovide et le Moi poétique "moderne" à la fin du Moyen Age: Jean Froissart et Christine de Pizan.' In *Modernité au Moyen Age: le défi du passé*. Ed. Brigitte Cazelles and Charles Méla. Recherches et rencontres, 1. Geneva: Droz, pp. 153–73.
—— 1991. 'The Image of History in Christine de Pizan's *Livre de la Mutacion de Fortune*.' In *Contexts: Style and Values in Medieval Art and Literature*. Ed. Daniel Poirion and Nancy Freeman Regalado. Yale French Studies Special Issue. New Haven, London: Yale University Press, pp. 44–56.
—— 1992. 'Discourses of the Self: Christine de Pizan and the *Romance of the Rose*.' In *Rethinking the 'Romance of the Rose': Text, Image, Reception*. Ed.

Kevin Brownlee and Sylvia Huot. Middle Ages Series. Philadelphia: University of Pennsylvania Press, pp. 234–61.

—— 1995a. 'Le Moi "lyrique" et la généalogie littéraire: Christine de Pizan et Dante dans le *Chemin de long estude*.' In *Musique*, pp. 105–39.

—— 1995b. 'Widowhood, Sexuality, and Gender in Christine de Pizan.' *Romanic Review*, 86, 339–53.

—— 1996. 'Rewriting Romance: Courtly Discourse and Auto-Citation in Christine de Pizan.' In *Gender and Text*, pp. 172–94.

—— 2000. 'Le projet "autobiographique" de Christine de Pizan: histoires et fables du moi.' In *Au champ*, pp. 5–23.

—— 2005. 'Christine de Pizan: Gender and the New Vernacular Canon.' In *Strong Voices*, pp. 99–120.

Brucker, Charles 1995. 'Le monde, la foi et le savoir dans quelques œuvres de Christine de Pizan: une quête.' In *Femme de lettres*, pp. 265–80.

—— 2001. 'Mouvement et fragilité humaine dans quelques œuvres de Christine de Pizan.' In *Riens ne m'est seur*, pp. 161–80.

Brundage, James A. 2000. 'Domestic Violence in Classical Canon Law.' In *Violence*, pp. 183–95.

Bugge, John 1975. *'Virginitas': An Essay in the History of a Medieval Ideal*. Archives Internationales d'histoire des idées: series minor, 17. The Hague: Nijhoff.

Burnley, J. D. 1986. 'Christine de Pizan and the So-Called *Style clergial*.' *Modern Language Review*, 81, 1–6.

Burrow, J. A. 1986. *The Ages of Man: A Study in Medieval Writing and Thought*. Oxford: Clarendon Press.

—— 2002. *Gestures and Looks in Medieval Narrative*. Cambridge Studies in Medieval Literature, 48. Cambridge: Cambridge University Press.

Callahan, Leslie Abend 2000. 'Filial Filiations: Representations of the Daughter in the Works of Christine de Pizan.' In *Au champ*, pp. 481–91.

Camargo, Martin 1991. *Ars dictaminis, Ars dictandi*. Typologie des sources du moyen âge occidental, 60. Turnhout: Brepols.

Campbell, P. G. C. 1924. *L'Epître d'Othéa: étude sur les sources de Christine de Pisan*. Paris: Champion.

Caraffi, Patrizia 1998. 'Autorità femminile e re-scrittura della tradizione: *La Cité des dames* di Christine de Pizan.' In *Tradizione letteraria, iniziazione, genealogia*. Ed. Carlo Donà and Mario Mancini. Biblioteca Medievale: saggi, 2. Milan, Trento: Luni, pp. 63–81.

—— 2000. 'Medea sapiente e amorosa: da Euripide a Christine de Pizan.' In *Au champ*, pp. 133–47.

—— 2002. 'Silence des femmes et cruauté des hommes: Christine de Pizan et Boccaccio.' In *Contexts*, pp. 175–86.

—— 2003. 'Il Libro e la Città: metafore architettoniche e costruzione di una genealogia femminile.' In *Città*, pp. 19–31.

Carruthers, Mary J. 1990. *The Book of Memory: A Study of Memory in Medieval Culture*. Cambridge Studies in Medieval Literature, 10. Cambridge: Cambridge University Press.

—— 1998. *The Craft of Thought: Meditation, Rhetoric, and the Making of Images, 400–1200*. Cambridge Studies in Medieval Literature, 34. Cambridge: Cambridge

University Press.
Case, Mary Anne C. 1998. 'Christine de Pizan and the Authority of Experience.' In *Christine Categories*, pp. 71–87.
Cayley, Emma J. 2003. 'Drawing Conclusions: The Poetics of Closure in Alain Chartier's Verse.' *Fifteenth-Century Studies*, 28, 51–64.
Cecchetti, Dario 1991. 'La nozione di letteratura come "Speculum humanae vitae" nel primo Umanesimo francese.' In *Recherches*, pp. 7–27.
Cerquiglini, Jacqueline 1985. *'Un engin si soutil': Guillaume de Machaut et l'écriture au XIVe siècle*. Bibliothèque du XVe siècle, 47. Paris: Champion.
—— 1988a. 'Le Dit.' In *GRLMA*, 8:1, 86–94.
—— 1988b. 'L'Etrangère.' *Revue des langues romanes*, 92, 239–51.
—— 1993a. 'Cadmus ou Carmenta: réflexion sur le concept d'invention à la fin du moyen âge.' In *What Is Literature?* pp. 211–30.
—— 1993b. *La Couleur de la mélancolie: la fréquentation des livres au XIVe siècle, 1300–1415*. Paris: Hatier.
—— 1993c. 'Le Matin mélancolique: relecture d'un topos d'ouverture aux XIVe et XVe siècles.' *CAIEF*, 45, 7–22.
—— 1994. 'Fondements et fondations de l'écriture chez Christine de Pizan: scènes de lecture et scènes d'incarnation.' In *City of Scholars*, pp. 79–96.
—— 2000. 'Le goût de l'étude: saveur et savoir chez Christine de Pizan.' In *Au champ*, pp. 597–608.
—— 2002. 'Voix et figures du lyrisme dans l'œuvre de Christine de Pizan.' In *Contexts*, pp. 187–202.
—— 2003. 'Christine de Pizan: dalla conocchia alla penna.' In *Città*, pp. 71–85.
Chance, Jane 1993. 'Gender Trouble in the Garden of Deduit: Christine de Pizan Translating the *Rose*.' *RLA: Romance Languages Annual*, 4, 20–28.
—— 1996. 'Introduction.' In *Gender and Text*, pp. 1–21.
Chareyron, Nicole 2002. 'Trois états du sentiment de l'irréversible et de la nostalgie dans le *Dit de Poissy* de Christine de Pizan.' In *Contexts*, pp. 243–56.
Cheyette, Fredric L., and Howell Chickering 2005. 'Love, Anger, and Peace: Social Practice and Poetic Play in the Ending of *Yvain*.' *Speculum*, 80, 75–117.
Chickering, Howell. *See* Cheyette, Fredric L., and Howell Chickering.
Cizek, Alexandru N. 1994. *Imitatio et tractatio: die literarisch-rhetorischen Grundlagen der Nachahmung in Antike und Mittelalter*. Rhetorik-Forschungen, 7. Tübingen: Niemeyer.
Collinson, Patrick 2004. 'La Bolaing.' *London Review of Books*, 26:22, 9–10.
Cooke, John Daniel 1927. 'Euhemerism: A Mediaeval Interpretation of Classical Paganism.' *Speculum*, 2, 396–410.
Copeland, Rita 1991. *Rhetoric, Hermeneutics, and Translation in the Middle Ages: Academic Traditions and Vernacular Texts*. Cambridge Studies in Medieval Literature, 11. Cambridge: Cambridge University Press.
Corti, Maria 1983. 'Structures idéologiques et structures sémiotiques dans les *sermones ad status* du XIIIe siècle.' In *Archéologie*, pp. 145–63.
Courcelle, Pierre 1967. *La Consolation de Philosophie dans la tradition littéraire: antécédents et postérité de Boèce*. Paris: Etudes Augustiniennes.
Crane, Susan 2002. *The Performance of Self: Ritual, Clothing, and Identity during the Hundred Years War*. Middle Ages Series. Philadelphia: University of Pennsylvania Press.

Cropp, Glynnis M. 1975. *Le Vocabulaire courtois des troubadours de l'époque classique*. Publications romanes et françaises, 135. Geneva: Droz.

—— 1981. 'Boèce et Christine de Pizan.' *Moyen âge*, 87, 387–417.

—— 2002. 'The Exemplary Figure of Alexander the Great in the Works of Eustache Deschamps and Christine de Pizan.' In *Contexts*, pp. 301–13.

Curnow, Maureen Cheney 1992. '"La pioche d'Inquisicion": Legal-Judicial Content and Style in Christine de Pizan's *Livre de la Cité des dames*.' In *Reinterpreting Christine*, pp. 157–72.

Curtius, Ernst Robert 1954. *Europäische Literatur und lateinisches Mittelalter*. 2nd rev. ed. Bern: Francke.

De Gendt, Anne-Marie Emma Alberta 1999. *Stratégies éducatives pour nobles damoiselles: 'Le Livre du Chevalier de la Tour Landry'*. Diss. Groningen. Groningen: Rijksuniversiteit Groningen.

Delany, Sheila 1987. '"Mothers to Think Back Through": Who Are They? The Ambiguous Example of Christine de Pizan.' In *Medieval Texts and Contemporary Readers*. Ed. Laurie A. Finke and Martin B. Shichtman. Ithaca, NY, London: Cornell University Press, pp. 177–97.

—— 1992. 'History, Politics, and Christine Studies: A Polemical Reply.' In *Politics*, pp. 193–206.

Delisle, Léopold 1907. *Recherches sur la librairie de Charles V*. 2 vols. Paris: Champion.

Del Mar Plaza Picón, Francisca. *See* González Doreste, Dulce Maria, and Francisca Del Mar Plaza Picón.

Delogu, Daisy 2005. 'Reinventing the Ideal Sovereign in Christine de Pizan's *Livre des fais et bonnes meurs du sage roy Charles V*.' *Medievalia et Humanistica*, 31, 41–58.

Demats, Paule 1973. *Fabula: trois études de mythographie antique et médiévale*. Publications romanes et françaises, 122. Geneva: Droz.

De Rentiis, Dina 1994. '"Sequere me": "imitatio" dans la "Divine Comédie" et dans le "Livre du chemin de long estude".' In *City of Scholars*, pp. 31–42.

Desmond, Marilynn 1994. *Reading Dido: Gender, Textuality, and the Medieval 'Aeneid'*. Medieval Cultures, 8. Minneapolis, London: University of Minnesota Press.

—— 2003. 'The *Querelle de la Rose* and the Ethics of Reading.' In *Casebook*, pp. 167–80.

Dörrie, Heinrich 1960. 'Untersuchungen zur Überlieferungsgeschichte von Ovids Epistulae Heroidum.' In *Nachrichten der Akademie der Wissenschaften in Göttingen aus dem Jahre 1960: Philologisch-Historische Klasse*. Göttingen: Vandenhoeck & Ruprecht, pp. 113–230, 359–423.

Dove, Mary 1986. *The Perfect Age of Man's Life*. Cambridge: Cambridge University Press.

Dowd, Maureen 2000. *New York Times*, July 17.

Dudash, Susan J. 2003. 'Christine de Pizan and the "menu peuple".' *Speculum*, 78, 788–831.

Dulac, Liliane 1973. 'Christine de Pizan et le malheur des "vrais amans".' In *Mélanges de langue et de littérature médiévales offerts à Pierre Le Gentil*. Paris: S.E.D.E.S. et C.D.U, pp. 223–33.

—— 1978. 'Un Mythe didactique chez Christine de Pizan: Sémiramis ou la Veuve héroïque (du *De Mulieribus claris* de Boccace à la *Cité des dames*).' In *Mélanges de philologie romane offerts à Charles Camproux*. 2 vols. Montpellier: Centre d'Etudes Occitanes, Montpellier III, pp. 315–43.

—— 1988. 'Unité et variations de la *sagesse* dans le *Livre des fais et bonnes meurs du sage roy Charles V*.' *Revue des langues romanes*, 92, 307–15.

—— 1990. 'Le *Livre du dit de Poissy* de Christine de Pizan: poème éclaté ou montage signifiant?' In *Ecrire pour dire: études sur le dit médiéval*. Ed. Bernard Ribémont. Sapience. Paris: Klincksieck, pp. 9–28.

—— 1991a. 'La Figure de l'écrivain dans quelques traités en prose de Christine de Pizan.' In *Figures de l'écrivain au moyen âge: Actes du Colloque du Centre d'Etudes Médiévales de l'Université de Picardie, Amiens 18–20 mars 1988*. Ed. Danielle Buschinger. Göppinger Arbeiten zur Germanistik, 510. Göppingen: Kümmerle, pp. 113–23.

—— 1991b. 'Les Ouvertures closes dans le *Livre de la Cité des Dames*: le *Topos* du "Veuvage qualifiant".' In *Vers un 'Thesaurus' informatisé: topique des ouvertures narratives avant 1800. Actes: Quatrième Colloque International SATOR, Université Paul-Valéry–Montpellier III, 25–27 octobre 1990*. Ed. Pierre Rodriguez and Michèle Weil. Montpellier: Presses de l'Imprimerie de Recherche–Université Paul-Valéry. Montpellier III, pp. 35–45.

—— 1992a. 'Authority in the Prose Treatises of Christine de Pizan: The Writer's Discourse and the Prince's Word.' In *Politics*, pp. 129–40.

—— 1992b. 'The Representation and Functions of Feminine Speech in Christine de Pizan's *Livre des trois vertus*.' In *Reinterpreting Christine*, pp. 13–22.

—— 1994. 'De l'art de la digression dans "Le Livre des Fais et bonnes meurs du sage Roy Charles V".' In *City of Scholars*, pp. 148–57.

—— 1998a. 'Littérature et dévotion: à propos des *Heures de contemplacion sur la Passion de Nostre Seigneur* de Christine de Pizan.' In *Miscellanea Mediaevalia*. Vol. 1, pp. 475–84.

—— 1998b. 'Thèmes et variations du *Chemin de long estude* à l'*Advision-Christine*: remarques sur un itinéraire.' In *Sur le chemin*, pp. 77–86.

—— 1999. 'La Représentation de la France chez Eustache Deschamps et Christine de Pizan.' In *Autour d'Eustache Deschamps: Actes du Colloque du Centre d'Etudes Médiévales de l'Université de Picardie–Jules Verne, 5–8 novembre 1998*. Ed. Danielle Buschinger. Médiévales, 2. Amiens: Presses du 'Centre d'Etudes Médiévales', Université de Picardie–Jules Verne, pp. 79–92.

—— 2000. 'La gestuelle chez Christine de Pizan: quelques aperçus.' In *Au champ*, pp. 609–26.

—— 2001. 'Sur les fonctions du bestiaire dans quelques œuvres didactiques de Christine de Pizan.' In *Riens ne m'est seur*, pp. 181–94.

Dulac, Liliane, and Christine Reno 1995. 'L'Humanisme vers 1400, essai d'exploration à partir d'un cas marginal: Christine de Pizan, traductrice de Thomas d'Aquin.' In *Pratiques de la culture écrite en France au XVe siècle: Actes du Colloque International du CNRS, Paris, 16–18 mai 1992, organisé en l'honneur de Gilbert Ouy par l'unité de recherche 'Culture écrite du Moyen Age tardif'*. Ed. Monique Ornato and Nicole Pons. Fédération Internationale des Instituts d'Etudes Médiévales: textes et études du moyen âge, 2. Louvain-la-Neuve: Fédération Internationale des Instituts d'Etudes Médiévales, Collège Thomas More, pp. 161–78.

—— 1997. 'Traduction et adaptation dans *L'Advision-Cristine* de Christine de Pizan.' In *Traduction*, pp. 121–31.
—— 2003. 'The *Livre de l'Advision Cristine.*' In *Casebook*, pp. 199–214.
Dziedzic, Andrzej 2002. 'A la recherche d'une figure maternelle: l'image de la mère dans l'œuvre de Christine de Pizan.' *Neophilologus*, 86, 493–506.
Echtermann, Andrea, and Sylvia Nagel 2000. 'Recuperating the Polyphony of Women's Speech: Dialogue and Discourse in the Works of Christine de Pizan.' In *Au champ*, pp. 493–515.
Edsall, Mary Agnes 2000. 'Like Wise Master Builders: Jean Gerson's Ecclesiology, *Lectio Divina*, and Christine de Pizan's *Livre de la Cité des Dames.*' *Medievalia et Humanistica*, 27, 33–56.
Edwards, Robert R. 1989. *Ratio and Invention: A Study of Medieval Lyric and Narrative*. Nashville, TN: Vanderbilt University Press.
Ehrhart, Margaret J. 1990. 'Christine de Pizan and the Judgment of Paris: A Court Poet's Use of Mythographic Tradition.' In *Mythographic*, pp. 125–56.
Enders, Jody 1994. 'The Feminist Mnemonics of Christine de Pizan.' *Modern Language Quarterly*, 55, 231–49.
—— 1999. 'Memory, Allegory, and the Romance of Rhetoric.' *Yale French Studies*, 95, 49–64.
Erler, Mary Carpenter 1990. 'Introduction.' In *Poems of Cupid, God of Love: Christine de Pizan's 'Epistre au dieu d'Amours' and 'Dit de la Rose', Thomas Hoccleve's 'The Letter of Cupid' – Editions and Translations with George Sewell's 'The Proclamation of Cupid'*. Ed. Thelma S. Fenster and Mary Carpenter Erler. Leiden, New York, Copenhagen, Cologne: Brill, pp. 159–74.
Faral, Edmond 1924. *Les Arts poétiques du XIIe et du XIIIe siècle: recherches et documents sur la technique littéraire du moyen âge*. Bibliothèque de l'Ecole des Hautes Etudes, 238. Paris: Champion.
Fenster, Thelma 1992. 'Did Christine Have a Sense of Humor? The Evidence of the *Epistre au dieu d'Amours.*' In *Reinterpreting Christine*, pp. 23–36.
—— 1995. '*Simplece* et sagesse: Christine de Pizan et Isotta Nogarola sur la culpabilité d'Ève.' In *Femme de lettres*, pp. 481–93.
—— 1998. '"Perdre son latin": Christine de Pizan and Vernacular Humanism.' In *Christine Categories*, pp. 91–107.
—— 2000. 'La Fama, la femme, et la Dame de la Tour: Christine de Pizan et la médisance.' In *Au champ*, pp. 461–77.
—— 2002. 'Possible Odds: Christine de Pizan and the Paradoxes of Woman.' In *Contexts*, pp. 355–66.
—— 2003. 'Who's a Heroine? The Example of Christine de Pizan.' In *Casebook*, pp. 115–28.
—— 2005. 'Strong Voices, Weak Minds? The Defenses of Eve by Isotta Nogarola and Christine de Pizan, Who Found Themselves in Simone de Beauvoir's Situation.' In *Strong Voices*, pp. 58–77.
Fernández Vuelta, María del Mar 1990. '*Meraugis de Portlesguez*: el *jeu-parti* y la ficción novelesca.' *Anuari de filología*, 13, 51–68.
Fleming, John V. 1971. 'Hoccleve's "Letter of Cupid" and the "Quarrel" over the *Roman de la Rose.*' *Medium Aevum*, 40, 21–40.
Forhan, Kate Langdon 1992. 'Polycracy, Obligation, and Revolt: The Body Politic in John of Salisbury and Christine de Pizan.' In *Politics*, pp. 32–52.

—— 1996. 'Respect, Interdependence, Virtue: A Medieval Theory of Toleration in the Works of Christine de Pizan.' In *Diffference and Dissent: Theories of Toleration in Medieval and Early Modern Europe*. Ed. Cary J. Nederman and John Christian Laursen. Lanham, MD, London: Rowman and Littlefield, pp. 67–82.

—— 2002. *The Political Theory of Christine de Pizan*. Women and Gender in the Early Modern World. Aldershot: Ashgate.

Fraioli, Deborah 1981. 'The Literary Image of Joan of Arc: Prior Influences.' *Speculum*, 56, 811–30.

Friedman, Lionel J. 1965. 'Gradus amoris.' *Romance Philology*, 19, 167–77.

—— 1989. 'La Mesnie faux semblant: homo interior =/= homo exterior.' *French Forum*, 14, Supplement 1, 435–45.

Friis-Jensen, Karsten 1995. 'Horace and the Early Writers of Arts of Poetry.' In *Sprachtheorien in Spätantike und Mittelalter*. Ed. Sten Ebbesen. Tübingen: Narr, pp. 360–401.

Frijda, Nico H. 1998. 'De structuur van emoties.' In *Emoties*, pp. 9–28.

Fumaroli, Marc 1997. *Le poète et le roi: Jean de la Fontaine en son siècle*. Paris: Fallois.

Galderisi, Claudio 2002. 'Du langage érotique au langage amoureux: représentations du *créaturel* dans le *Petit Jehan de Saintré* et dans la nouvelle XCIX des *Cent Nouvelles Nouvelles*.' *Le Moyen français*, 50, 13–29.

Gaunt, Simon 1995. *Gender and Genre in Medieval French Literature*. Cambridge Studies in French, 53. Cambridge: Cambridge University Press.

Gauvard, Claude 1988. 'De la théorie à la pratique: justice et miséricorde en France pendant le règne de Charles VI.' *Revue des langues romanes*, 92, 317–25.

—— 1991. *'De grace especial': crime, état et société en France à la fin du moyen âge*. Université de Paris I (Panthéon-Sorbonne): Histoire ancienne et médiévale, 24. 2 vols. Paris: Publications de la Sorbonne.

—— 1995. 'Christine de Pizan et ses contemporains: l'engagement politique des écrivains dans le royaume de France aux XIVe et XVe siècles.' In *Femme de lettres*, pp. 105–28.

González Doreste, Dulce M.ª 1997. '¿Palas o Minerva?: la recreación del mito clásico en dos textos literarios franceses de la Edad Media.' *Revista de filología románica*, 14:2, 183–95.

González Doreste, Dulce Maria, and Francisca Del Mar Plaza Picón 2002–03. 'A propos de la compilation: du *De claris mulieribus* de Boccace à *Le Livre de la Cité des Dames* de Christine de Pizan.' *Moyen français*, 51–53, 327–37.

Gottlieb, Beatrice 1985. 'The Problem of Feminism in the Fifteenth Century.' In *Women of the Medieval World: Essays in Honor of John H. Mundy*. Ed. Julius Kirshner and Suzanne F. Wemple. Oxford: Blackwell, pp. 337–64.

Green, Monica H. 1998. '"Traittié tout de mençonges": The *Secrés des dames*, "Trotula," and Attitudes toward Women's Medicine in Fourteenth- and Early-Fifteenth-Century France.' In *Christine Categories*, pp. 146–78.

Gros, Gérard 1990. '"Mon oroison entens …": étude sur les trois opuscules pieux de Christine de Pizan.' *Bien dire et bien aprandre*, 8, 99–112.

Gründel, Johannes 1963. *Die Lehre von den Umständen der menschlichen Handlung im Mittelalter*. Beiträge zur Geschichte der Philosophie und Theologie des Mittelalters: Texte und Untersuchungen, 39:5. Münster Westfalen: Aschendorff.

Guarinos, Marion 1998. 'Individualisme et solidarité dans *Le Livre des Trois Vertus* de Christine de Pizan.' In *Sur le chemin*, pp. 87–99.

Haasse, Hella S. 1996. 'Vriendschap in de achttiende eeuw.' In her *Uitgesproken, opgeschreven: essays over achttiende-eeuwse vrouwen, een bosgezicht, verlichte geesten, vorstenlot, satire, de pers en Vestdijks avondrood*. Amsterdam: Querido, pp. 24–34.

Hahn, Stacey Layne 1988. 'Patterned Diversity: Hierarchy and Love in the Prose *Lancelot*.' Diss. University of Wisconsin-Madison.

Haidu, Peter 2004. *The Subject Medieval/Modern: Text and Governance in the Middle Ages*. Figurae. Stanford, CA: Stanford University Press.

Hanawalt, Barbara A. 2000. 'Violence in the Domestic Milieu of Late Medieval England.' In *Violence*, pp. 197–214.

Hauck, Johannes 1995. 'Der notwendige "descort" der höfischen Liebenden: zur Liebeslyrik von Christine de Pizan.' In *Musique*, pp. 211–59.

Heitmann, Klaus 1963. 'Typen der Deformierung antiker Mythen im Mittelalter: am Beispiel des Orpheussage.' *Romanistisches Jahrbuch*, 14, 45–77.

Hicks, Eric 1988. 'Discours de la toilette, toilette du discours: de l'idéologie du vêtement dans quelques écrits didactiques de Christine de Pizan.' *Revue des langues romanes*, 92, 327–41.

—— 1995a. 'Une femme dans le monde: Christine de Pizan et l'évidence de la politique.' In *L'Hostellerie de pensée: études sur l'art littéraire au Moyen Age offertes à Daniel Poirion*. Ed. Michel Zink and Danielle Bohler, with Eric Hicks and Manuela Python. Cultures et civilisations médiévales, 12. Paris: Presses de l'Université de Paris-Sorbonne, pp. 233–43.

—— 1995b. 'Situation du débat sur le *Roman de la rose*.' In *Femme de lettres*, pp. 51–67.

—— 2000. 'Excerpts and Originality: Authorial Purpose in the *Fais et bonnes meurs*.' In *Christine 2000*, pp. 221–31.

Hindman, Sandra L. 1986. *Christine de Pizan's 'Epistre Othéa': Painting and Politics at the Court of Charles VI*. Studies and Texts, 77. Toronto: Pontifical Institute of Mediaeval Studies.

Holderness, Julia Simms 2000. 'Christine et ses "bévues": sens et portée de quelques assimilations abusives.' In *Au champ*, pp. 149–60.

—— 2002. 'Fiction and Truth in Ballad 15 of the *Cent balades*.' In *Contexts*, pp. 421–29.

Huizinga, Johan 1997. *Herfsttij der middeleeuwen: studie over levens- en gedachtenvormen der veertiende en viftiende eeuw in Frankrijk en de Nederlanden*. Ed. Anton van der Lem. [Antwerp]: Contact.

Huot, Sylvia 1985. 'Seduction and Sublimation: Christine de Pizan, Jean de Meun, and Dante.' *Romance Notes*, 25, 361–73.

—— 1987. *From Song to Book: The Poetics of Writing in Old French Lyric and Lyrical Narrative Poetry*. Ithaca, NY, London: Cornell University Press.

—— 1993a. *The 'Romance of the Rose' and Its Medieval Readers: Interpretation, Reception, Manuscript Transmission*. Cambridge Studies in Medieval Literature, 16. Cambridge: Cambridge University Press.

—— 1993b. 'Sentences and Subtle Fictions: Reading Literature in the Later Middle Ages.' In *What Is Literature?* pp. 197–209.

Jaeger, C. Stephen 1999. *Ennobling Love: In Search of a Lost Sensibility*. Middle

Ages Series. Philadelphia: University of Pennsylvania Press.
Johnson, Leonard W. 1990. *Poets as Players: Theme and Variation in Late Medieval French Poetry*. Stanford, CA: Stanford University Press.
Jung, Marc-René 1971. '*Poetria*: zur Dichtungstheorie des ausgehenden Mittelalters in Frankreich.' *Vox Romanica*, 30, 44–64.
—— 1996. *La Légende de Troie en France au moyen âge: analyse des versions françaises et bibliographie raisonnée des manuscrits*. Romanica Helvetica, 114. Basel, Tübingen: Francke.
Kantorowicz, Ernst H. 1957. *The King's Two Bodies: A Study in Mediaeval Political Theology*. Princeton: Princeton University Press.
Kay, Sarah 1990. *Subjectivity in Troubadour Poetry*. Cambridge Studies in French. Cambridge: Cambridge University Press.
Kellogg, Judith L. 1990. 'Christine de Pizan as Chivalric Mythographer: *L'Epistre d'Othea*. In *Mythographic*, pp. 100–24.
—— 2003. '*Le Livre de la cité des dames*: Reconfirming Knowledge and Reimagining Gendered Space.' In *Casebook*, pp. 129–46.
Kelly, Douglas 1969. 'Theory of Composition in Medieval Narrative Poetry and Geoffrey of Vinsauf's *Poetria Nova*.' *Mediaeval Studies*, 31, 117–48.
—— 1972. '"Li chastiaus ... Qu'Amors prist puis par ses esforz": The Conclusion of Guillaume de Lorris' *Rose*.' In *A Medieval French Miscellany: Papers of the 1970 Kansas Conference on Medieval French Literature*. Ed. Norris J. Lacy. University of Kansas Humanistic Studies, 42. Lawrence: University of Kansas Publications, pp. 61–78.
—— 1978. *Medieval Imagination: Rhetoric and the Poetry of Courtly Love*. Madison, London: University of Wisconsin Press.
—— 1981. 'Les Inventions ovidiennes de Froissart: réflexions intertextuelles comme imagination.' *Littérature*, 41, 82–92.
—— 1983. 'La Spécialité dans l'invention des topiques.' In *Archéologie*, pp. 101–25.
—— 1985. 'Assimilation et montage dans l'amplification descriptive: la démarche du poète dans le Dit du XIVe siècle.' In *Mittelalterbilder*, pp. 289–301.
—— 1991. *The Arts of Poetry and Prose*. Typologie des sources du moyen âge occidental, 59. Turnhout: Brepols.
—— 1992. *The Art of Medieval French Romance*. Madison, London: University of Wisconsin Press.
—— 1994a. 'Amitié comme anti-amour: au-delà du *fin amour* de Jean de Meun à Christine de Pizan.' In *Anteros: Actes du Colloque de Madison (Wisconsin) mars 1994*. Ed. Ullrich Langer and Jan Miernowski. L'Atelier de la Renaissance, 4. Orléans: Paradigme, pp. 75–97.
—— 1994b. 'Titles, Openings, and Adventures in Marie de France's Lays.' In *Europäische Literaturen im Mittelalter: Mélanges en l'honneur de Wolfgang Spiewok à l'occasion de son 65ème anniversaire*. Ed. Danielle Buschinger. WODAN. Greifswalder Beiträge zum Mittelalter, 30. Series 3: Tagungsbände und Sammelschriften, 15. Greifswald: Reineke, pp. 231–39.
—— 1995a. *Internal Difference and Meanings in the 'Roman de la rose'*. Madison, London: University of Wisconsin Press.
—— 1995b. 'The Invention of Briseida's Story in Benoît de Sainte-Maure's *Troie*.' *Romance Philology*, 48, 221–41.

—— 1996. 'Les mutations de Christine de Pizan.' In *'Ensi firent li ancessor': Mélanges de philologie médiévale offerts à Marc-René Jung*. Ed. Luciano Rossi with Christine Jacob-Hugon and Ursula Bähler. 2 vols. Alessandria: Edizioni dell'Orso. Vol. 2, pp. 599–608.

—— 1998. 'Imitation, Metamorphosis, and Froissart's Use of the Exemplary *Modus tractandi*.' In *Froissart across the Genres*. Ed. Donald Maddox and Sara Sturm-Maddox. Gainesville: University Press of Florida, pp. 101–18.

—— 1999a. *The Conspiracy of Allusion: Description, Rewriting, and Authorship from Macrobius to Medieval Romance*. Studies in the History of Christian Thought, 97. Leiden, Boston, Cologne: Brill.

—— 1999b. 'Forlorn Hope: Mutability *Topoi* in Some Medieval Narratives.' In *The World and Its Rival: Essays on Literary Imagination in Honor of Per Nykrog*. Ed. Kathryn Karczewska and Tom Conley. Faux Titre, 172. Amsterdam, Atlanta: Rodopi, pp. 59–77.

—— 1999c. 'The Genius of the Patron: The Prince, the Poet, and Fourteenth-Century Invention.' In *Chaucer's Contemporaries*, pp. 1–27.

—— 2000. 'The Poem as Art of Poetry: The Rhetoric of Imitation in the *Grand chant courtois*.' In *Medieval Lyric*, pp. 191–208.

—— 2001. 'The Implications of Age and Aging in the *Roman de la rose*.' In *Riens ne m'est seur*, pp. 91–103.

—— 2004. 'La Norme et l'anomalie dans le roman au milieu du XVe siècle.' In *Du roman courtois au roman baroque: actes du colloque du 2–5 juillet 2002*. Ed. Emmanuel Bury and Francine Mora. Paris: Belles Lettres, pp. 353–66.

—— 2005. 'How Did Guiolete Come to Court? Or, the Sometimes Inscrutable Paths of Tradition.' In *'De sens rassis': Essays in Honor of Rupert T. Pickens*, Faux Titre, 259. Amsterdam, New York: Rodopi, pp. 309–23.

Kennedy, Angus J. 1984. *Christine de Pizan: A Bibliographical Guide*. Research Bibliographies and Checklists, 42. London: Grant and Cutler.

—— 1994. *Christine de Pizan: A Bibliographical Guide. Supplement 1*. Research Bibliographies and Checklists, 42:1. London: Grant and Cutler.

—— 1998. 'Christine de Pizan's *Livre du corps de policie*: Some Problems in the Identification and Analysis of Her Sources.' In *Miscellanea mediaevalia*. Vol. 1, pp. 733–43.

—— 2004. *Christine de Pizan: A Bibliographical Guide. Supplement 2*. Research Bibliographies and Checklists: New Series, 5. Woodbridge, Suffolk: Tamesis; Rochester, NY: Boydell and Brewer.

Kiehl, Carole 2002. 'Christine de Pizan and Fortune: A Statistical Survey.' In *Contexts*, pp. 443–52.

Klee, Wanda G. 1997. 'Die Autorin zwischen Werk und Wirklichkeit: eine andere Lesart der Frauenbilder in Christine de Pizans *Livre de la Cité des dames*.' *Germanisch-romanische Monatsschrift*, 47, 363–77.

Kleinschmidt, Erich 1974. *Herrscherdarstellung: zur Disposition mittelalterlichen Aussageverhaltens, untersucht an Texten über Rudolf I. von Habsburg*. Bibliotheca Germanica, 17. Bern, Munich: Francke.

Kooper, Erik 2004. 'Christine de Pizan en Thomas Hoccleves *Letter to Cupid*.' In *Christine vrouw*, pp. 75–88.

Kosta-Théfaine, Jean-François 1998. 'Entre poésie et prophétie: les sources du *Ditié de Jehanne d'Arc* de Christine de Pizan.' *Romanische Zeitschrift für*

Literaturgeschichte–Cahiers d'Histoire des Littératures romanes, 22, 41–56.

Kottenhoff, Margarete 1994. *'Du lebst in einer schlimmen Zeit': Christine de Pizans Frauenstadt zwischen Sozialkritik und Utopie*. Cologne, Weimar, Vienna: Böhlau.

Krueger, Roberta L. 1993. *Women Readers and the Ideology of Gender in Old French Verse Romance*. Cambridge Studies in French, 43. Cambridge: Cambridge University Press.

—— 1998. 'Christine's Anxious Lessons: Gender, Morality, and the Social Order from the *Enseignemens* to the *Avision*.' In *Christine Categories*, pp. 16–40.

—— 2003. 'Christine's Treasure: Women's Honor and Household Economies in the *Livre des trois vertus*.' In *Casebook*, pp. 101–14.

Krynen, Jacques 1981. *Idéal du prince et pouvoir royal en France à la fin du Moyen Age (1380–1440): étude de la littérature politique du temps*. Paris: Picard.

Lacarra Lanz, Enkene 2001. 'Las Enseñanzas de *Le livre des trois vertus* à *l'enseignement des dames* de Christine de Pizan y sus primeras lectoras.' *Cultura neolatina*, 61, 335–60.

Laennec, Christine Moneera 1993. 'Christine *Antygrafe*: Authorial Ambivalence in the Works of Christine de Pizan.' In *Anxious Power: Reading, Writing, and Ambivalence in Narrative by Women*. Ed. Carol J. Singley and Susan Elizabeth Sweeney. SUNY Series in Feminist Criticism and Theory. Albany: State University of New York Press, pp. 35–49.

—— 1995. 'Prophétie, interprétation et écriture dans *L'Avision-Christine*.' In *Femme de lettres*, pp. 131–38.

Laidlaw, J. C. 1983. 'Christine de Pizan – An Author's Progress.' *Modern Language Review*, 78, 532–50.

—— 1986. 'Christine de Pizan – A Publisher's Progress.' *Modern Language Review*, 82, 35–75.

—— 1994. 'L'unité des "Cent Balades".' In *City of Scholars*, pp. 97–106.

—— 1998a. 'The *Cent Balades*: The Marriage of Content and Form.' In *Christine Lyric*, pp. 53–82.

—— 1998b. 'Les virelais de Christine de Pizan.' In *Sur le chemin*, pp. 111–25.

—— 2003. 'Christine and the Manuscript Tradition.' In *Casebook*, pp. 231–49.

—— 2004. 'De *Cent balades* van Christine de Pizan.' In *Christine vrouw*, pp. 25–88.

Laird, Judith, and Earl Jeffrey Richards 1998. '*Tous parlent par une mesmes bouche*: Lyrical Outbursts, Prosaic Remedies, and Voice in Christine de Pizan's *Livre du Duc des vrais amans*.' In *Christine Lyric*, pp. 103–31.

Latzke, Therese 1979. 'Der Fürstinnenpreis.' *Mittellateinisches Jahrbuch*, 14, 22–65.

Lausberg, Heinrich 1973. *Handbuch der literarischen Rhetorik: eine Grundlegung der Literaturwissenschaft*. Rev. ed. Munich: Hueber.

Leake, Roy E., with David B. and Alice Elder Leake 1981. *Concordance des Essais de Montaigne*. 2 vols. Geneva: Droz.

LeBlanc, Yvonne 1995. *Va Lettre Va: The French Verse Epistle (1400–1550)*. Birmingham, AL: Summa.

Le Brun-Gouanvic, Claire 2001a. 'Christine de Pizan et l'édification de la cité éternelle.' *Etudes françaises*, 37, 51–65.

—— 2001b. 'Spectacles aristocratiques et spectacles bourgeois chez Christine de

Pizan.' In *Les Arts du spectacle dans la ville (1404–1721)*. Ed. Marie-France Wagner and Claire Le Brun-Gouanvic. Colloques, Congrès et Conférences sur la Renaissance, 24. Paris: Champion, pp. 19–36.

Lechat, Didier 2000. 'L'Utilisation par Christine de Pizan de la traduction de Valère Maxime par Simon de Hesdin et Nicolas de Gonesse dans *Le Livre du Chemin de long estude*.' In *Au champ*, pp. 175–96.

—— 2002. 'L'art du portrait dans *Charles V*.' In *Contexts*, pp. 515–29.

Lefèvre, Sylvie 1988. 'Le poète et la pastoure.' *Revue des langues romanes*, 92, 342–58.

Lemaire, Jacques 1994. *Les Visions de la vie de cour dans la littérature française de la fin du Moyen Age: Mémoire présenté au concours de l'Académie Royale de langue et de littérature françaises – octobre 1990*. Brussels: Palais des Académies, Paris: Klincksieck.

Leppig, Linda 1992. 'The Political Rhetoric of Christine de Pizan: *Lamentacion sur les maux de la guerre civile*.' In *Politics*, pp. 141–56.

Lewis, C. S. 1942. *A Preface to Paradise Lost*. London: Oxford University Press.

—— 1964. *The Discarded Image: An Introduction to Medieval and Renaissance Literature*. Cambridge: Cambridge University Press.

Lindberg, David C. 1992. *The Beginnings of Western Science: The European Scientific Tradition in Philosophical, Religious, and Institutional Contexts, 600 B.C. to A.D. 1450*. Chicago, London: University of Chicago Press.

Lorcin, Marie-Thérèse 1988. 'Pouvoirs et contre-pouvoirs dans le *"Livre des trois vertus"*.' *Revue des langues romanes*, 92, 359–68.

—— 1989. 'Mère nature et le devoir social: la mère et l'enfant dans l'œuvre de Christine de Pizan.' *Revue historique*, 282, 29–44.

—— 1991. 'Au moyen âge, l'amitié au féminin: le témoignage de Christine de Pizan.' *Cahiers d'histoire*, 36, 89–100.

—— 1994. 'Christine de Pizan analyste de la société.' In *City of Scholars*, pp. 197–205.

—— 1995. 'Le *Livre des trois vertus* et le *Sermo ad status*.' In *Femme de lettres*, pp. 139–49.

—— 2002. '"Seulete suy et seulete vueil estre ...".' In *Contexts*, pp. 549–60.

Luff, Robert 1999. *Wissensvermittlung im europäischen Mittelalter: 'Imago mundi'-Werke und ihre Prologe*. Texte und Textgeschichte, 47. Tübingen: Niemeyer.

Maddox, Donald 2000. *Fictions of Identity in Medieval France*. Cambridge Studies in Medieval Literature, 43. Cambridge: Cambridge University Press.

Malosse, Pierre-Louis 2000. 'Sans mentir (ou presque): la dissimulation des faits gênants dans la rhétorique de l'éloge, d'après l'exemple des discours royaux de Libanios.' *Rhetorica*, 18, 243–63.

Marchello-Nizia, Christiane 1985. 'La Rhétorique des songes et le *songe* comme rhétorique dans la littérature française médiévale.' In *I Sogni nel medioevo: seminario internazionale, Roma, 2–4 ottobre 1983*. Ed. Tullio Gregory. Lessico Intellettuale Europeo, 35. Rome: Ateneo, pp. 245–59.

Margolis, Nadia 1986. 'Christine de Pizan: The Poetess as Historian.' *Journal of the History of Ideas*, 47, 361–75.

—— 1992. 'Christine de Pizan and the Jews: Political and Poetic Implications.' In *Politics*, pp. 53–73.

—— 1996. '"The Cry of the Chameleon": Evolving Voices in the Epistles of

Christine de Pizan.' *Disputatio*, 1, 37–70.

—— 1997. 'Les Terminaisons dangereuses: lyrisme, féminisme et humanisme néologiques chez Christine de Pizan.' *Moyen Français*, 39-40-41, 381–404.

—— 1998. 'Clerkliness and Courtliness in the Complaintes of Christine de Pizan.' In *Christine Lyric*, pp. 135–54.

—— 2000. 'Culture vantée, culture inventée: Christine, Clamanges et le défi de Pétrarque.' In *Au champ*, pp. 269–308.

Marquard, Odo. *See* Von Graevenitz, Gerhart, and Odo Marquard.

McGrady, Deborah 2000. 'Authorship and Audience in the Prologues to Christine de Pizan's Commissioned Poetry.' In *Au champ*, pp. 25–40.

McKinley, Mary 1992. 'The Subversive "Seulette".' In *Politics*, pp. 157–69.

McLeod, Glenda 1991. *Virtue and Venom: Catalogs of Women from Antiquity to the Renaissance*. Ann Arbor: University of Michigan Press.

—— 1992. 'Poetics and Antimisogynist Polemics in Christine de Pizan's *Li Livre de la Cité des dames*.' In *Reinterpreting Christine*, pp. 37–47.

McMunn, Meradith T. 2000. 'Programs of Illustration in *Roman de la Rose* Manuscripts Owned by Patrons and Friends of Christine de Pizan.' In *Au champ*, pp. 737–53 + 7 plates.

McWebb, Christine 1998. 'Lyrical Conventions and the Creation of Female Subjectivity in Christine de Pizan's *Cent ballades d'Amant et de Dame*.' In *Christine Lyric*, pp. 168–83.

Meier, Christel 1979. 'Zwei Modelle von Allegorie im 12. Jahrhundert: das allegorische Verfahren Hildegards von Bingen und Alans von Lille.' In *Formen und Funktionen der Allegorie*. Symposion Wolfenbüttel 1978. Ed. Walter Haug. Germanistische Symposien: Berichtsbände, 3. Stuttgart: Metzler, pp. 70–89.

Messelaar, P. A. 1963. *Le vocabulaire des idées dans le 'Tresor' de Brunet Latin*. Assen: Van Gorcum.

Meyenberg, Regula 1992. *Alain Chartier prosateur et l'art de la parole au XVe siècle*. Romanica Helvetica, 107. Bern: Francke.

Minnis, A. J. 1984. *Medieval Theory of Authorship: Scholastic Literary Attitudes in the Later Middle Ages*. London: Scolar Press.

—— 1991. 'Theorizing the Rose: Commentary Tradition in the *Querelle de la Rose*.' In *Poetics: Theory and Practice in Medieval English Literature. The J. A. W. Bennett Memorial Lectures, Seventh Series, Perugia, 1990*. Ed. Piero Boitani and Anna Torti. Cambridge: Brewer, pp. 13–36.

—— 2001. *Magister amoris: The 'Roman de la rose' and Vernacular Hermeneutics*. Oxford: Oxford University Press.

Momigliano, Arnaldo 1971. *The Development of Greek Biography: Four Lectures*. Cambridge, MA: Harvard University Press.

Monahan, Jennifer 2002. '*Querelles*: Medieval Texts and Modern Polemics.' In *Contexts*, pp. 575–84.

Monson, Don A. 2005. *Andreas Capellanus, Scholasticism, and the Courtly Tradition*. Washington, DC: The Catholic University of America Press.

Morse, Ruth 1996. *The Medieval Medea*. Cambridge: Brewer.

Moss, Ann 2002. *Les Recueils de lieux communs: méthode pour apprendre à penser à la Renaissance*. Trans. Patricia Eichel-Lojkine [et alii]. Titre courant, 23. Geneva: Droz.

Muckelbauer, John 2003. 'Imitation and Invention in Antiquity: An Historical-

Theoretical Revision.' *Rhetorica*, 21, 61–88.

Mühlethaler, Jean-Claude 1983. 'Le Poète et le prophète: littérature et politique au XVe siècle.' *Moyen Français*, 13, 37–57.

—— 1992. '"Les poètes que de vert on couronne". En marge du nouveau "Dictionnaire du moyen français": réflexions sur quelques changements dans le champ lexical de la création poétique au XVe siècle.' *Moyen Français*, 30, 97–112.

—— 2002. '"Traictier de vertu au proufit d'ordre de vivre": relire l'œuvre de Christine de Pizan à la lumière des miroirs des princes.' In *Contexts*, pp. 585–601.

—— *See also* Blanchard, Joël, and Jean-Claude Mühlethaler.

Mulder, Etty Martha 1978. *Guillaume de Machaut, een grensbewoner: samenhang van allegorie en muziek bij een laat-Middeleeuws dichter-componist*. Diss. Utrecht. Amsterdam: Stichting Musicater.

Nabert, Nathalie 1997. 'La Référence à Clovis chez Jean Gerson et chez Christine de Pisan.' In *Clovis: histoire et mémoire*. Vol. 2: *Le Baptême de Clovis, son écho à travers l'histoire*. Ed. Michel Rouche. Paris: Presses de l'Université de Paris-Sorbonne, pp. 231–48.

Nagel, Sylvia 2000. *Spiegel der Geschlechterdifferenz: Frauendidaxen im Frankreich des späten Mittelalters*. Ergebnisse der Frauenforschung, 54. Stuttgart, Weimar: Metzler.

—— *See* Echtermann, Andrea, and Sylvia Nagel.

Neumeister, Sebastian 1999. 'Vier Stationen der Selbstkonstitution weiblicher Subjektivität in der höfischen Lyrik: Na Castelloza–Christine de Pizan–Gaspara Stampa–Sor Juana Inés de la Cruz.' In *Mittelalter und frühe Neuzeit: Übergänge, Umbrüche und Neuansätze*. Ed. Walter Haug. Fortuna Vitrea, 16. Tübingen: Niemeyer, pp. 100–27.

Nichols, Stephen G. 1992. 'Prophetic Discourse: St. Augustine to Christine de Pizan.' In *The Bible in the Middle Ages: Its Influence on Literature and Art*. Ed. Bernard S. Levy. Medieval and Renaissance Texts and Studies, 89. Binghamton, NY: Medieval and Renaissance Texts and Studies, pp. 51–76.

Nouvet, Claire 1996. 'Writing (in) Fear.' in *Gender and Text*, pp. 279–305.

O'Leary, Susan Jane 1980. 'A Semiotics of Allegory (An Allegory of Semiotics): A Study of Guillaume de Lorris' *Roman de la rose*.' Diss. University of Wisconsin-Madison.

Orbán, Arpad P. 2004. 'Christine de Pizan en de Oudheid.' In *Christine vrouw*, pp. 111–39.

Ouy, Gilbert, and Christine M. Reno 2000. 'Où mène le *Chemin de long estude*? Christine de Pizan, Ambrogio Migli, et les ambitions impériales de Louis d'Orléans (A propos du ms. BNF fr. 1643).' In *Christine 2000*, pp. 177–95, 325–28.

Paden, William D. 1994. 'Christine de Pizan as a Reader of the Medieval Pastourelle.' In *Conjunctures: Medieval Studies in Honor of Douglas Kelly*. Ed. Keith Busby and Norris J. Lacy. Faux Titre, 83. Amsterdam, Atlanta: Rodopi, pp. 387–405.

—— 1996. 'Flight from Authority in the Pastourelle.' In *The Medieval 'Opus': Imitation, Rewriting, and Transmission in the French Tradition. Proceedings of the Symposium Held at the Institute for Research in the Humanities, October 5–7 1995, The University of Wisconsin-Madison*. Ed. Douglas Kelly. Faux Titre,

116. Amsterdam, Atlanta: Rodopi, pp. 299–325.

Pagot, Simone 1995. 'Du bon usage de la compilation et du discours didactique: analyse du thème "guerre et paix" chez Christine de Pizan.' In *Femme de lettres*, pp. 39–50.

Pairet, Ana 2002. *Les Mutacions des fables: figures de la métamorphose dans la littérature française du moyen âge*. Essais sur le moyen âge, 26. Paris: Champion.

Paradis, Françoise 1990. 'Une Polyphonie narrative: pour une description de la structure des *Cent ballades d'amant et de dame*.' *Bien dire et bien aprandre*, 8, 127–40.

Paré, Gérard 1947. *Les Idées et les lettres au XIIIe siècle: le 'Roman de la rose'*. Université de Montréal: Bibliothèque de philosophie, 1. Montréal: Centre de Psychologie et de Pédagogie.

Parussa, Gabriella 1993. 'Le Concept d'intertextualité comme hypothèse interprétative d'une œuvre: l'exemple de l'"*Epistre Othea*" de Christine de Pizan.' *Studi francesi*, 111, 471–93.

—— 1996. 'Instruire les chevaliers et conseiller les princes: L'*Epistre Othea* de Christine de Pizan.' In *Studi di storia della civiltà letteraria francese: mélanges offerts à Leonello Sozzi*. Bibliothèque Franco Simone, 25. 2 vols. Paris: Champion, pp. 129–55.

—— 1997. 'Christine de Pizan: une lectrice avide et une vulgarisatrice fidèle des *Rumigacions du latin et des parleures des belles sciences*.' In *Traduction*, pp. 161–75.

Patterson, Lee 2001. 'Chaucer's Pardoner on the Couch: Psyche and Clio in Medieval Literary Studies.' *Speculum*, 76, 638–80.

Paupert, Anne 1993. 'Le "Je" lyrique féminin dans l'œuvre poétique de Christine de Pizan.' In *Hommage Dufournet*, pp. 1057–71.

—— 2000. '"La narracion de mes aventures": des premiers poèmes à l'*Advision*, l'élaboration d'une écriture autobiographique dans l'œuvre de Christine de Pizan.' In *Au champ*, pp. 51–71.

—— 2002a. 'Christine et Boèce. De la lecture à l'écriture, de la réécriture à l'écriture du moi.' In *Contexts*, pp. 645–62.

—— 2002b. '"Soubz figure de methaphore": théorie et pratique de l'allégorie chez Christine de Pizan, ou: une "Poetria Nova" du début du XVème siècle.' In *'Ce est li fruis selonc la letre': mélanges offerts à Charles Méla*. Ed. Olivier Collet, Yasmina Foehr-Janssens, and Sylviane Messerli. Colloques, Congrès et Conférences sur le moyen âge, 3. Paris: Champion, pp. 511–26.

Pereira, Michela 2000. '*La Città delle dame* e la mistica: riflessioni a margine.' *Medioevo romanzo*, 24, 126–33.

Pernot, Laurent 1993. *La Rhétorique de l'éloge dans le monde gréco-romain*. Collection des Etudes Augustiniennes: série Antiquité, 137–38. 2 vols. Paris: Etudes Augustiniennes.

Perrand, Françoise 1998. 'Le "Féminisme" de Christine de Pizan: désirs et trahisons dans les *Cent Ballades d'amant et de dame*.' *RLA: Romance Languages Annual*, 10, 117–21.

Perugi, Maurizio 1998. 'Des farcitures en forme de gloses: les Héroïdes vernaculaires entre roman farci et commentaire à citations.' In *L'Antichità nella cultura europea del Medioevo–L'Antiquité dans la culture européenne du moyen âge:*

Ergebnisse der internationalen Tagung in Padua, 27.09.–01.10.1997. Ed. Rosanna Brusegan and Alessandro Zironi, with Anne Berthelot and Danielle Buschinger. WODAN, 75. Greifswalder Beiträge zum Mittelalter, 62. Reihe 3: Tagungsbände und Sammelschriften, 43. Greifswald: Reineke, pp. 3–20.

Picherit, Jean-Louis G. 1994. *La Métaphore pathologique et thérapeutique à la fin du moyen âge*. Beiträge zur Zeitschrift für romanische Philologie, 260. Tübingen: Niemeyer.

—— 1995. 'Les Références pathologiques et thérapeutiques dans l'œuvre de Christine de Pizan.' In *Femme de lettres*, pp. 233–44.

Pickens, Rupert T. 2000. 'The Old Occitan Arts of Poetry and the Early Troubadour Lyric.' In *Medieval Lyric*, pp. 209–41.

Picoche, Jacqueline 1976. *Le Vocabulaire psychologique dans les Chroniques de Froissart*.Vol. 1. Bibliothèque française et romane, A32. Paris: Klincksieck.

—— 1978. 'Humilité et modestie: histoire lexicale et histoire des mentalités.' In *Mélanges de littérature du moyen âge au XXe siècle offerts à Mademoiselle Jeanne Lods*. 2 vols. Paris: Ecole Normale Supérieure de Jeunes Filles. Vol. 1, pp. 485–94.

Pinet, Marie-Josèphe 1927. *Christine de Pisan 1364–1430: étude biographique et littéraire*. Paris: Champion.

Plebani, Tiziana 2003. 'All'origine della rappresentazione della lettrice et della scrittrice: Christine de Pizan.' In *Città*, pp. 47–58.

Poirion, Daniel 1965. *Le poète et le prince: l'évolution du lyrisme courtois de Guillaume de Machaut à Charles d'Orléans*. Université de Grenoble: Publications de la Faculté des Lettres et Sciences Humaines, 35. Paris: Presses Universitaires de France.

—— 1983a. 'De la signification selon Jean de Meun.' In *Archéologie*, pp. 165–85.

—— 1983b. *Précis de littérature française du Moyen Age*. Paris: Presses Universitaires de France.

Pons, Nicole 2000. '*Pour ce que manifestation de la Verité*: un thème du débat politique sous Charles VI.' In *Penser*, pp. 343–63.

Potansky, Peter 1972. *Der Streit um den Rosenroman*. Münchener romanistische Arbeiten, 33. Munich: Fink.

Pratt, Karen 1994. 'Analogy or Logic; Authority or Experience? Rhetorical Strategies for and against Women.' In *Literary Aspects of Courtly Culture: Selected Papers from the Seventh Triennial Congress of the International Courtly Literature Society, University of Massachusetts, Amherst, USA, 27 July–1 August 1992*. Ed. Donald Maddox and Sara Sturm-Maddox. Cambridge: Brewer, pp. 57–66.

—— 1997. 'The Image of the Queen in Old French Literature.' In *Queens and Queenship in Medieval Europe: Proceedings of a Conference Held at King's College London April 1995*. Ed. Anne J. Duggan. Woodbridge: Boydell Press, pp. 235–59.

—— 2002a. 'The Context of Christine's *Livre des trois vertus*: Exploiting and Rewriting Tradition.' In *Contexts*, pp. 671–84.

—— 2002b. 'The Strains of Defense: The Many Voices in Jean LeFèvre's *Livre de Leesce*.' In *Gender in Debate from the Early Middle Ages to the Renaissance*. Ed. Thelma S. Fenster and Clare A. Lees. The New Middle Ages. New York, Basingstoke: Palgrave, pp. 113–33.

Quadlbauer, Franz 1962. *Die antike Theorie der genera dicendi im lateinischen Mittelalter*. Österreichische Akademie der Wissenschaften: philologisch-historische Klasse, Sitzungsberichte, 241.2. Graz, Vienna, Cologne: Böhlaus.

Quereuil, Michel. *See* Blanchard, Joël, and Michel Quereuil.

Quillet, Jeannine 2002. 'Note sur le *Livre du corps de policie*.' In *Contexts*, pp. 685–91.

Quilligan, Maureen 1991. *The Allegory of Female Authority: Christine de Pizan's 'Cité des dames'*. Ithaca, NY, London: Cornell University Press.

Ramsay, Alison 2002. 'On the Link between Rape, Abduction and War in Christine de Pizan's *Cité des dames*.' In *Contexts*, pp. 693–703.

Regalado, Nancy Freeman 1970. *Poetic Patterns in Rutebeuf: A Study in Noncourtly Poetic Modes of the Thirteenth Century*. New Haven, London: Yale University Press.

—— 1981. '"Des contraires choses": la fonction poétique de la citation et des *exempla* dans le "Roman de la rose" de Jean de Meun.' *Littérature*, 41, 62–81.

Reno, Christine 1980. 'Feminist Aspects of Christine de Pizan's "Epistre d'Othea à Hector".' *Studi francesi*, 71, 271–76.

—— 1981. 'Virginity as an Ideal in Christine de Pizan's *Cité des dames*.' In *Ideals*, pp. 69–90.

—— 1992a. 'Christine de Pizan: "At Best a Contradictory Figure"?' In *Politics*, pp. 171–91.

—— 1992b. 'The Preface to the *Avision-Christine* in ex-Phillipps 128.' In *Reinterpreting Christine*, pp. 207–27.

—— *See also* Dulac, Liliane, and Christine Reno.

—— *See also* Ouy, Gilbert, and Christine M. Reno.

Rheinfelder, Hans 1928. *Das Wort 'Persona': Geschichte seiner Bedeutungen mit besonderer Berücksichtigung des französischen und italienischen Mittelalters*. Beihefte zur Zeitschrift für romanische Philologie, 77. Halle/S.: Niemeyer.

Ribémont, Bernard 1991. 'Du temps de Christine de Pizan, le temps de cent ballades …' *Studi francesi*, 104, 285–93.

—— 1995. 'Christine de Pizan: entre espace scientifique et espace imaginé (*Le Livre du Chemin de long estude*).' In *Femme de lettres*, pp. 245–61.

—— 2000. 'Christine de Pizan et la figure de la mère.' In *Christine 2000*, pp. 149–61, 324.

—— 2002a. 'Christine et la nouveauté.' In *Contexts*, pp. 731–45.

—— 2002b. '"Quand écrire est se remémorer" … Le motif du souvenir comme déclencheur de l'écriture chez Christine de Pizan.' In *Das Schöne im Wirklichen–das Wirkliche im Schönen: Festschrift für Dietmar Rieger zum 60. Geburtstag*. Ed. Anne Amend-Söchting [et alii]. Studia Romanica, 110. Heidelberg: Winter, pp. 255–64.

—— 2003. 'L'"automne" de Christine de Pizan.' In *Progrès, réaction, décadence dans l'Occident médiéval*. Ed. Emmanuèle Baumgartner and Laurence Harf-Lancner. Publications romanes et françaises, 231. Geneva: Droz, pp. 79–91.

Richards, Earl Jeffrey 1992. 'French Cultural Nationalism and Christian Universalism in the Works of Christine de Pizan.' In *Politics*, pp. 75–94.

—— 1993. '"*Seulette a part*" – The "Little Woman on the Sidelines" Takes Up the Pen: The Letters of Christine de Pizan.' In *Dear Sister: Medieval Women and the Epistolary Genre*. Ed. Karen Cherewatuk and Ulrike Wiethaus. Middle Ages

Series. Philadelphia: University of Pennsylvania Press, pp. 139–70.
—— 1994. 'Christine de Pizan and Sacred History.' In *City of Scholars*, pp. 15–30.
—— 1996. 'Rejecting Essentialism and Gendered Writing: The Case of Christine de Pizan.' In *Gender and Text*, pp. 96–131.
—— 1998a. 'Christine de Pizan and the Freedom of Medieval French Lyric: Authority, Experience, and Women in the Republic of Letters.' In *Christine Lyric*, pp. 1–24.
—— 1998b. 'Poems of Water without Salt and Ballades without Feeling, or Reintroducing History into the Text: Prose and Verse in the Works of Christine de Pizan.' In *Christine Lyric*, pp. 206–29.
—— 2000a. 'Christine de Pizan and Jean Gerson: An Intellectual Friendship.' In *Christine 2000*, pp. 197–208, 328–30.
—— 2000b. 'Christine de Pizan: la libertà della città e delle dame.' *Medioevo romanzo*, 24, 114–26.
—— 2002. 'Christine de Pizan and Medieval Jurisprudence.' In *Contexts*, pp. 747–66.
—— 2003. 'Somewhere between Destructive Glosses and Chaos: Christine de Pizan and Medieval Theology.' In *Casebook*, pp. 43–55.
—— See also Laird, Judith, and Earl Jeffrey Richards.
Rivera Garretas, María Milagros 2003. 'La *Querelle des femmes* nella *Città delle Dame*.' In *Città*, pp. 87–97.
Robertson, D. W., Jr. 1946. 'A Note on the Classical Origin of "Circumstances" in the Medieval Confessional.' *Studies in Philology*, 43, 6–14.
Romagnoli, Patrizia 2000. 'Les formes de la voix: masques et dédoublements du moi dans l'œuvre de Christine de Pizan.' In *Au champ*, pp. 73–90.
Rossiaud, Jacques 1986. 'Les métamorphoses de la prostitution au XVe siècle: essai d'histoire culturelle.' In *Condición*, pp. 155–85.
—— 1988. *La prostitution médiévale*. Paris: Flammarion.
Roussel, Claude 1994. 'Le Legs de la rose: modèles et préceptes de la sociabilité médiévale.' In *Pour une histoire des traités de savoir-vivre en Europe*. Ed. A. Montandon. Librairie Européenne des idées: Littératures. Clermont-Ferrand: Association des Publications de la Faculté des Lettres et Sciences Humaines de Clermont-Ferrand, pp. 1–90.
Ruhe, Doris 2000. '*La langue de Christine*: zum Selbstverständnis der Christine de Pizan.' In *Au champ*, pp. 91–109.
Ruhe, Ernstpeter 1975. *De amasio ad amasiam: zur Gattungsgeschichte des mittelalterlichen Liebesbriefes*. Beiträge zur romanischen Philologie des Mittelalters, 10. Munich: Fink.
Sazaki, Shigemi 1988. 'Le poète et Pallas, dans le *Chemin de long estude* (1402–1403) (vv. 787–1170 et 1569–1780).' *Revue des langues romanes*, 92, 369–80.
Schilperoort, Johanna Catharina 1936. *Guillaume de Machaut et Christine de Pisan (étude comparative)*. Diss. Leiden. The Hague: De Swart.
Schmolke-Hasselmann, Beate 1982. 'Accipiter et chirotheca: die Artusepisode des Andreas Capellanus – eine Liebesallegorie?' *Germanisch-romanische Monatsschrift*, 32, 383–417.
Schnell, Rüdiger 1985. *Causa amoris: Liebeskonzeption und Liebesdarstellung in der mittelalterlichen Literatur*. Bibliotheca Germanica, 27. Bern, Munich:

Francke.
—— 1998a. 'The Discourse on Marriage in the Middle Ages.' *Speculum*, 73, 771–86.
—— 1998b. *Frauendiskurs, Männerdiskurs, Ehediskurs: Textsorten und Geschlechterkonzepte in Mittelalter und Früher Neuzeit*. Geschichte und Geschlechter, 23. Frankfurt/M., New York: Campus.
Schnerb, Bertrand 2001. *Les Armagnacs et les Bourguignons: la maudite guerre*. Paris: Perrin.
Schreiner, Elisabeth 2000. 'L'image de la Nature dans la poésie de Christine de Pizan.' In *Au champ*, pp. 639–50.
Schwarze, Michael 2003. *Generische Wahrheit–höfischer Polylog im Werk Jean Froissarts*. Text und Kontext, 19. Stuttgart: Steiner.
Sedgwick, W. B. 1927. 'Notes and Emendations on Faral's *Les Arts poétiques du XIIe et du XIIIe siècle*.' *Speculum*, 2, 331–43.
Segre, Cesare 1968. 'Le forme et le tradizioni didattiche.' In *GRLMA*, 6:1, 58–145.
Semple, Benjamin 1995. 'The Consolation of a Woman Writer: Christine de Pizan's Use of Boethius in *Lavision-Christine*.' In *Women, the Book and the Worldly: Selected Proceedings of the St Hilda's Conference, 1993*. Vol. 2. Cambridge: Brewer, pp. 39–48.
—— 1998a. 'Christine de Pizan's Phenomenology of Beauty in the Lyric and the Dream Vision.' In *Christine Lyric*, pp. 187–205.
—— 1998b. 'The Critique of Knowledge as Power: The Limits of Philosophy and Theology in Christine de Pizan.' In *Christine Categories*, pp. 108–27.
Seznec, Jean 1953. *The Survival of the Pagan Gods: The Mythological Tradition and Its Place in Renaissance Humanism and Art*. Trans. Barbara F. Sessions. Harper Torchbooks/The Bollingen Library. New York: Harper and Brothers.
Shapley, C. S. 1970. *Studies in French Poetry of the Fifteenth Century*. The Hague: Nijhoff.
Sigal, Pierre André 2002. 'Christine de Pizan et le peuple.' In *Contexts*, pp. 811–28.
Skemp, Mary L. 1996. 'Autobiography as Authority in *Lavision-Christine*.' *Moyen Français*, 35–36, 17–31.
Slerca, Anna 1998. 'Le *Livre du chemin de long estude* (1402–1403): Christine au pays des merveilles.' In *Sur le chemin*, pp. 135–47.
Smith, Geri L. 1999. 'Christine de Pizan's *Dit de la pastoure* – A Feminization of the Pastourelle.' *Romance Notes*, 39, 285–94.
Solente, S. 1974. 'Christine de Pisan.' *Histoire littéraire de la France*, 40, 335–422.
Solterer, Helen 1995. *The Master and Minerva: Disputing Women in French Medieval Culture*. Berkeley, Los Angeles, London: University of California Press.
Stäblein-Harris, Patricia 1992. 'Orléans, the Epic Tradition, and the Sacred Texts of Christine de Pizan.' In *Reinterpreting Christine*, pp. 272–84.
Stakel, Susan 1991. *False Roses: Structures of Duality and Deceit in Jean de Meun's 'Roman de la rose'*. Stanford French and Italian Studies, 69. Saratoga, CA: ANMA Libri.
Stanesco, Michel 1988. *Jeux d'errance du chevalier médiéval: aspects ludiques de*

la fonction guerrière dans la littérature du Moyen Age flamboyant. Brill's Studies in Intellectual History, 9. Leiden, New York, Copenhagen, Cologne: Brill.

Stedman, Gesa 2002. '"Where is the shade of the worthy Christine today?" – Alice Kemp-Welch's Early Feminist Reading of *The Book of the Duke of True Lovers*.' In *Contexts*, pp. 829–41.

Stierle, Karlheinz 1972. 'L'Histoire comme exemple, l'exemple comme histoire: contribution à la pragmatique et à la poétique des textes narratifs.' *Poétique*, 10, 176–98.

Strubel, Armand 1995. 'Le Style allégorique de Christine.' In *Femme de lettres*, pp. 357–72.

—— 2000. 'Le "chevauchier" de Charles V: Christine de Pizan et le spectacle de la majesté royale.' In *Penser*, pp. 385–99.

—— 2002. *'Grant senefiance a': allégorie et littérature au moyen âge*. Moyen Age–outils de synthèse, 2. Paris: Champion.

Stuip, R. E. V. 1998. 'Huilende helden?' In *Emoties*, pp. 183–98.

—— 2004. 'Christine, kennis en boeken.' In *Christine vrouw*, pp. 141–58.

Suard, François 1993. 'Christine de Pizan: *Le Ditié de Jehanne d'Arc*.' In *Studies in Honor of Hans-Erich Keller: Medieval French and Occitan Literature and Romance Linguistics*. Ed. Rupert T. Pickens. Kalamazoo: Medieval Institute Publications, Western Michigan University, pp. 247–58.

Szkilnik, Michelle 2003. *Jean de Saintré: une carrière chevaleresque au XVe siècle*. Publications romanes et françaises, 232. Geneva: Droz.

Tarnowski, Andrea 1993. 'Le Geste prophétique chez Christine de Pizan.' In *Apogée*, pp. 225–36.

—— 1994. 'Maternity and Paternity in "La Mutacion de Fortune".' In *City of Scholars*, pp. 116–26.

—— 1998. 'Pallas Athena, la science et la chevalerie.' In *Sur le chemin*, pp. 149–58.

—— 2000. 'Perspectives on the *Advision*.' In *Christine 2000*, pp. 105–14, 317–18.

—— 2003. 'The Lessons of Experience and the *Chemin de long estude*.' In *Casebook*, pp. 181–97.

Taylor, Jane H. M. 2002. 'Christine de Pizan and the Poetics of the *Envoi*.' In *Contexts*, pp. 843–54.

Thompson, John Jay 1999. 'Medea in Christine de Pizan's *Mutacion de Fortune*, or How to Be a Better Mother.' *Forum for Modern Language Studies*, 35, 158–74.

Thoss, Dagmar 1972. *Studien zum locus amoenus im Mittelalter*. Wiener romanistische Arbeiten, 10. Vienna, Stuttgart: Braumüller.

Trachsler, Richard 2000. *Disjointures–conjointures: étude sur l'interférence des matières narratives dans la littérature française du Moyen Age*. Romanica Helvetica, 120. Tübingen, Basel: Francke.

Tuve, Rosemond 1966. *Allegorical Imagery: Some Mediaeval Books and Their Posterity*. Princeton: Princeton University Press.

Tyssens, Madeleine 1992. 'Voix de femmes dans la lyrique d'oïl.' In *Femmes*, pp. 373–87.

Van der Helm, José 2004. 'Het *Livre de la cité des dames* en Boccaccio.' In *Christine vrouw*, pp. 89–109.

Van Gijsen, Annelies 1998. 'De dramatisering van begeerte en vrees.' In *Emoties*, pp. 157–82.
Van Hemelryck, Tania 2000. 'Christine de Pizan et la paix: la rhétorique et les mots pour le dire.' In *Au champ*, pp. 663–89.
Vincensini, Jean-Jacques 1999. 'Désordre de l'abjection et ordre de la courtoisie: le corps abject dans *Paris et Vienne* de Pierre de la Cépède.' *Medium Aevum*, 68, 292–304.
Vincent-Cassy, Mireille 1986. 'Péchés de femmes à la fin du Moyen Age.' In *Condición*, pp. 501–17.
—— 1992. 'Quand les femmes deviennent paresseuses.' In *Femmes*, pp. 431–47.
Von Graevenitz, Gerhart, and Odo Marquard 1998. *Kontingenz*. Poetik und Hermeneutik, 17. Munich: Fink.
Von Moos, Peter 1988. *Geschichte als Topik: das rhetorische Exemplum von der Antike zur Neuzeit und die 'historiae' im 'Policraticus' Johanns von Salisbury*. Ordo, 2. Hildesheim, Zürich, New York: Olms.
—— 2002. 'Le sens commun au moyen âge: sixième sens et sens social. Aspects épistémologiques, ecclésiologiques et eschatologiques.' *Studi medievali*. Ser. 3, 43, 1–58.
Waaldijk, Berteke 2004. 'Christine de Pizan en Vrouwenstudies.' In *Christine vrouw*, pp. 191–202.
Walters, Lori J. 1989. 'The Woman Writer and Literary History: Christine de Pizan's Redefinition of the Poetic *Translatio* in the *Epistre au Dieu d'amours*.' *French Literature Series*, 16, 1–16.
—— 1994. 'Chivalry and the (En)Gendered Poetic Self: Petrarchan Models in the "Cent Balades".' In *City of Scholars*, pp. 43–66.
—— 1996. 'Boethius and the Triple Ending of the *Cent Balades*.' *French Studies*, 50, 129–37.
—— 1998. '*Translatio studii*: Christine de Pizan's Self-Portrayal in Two Lyric Poems and in the *Livre de la mutacion de Fortune*.' In *Christine Lyric*, pp. 155–67.
—— 2002a. 'Christine de Pizan, Primat, and the "noble nation françoise".' *Cahiers de recherches médiévales (XIIIe–XVe s.)*, 9, 237–46.
—— 2002b. 'The Royal Vernacular: Poet and Patron in Christine de Pizan's *Charles V* and the *Sept Psaumes allégorisés*.' In *The Vernacular Spirit: Essays on Medieval Religious Literature*. Ed. Renate Blumenfeld-Kosinski, Duncan Robertson, and Nancy Bradley Warren. New York: Palgrave, pp. 145–82.
—— 2003a. 'Christine de Pizan as Translator and Voice of the Body Politic.' In *Casebook*, pp. 25–41.
—— 2003b. 'Constructing Reputations: *Fama* and Memory in Christine de Pizan's *Charles V* and *L'Advision Cristine*.' In *Fama: The Poetics of Talk and Reputation in Medieval Europe*. Ed. Thelma Fenster and Daniel Lord Smail. Ithaca, NY, London: Cornell University Press, pp. 118–42.
Wandruszka, Nikolai 2000. 'The Family Origins of Christine de Pizan: Noble Lineage between City and *Contado* in the Thirteenth and Fourteenth Centuries.' In *Au champ*, pp. 111–30.
Weil, Michèle 1995. '"Je suis comme toy": dialogie de Christine de Pizan.' In *Femme de lettres*, pp. 373–81.
Wetherbee, Winthrop 1976. 'The Theme of Imagination in Medieval Poetry and the

Allegorical Figure of "Genius".' *Medievalia et Humanistica*, 7, 45–64.
White, Stephen D. 1998. 'The Politics of Anger.' In *Anger's Past: The Social Uses of an Emotion in the Middle Ages*. Ed. Barbara H. Rosenwein. Ithaca, NY, London: Cornell University Press, pp. 127–52.
Whitman, Jon 1987. *Allegory: The Dynamics of an Ancient and Medieval Technique*. Cambridge, MA: Harvard University Press.
Willard, Charity Cannon 1980. 'Christine de Pizan: The Astrologer's Daughter.' In *Mélanges à la mémoire de Franco Simone*. 4 vols. Geneva: Slatkine. Vol. 1, pp. 95–111.
—— 1981a. 'Christine de Pizan and the Order of the Rose.' in *Ideals*, pp. 51–67.
—— 1981b. 'Christine de Pizan's *Cent Ballades d'Amant et de Dame*: Criticism of Courtly Love.' In *Court and Poet: Selected Proceedings of the Third Congress of the International Courtly Literature Society (Liverpool 1980)*. Ed. Glyn Burgess [et alii]. Arca: Classical and Medieval Texts, Papers and Monographs, 5. Liverpool: Cairns, pp. 357–64.
—— 1981c. 'Christine de Pizan's *Livre des trois vertus*: Feminine Ideal or Practical Advice?' In *Ideals*, pp. 91–116.
—— 1981d. 'Lovers' Dialogues in Christine de Pizan's Lyric Poetry from the *Cent Ballades* to the *Cent Ballades d'amant et de dame*.' *Fifteenth-Century Studies*, 4, 167–80.
—— 1981e. 'A New Look at Christine de Pizan's *Epistre au Dieu d'Amour*.' In *Seconda Miscellanea di studi e ricerche sul Quattrocento francese*. Ed. Franco Simone, with Jonathan Beck and Gianni Mombello. Chambéry, Turin: Centre d'Etudes Franco-Italien, Ann Arbor, MI: UMI Monographs, pp. 71–92.
—— 1984. *Christine de Pizan: Her Life and Works*. New York: Persea.
—— 1987. 'Punishment and Reward in Christine de Pizan's Lyric Poetry.' In *Rewards and Punishments in the Arthurian Romances and Lyric Poetry of Mediaeval France: Essays Presented to Kenneth Varty*. Ed. Peter V. Davies and Angus J. Kennedy. Arthurian Studies, 17. Cambridge: Brewer, pp. 165–74.
—— 1990a. 'L'Idée du bonheur chez Christine de Pizan.' In *L'Idée de bonheur au moyen âge: Actes du Colloque d'Amiens de mars 1984*. Ed. Danielle Buschinger. Göppinger Arbeiten zur Germanistik, 414. Göppingen: Kümmerle, pp. 97–102.
—— 1990b. 'Jean de Werchin, Seneschal de Hainaut: Reader and Writer of Courtly Literature.' In *Courtly Literature: Culture and Context. Selected Papers from the 5th Triennial Congress of the International Courtly Literature Society, Dalfsen, The Netherlands, 9–16 August 1986*. Utrecht Publications in General and Comparative Literature, 25. Amsterdam, Philadelphia: Benjamins, pp. 595–603.
—— 1992. 'Christine de Pizan: From Poet to Political Commentator.' In *Politics*, pp. 17–32.
—— 1998. 'Christine de Pizan on the Art of Warfare.' In *Christine Categories*, pp. 3–15.
Wisman, Josette A. 1997. 'Christine de Pizan and Arachne's Metamorphoses.' *Fifteenth-Century Studies*, 23, 138–51.
Wittgenstein, Ludwig 1972. *Über Gewißheit–On Certainty*. Ed. G. E. M. Anscombe and G. H. von Wright; trans. Denis Paul and G. E. M. Anscombe. New York: Harper.
Wolf-Bonvin, Romaine 1998. *Textus: de la tradition latine à l'esthétique du roman médiéval. Le Bel Inconnu, Amadas et Ydoine*. Nouvelle Bibliothèque du Moyen

Age, 41. Paris: Champion.

Wolfthal, Diane 1998. '"Douleur sur toutes autres": Revisualizing the Rape Script in the *Epistre Othea* and the *Cité des dames*.' In *Christine Categories*, pp. 41–70.

Wolfzettel, Friedrich 1984. 'Zur Poetik der Subjektivität bei Christine de Pisan.' In *Lyrik des ausgehenden 14. und des 15. Jahrhunderts*. Ed. Franz V. Spechtler. Chloe, 1. Amsterdam: Rodopi, pp. 379–97.

—— 1995. 'Abundante Rhetorik: Selbstverständnis und historische Funktion der lyrischen Sprache von Machaut zu den Grands Rhétoriqueurs.' In *Musique*, pp. 75–104.

Zimmermann, Margarete 1991. 'La Littérature française à la fin du moyen âge: une littérature de crise?' In *Recherches*, pp. 207–19.

—— 1993. '*Wirres Zeug und übles Geschwätz*': Christine de Pizan über den Rosenroman. Schriftenreihe Rosenmuseum Steinfurth. Bad Nauheim: Rosenmuseum Steinfurth.

—— 1994. 'Mémoire – tradition – historiographie: Christine de Pizan et son "Livre des Fais et bonnes meurs du sage Roy Charles V".' In *City of Scholars*, pp. 158–73.

—— 1995. 'Les *Cent Balades d'amant et de dame*: une réécriture de l'*Elegia di madonna Fiammetta* de Boccace?' In *Femme de lettres*, pp. 337–46.

—— 2002. *Christine de Pizan*. Rowohlts Monographien 50437. Reinbek bei Hamburg: Rowohlt.

—— 2003a. 'Memory's Architect.' In *Casebook*, pp. 57–77.

—— 2003b. 'La Scrittrice della memoria.' In *Città*, pp. 33–45.

Zink, Gaston 1995. 'La phrase de Christine de Pizan dans le *Livre du corps de policie*.' In *Femme de lettres*, pp. 383–95.

Zink, Michel 1979. *Roman rose ou rose rouge: le Roman de la Rose ou de Guillaume de Dole de Jean Renart*. Paris: Nizet.

—— 1985. *La Subjectivité littéraire: autour du Siècle de saint Louis*. Ecriture. Paris: Presses Universitaires de France.

Zühlke, Bärbel 1994. *Christine de Pizan in Text und Bild: zur Selbstdarstellung einer frühhumanistischen Intellektuellen*. Ergebnisse der Frauenforschung, 36. Stuttgart, Weimar: Metzler.

Zumthor, Paul 1955. 'Note sur les champs sémantiques dans le vocabulaire des idées.' *Neophilologus*, 39, 175–83, 241–49.

—— 1956. 'Pour une histoire du vocabulaire français des idées.' *Zeitschrift für romanische Philologie*, 72, 340–62.

—— 1972. *Essai de poétique médiévale*. Paris: Seuil.

Index

Adams, Tracy, 137–38, 139
Adultery and pregnancy, 93
Aelred de Rievaulx, 83 n. 29
Aevum. *See* Great Beyond
Affection, Conjugal (*affectio coniugalis*), 69, 128
Agincourt, Battle of, 116, 147, 178
Alain de Lille: *Anticlaudianus*, 28, 35–36, 38, 39 n. 120, 47 n. 23, 70, 102 n. 99, 165 n. 106; *De planctu Naturae*, 35 n. 108, 38, 149–50; *Distinctiones*, 35 n. 109; mentioned, 37, 39
Alba, 128
Alchemists, Farcical, 89
Allegory: Subtle, 28, 29; and *aviser-deviser* paradigm, 42; Mode of, 50; in *Advision*, 70–72, 75, 169; and opinion, 70–74, 169–70; of widow's bereavement, 138 n. 130; mentioned, 84, 138 n. 130, 169. *See also Modus poeticus*
Allen, Judson Boyce, 44
Andreas Capellanus: *De amore*, 109, 116 n. 32, 119 n. 46, 127–28, 130, 132, 136 n. 120, 175
Angeli, Giovanna, 73
Anger, Amant's, 26
Anomaly: as deviation from norm, 100–03, 105; Christine as, 170–72, 173, 174, 177; in medieval authors, 170; for women, 171; mentioned, 4
Antigraphe (Philographe), 70, 71, 81
Antiphrasis, 38, 39, 84–85, 88, 117 n. 40, 119, 124, 155, 165
Antithesis, 128
Anxiety, Christine's, 157, 171–72
Apo koinu principle, 113 n. 26, 139 n. 134
Apostrophe, 61
Appearance (*semblance*), 34, 111

Apprehensive, 83
Aquinas, Thomas: Commentary on Aristotle's *Metaphysics*, 32, 45 n. 16, 46 ns. 18–19; on love, 109 n. 8; mentioned, 3, 17, 19 n. 49, 77
Archetypus: as blueprint, 129; *Status*, 159 n. 82
Architecture and composition, 51 n. 41
Arenga (arrenge, ars arengandi): and *ars dictaminis*, 46 n. 21; mentioned, 46–47, 82, 99
Arianism, 45
Aristotle, 17, 22, 26 n. 77, 32, 45, 46 n. 19, 50, 78, 81, 98, 116
Array: Orderly, 44; of good women, 103; of virtues, 156, 160, 164; of vices, 164
Astrological predictions, 37 n. 114
Astrology and hypothesis, 67 n. 105
Attwood, Catherine, 141 n. 145, 177
Audience: and individual opinions, 42, 72, 139–40, 152, 169–70, 175–76; and rhetoric, 46, 66–67; Christine's, 88, 105; for lyric poetry, 113
Augustine, Saint, 81, 92 n. 69
Author (*auctor*), 17, 18 n. 47
Authority: Misogynist, 78, 80, 90, 99, 172, 173; and opinion, 78–80, 97
Autobiographical assumption, 178–79
Auxerre, Treaty of, 167
Aviser (avis): in *aviser-deviser* paradigm, 30 n. 89, 41–42, 52–53, 82–83, 153; as opinion, 31; as *consideracion* and *discrecion*, 48 n. 26; mentioned, 149, 150 n. 33, 158, 162
Awakening (reawakening), 63 n. 88, 152–53

Babel, Tower of, 90, 148

Babylonian exile, 14
Baudet Harenc: *Accusations against the Belle Dame sans mercy*, 113 n. 26
Baudouin in *jeu-parti*, 176
Beaune, Colette, 151 n. 36
Beauty: Christine's, 21–22, 156; Ideal, 164
Beer, Jeanette M. A., 149 n. 29
Bellatores: as women, 91; mentioned, 147
Benoît de Sainte-Maure: *Roman de Troie*, 56 n. 55
Bernardus Silvestris: *Cosmographia*, 70 n. 116
Bible (Scripture), 19, 28, 33, 49, 80, 92, 99
Biblical characters: Adam, 19, 23, 45, 47, 59 n. 72, 65 n. 98, 77, 83 n. 29; Angels, 39; David, 14; Devil (Satan), 45 n. 13, 47, 59 n. 72; Esther, 21 n. 57; Eve, 19, 21 n. 57, 23, 45, 47, 59 n. 72, 65 n. 98, 80, 83–84, 98; Hebrews, 166; Holophernes, 91; Jesus Christ, 16, 17, 90 n. 58; Judith, 21 n. 57; 53 n. 46, 91; Mary, 90, 104, 163, 164, 167; Nebuchadnezzar, 24; Nimrod, 90; Trinity, 35, 37
Biography: and autobiography, 72 n. 118; Panegyric (*Herrscherlob*), 153–54, 157; as description, 158–59; as florilegium, 158
Blanchard, Joël, 29 n. 85, 112, 139–40, 143 n. 8, 178 n. 41
Bluestocking, 45
Blumenfeld-Kosinski, Renate, 53 n. 45, 70 n. 116, 176
Boccaccio: *De casibus*, 39 n. 124; and Christine, 54 n. 48, 59–60, 84, 102 n. 97
Body (Bodies): Nature's, 21, 31 n. 90, 101, 164, 165; Christine's, 21–22, 36; politic, 4, 142, 145, 152, 163; King's and queen's two, 163; Noble, 165; mentioned, 155 n. 56
Boerdam, Jaap, 62 n. 85
Boethius: *Consolation of Philosophy*, 16–17, 18–20, 28, 46, 47, 49–50, 60–61, 74 n. 127, 82, 92 n. 69, 98 n. 86; *De differentiis topicis*, 60 n. 79; in arts of poetry, 60 n. 80; and virtuous love, 109 n. 8; mentioned, 3, 14, 21, 71, 74, 77, 116, 141, 143, 149, 157, 166
Bonaventure, Saint, 18 n. 47
Brandenberger, Tobias, 105 n. 111
Brown-Grant, Rosalind, 54, 71 n. 117, 75
Brownlee, Kevin, 60 n. 77
Busby, Keith, 57 n. 65

Carruthers, Mary J., 23 n. 66
Castle, Fortune's, 15, 148, 149
Cause: First, 19, 46, 81; Material, 33, 46, 47, 81; Formal, efficient, and final, 46 n. 19; Opinion as, 49, 74, 77; mentioned, 22
Cayley, Emma J., 176 n. 27
Cecco d'Ascoli: *Acerba*, 85, 88
Cerquiglini, Jacqueline, 41
Certainty, Subjective, ix, 31, 49, 151
Chansons féminines, 124
Chaos: Moral and social, vii, 168, 171; France's, 23, 47, 70–71, 75, 142–43, 147, 168, 177; in *Advision*, 70–72; created by God, 70 n. 116; as shame, 70 n. 116; as confusion, 71; Emotional, 121; in Christine's life, 153, 167–68
Chareyron, Nicole, 153
Charity, 93
Charivari, 94 n. 74
Charles d'Orléans, 175, 179
Chartier, Alain: *Quadrilogue invectif*, 18 n. 48, 47 n. 22; *Livre de l'esperance*, 82 n. 25, 117 n. 38; *Belle Dame sans mercy*, 113 n. 26, 115, 127 n. 87; *Livre des quatre dames*, 113 n. 26, 115–16; Poems, 115, 122 n. 58; mentioned, 175
Chastity of women, 91–92, 103
Chaucer, Geoffrey: *Troilus and Criseyde*, 134 n. 107; mentioned, 9 n. 10
Chivalry: and love, 4, 107–08; Charles V's, 155, 160, 163, 164
Chrétien de Troyes: *Yvain*, 91 n. 64, 93, 128; *Lancelot (Chevalier de la charrette)*, 128, 164; *Erec et Enide*, 128 n. 90
Christine de Pizan: *Advision Cristine*, vii, 1, 2, 3, 7–8, 10, 13 n. 29, 15, 16, 17, 18–19, 20, 21–22, 23, 26 n. 74, 27,

28, 30, 32–35, 39, 40, 43–50, 61, 63 n. 88, 65, 67–68, 70–72, 74–75, 77, 80, 81, 82, 89, 90, 95, 98, 105 n. 112, 106, 108 n. 4, 117, 118, 120 n. 48, 121 n. 53, 122, 123 n. 63, 125 ns. 73 and 77, 131 n. 102, 132, 139, 141, 144, 145, 149, 150 n. 33, 152, 153, 156, 157 n. 71, 166, 169–70, 171, 173, 178 n. 41, 179

Autres balades: *AB* 6: 81, 125 n. 77, 126; *AB* 8: 128; *AB* 9–10, 129 n. 95; *AB* 26: 126, 128; *AB* 29–31, 33 and 52: 108 n. 4; *AB* 35: 126

Cent balades: *CB* 1: 115, 118; *CB* 3: 117 n. 38; *CB* 5–20: 128; *CB* 11: 172; *CB* 13: 122 n. 60; *CB* 14, 17 and 19: 118; *CB* 40: 108; *CB* 41, 42, 46, 48 and 49: 114; *CB* 50: 114, 115 n. 30, 116; *CB* 50–90: 112; *CB* 51: 115 n. 30; *CB* 51–89: 114; *CB* 61: 116 n. 35; *CB* 78: 89, 136; *CB* 96: 114; *CB* 97: 116; *CB* 98 and 99: 117; *CB* 100: 118; mentioned, 95, 112–19, 141, 175, 177

Cent ballades d'amant et de dame, 9 n. 9, 84 n. 32, 107, 111, 112, 115 n. 31, 137–40, 175, 177

Charles V, 51 n. 41, 59 n. 71, 66–67, 72, 75, 84–85, 98–99, 100–01, 119–22, 123, 125, 145–46, 147, 153–56, 158–65

Chemin de long estude, 19–20, 23, 29, 32 n. 94, 34, 35, 36–39, 40, 41–42, 45, 46 n. 17, 52–53, 63 n. 88, 65, 70, 75 n. 130, 99 n. 89, 100 n. 93, 109, 122 n. 58, 135, 143, 144–45, 147, 148, 149–53, 155, 156, 163, 165–66, 171, 179

Cité des dames, 20, 34, 40, 46 n. 20, 51 n. 41, 52, 53 n. 46, 59–60, 63 ns. 88–89, 65–67, 72, 75 n. 129, 78–79, 80, 81–85, 87, 88, 89, 90–91, 94–95, 97–98, 99–105, 107, 110 n. 12, 114, 125, 128, 140, 145–46, 147, 154, 156, 161, 162–63, 164, 165, 166 n. 109, 171, 172, 173–74, 180 n. 49

Débat de deux amants, 11 n. 18, 25 n. 73, 69 n. 111, 85 n. 36, 109 n. 7, 112 n. 16

Dit de la pastoure, 53 n. 45, 57–58, 100, 107, 111, 112, 114, 126, 137–40, 174, 175

Dit de la rose, 107, 109, 110, 112, 119, 121 n. 52, 123 n. 62, 124, 125, 128, 174

Dit de Poissy, 21 n. 57, 109 n. 7, 111 n. 14, 115, 177 n. 35

Ditié de Jehanne d'Arc, 137 n. 126, 148, 151 n. 36, 166–67, 178

Duc des vrais amants, 95, 107, 108 n. 5, 109–11, 118, 127, 129–40, 171, 174–75

Encore aultres balades, *EAB* 9: 108 n. 4

Enseignemens moraux, 23 n. 67, 81 n. 22, 109 n. 8, 110–11, 127, 137 n. 126, 158

Epistre au dieu d'amours, 13 n. 28, 59 n. 72, 83, 84 n. 32, 100 n. 93, 107, 109, 112, 124, 125, 128, 174

Epistre de la prison de vie humaine, 24, 115

Epistre Othea, viii n. 5, 15, 26 n. 77, 28, 29, 30, 36, 47 n. 23, 56 n. 55, 59, 65–66, 72, 84, 95, 98, 105, 109 n. 8, 110, 111, 126, 127, 136, 155 n. 56, 161, 165

Epître à la reine, 72 n. 119, 147

Fais d'armes, 101 n. 94, 108 n. 4, 157 n. 72

Livre de la paix, 23, 38 n. 117, 42, 43 n. 4, 46 n. 20, 72, 85 n. 39, 105 n. 108, 120 n. 48, 121 n. 53, 143 n. 6, 144, 146, 147, 148 n. 26, 154, 157 n. 71, 162, 165, 167

Livre de prudence, 148 n. 26

Livre des trois jugemens, 109 n. 7, 111 n. 14, 115 n. 30, 116 n. 32

Livre du corps de policie, 3, 20, 43 n. 4, 52 n. 44, 65 n. 95, 67 n. 105, 73 n. 122, 88 n. 48, 91 n. 62, 99 n. 91, 109 n. 9, 122 n. 58, 123 n. 63, 143, 144, 145, 146, 147, 148 n. 26, 154, 161 n. 92, 162, 165, 174 n. 22

Mutacion de Fortune, vii, 14–16, 17–

18, 19, 20–23, 24–25, 27 n. 78, 29, 31 n. 90, 45 n. 12, 49, 51 n. 41, 52, 57, 60, 63, 66 n. 100, 67, 74, 81, 84 n. 33, 85 ns. 36 and 38, 88, 90, 94–96, 98, 112, 117, 119, 122, 128, 144, 148–49, 154, 162, 166, 173
Prouverbes, 89 n. 54, 99, 102, 150 n. 33, 157, 165
XV joies nostre Dame, 104 n. 105
Rondeaux: *R* 1: 118; *R* 1–7: 128; *R* 7 and 11: 115; *R* 42: 136 n. 114; *R* 56: 122 n. 58
Trois vertus, 53 n. 45, 67 n. 103, 68, 69, 72–73, 75 ns. 129–30, 88, 90–94, 95, 98 n. 86, 102 n. 99, 104, 105, 111, 114, 120, 123 n. 65, 125–26, 127, 128, 129, 134 n. 106, 135, 137, 140, 146 n. 18, 154, 156, 157 ns. 71–72, 165, 180 n. 49
Virelais: *V* 1 and 15: 115
Cicero: *De inventione*, 46 n. 20, 59 n. 70; *De senectute*, 120 n. 48; mentioned, 63–64
Circumspection (*circonspection*), 23, 24 n. 68
Circumstances (*circumstantiae*; *Quis quid ubi quibus auxiliis cur quomodo quando*), 55, 58, 61, 62, 63, 127, 146, 158, 174, 175
City of Ladies, 65, 66, 83–84, 90, 91, 97–98, 100 n. 92, 102 n. 99, 103, 105, 146 n. 16, 162–63, 164, 167
Cleric, Woman (*clergesse*), 141 n. 143, 170
Col: Gontier, 87 n. 46; Pierre, 10, 11, 12, 32, 48 n. 26, 62, 87, 88, 97 n. 82. *See also* Wife, Gontier Col's
Commeres as promiscuous men, 121–22 n. 58
Common places and commonplaces, Distinction between, 51. *See also* Invention
Commonweal: and misogyny, 103, 146; and Lady Philosophy, 106; and France, 143, 153, 154; mentioned, 4, 148
Communication between lovers, 136, 138, 139
Compilation (*compillacion*), 1, 16–18, 19, 154, 158

Composition of *Advision*, 169–70
Confession, 55, 61, 172–73
Coniecturale argumentum, 63–64
Cons, Young and old, in the *Roman de la rose*, 123
Conscience (*conscience*), 4, 30, 34, 48, 91, 92, 94, 170, 172, 173
Consent in *Roman de la rose*, 64 n. 93
Conservatio amoris. *See Gradus*
Consideration (*consideracion*). *See* Virtues, Intellectual
Consolation: and the intellectual virtues, 24, 82, 92 n. 68; and conscience, 92 n. 68; Religious, 177
Conspiratio, 18 n. 47
Constancy in love, 103, 111, 124, 135, 136, 137–38, 175
Contingency, 4, 170, 171, 172, 174, 175, 178
Continuatio amoris. *See Gradus*
Contraires choses, 12, 26, 123–24, 143, 155, 161
Copia (*coppie d'eloquence*), 24–25
Corneille, Pierre: *Horace*, 76 n. 132
Corti, Maria, 91 n. 62, 179
Covetousness: as virtue, 20, 143, 174; as vice, 149, 174
Cow as promiscuous woman, 56, 116 n. 35
Creintis (*craintive*), 91, 171
Cropp, Glynnis M., 16–17, 18, 153

Dante: *Divine Comedy*, 29, 37, 38, 39–40, 72, 105 n. 111; *Epistula Can Grande*, 72; mentioned, 7
Death: of husband, 67–68, 74, 96, 114, 117 n. 38, 122, 124, 141, 147, 171, 172; of beloved, 113, 114, 115–16, 134, 139, 147, 175, 176–77; of love, 113; Christine's, 167–68, 170; in war, 115–16, 175, 177.
Debate: on *Roman de la rose*, 1, 2, 4, 8–14, 30–32, 35 n. 108, 39, 45, 46, 48 n. 26, 50, 56, 59 n. 72, 60, 61–62, 64, 69, 76, 80, 87, 89 n. 54, 95, 96, 99, 108, 109, 111, 112, 114, 124–25, 127, 129, 132, 143, 152, 174; Epistolary, 10 n. 13; in *Chemin de long estude*, 41–42, 143, 144–45, 150–52, 155; and

arenga, 46, 99; among theologians, 99; Political, 142; Internal, 173–74; poems (*jeux partis*), 176; Inconclusiveness (irresolution) of, 176 n. 27
Deception and seduction, 96, 109, 124–25, 134, 139
Decorum: in the *Roman de la rose*, 11, 50; and character, 50
Deminutio amoris. See Gradus
Depravity, Women's alleged, 78–79, 81, 83
Deschamps, Eustache, 16 n. 37, 51
Description, Art of, 3, 21 n. 57, 41, 42, 50–64, 84, 146 n. 18, 153, 155, 156, 162, 164
Desire to know: and opinion, 41; Christine's, 117, 156
Deviser. See Aviser
Differences between men and women, 100–03
Disciples of Jean de Meun, viii, 1, 2, 10, 11, 13 ns. 25 and 31, 14, 31–32, 33, 34, 62, 64, 68, 80, 84 n. 35, 87, 96
Discretion (*discrecion*). *See* Virtues, Intellectual
Dissimulation, 146 n. 18
Dowd, Maureen, 125
Dream: as thought, 70, 71; True, 114
Dulac, Liliane, 28 n. 83, 35, 45 n. 16, 59–60, 70 n. 116, 110, 136
Du secret des femmes (*De secretis mulierum*), 85, 88

Eberhard the German: *Laborintus*, 60 n. 80
Echtermann, Andrea, 50, 75 n. 129
Education, Christine's, 10 n. 13, 20, 34, 38, 46 n. 17, 49–50, 51–52, 77, 126 n. 83, 179
Elements, Four: Harmony of, 36, 39 n. 120; Rebellion of, 38–39; Discord of, 39 n. 120; mentioned, 33
Eloquence. *See* Faculties, Intellectual, *and* Rhetoric, Art of
Emperor, Holy Roman, 151
Emulation (*aemulatio*): in writing, 18; of virtues, 154; of good women, 163; of ancestors, 165

Encomium: in *Charles V*, 67, 84, 161; in *Cité des dames*, 84–85; for Virgin Mary, 163 n. 99
Engin (*engien*), 11, 27
Enlightened self-interest. *See* Self-interest, Enlightened
'Entindividualisierung' of ideal king, 159
Envy: and conscience, 92 n. 68; God's, 98
Epideixis, 66, 153–58, 166
Esplucher, 27, 35, 48, 61, 62, 78, 82, 83, 85 n. 36, 88, 92, 100
Essentialism, 94 n. 76
Euhemerism, 36, 65–67, 102, 105, 161. *See also* Integument
Exaggeration (*exaggeratio*), 97
Examples: Pagan, 65; Common places in, 155; Historical, 158–59
Experience: and opinion, 34, 48, 49, 69, 74, 77, 80, 98, 118, 122, 170–72, 175; Reading, 78; and authority, 79–80, 81, 89; and reason, 82, 89; and farce, 88; of anomalies and contingencies, 174
Extraction by topical invention, 55

Faculties: Intellectual, as Reason (*raison*), 4, 24, 25, 30, 33, 34, 48, 49, 69, 75, 79, 88, 98, 101, 105, 106, 119–20, 121, 122, 140, 154, 170, 171, 173, 179; as Eloquence (*eloquence, loquence*), 10–11, 24–25, 33, 99, 154; as Understanding, Rational (*entendement, entendement de raison*), 11, 15, 21, 22, 25–26, 27, 28, 30–31, 40, 42, 74, 82, 83, 101, 116, 119–20, 154, 173
Imagination, 12, 31, 34, 39, 42; Five senses, 34, 35; Fantasy (*fantasie*), 43–44; mentioned, 20, 24–26, 30, 42, 87, 142, 154
Faith: and opinion, 1–2, 19, 30, 32, 35–36, 69, 74, 93, 98–106, 154, 170, 173; False, 45; and philosophy, 47, 117; and misogynist authority, 78, 83; and conscience, 92; and misogyny, 98, 101; and theology, 99; and justice, 105; and Providence, 167. *See also* Religion
False goods, 16, 74, 87, 98, 117, 143, 175

Farce: as *trufferie*, 88–89; as *goliardise* and *deshonnesteté*, 89
Fathers, Church, 17, 19, 28, 80
Fauvel, Roman de, 47 n. 23
Felicity, 20, 143
Feminism, Christine's, viii n. 7
Femme forte. See Virago
Fille d'escole or *d'escolle*, 44–45, 47–48, 74, 98, 156
Finis amoris. See Gradus
Flattery (*blandice*) and laudation (*louange*), 153 n. 48
Foreplay, 126
Forhan, Kate Langdon, 35 n. 107, 75, 147–48, 151–52, 180 n. 49
Fortitude (*force*): of fearful women, 85, 91, 102; of Charles V and Du Guesclin, 166 n. 109
Fortune: and opinion, 3, 15, 16, 18–20, 49–50, 75, 77, 90, 98, 141, 144, 149; Mutability of, 28; Names for, 47 n. 23; and God's chosen people, 90 n. 56; in history, 148–49; and nobility, 165; and Providence, 166
Foulechat, Denis: *Policratique*, 2 n. 5, 79 n. 5, 155 n. 63
Fountain of Wisdom, 41
France: the nation, 74, 75, 141–48, 149–53, 167, 177; Allegory of, 75, 144; and the king, 161, 163, 165–66. See also Chaos
Frequentatio, 97 n. 83
Froissart, Jean: *Chroniques*, 93 n. 69; *Meliador*, 132 n. 103, 178–79; mentioned, 47 n. 23, 118, 170 n. 6, 179
Fulgentius, 65

Gaunt, Simon, 86
Gautier d'Arras: *Ille et Galeron*, 107
Gauvard, Claude, vii, 161 n. 93
Gender barriers and boundaries, 34, 94–96.
Geocentric (Finite) universe, 29, 35, 36, 37, 179
Geoffrey of Vinsauf: *Poetria nova*, 51 n. 41, 53–54, 58, 159 n. 82, 164; *Documentum*, 53; mentioned, 55
Gerson, Jean, 1 n. 2, 9–10, 11, 12, 33, 34, 35 n. 108, 56, 61–62, 71 n. 117, 81 n. 22, 99, 117 n. 39, 149 n. 31
Gifts, God's, 21–22, 155 n. 56, 163–64
Gigolo, Fol Amoureux as, 123
Gossip and love, 125, 134, 135–36, 140. See also Slander
Gradus: as topos, 53–54; *amoris*, 53 n. 45, 54, 55, 69, 112–13, 114, 117–19, 120, 121 n. 58, 127–36, 137, 139, 141; *irae*, 53 n. 46; *aetatum* (ages of life), 54, 119–22, 160–61; and *finis amoris*, 113 n. 26, 119, 128, 137; and *deminutio amoris*, 114, 119, 136, 137, 141; and *continuatio amoris*, 119, 139; and *conservatio amoris*, 128, 135, 136, 137, 139
Grandes Chroniques de France, 159
Great Beyond (*aevum*, Heaven), 35, 36, 37, 40, 45, 90
Greban, Arnould: *Mystère de la Passion*, 77
Gros, Gérard, 178 n. 42
Guillaume de Lorris, 100 n. 93, 117 n. 39, 118 n. 41, 129, 130, 135. See also Roman de la rose

Haasse, Hella S., viii, 5, 64, 90, 127 n. 85
Hauck, Johannes, 116 n. 32
Heaven. See Great Beyond
Heitmann, Klaus, 136 n. 121
Hell, 37, 45
Heresy, 18–19, 33, 48, 71, 79, 85 n. 36, 173
Hicks, Eric, 82 n. 25, 161
Hindman, Sandra L., 18 n. 48
Histoire ancienne jusqu'à César, 56 n. 55, 57–58
Historical persons and characters: Affre, 66; Aghinolfo (Christine's brother), 98 n. 86, 126 n. 83; Alexander, 29; Artemisia, 103; Berry, Duke of, 167; Charlemagne, 100 n. 93, 144; Charles IV, Emperor, 162; Charles V, vii, 11 n. 19, 23, 59 n. 71, 66–67, 71, 75–76, 99, 100–01, 103, 119–22, 123, 144, 145, 147–48, 149, 152, 153–62, 165, 166, 171, 177; Charles VI, vii, 147, 152, 166, 171; Charles VII (the Dauphin), 147, 151 n. 36, 166, 178;

Clovis, 144; Cyrus, 15; Daughter, Christine's, 74 n. 127; Du Guesclin, Bertrand, as lover, 109–12, 114, 117, 119, 124, 127, 128, 129, 130, 132, 134 n. 107, 136, 141, 174, 175, as 'omme fort', 166 n. 109; Elizabeth I, 164 n. 105; Etienne de Castel (Christine's husband), 52, 60, 74, 122, 147, 171, 173; Family, Boethius's, 98 n. 86; Family, Christine's, 52, 60, 98 n. 86, 126 n. 83, 147 n. 22, 156; Father, Christine's, 37 n. 114, 51, 52, 60, 63, 147, 156; Father-in-law, Christine's, 98 n. 86; Heloise, 66, 84, 97 n. 82, 162 n. 98; Hitler, 3; Isabeau de Bavière, Queen, 12, 147, 166 n. 107, 171; Jean de Castel (Christine's son), 22, 74 n. 127, 111, 147 n. 22; Jean de Werchin as lover, 109, 117; Jean sans Peur, 147, 167; Jeanne de Bourbon, 154, 159, 171; Joan of Arc, vii, 100, 101, 103, 137 n. 126, 144, 147, 148, 166–68, 171, 177, 178; Julius Caesar, 65 n. 95; King, Martin Luther, 3; Leonce, 97, 125; Louis VIII, 144; Louis IX, 144; Louis de Guyenne, 23, 72, 147, 154, 162, 165, 166, 167–68, 171; Louis d'Orléans, 99 n. 91, 136 n. 122, 147, 152 n. 42; Marie de Berry, 24; Mother, Christine's, 51, 52, 63, 79, 101 n. 95, 152, 174; Paolo (Christine's brother), 98 n. 86, 126 n. 83; Philippe the Bold, duke of Burgundy, 66–67, 154; Plato, 123 n. 63; Proba, 16 n. 40, 17; Saint, 161; Sappho, 123 n. 63; Semiramis, 53 n. 46, 54 n. 48, 59–60, 66 n. 100, 84, 100, 102; Solomon, 138–39, 151; Son, Christine's anonymous, 147 n. 22; Tarquin, 62; Theophrastus, 97; Verres, 63–64, 68; Xerxes, 15

Historiography, Medieval, 153

History: Jewish, 148–49, 166 n. 111; Repetitive, 148; Eye-witness, 155, 157; Epideictic, 159

Hoccleve, Thomas, 9 n. 10

Homosexuality and misogyny, 86

Honor, 91–93, 132, 134, 135, 137, 140, 171, 175

Horace, 53 n. 47, 67 n. 106

Household as woman's office, 101

Huizinga, Johan, vii, viii, 168

Humbert de Romans: *De eruditione praedicatorum*, 91 n. 62

Humility in women and aristocrats, 92–93

Humors, 142

Hundred Years War, 4, 115, 166, 177

Husband: as false good, 74, 117; Complacent, 89; Jealous, 89; Abusive, 89, 94, 171; Absent, 135

Hyperbole: Philogynist and Misogynist, 84–85, 97, 127; in description, 103–04

Hypocrisy ('Juste ypocrisie'), 93

Hypothesis and thesis, Rhetorical, 67–69, 74, 152

Ignorance, Christine's, 156

Ihle, Sandra, 125 n. 76

Immaculate Conception, 32, 36

Infanticide: Medea's, 66, 84 n. 33 ; as martyrdom, 66 n. 100

Infidelity, 128, 136, 137–38

Infratextuality, Christine's, 3 n. 9

Inspiration, 16, 18, 19, 158

Integument (*integument, couverture*), 27, 50. *See also* Euhemerism

Intelligence and physical weakness, 100–01

Intention and topical invention, 51

Introspection: and self-knowledge, 89–90, 103, 172–73; and correction, 90; Psychoanalytical, 142

Invective: Christine's, 13 n. 31, 121–22; Misogynist, 67; and epideictic, 69, 119

Invention: mentioned, 45, 50
  of common places (topoi): place (*locus*), 7 n. 4, 58, 59, 64; time (*tempus*), 7 n. 4, 58, 59; name (*nomen*), 40, 58–59; age (*aetas*) 51, 58, 59, 60; family (*cognatio*), 51, 59, 60, 63, 156; gender (*sexus*), 51, 52, 58, 59, 60, 63, 73, 85 n. 38, 88, 94 n. 76, 124, 146; language (*natio*) and nationality (*patria*), 51, 52 n. 44, 59, 60; character (*habitus*), 52, 58–59, 156; person (*persona*), 52, 58–59, 88, 159, 179; way of life (*convictus*), 52, 58–59; object

(*res*), 58; action (*negotium*), and action preceding the action described (*ante rem*), action accompanying the action described (*cum re*), and action following the action described (*post rem*), 58–59; appetites (*affectio, affectus*), 58–59, 125, 156; cause of the action (*causa facti*), 58–59, 159; condition (*conditio*), 58; eloquence (*orationes*), 58–59; event (*eventus*), 58; exploits (*facta*), 58–59; fortune (*fortuna*), 58–59, 60 n. 77, 73; gist of the action (*summa facti*), 58–59; goals (*studium*), 58–59, 156; judgment (*consilium*), 58–59; luck (*casus*), 58–59, 60 n. 77, 73; nature (*natura*), 58–59, 60 n. 77, 87; care with which the action was done (*facultas faciendi*), 59; quality of the action (*qualitas facti*), 59; material (*materia*), 59 n. 71; opinion, 68; example (*ab exemplo*), 155 n. 65

Topical, 51–54, 56 n. 55, 59 n. 71, 60, 67–68, 73, 84, 104, 112–13, 127, 153, 156, 173, 174, 176; by rewriting common places (topoi), 55–64, 84 n. 30, 97, 117–18; and euhemerism, 65–67

of commonplaces: *puer senex*, 121; love promotes valor, 124; erotic pleasure and its consequences, 125; women desire rape, 56–58, 125; separation of lovers is sad, 137; Golden Age, 146–47; image of Fortune, 149; *translatio imperii*, 157; in stereotypes, 164, 173, 176; of nobility, 165; see also Death of beloved, Gradus aetatum, Rabbit hunt

Isidore of Seville: *Etymologiae*, 12 n. 24, 32–33, 67 n. 104; *Synonyms*, 32 n. 93

Jacques d'Autun, 128 n. 91
Jaeger, C. Stephen, 108 n. 5
Jean de Meun: *Testament*, 13 n. 30; translation of Aelred de Rievaulx, 83–84 n. 29; mentioned, 3, 7, 9–14, 38, 39, 43 n. 4, 61–62, 69, 84, 86, 87, 89, 96, 97, 100 n. 93, 116, 117, 119–22, 127, 129, 130, 138, 146 n. 18, 174 n. 22. See also Roman de la rose
Jean de Montreuil (Jehan Jehannez), 10 n. 15, 13 n. 31, 97 n. 82, 125
Jean de Werchin: *Songe de la barge*, 176 n. 27
Jean Renart: *Guillaume de Dole*, 151 n. 37
Jeux partis. See Debate poems
John of Salisbury: *Policraticus*, 2 n. 5, 79 n. 5, 155; mentioned, 157 n. 76
Johnson, Leonard W., 115 n. 29
Joinville, Jean de: *Vie de Saint Louis*, 157 n. 76
Jung, Marc-René, 57 ns. 62 and 65
Justice: as virtue, 106, 161 n. 93; Divine, 171

Kant, Immanuel, 14 n. 34
Kantorowicz, Ernst H., 155
Kay, Sarah, 169 n. 1, 175, 178
Kiehl, Carole, 19 n. 49
King: Divine right of, 33, 98, 142, 152, 171; Good, 149, 151–52, 165; Abstract, 155, 158–59, 161
Kleinschmidt, Erich, 160
Knighthood (*chevalerie*) and opinion, 44 n. 10
Krueger, Roberta L., 72 n. 119

Laboratores: Women as, 91; mentioned, 93, 147
La Bruyère: *Les Caractères*, 91 n. 64
Ladder of Speculation, 36, 37–38, 39, 99 n. 89
Laidlaw, J. C., 3 n. 10, 113
Lancelot, Prose, 108 n. 4, 164
Language (*raison*): Crude, 11, 56 n. 57, 69; and reason, 24
Largess (*largesse*), 23, 151, 162 n. 95
La Rochefoucauld, 143, 158
Latin, Christine's knowledge of, 17 n. 41, 52, 57
Latini, Brunetto: *Tresor*, 2, 8, 9, 12, 20, 22 n. 62, 23, 24 n. 70, 25, 27, 46 n. 20, 51–52, 56 n. 57, 59 n. 70, 63 n. 86, 93 n. 69, 148 n. 27, 153, 157 n. 70, 159 n. 82 ; mentioned, 34

Latzke, Therese, 163
Laurent de Premierfait, 39–40
Lausberg, Heinrich, 12–13 n. 24
Leaf in *Roman de la rose*, 132
Lechat, Didier, 59 n. 71
Le Fèvre, Jean: *Lamentations* (*Matheolus*) and *Livre de Leesce*, 78 n. 3, 91 n. 63
Lefèvre, Sylvie, 138 n. 130
Lewis, C. S., 162 n. 96
Liberal arts, 35, 51, 102
Life: Active, 91; Contemplative, 91, 93 n. 70, 102 n. 99, 144
Literary characters: Agricol li Bials Parliers, 108 n. 4; Arnolphe, 89; Belle Dame sans mercy, 115, 179; Boort, 108 n. 4; Cousin of the Duc des vrais amants, Male, 134; Dame and damoiselle in the *Cent balades*, 112, 114, 115, 116; Dame de la Tour Landry, 135 n. 109; Damsel in *Meliador*, 178–79; Duke (Duc des vrais amants), 109–10, 129–36, 175; Gauvain, 163 n. 98; Griselda, 94; Herdsman in *Yvain*, 91 n. 64; Hermondine, 132 n. 103; Lady and lover in *Cent ballades d'amant et de dame*, 138–39 ; Lancelot, 163 n. 98, 164; Laudine, 93; Lorete, 57, 112, 137; Lunete, 93; Marote, 57, 58, 137, 140; Meliador, 132 n. 103; Pandarus, 134 n. 107; Perceval, 163 n. 98; Prince in *Pastoure*, 137, 140; Princess in *Duc des vrais amants*, 109 n. 8, 130–36; Sebile de Monthault, 95, 110, 111, 112, 124, 126, 127, 129 n. 93, 132, 134–36, 137, 139, 174, 175
Love: Chivalric (Courtly, Ideal, Noble, Pure, *amor sapiens*, *fin'amour*), 3, 75, 77, 107, 109, 110, 112, 113, 114, 117, 119, 124, 126–27, 128–29, 130, 136, 138, 141, 171, 174, 175, 177; Description and definition of, 26; Incestuous, 66 n. 100, 102, 129 n. 93; and opinions, 68, 107–41; and misogyny, 80, 107, 124; Foolish (*amor stultus*), 85 n. 36, 121, 128, 129, 138; and valor or prowess, 92 n. 67, 108–11, 124, 130, 134, 135, 136, 175; Mutability or instability of, 107–08, 111, 125, 139; and virtue, 108, 119; as *amor purus*, 109, 132; and abstinence (continence), 91, 109, 110, 125; Extramarital, 112–17, 119, 124, 125; Unequal (*amour disproportionné*), 111 n. 13, 137; New, 113 n. 26, 114, 115–16, 125; Carnal, 117; Conjugal, 117, 125 n. 73, 128, 129; Varieties of, 127–29; Young, 128, 129; Lancelot's, 164. *See also* Historical persons and characters: Du Guesclin, Bertrand, as lover *and* Jean de Werchin as lover
Lust (*luxure*), 2, 9, 39, 68, 69, 86, 109, 174
Lyric: sequence or cycles, 112–13, 114–15, 116, 139, 175; insertions, 113, 126

Machaut, Guillaume de: *Remede de Fortune*, 109 n. 8, 118, 131 n. 100, 177; *Jugement dou roy de Behaigne* and *Jugement dou roy de Navarre*, 176–77; *Voir-dit*, 179; mentioned: 128 n. 90
Macrobius, 18 n. 47
Magnanimity, 85 n. 39
Majesty and ceremony, 162
Manicheism, 45
Mann, Thomas: *Doktor Faustus*, viii
Manuscript: of Christine's writings, 3 n. 10, 18 n. 48, 67 n. 103, 110 n. 12, 156 n. 68; illustrations of *Roman de la rose*, 9 n. 10; London BL Royal 20 D.I., 57; Paris BNF fr. 301, 57 n. 65; of Jean Le Fèvre's works, 91 n. 63; ex-Phillipps, 169; mentioned, 176
Marchello-Nizia, Christiane, 143 n. 5
Marcus, Sharon, 53–54
Marie de France: Prologue to *Lais*, 73; mentioned, 128, 139 n. 134
Marriage: Happy, and fortune, 67–68, 171; and love (*affectio coniugalis*), 108, 111, 128–29; Christine's, 48 n. 27, 112, 125 n. 73, 141, 171; for *mal-mariées*, 128
Martyrs (martyrdom), 66 n. 100, 101–02
Materia Commentary on Horace's *Art of Poetry*, 53 n. 47
Material Style, 50
Matheolus: *Lamentations*, 78, 79, 80, 88,

135 n. 113, 164, 172; mentioned: 20, 84, 89, 90 n. 57, 98
Matthew of Vendôme: *Ars versificatoria*, 40, 54, 55–56, 58–59, 60 n. 77, 63, 67 n. 106, 164 n. 103
McLeod, Glenda, 46 n. 20, 90 n. 58
McMunn, Meradith T., 9 n. 10
Measuring cup of Justice, 89, 90, 104
Mechanical arts: and opinion, 40, 44 n. 10; mentioned, 102
Memory (*memoire*). *See* Virtues, Intellectual
Messelaar, P. A., 2 n. 3, 20, 29
Metamorphosis (gender change), Christine's, 49, 63, 94, 96, 98, 122
Meyenberg, Regula, 13 n. 24
Military activity. *See* Warfare
Minnis, A. J., 17
Miracles, 99
Mirror: Prudence's, 36; Reason's, 89–90, 103; for princes, 155
Misandry, 127, 136 n. 121
Misogamy, 78
Misogyny, 3, 13, 20, 34, 75, 77–106, 107, 111, 121, 124, 127, 136 n. 121, 146, 153, 164, 172–73, 177, 178 n. 43, 179
Mode (*Modus*): Epideictic, 4, 84–85, 90, 119
    of treating (*tractandi*), 7, 84–85, 155: allegorical or poetic (*poeticus*), 7, 50, 70, 72, 73, 74, 75, 95, 102, 104, 144, 173, 174; of definition (*diffinitivus*), 7, 155, 160; of demonstrative logic (*probativus vel improbativus*), 7, 83; descriptive (*descriptivus*), 7, 155, 160–61; digressive (*digressivus*), 7; fictional (*fictivus*), 7; metaphorical (*transumptivus*), 7; of supporting examples (*exemplorum positivus*), 7, 83
    Debate, 9, 50; Ovidian, 13; of satire, 13 n. 31; Hortatory, 90–91; Invective, 119; of the treatise (*tractatus*), 155, 163. *See also* Treatise
Molière: *Ecole des femmes* and *Femmes savantes*, 89; *La Critique de l'Ecole des femmes* and *L'Impromptu de Versailles*, 89 n. 51
Molinet, Jean, 117 n. 40
Mollesse (*mous*), 2, 122 n. 58
Montaigne: *Essais*, 41, 48 n. 26; mentioned, 4, 170
Morse, Ruth, 17–18
Mouvoir opinions, 12, 14, 33, 41
Mühlethaler, Jean-Claude, 29 n. 85
Mutatis mutandis and reading, 72–73
Mythological and legendary characters: Adonis, 116; Alcyone, 95 n. 79; Amazons, 53 n. 46, 102 n. 99; Arachne, 84 n. 33; Briseida, 56 n. 55, 65, 66, 69, 84, 98, 110, 111, 162 n. 98; Cassandra, 56; Ceres, 65; Ceyx, 95 n. 79; Dido, 65, 66, 69, 84, 91, 102, 162 n. 98; Echo, 113 n. 26; Hector, 36; Helen, 56, 57–58, 59, 84 n. 32; Hero, 117 n. 38; Isis, 65 n. 95; Jason, 66, 111; Juno, 116; Jupiter, 116 n. 35; Leander, 117 n. 38; Mars, 116; Medea, 65, 66, 84, 91, 102, 162 n. 98; Minerva (Pallas), 35 n. 110, 47 n. 23, 65; Morpheus, 114; Narcissus, 113 n. 26, 129; Oenone (Cenona), 56–58; Orpheus, 136; Othea, 36, 47 n. 23; Paris, 56, 57, 84 n. 32; Penthesilea, 47 n. 23; Pygmalion, 28; Saturn, 11 n. 18; Sibyl, 19 n. 51, 34, 37, 38, 45 n. 10, 70, 85 n. 39, 135, 156; Thisbe, 162 n. 98; Tiresias, 95; Ulysses, 95; Venus, 65, 116; Yplis, 95

Nagel, Sylvia, 50, 75 n. 129, 146
Narcisus, 113 n. 26
Necromancy, 66, 102
Nicolas de Clamanges, vii
Nicopolis, Battle of, 115, 116, 147, 177
Nobility: Inherited and virtuous, 4, 92–93, 157, 165; Complexion of, 91 n. 64; Christine's, 156, 157 n. 71; Charles V's, 155, 160, 163, 164

'Oiseuse,' 121, 174
Ombre, 1, 43–44, 104
Opinion (*opinio, opinor*): Scholarly, on Christine, viii n. 7, 4–5; in Latin, 2 n. 5; Definition of, 8, 41, 156; False, 16, 19, 92 n. 67; Subjective, 31, 67;

and God, 45; Kinds of, 75–76, 151; Error and correction of, 74, 90; Foolish, 135; Reader's, 138, 139–40
Orator (*orator*): Ideal, 12–13, 99; Woman as, 91; mentioned, 91, 147
Oratory, Demonstrative, judicial, and deliberative, 153
Order: in character and conduct, 160–62; in government and governance, 160–66; and ceremony, 162
Ordo artificialis, 115, 148 n. 27
Oton de Grandson, 175
Ouy, Gilbert, 152 n. 42
Ovid: *Heroides*, 56–58; *Ars amatoria*, 85, 88; mentioned, 54, 58, 60, 62, 89, 96
Oxymoron, 143

Paden, William D., 138 n. 130
Panegyric: and invective, 69, 155; as model, 153. *See also* Epideixis
Paradise, 39
Paradox, 79 n. 7, 172, 174
Parussa, Gabriella, 65, 155 n. 56
Pascal, Blaise: *Pensées*, 99 n. 90, 158
Passion: of *femme passionnée*, 3, 143; mentioned, 3, 121, 129–30, 138–39
Patience, 94, 105
Patron, 66–67, 123, 152, 175–76
Patterson, Lee, viii
Pedestal, Moral, 92–93
Pen (*calamus*), 36, 70
Personification: of Opinion, 3, 43; Names of, 40, 47 n. 23, 49; of king, 161
Personifications and types: Ami, 134, 141; Avis, Maistre, 152; Bel Acueil, 64 n. 93, 123, 132; Bigamist, 78, 88; Chaos, 39, 44, 47, 70–71, 153; Chastity, 9, 56, 91 n. 66; Chivalry (Chevalerie), 131 n. 102, 132; Deduit, 129; Désir de savoir, 45, 156; Eloquence Theologienne, 33, 34, 99; Envy (Envie), 48; Fama, 8; Faux Semblant, 13 n. 29, 43 n. 4, 44 n. 8, 96, 146 n. 18; Fol Amoureux (Amant), 11, 25–26, 27, 61, 62, 121, 122, 123, 127, 129–30, 132, 150 n. 35; Fortune, 15, 16, 19–20, 47 n. 23, 60 n. 77, 67, 74, 90, 116, 148, 149, 165; France (Libera), 47, 70–71, 81 ns. 19 and 24, 149 n. 32, 150 n. 33; Fraude, 13 n. 29, 44 n. 8; Genius, 39, 121 n. 56; Hearing, 35–36; Honte, 9; Ignorance, 45, 48, 156; Imagination, 36, 37, 39; Jealous Husband, 141; Justice, 75 n. 129, 82, 89, 99, 104–05, 164, 171; Justice Canonique, 9; Knighthood (Chevalerie), 53, 143, 145, 150, 151; Love, God of, 129, 130; Loyalty, 123 n. 62; Lust, 131 n. 102, 132; Malebouche, 134; Nature, 21, 27, 38, 39 n. 120, 44 n. 8, 60, 63, 71, 77, 92 n. 69, 101, 116, 119, 149, 154, 164, 165; Nobility (Noblesse), 53, 143, 150, 151, 165 n. 106; Opinion, vii, 1, 2, 3, 7–8, 15, 18–19, 26 n. 74, 30, 32, 34, 40, 42–49, 65 n. 98, 68, 71, 74, 90, 104, 156, 168, 169, 178 n. 41, 179 n. 47; Paour (Fear), 9, 91 n. 66; Philosophy (Theology, Sapience, Serenité), 3, 15, 18–19, 22, 30, 32, 33, 46–48, 49, 61, 68, 71, 74, 82, 105 n. 112, 106, 117, 118, 166 n. 110, 171; Prudence (Minerva, Phronesis, Sapientia, Sophia), 35–36, 38, 47 n. 23, 94, 99, 102 n. 99; Prudence Mondaine, 102 n. 99; Reason (Raison), 3–4, 9, 11 n. 18, 25–26, 29, 35, 36, 40, 56 n. 57, 61, 69, 75 n. 129, 81–82, 83, 85 n. 36, 92 n. 69, 99–104, 105, 121, 123, 124 n. 68, 135, 143, 149–52, 155, 156, 163, 164, 171; Rectitude (Droiture), 75 n. 129, 82, 89, 99, 103–04, 105, 164; Ribaud (the Vieille's lover), 122; Terre (Terra), 70, 149; Vieille (Vetula insipiens), 87, 121–23, 134–35, 136, 141; Vetulus insipiens, 121, 122; Wealth (Richesse), 53, 143, 150, 151, 152; Wife, Jealous Husband's, 141; Wisdom (Sagesse), 52–53, 81, 143, 145, 150–51
Petrarch, 9 n. 10, 84, 102 n. 97
Philosophies (Philosophers), Errors of, 19, 22, 28, 32, 45
Pierre de la Cépède: *Paris et Vienne*, 170 n. 6
Pilgrimage, Christine's, 70

Pinet, Marie-Josèphe, 80 n. 15
Plague in Machaut's *Jugement Navarre*, 177
Planctus: *Naturae* and *Terrae*, 149; *Liberae* (*Franciae*), 149 n. 32; mentioned, 149 n. 32
Plumb line, Rectitude's, 89, 90
Poet: and prophet, 36, 38; Christine as, 37
Poetry: Subtle, 27, 72; Courtly, 34; and allegory, 95
Poirion, Daniel, 68, 124
Pregnancy, 93, 146 n. 18
Presumption (*cuidier*, *oultrecuidance*), 2, 15, 16, 31, 32, 47, 49, 79, 111, 135, 150 n. 33
Pride: as mockery of the gods, 98–99; Noble's, as false opinion, 99, 157; as vainglory, 170
Prophecy and France, 167
Prophet: in Alain de Lille's *Anticlaudianus*, 35–36, 70; women as, 103, 135
Prostitution, 122, 126, 140
Providence, 148, 149, 166–67, 171
Prudence: as discretion, 23, 42, 120; and description, 42; in *Trois vertus*, 82 n. 25, 92, 94; of the virago, 95; as foresight, 102, 149; as virtue, 106, 158, 162; and self-interest, 148
Psychology and psychiatry in Christine's time, 142
Purgatory, 37

Quereuil, Michel, 143 n. 8, 178 n. 41
Quilligan, Maureen, 102 n. 98
Quinze joies de mariage, 89 ns. 52–53, 122 n. 58
Quis quid ubi etc. *See* Circumstances
Quotation, Selective, 54

Rabbit (*connin*) hunt, 133–34
Rabelais: *Pantagruel*, 104; mentioned, 4
Raoul de Houdenc: *Meraugis de Portlesguez*, 176
Rape, 53–54, 55, 56, 57–58, 64, 68, 97, 125, 140, 144 n. 10
Reading: poetry, 27; Subtle, 27–29, 30, 71–72, 73; program, 28, 72–74, 75, 170; by men and women, 72–73; and reader response, 78–79, 170, 172; examples, 158; Autobiographical, 178–80
Reason (*raison*). *See* Faculties, Intellectual
Rebellion: Man's, 38; Universal, 38–39; against authority, 79, 99; in France, 145, 167, 171; Caboche, 167
Recreantise, 110, 131 n. 102, 136, 175
Rectitude as virtue, 106
Relics, 99
Religion (*loy*): and opinion, 1–2, 4, 29–30, 33–34, 48, 49, 75, 98, 105, 122, 170; as faith, 34, 47, 79, 170; mentioned, 148, 166
René d'Anjou: *Cuers d'amours espris*, 113 n. 25
Reno, Christine, 28 n. 83, 34–35, 45 n. 16, 70 n. 116, 71–72, 152 n. 42
Renown, Christine's, 156, 179 n. 47
Rent robe, Philosophy's, 18–19, 71
Repetitiveness of misogyny, 79 n. 6
Retention (*Retentive*). *See* Virtues, Intellectual
Retraction, Jean de Meun's, 13 n. 30
Rhetoric (*Rethorique*): Art of, 3, 10–13, 24–25, 27, 34, 46, 50, 99; Deliberative, 50; of love, 69, 127; of courtship and seduction, 176
Richards, Earl Jeffrey, 80, 86 n. 40, 146 n. 16
Robertson, D. W., Jr., 55, 61, 62 n. 85
Role: Gender, 96, 173; playing, 176
Romancers, 115
Roman de la rose: Opinions on, viii, 33, 39, 64, 69, 79, 103, 117, 119–24, 127, 136, 146 n. 17; as compilation, 16; and integuments, 27; and audience, 46 n. 17; and misogyny, 79, 80; and Fear, 91 n. 66; mentioned, 68, 88, 109, 118, 128, 129–30, 133, 139 n. 134, 140–41, 149–50, 152, 164–65, 170 n. 6, 171. *See also* Debate, Guillaume de Lorris, *and* Jean de Meun
Rose: White and red, 39; in *Roman de la rose*, 129–30, 132
Rossiaud, Jacques, 87 n. 46, 126, 140
Rousseau, Jean-Jacques: *Confessions*, 52; mentioned, 179

Rumigacion, 17 n. 41

Saint Alexis, 146
Saintly scenario, 53 n. 45
Satire: and ambiguity, 13–14; in Jean's *Roman de la rose*, 13 n. 31; and irony in Andreas Capellanus's *De amore*, 116 n. 32
Schism, vii, 71, 98, 147, 148
Schnell, Rüdiger, 101, 105
Scholar, Christine as, 171
School of thought and opinion, 43, 44–45
Script, 53–54, 97, 156
Scripture. *See* Bible
Seduction. *See* Deception
Self-correction and opinion, 74–76
Self-interest, 3, 4, 75, 77, 141, 143–48, 149, 150, 152, 153, 170; Enlightened, 4, 76, 141, 143, 145, 148, 152, 154, 163, 165
Semantic range of ideas and words, 2, 30 n. 86, 43 n. 4, 47 n. 23
Semple, Benjamin, 43, 68 n. 108
Sensus communis, 142 n. 2
Sentement: Vray, 3, 33, 34, 35, 48, 78, 80, 86, 92, 94–98, 101, 105, 124, 154, 167, 179; Personal (*de sentement*): 34–35, 79–80, 118, 154, 156, 172, 177; Homosexual's, 86; Misogynist's, 86–90; Virtuous, 86; and self-knowledge, 87–88, 89–90, 101; and conscience, 92; of others (*d'autrui*), 95, 97, 138; and allegory, 96; and experience, 118; mentioned, 80, 97
Sermo ad status feminarum, 91
Seulete, 171–72, 179
Seznek, Jean, 65
Shapley, C. S., 176
Shipwreck, vii, 96, 122
Sicily, Description of, 63–64, 68
Sin, Original, 19, 23, 83, 84 n. 30
Sincerity of love, 80, 111, 118, 123, 127–28, 138; mentioned, 176
Slander (*médisance*) and love, 68, 122 n. 61, 125, 135. *See also* Gossip
Slut, 125
Sobriety of women, 91, 92
Social status: as hierarchy, 73, 91–93, 100, 105–06, 114, 145, 146, 164, 165, 167, 175, 179–80; and virtue, 92–93; and misogyny, 106; and choice of wife, 111
Solempne, 162 n. 96
Solente, S., 12 n. 24, 156 n. 68, 162
Solomon: *Proverbs*, 95 n. 77
Sovereignty of Charles V, 154
Speculation: in philosophy, 33, 45; Theological, 34; and visions, 36; Christine's 38, 40. *See also* Ladder of Speculation
Stäblein-Harris, Patricia, 117 n. 40
Stakel, Susan, 13 n. 28
Stand-up comedy, 176
Stereotype. *See* Invention of commonplaces
Stierle, Karlheinz, 14 n. 34
Strubel, Armand, 169 n. 3
Style (*stille*), Christine's, 27, 50
Subject: Poetic, 174, 175–76; Fragmentation of, 175; Autobiographical and fictitious, 176
Subjectivity: and truth, 4, 75; in debate, 31; and Christine's love poems, 80; and opinion, 169–80; Christine's, 172–74
Subtlety (*soutilleté*): and rhetoric, 24–25, 27; in poetry, 27–30, 84 n. 30
Sufficiency (*souffisance*), 49, 109 n. 8
Suicide, 117 n. 38
Surplus de san, 73
Suspicion and distrust in love, 110, 138–39
Sydney, Sir Philip, 164 n. 105
Synecdoche, 144

Tarnowski, Andrea, 73–74
Taste and judgment, 14
Theologians, 17, 99
Thesis. *See* Hypothesis and thesis
Thibaut de Champagne: *Chansons* 37 and 47, 176
Three-part division, 137 n. 124, 154–55, 160, 163, 164, 167
Topos (topoi). *See* Invention
Tower, Reason's, 3–4, 150, 152
Translatio: *studii*, 51, 100; of *chevalerie* and *clergie*, 100; *imperii*, 100, 157

Translations of Christine's writings, 67 n. 103
Treatise (*traittié*), 155. See also *Modus tractandi* and *Modus tractatus*
Tree of Knowledge of Good and Evil, 45
Troubadours, 80, 113, 115
Trouvères, 113
Troy: Fall of, 62; and lineage, 151, 160; mentioned, 57
Tuve, Rosemond, 109 n. 8

Uncertainty, Operation of, 139–40
Understanding, Rational. *See* Faculties, Intellectual
University and Lady Opinion, 44, 47

Valerius Maximus: *Facta et dicta memorabilia*, 158
Van der Helm, José, 54 n. 48
Varty, Kenneth, 112
Vergil, 17
Vices. *See* Array of vices
Villainy: and complexion, 91 n. 64; of nobles, 165
Villenie (*chose vilaine*) as intercourse, 110, 121, 131–32, 135–36
Villon, 179
Violence: against women, 53, 126 n. 81, 140–41; by women, 53, 85; among French, 70
Virago (*femme forte, preude femme*), 52 n. 44, 77, 85, 91, 94, 95, 102–04, 122 n. 58, 164 n. 104, 166 n. 109
Virgin: birth, 36; and rape, 55, 56
Virtue: and felicity, 20; and beauty, 21, 164; and orderly array, 44; in the City of Ladies, 66, 163; and complexion, 91 n. 64; and body, 93 n. 72; Physical and moral, 102–03; and love, 107–08; King's, 119–22, 144, 149, 154, 160–63; Queen's, 144, 154, 171; in history, 149; in government and governance, 160; Definition of, 164 n. 104; and contingencies, 175
Virtues, Intellectual: as *biens de Nature* and *vertus de l'ame*, 21; Consideration (*consideracion*), 21, 22, 23, 24 n. 68, 26, 48 n. 26, 61, 63, 76 n. 132, 82, 83, 100, 116, 162, 173, 179; Discretion (*discrecion*), 21, 22–23, 26, 27, 42, 48 n. 26, 61, 63, 74, 76 n. 132, 82, 83, 85 n. 36, 100, 116, 118, 120, 152, 162, 173, 174 n. 22; Memory (*memoire*), 21, 23, 26, 61, 63, 83, 100, 154, 173; Retention (recall, *retentive*), 21, 23, 26, 61, 83, 173; and *circonspection*, 23; mentioned: 20–24, 25, 30, 42, 82–85, 87, 116–17, 142. *See also* Array of virtues
Vita as genre, 161
Von Moos, Peter, 78, 142 n. 2, 155, 159

Wandruszka, Nicolai, 126 n. 83
Warfare: and opinion, 40, 44 n. 10, 70; Life as, 68
Wheel of Fortune, 18 n. 48, 149
White, Stephen D., 53 n. 46
Widow (widowhood), 60, 63, 67–68, 69, 78 n. 3, 80, 89, 90, 94, 98 n. 86, 105, 112, 115, 116, 117, 118, 122–23, 125, 126, 135, 138 n. 130, 140–41, 171, 173, 175
Wife: Gontier Col's, 87 n. 46; Patient, 94; Choice of, 111
Willard, Charity Cannon, 44–45, 157
Wisdom (*sagece*): Divine, 92; King's, 155, 160, 163, 164
Wittgenstein, Ludwig, ix
Wolf-Bonvin, Romaine, 13–14
Woman: Natural, 85, 90–94; and men, 85 n. 39; Unnatural, 92, 98; Dissolute, 98

Youth: Christine's, 98 n. 85; Education of, 105; in *gradus aetatum*, 119–21

Zink, Michel, vii, 4, 79 n. 7, 151 n. 37, 169 n. 1, 172–74, 178 n. 42
Zühlke, Bärbel, 51–52
Zumthor, Paul, 20, 30 n. 86, 51, 178 n. 42